The International Library of Sociology

TRANSFORMATION SCENE

Founded by KARL MANNHEIM

The International Library of Sociology

THE SOCIOLOGY OF DEVELOPMENT
In 18 Volumes

I	Caste and Kinship in Central India	*Mayer*
II	Economics of Development in Village India	*Haswell*
III	Education and Social Change in Ghana	*Foster*
	(The above title is not available through Routledge in North America)	
IV	Growing up in an Egyptian Village	*Ammar*
V	India's Changing Villages	*Dube*
VI	Indian Village	*Dube*
VII	Malay Fishermen	*Firth*
VIII	The Mende of Sierra Leone	*Little*
IX	The Negro Family in British Guiana	*Smith*
X	Peasants in the Pacific	*Mayer*
XI	Population and Society in the Arab East	*Baer*
XII	The Revolution in Anthropology	*Jarvie*
XIII	Settlement Schemes in Tropical Africa	*Chambers*
XIV	Shivapur: A South Indian Village	*Ishwaran*
XV	Social Control in an African Society	*Gulliver*
XVI	State and Economics in the Middle East	*Bonne*
XVII	Tradition and Economy in Village India	*Ishwaran*
XVIII	Transformation Scene	*Hogbin*

TRANSFORMATION SCENE

The Changing Culture of a New Guinea Village

by

H. IAN HOGBIN

First published in 1951
by Routledge

Reprinted in 1998, 2001
by Routledge
2 Park Square, Milton Park, Abingdon, Oxon, OX14 4RN
or
270 Madison Avenue, New York, NY 10016

First issued in paperback 2010

Routledge is an imprint of the Taylor & Francis Group

British Library Cataloguing in Publication Data
A CIP catalogue record for this book
is available from the British Library

Transformation Scene
ISBN 978-0-415-17585-2 (hbk)
ISBN 978-0-415-60553-3 (pbk)
The Sociology of Development: 18 Volumes
ISBN 978-0-415-17822-8
The International Library of Sociology: 274 Volumes
ISBN 978-0-415-17838-9

Publisher's Note
The publisher has gone to great lengths to ensure the quality of this reprint
but points out that some imperfections in the original may be apparent

To

J. K. MURRAY

and the other builders
European and native
of the new New Guinea

'There is no turning back, even if this were thought desirable. There is only one-way traffic in Time.'

JAWAHARLAL NEHRU
The Discovery of India

Acknowledgements

My chief debt is to Colonel J. K. Murray, head of the New Guinea Administration since 1945. He made it possible for me to carry out the later stages of the field work on which the book is based and at all times gave me his full support and encouragement. The dedication is a return for what I owe to him and also a tribute to his devotion to the country which he is so ably serving.

In the field I had practical help from Colonel A. A. Conlon, sometime Director of Research and Civil Affairs in the Australian Army; from Mr. H. J. Jones, Director of District Services and Native Affairs in the New Guinea Government from 1944 to 1949; and from the successive officers who have been in charge of the Morobe District since 1944—Mr. A. Bloxham, Mr. R. Farlow, Mr. A. Roberts, and Mr. H. Niall.

I have to express my thanks also to the Council of the Australian National University. The main part of the MS. was prepared during the period when I held one of its Fellowships. This enabled me to travel overseas and re-examine the problems of culture contact with anthropologists who had been working outside the Pacific area. Discussions with Professor Raymond Firth, Dr. L. P. Mair, and other members of the seminar group at the London School of Economics were of particular value.

Finally, I wish to record my indebtedness to Mr. W. Conroy for supplying the botanical names of the food crops, to Miss M. Turner Shaw for preparing the diagrams and maps, to Miss C. Eppers for rectifying some of my worst lapses from standard English, and to Professor A. P. Elkin, editor of *Oceania*, and Mr. C. R. H. Taylor, editor of the Polynesian Society's *Journal*, for allowing me the use of several photographic blocks.

H. Ian Hogbin

Busama, Territory of New Guinea
January 31, 1950

Contents

I. WAR   page 1

II. PEOPLE AND VILLAGE   24

III. DAILY ROUTINE   34

IV. WORK   54

V. TRADE   81

VI. SOCIAL GROUPING   96

VII. STATUS AND LEADERSHIP   118

VIII. NATIVE ADMINISTRATIVE OFFICIALS   150

IX. COUNCILS AND COURTS   164

X. WAGE LABOUR   183

XI. PAGAN RELIGION.   204

XII. CHRISTIANITY   232

XIII. RACE RELATIONS   276

APPENDICES

A. VITAL STATISTICS   293

B. FOOD SURVEYS   296

C. WAR DAMAGE CLAIMS   302

D. DAILY WORK SCHEDULES   304

E. WORK DIARIES   308

F. HOUSEHOLD GARDENS   314

G. TIME AND LABOUR IN HOUSE BUILDING 317

INDEX   319

ix

Illustrations

1. Wielding a digging stick in the garden   *facing page* 18

2*a*. New house built after the return of the conscripts   19

2*b*. Completing one of the new school buildings, January, 1950   19

3*a*. An expert builder sketching the plan for a house   34

3*b*. Flooring material for a new house   34

4. Bumbu before dismissal. His white-topped cap is the mark of a paramount luluai   35

5. Busama rebuilt. The view looking southwards from Schneider Point   66

6*a*. Mother and child   67

6*b*. Housewife with a load of firewood   67

7. Group of men at a house-building feast. The palmwood flooring in the background   82

8. Cooking sago gruel for a feast   83

9. Fishing with spear. The Buang Range in the background   162

10*a*. Repairing the seine   163

10*b*. Hauling in the seine   163

11*a*. Pounding sago pith   178

11*b*. Washing sago   178

12. Girl with net for catching freshwater fish   179

13. Pot maker of Lababia village. The bowl containing the rolls of clay came from the Tami Islands   242

ILLUSTRATIONS

14. Dance by the residents of Busama in Buakap village. The performers are in circular formation, with the women in pairs on the outside and the men in the middle   *facing page* 243

15. Dancer with hand drum. His garment is made from painted bark cloth: and he is also wearing a headdress of feathers, small cowrie shells, and dogs' teeth, together with a breast ornament of dogs' teeth   258

16*a*. Tami Island figure in the traditional style of the Huon Gulf. The figure is fifteen inches high and, except for the whitened base, is painted dark grey, the inlay is lime, with the highlights (hair, eyes, nipples, etc.) picked out in red ochre   259

16*b*. Model of a club house in the traditional style (courtesy of Australian Museum, Sydney)   259

MAPS

Territory of New Guinea, Papua, and the Solomon Islands   *page* xiii

Huon Gulf. Language Distribution   xiv

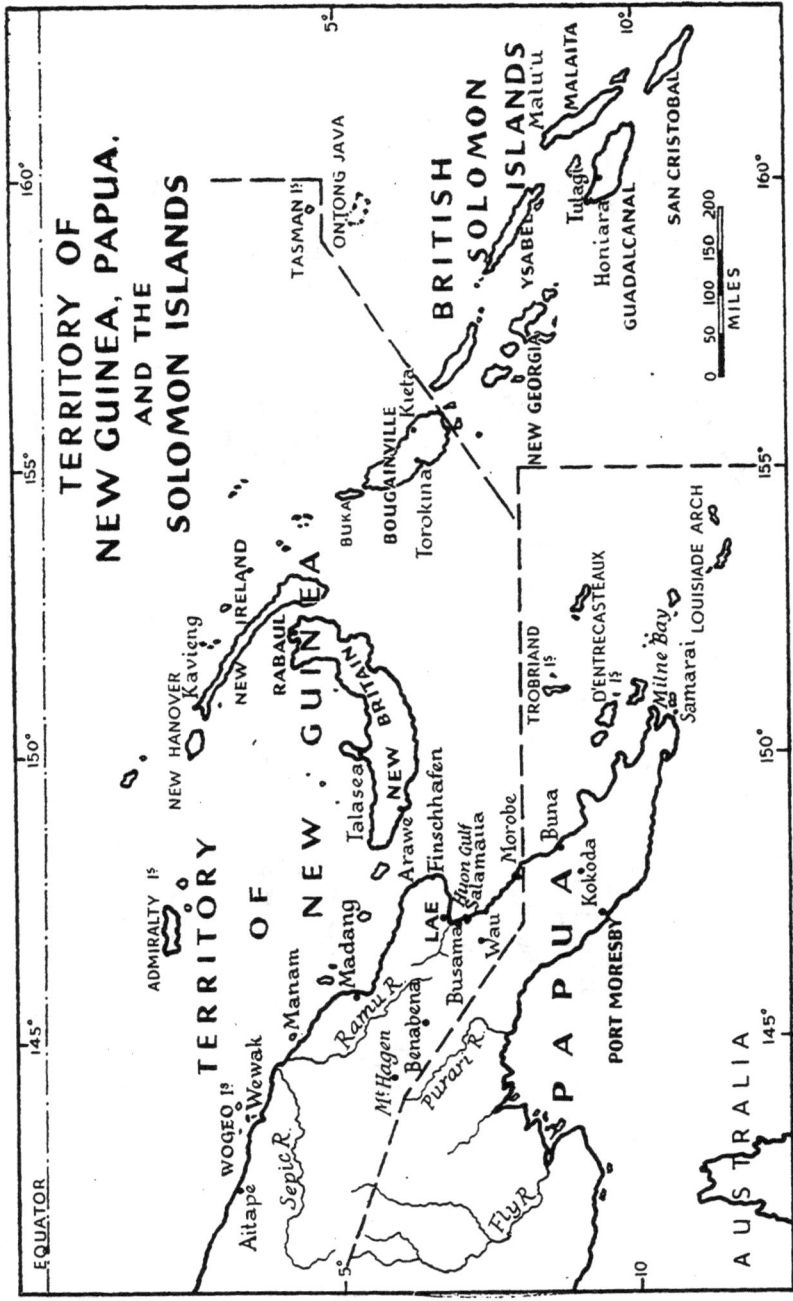

TERRITORY OF
NEW GUINEA, PAPUA.
AND THE
SOLOMON ISLANDS

HUON GULF
LANGUAGE DISTRIBUTION

APIM (YABIM)	GAIDEMOE	
DAMBI	BUASI'	
GAWA'	GELA	
WAIN	GAI	
APU'	GAIWA	
LAHIWAPA		

Names are in their Gawa' forms

HUON PENINSULA

FINSCHHAFEN

Mape R.
Ngasigelatu
Tami Is.
Manggei
Tamigidu
Bulum R.
Bukawa
147°30'
147°
6°30'
Busu R.
Wagang
Buibara
Apo
LAE
Labu'Mete
Labu'Tali
Yalu
Labu'Butu
Labu
Lagoon
Gabanses
Busi (Markham) R.
Busi (Markham) R.
Buang R.
Mapuss
Buasi'
Buasi R.
Wakop
Gwado
Maialo
Hote
Busama
Wamasu'
Bualkap
Lutu
SALAMAUA
Taugwi'
Nuknuk
Laukanu
Salus
Lebabia
Fly Islands
Busu (Francisco)
Bitoi R.
Wampit R.
6°30'
7°
7°
147°

MILES
0 4 8 12 16 20

Chapter One

WAR

'They brought the elephant of Asia to convey the artillery of Europe to dethrone one of the kings of Africa, and to hoist the standard of Saint George upon the mountain of Rasselas.'—BENJAMIN DISRAELI, moving a vote of thanks in the House of Commons to Sir Robert Napier's army after the Abyssinian campaign in 1868.

THIS is a descriptive study of the village of Busama, which is situated on the upper part of the west coast of the Huon Gulf, north-eastern New Guinea. I have known it well since 1944, at the height of the recent war, when the people were suffering acute hardships. Their dwellings had been bombed, their goods destroyed, their livestock killed, and their agricultural work suspended. Not until the beginning of 1950 was physical rehabilitation complete and the settlement normal.

But the clash of the opposing armies was not the natives' first taste of the modern world. Europeans entered the area before 1900, and for two generations the old way of life was being steadily modified. Government officers stamped out raiding and introduced a different set of laws; missionaries preached the Christian religion and established a church and a school; labour recruiters took the young men away to work in distant places; and traders operated stores in the neighbouring towns where cash earned as wages could be exchanged for tools more effective than those made of stone and volcanic glass.

The difficulties brought about by the war and the way in which the destitute families were able to set themselves on their feet will be the theme of the first part of the book. But I am also concerned with culture change in general, and the later chapters are devoted to the problem of how a society with simple needs and simple material apparatus has adapted itself to the values and techniques of industrial civilisation. This section of the work is in line with recent investigations carried out elsewhere in the Pacific, and in Asia, Africa, and the Americas, to discover what is retained from the past and what lost, what is accepted from ourselves and what rejected. I shall place emphasis throughout on personal relations as illustrative of structural principles.

Money has affected the economic system to some extent, but the natives still build houses of the same materials, still grow the same crops by identical methods, and still supplement their diet by fishing and raising livestock. Co-operation is as necessary as it used to be, and the social groups, which are bound up with production, remain almost unaltered. The ancient political authorities, on the other hand, have disappeared in favour of others set up by the Administration. Despotism has sometimes resulted, to the distress of the people and the disappointment of Government officers. The absence of the young men in employment has also upset the old order, and the introduction of Christianity has had repercussions which the early missionaries did not foresee. They would have been gratified to know that the implications of the new moral code are so thoroughly comprehended, but chagrined at the pagan survivals and deeply shocked at the use of prayer as a substitute for magic.

The investigation has been officially sponsored, in the early stages by the Army and later by the Administration. Victory in the Pacific was so certain by the middle of 1944 that the Australian Cabinet could at length consider the future of the ravaged dependencies in the north. The colonial Governments had been suspended shortly after the enemy landing in 1942, and much of the planning had to be done in association with the Army, which was then in control. Anthropologists in the Forces were called upon for background information, and to me fell the task of surveying the Huon Gulf area, scene of some of the bitterest fighting and allegedly of much native discontent. Busama was my chief place of residence, and prior to demobilisation early in 1946 I had spent eight months there, sufficient for the immediate purpose. The civil Administration was by that time restored and subsequently invited me to broaden the scope of the study. This involved concentrating on the one settlement.

As a subsidiary aim, I have to furnish officials with data. Busama has been selected for social experiments, and the staff which will carry them out requires a knowledge of the native culture and of the human material available.

Problems of kinship and the indigenous system of education have an obvious relevance both for theoretical anthropology and practical affairs, but treatment of these subjects must be deferred for a second volume.

The Setting

The Huon Gulf has some of the finest tropical scenery in the world. On the north side is the Huon Peninsula, formed by the Rawlinson Mountains, an extension of the great Finistere block, which rises to a height of over 10,000 feet within eleven miles of the sea. To the south of the range, running inland from the base of the Gulf, is a broad rift valley, which forms the natural gateway to the interior. The Markham River (Busi to the natives) winds through the south-eastern end to empty itself into the Gulf, but beyond the headwaters, about one hundred miles inland, is the Ramu River flowing in the opposite direction towards the Sepik swamps of western New Guinea. The slight rise dividing the two is scarcely perceptible if one is on foot, and from the air it cannot be located at all. On the right bank of the Markham estuary is an extensive area of waters known as Labu Lagoon or Lake Herzog, and the mountains then begin again. The twin peaks of Mount Songol, nearly 11,000 feet high, serve as a buttress for the unbroken chain which continues down the full length of the west coast of the Gulf. A separate name is given to each different section, and the most northerly, twenty miles long, from the Markham to the Francisco or Buu River, is known as the Buang Range. At the mouth of the Francisco the crescent-shaped promontory of Salamaua juts three miles into the sea to form Samoa Harbour, a safe anchorage for large ocean-going steamers. Smaller rivers have cut into the eastern slopes of the Buangs and worn a series of flat-bottomed valleys admirably suited to cultivation, but farther south the rise is more abrupt, and the streams rush through narrow gorges.

The variation of temperature is small, and the thermometer seldom drops below seventy-five degrees or rises above ninety. The alternation of trade winds and monsoons, however, gives a regular change of seasons, one much wetter than the other. The only rainfall figures available are for Lae, at the mouth of the Markham, where the average for the year is 189 inches. Nine of these fall in January, the dryest month, and twenty-five in July, the wettest.

In such a climate the growth is prodigious, and a year after the Pacific war ended the jungle had reclaimed its own, leaving scarcely a scar. The mountains are clothed with rain forest on the lower slopes and with moss forest above, but over the Markham flood plain in the rift valley the trees give place to a coarse man-high grass known as kunai.

The Gulf country is part of the Mandated (now Trust) Territory of New Guinea,[1] a dependency consisting of the north-eastern section of the main island from the 141st meridian of east longitude to the Waria River just south of the Gulf, together with the Bismarck Archipelago—New Britain, New Ireland, New Hanover, and the Admiralties—and Bougainville and Buka of the north-western Solomons.[2] Originally a German colony, it was captured by Australian troops in 1914 and six years later entrusted to the Australian Government by the League of Nations. The north coast of the mainland from the Waria River eastwards, the whole of the south-eastern part, and the island groups to the east—the D'Entrecasteaux, the Trobriands, and the Louisiades—make up a second dependency, the Territory of Papua. This was annexed by Britain in 1884, and handed over to Australia in 1906. The two Territories have been administered jointly since 1942.

The Germans, after three previous choices, selected Rabaul, on the north-east corner of New Britain, as the capital for the New

[1] The title Mandated Territory of New Guinea is generally shortened to 'New Guinea'. Confusion is sometimes caused, but in the following pages the reader will be able to gather from the context whether I am referring to the whole island or the colony which is a part of it.

[2] The central and south-eastern Solomons are a British Protectorate administered from Fiji by the High Commissioner for the Western Pacific.

Guinea Territory. The site is encircled by volcanoes, and when a severe eruption took place in 1937 it was agreed to move the seat of Government to Salamaua and Lae. The change-over was in progress when war intervened. Port Moresby, in Papua is now the capital of the combined Territories of Papua and New Guinea.

The Territory of New Guinea is divided for purposes of administration into eight Districts. The Huon Gulf is in Morobe District, named after the harbour at the mouth of the Waria River where the Germans set up the first Government station. In 1926, when gold had been discovered at Edie Creek and Wau in the interior, the official centre was transferred to Salamaua. A thriving port soon grew up on the isthmus of the promontory, and by 1939 the European population numbered some hundreds.

All traffic with the goldfields in pre-war years was by plane. The terrain at Salamaua, however, is such that only a small runway could be constructed, and the main airfield had to be located at Lae, on the left bank of the Markham estuary, where there is no harbour.

Lae, with the rift valley behind, was considered to be more suitable for development as a military and air base than Salamaua, and in 1944, shortly after the Japanese invaders had been expelled, the First Australian Army chose it as headquarters. The Americans had Forces stationed alongside, and for a time this was one of the chief nerve-centres of the Pacific. Hundreds of miles of roads were built, including a highway to the goldfields—though these were not then being worked—and a huge airfield carved out of the kunai twenty-five miles up the Markham River at Nadzab.

The Morobe station remained at Salamaua during the later war period, but after the departure of the Army the Government decided to take advantage of the installations at Lae. The shift across took place in 1946. The commercial community followed; and a few shell holes, some rusted iron frames, and a quantity of smashed concrete are now all that remains of the former port.[1]

Native villages are located every few miles (see map p. xiv). The average number of inhabitants in each is between two hundred and three hundred, though a few have more, and Busama's exceed six hundred (see Appendix A). This is large both for Morobe and

[1] The lack of a harbour is Lae's only disadvantage. It is possible that a road may eventually have to be built to Salamaua and wharves constructed there.

for New Guinea as a whole—indeed, very few communities anywhere in the South Pacific have so many.

Till 1943 Busama was situated on the two sides of Schneider Point, a headland eight miles from Salamaua in the south and fourteen from Lae in the north. A narrow shelf of sand here borders the base of green jungle-clad cliffs, allowing just room enough for the dwellings. The stream known as Bu-samang gives the place its name (*bu*='water', 'spring', 'river', 'lake'); it trickles gently from the rocks in the middle of the settlement.[1] The houses were all stout structures, and the people had many possessions of European origin, including sewing-machines (almost always used by men, bicycles, carpenter's tools, furniture, crockery, and lamps. But when I first arrived, in September, 1944, nothing of this village remained: every building had been destroyed, and the villagers were living in crude huts hidden in a bush clearing nearly half a mile from the sea. Most of their belongings were gone and all their domestic animals. To understand how such a disaster had come about one must know something of the campaign, and it is with an account of this that I shall begin.

The Japanese Occupation[2]

The first Japanese moves were directed against Rabaul in New Britain. The small garrison could offer little opposition, and the town fell on January 23, 1942. The civil Administration was shortly afterwards suspended, and within a few weeks joint control of the two Australian Territories passed to a military organisation set up for the purpose. This had the title Australian New Guinea Administrative Unit but was generally referred to as ANGAU.

Members of the Government who were not too old for active service were quickly enlisted and continued, as far as possible, to

[1] The correct spelling is Busamang, but it would be pedantic to use this now that Busama has come to be accepted. Most native names in New Guinea have suffered a similar fate—and if by a miracle spelt correctly they are usually mispronounced. Lae, for example, should rhyme with 'die'; as spoken by Europeans it rhymes with 'day'.

[2] The general information in this and the following sections came from official sources, the account of what happened in Busama from the natives.

carry out their old jobs. Their numbers were inadequate to meet the new conditions, however, and in course of time other men had to be added, many of them with no previous knowledge of the island area. But ANGAU had other functions besides native administration, one of the most important being the supervision of the labour required to assist the combatant units.[1] A nucleus of staff for this work was provided by persons who had had experience handling native workers on the plantations and goldfields, but as the needs of the Army grew these also were supplemented by new recruits.

Air raids on the towns of the mainland of New Guinea followed the capture of Rabaul, and in February Salamaua station was moved inland to Wau, on the goldfields. The remaining civilians also withdrew, and the European settlements on the coast were soon deserted. Such of the native employees of the various firms as could do so made their way home, but for the majority this was impossible. They had been brought from the Sepik River, Madang, and other places hundreds of miles away, and, as ships were not now available, they had to stop where they were. Some were given refuge in the surrounding villages, and the rest set up camps, using abandoned supplies for food.

A Japanese Force landed at Salamaua during March with a fair quantity of equipment. Cargo vessels at first used the harbour, but after a couple of these had been sunk by Allied bombers, reinforcements and stores came in by submarines, which were unloaded at night.

A few days after the landing a small detachment of Japanese military police, including an interpreter who spoke pidgin English, went around the countryside with orders that the village officials should attend at the headquarters to receive instructions. Each settlement had two such leaders recognised by the Australian Administration, a senior called the luluai and an assistant referred to as the tultul. The Busama luluai, a man named Bumbu (Plate 4), whose story I shall be giving in full in Chapter VIII, had gone into hiding, but the tultul, Isom, thought it advisable to recognise the *de facto* authority and make the journey. In the absence of his superior, who was later imprisoned for disobedience, he was created

[1] Many members of ANGAU also played an operational rôle, but their activities will not concern us here.

headman and invested with appropriate insignia. The chief of the military police stated that all orders would be issued through Isom and that he was to inform the villagers of the probability of future requests for food and casual labourers. Everything would be paid for in invasion currency, which could be spent in shops to be set up when the war was over.

Village affairs went along smoothly for two or three months. The Japanese bought pigs and fruit and occasionally sought the services of a group of men for a few days to unload a submarine or assist in dragging guns and other gear into position, but they never interfered in purely domestic matters. A rumour circulated at one stage that a brothel of single native girls was to be set up for the use of the troops, and several marriages were speedily arranged in consequence, but the story apparently had no foundation.[1] The lack of trade stores where worn-out tools could be replaced was as yet not a serious problem, and the only real disability which the people suffered was a lack of medical attention.

About this time, in June 1942, an American fighter aircraft crashed in the sea near Schneider Point. The wounded pilot managed to swim ashore, where some of the Busama gave him medical treatment, provided him with food, and furnished men to take him over the mountains to the nearest Australian outpost. The guides selected were refugee labourers, for the people of the village feared to go lest the news should leak out and their relatives be punished.

The luluai Bumbu was now released from his imprisonment.

[1] Much later, in the final stages of the war, the natives of Bougainville and the Wewak-Aitape hinterland of western New Guinea suffered severely. Large enemy Forces were by that time cut off without any chance of replenishing their dwindling supplies. They therefore took to plundering the local gardens, killing anyone who resisted them. It has been estimated that about one-fifth of the population of Bougainville succumbed either to starvation or to violence. Yet although between 1943 and 1945 I visited almost every area from Guadalcanal in the Solomons to Aitape I found that not a single charge of rape against a Japanese could be substantiated; nor did I see one Japanese half-caste. The tales which gained wide currency amongst Allied troops of the mutilation of native women also remain unproven. The abstract of the report prepared by Sir William Webb for the Australian Government published in the *Sydney Morning Herald* on September 11, 1945, included at least one account of an alleged atrocity which, from conversations with the victim, I believe to be exaggerated.

Burning with resentment at his dismissal, he sent word through his daughter to ANGAU officers inland at Wau that the villagers, led by Isom, were giving the enemy willing assistance. A raid by native police under the command of two white men was accordingly arranged to bring the new headman to trial. The plan was for a night surprise, but in the darkness friend and foe were indistinguishable. An old woman and a youth were shot dead by the police and another youth bayonetted, but Isom made his escape.

A couple of months afterwards, in September, a party of three native policemen who were scouting for the Allied Forces walked into one of the refugee camps. The labourers promptly seized them, bound their wrists, and marched them to Busama, where the leader told the people to hand them over to the Japanese. If this was not done, he said, he would lay information at Salamaua, and doubtless everyone would be punished. What prompted the man to take this action I cannot say—my endeavours to locate him for interrogation were fruitless—but I suspect a private grudge, possibly against the police force, whose actions in the pre-war years had made them generally unpopular. The villagers felt bound to obey, and the captives were soon incarcerated.

An order immediately went out for the Busama elders to appear before the Japanese commander. He addressed them through an interpreter and asked those related to the persons killed in the earlier raid to stand. The deaths of the police, it was suggested, might be a fitting return for the murders : did everyone agree? Again I cannot tell what the real feelings of those present were, but they clearly had no alternative but to say 'yes', and next day the three men were shot.

The Recapture of Salamaua

The year 1942 was now drawing to a close, and as the months passed the efforts of the Allies began to meet with success. The battles of Milne Bay, Kokoda, and Buna were won, and it became possible to send a strong Force to Wau. A Japanese attack on the town was repulsed on January 30, 1943, and the slow descent to Salamaua began from that date. Every foot of the way was contested, and the enemy was at length compelled to make a round-up of the coast villages for carriers to bring supplies to the forward lines.

WAR

The natives faced danger on both sides—if they ran away they were shot by the Japanese, and if they advanced our fire confronted them. Several lost their lives, including some of the Busama.

Air raids also increased in intensity, and bombs were dropped not only on Salamaua but on the villages. Busama, along with several others, was obliterated and many persons killed. The people fled to the jungle, taking such of their belongings as they could conveniently carry. Everything left behind was destroyed by the bombing—canoes, nets, clothing, tools, utensils, all went. The pigs and fowls ran away, and no new ground could be broken for gardens. It was feared, and with reason, that if fresh areas were cleared the planes would be drawn by the smoke of the burning rubbish and turn their machine-guns on those working in the vicinity.

Salamaua was eventually recaptured on September 14, 1943, eighteen months after its occupation. Large Forces were soon concentrated nearby, and the Busama village site served as a convalescent camp. Within a few months, however, early in 1944, the base was moved across to Lae. After the transfer the only troops left at Salamaua were those connected with the ANGAU District Office, which had been reopened at once, a Fisheries Unit to supply sea foods to the hospitals, some signallers, and a War Graves detachment. Much later, in 1945, a rest camp for Army nurses was also set up, though long before this the coast for twenty miles on each side of Lae was regularly visited by leave parties. Upwards of five hundred were sometimes to be seen picnicking and bathing on the Busama beaches.

One of the District Officer's first moves was to despatch a posse of police to arrest Isom and the men who had captured the three scouts. Forewarned, Isom took to the hills. The police did not follow but sent one of his kinsmen to inform him that they intended to surround his house and carry out a mass rape of the womenfolk until such time as he gave himself up. This threat was actually carried out, and he came in within twenty-four hours. He was kept in confinement for a year but then liberated without being brought to trial (he died of what I took to be tuberculosis during 1948). No action was taken against the police.

Bumbu lost no time in paying his respects to ANGAU. The Administration had for years reposed trust in him, and his claim that he had been imprisoned and tortured for refusing to co-operate with the Japanese was given full credence. The District Officer recommended a decoration, and a Loyal Service Medal was eventually awarded. To heighten the effect and pay back a few old scores Bumbu also circulated the untruth that the rest of the Busama had openly courted the enemy and done all in their power to bring about a Japanese victory. The story was repeated so often, with more and more circumstantial details as time went on, that some officials came to refer to the village as 'disloyal'.

'When I use a word,' Humpty-Dumpty told Alice, 'it means what I choose it to mean—neither more nor less.' If words are to retain their ordinary implications, however, it is surely impossible for anyone to be 'disloyal' to an alien Government which is none of his choosing, or 'disloyal' to a cause which he has no power to accept or reject [1]—a cause, moreover, which he does not have the necessary background to comprehend.[2] In New Guinea, too, the German Administration had been overthrown in 1914, and the people were not to know that our departure twenty-eight years later would be less permanent.

The reply which a Busama native gave to this former employer when asked in my presence why he had not joined up at once with the Allies has much point. 'The negroes stuck to the Americans,' said the employer. 'Why didn't you do the same?' 'The American Government taught the negroes to read and write and so made it possible for them to understand all about the war,' was the reply. 'Our Government gave us nothing. The little learning that we had came from the Missions. The Americans also furnished the negroes with weapons, but what guns did we receive?'

The usual Busama attitude, at least in the beginning, was one of neutrality: the people were neither pro-Japanese nor anti-Japanese. But so long as the enemy had the power of punishment it was obviously inexpedient to neglect his orders. Increasing familiarity, however, aroused contempt. The natives were disgusted by the filth of the Japanese Army, by its neglect of the wounded, and by

---

[1] The Papuan natives, unlike those of the Territory of New Guinea, are technically British subjects and could thus be charged with treason. The Australian Army commander insisted that those found guilty should be hanged.

[2] I know several Europeans who in 1940 and 1941 did their best to keep the war news from their native servants. It was thought that a knowledge of our repeated defeats would be bad for the masters' prestige.

its indifference to hygiene. The ordinary soldiers are said to have defecated outside their quarters in preference to using latrines.[1]

Many, perhaps the majority, were neutral also to the Allies and gave them assistance no less but no more willingly. A certain number had in the preceding years developed close ties with particular white men and on this account were prepared to stand beside them in hardship and danger; but such conduct was a matter of personal trust and had nothing to do with political conviction.

The aid which was given to the Japanese voluntarily by individual natives in other parts of New Guinea may possibly be attributable in some instances to similar friendships, but real or fancied grievances against Europeans are the more common explanation.

Later, in March 1944, the New Guinea native infantry battalion was formed. Volunteers were found without difficulty, and the detachment earned a fine name for itself, winning several decorations. It would be rash to assume from this, nevertheless, that there was any belief in the Allies having a monopoly of right and justice. Some men joined to carry on the warrior traditions of their fathers, some for adventure, some for the high pay, some for the glamour of a uniform, some to see the world, some because their friends had already done so, some as an escape from unhappy domesticity.

Conscription of Labourers [2]

From September 1943 till the end of the year the Busama, together with their neighbours, were mainly occupied in clearing up Salamaua and building the convalescent camp. Little time was left over for their own concerns, though they managed to erect the huts in which they were still living a year later. A large number of the able-bodied men were then conscripted to act as carriers in the Markham-Ramu campaign and later for work in Lae and elsewhere.

Bringing supplies over mountain barriers to the forward areas

---

[1] I heard this many times in different places. Cf. K. E. Read, 'Effects of the Pacific War in the Markham Valley,' *Oceania*, Vol. X̄VIII, pp. 104-5. Parents nowadays scold a child who has made a mess by telling him that he is a Japanese.

[2] Early in 1944, before my initial visit to Busama, I carried out a survey of all aspects of the labour situation as part of my military duties.

was tough work and transporting the wounded on the return journey up and down precipices still more exacting. ANGAU aimed at having one day per week set aside for rest, but the exigencies of the fighting often rendered this impossible. Not many of the conscripts shirked their jobs, nevertheless, and some went on till they collapsed in their tracks. Army commanders have often admitted that the native carriers and stretcher-bearers were a deciding factor in the ultimate victory.

Duties in Lae and the other bases included building camps, loading and unloading trucks and planes, stacking cargo from ships, spraying pools to prevent the breeding of mosquitoes, and serving in some of the messes. General labour of this kind was arduous but not unduly so, and the hours were reasonably regular. The compounds where the men were housed, too, differed little from those to which they had become accustomed in the days of peace, the food was superior, and the war atmosphere made life more exciting. The lads with few home ties were not unhappy, and some told me that they had enjoyed themselves. The married men, on the contrary, were seriously worried about their dependants. A pathetic incident occurred when I paid a call on one of them who was working in the kitchen at the Lae Officers' Club. I had gone across from Busama for a few days to attend a conference and had promised his three youngsters, with whom I had become friendly, to take him a message. On my making myself known he burst into tears and, sobbing into his pots and pans, begged me to intercede for his release.

Papuan labourers from the south similarly conscripted composed a song in pidgin Motu, their *lingua franca*, to express their homesickness. I asked one whom I met at Milne Bay to prepare a translation, which I reproduce here as it was handed to me, the oddities of spelling and punctuation uncorrected.

SONG THAT IS SUNG IN REMEMBRANCE OF
HOMES LEFT BEHIND

We have left our homes and beaches
To labour for the war in different places,
In far flung places. In these hard times
We wander aimlessly away from home.

WAR

Places that were never seen before
We now have seen by toil and sweat
Who has caused this dredded parting ? ? ?
To be out on scatterd places

In our little homes before the war
Partings from dear ones was unknown.
We have worked in different places.
To return is something dim.

We now wonder by our camp fires
Of our homes, our dear ones, and our wive's
Longing, hoping, Praying deeply,
To return to home onece more.

Village Affairs

If those left behind after the labourers were taken away had been freed from further outside work the difficulties of poor housing and inadequate gardens might in time have been overcome. Instead, Busama was now ordered to supply 1,600 sheets of thatch weekly for the increasing number of buildings going up in Lae. (Each sheet consists of a stick six to eight feet long over which a row of leaflets from a sago palm are folded and then skewered in position: the leaflets are cut from living palms, whose growth is thereby somewhat hindered: palms which have been cut back too severely may die.) A certain amount of rations was issued and payment promised. Eventually, two years later, the money was handed over, one shilling for every ten sheets.

When I first reached Busama, in September 1944, the conscripts with four or more children—men who in peace-time would never have gone away—had just been allowed to return, but thatch making, which had then been going on for nine months, was still in progress. The fulfilment of the quota took up three days in the week, and Bumbu, in addition, was making inroads on the remainder by demanding services to which he was entitled neither by tradition nor law. The huts, poor to begin with, were now on the point of collapse—one was blown down in a squall during the week in which I arrived—the area under cultivation had decreased from over one hundred acres to less than nine, fish were not being caught because replacement of the canoes and nets was impossible, and there were still no livestock. The ANGAU staff at Salamaua had been changed a couple of weeks before my coming. The new District Officer quickly realised something of the seriousness of the situation, and it was at his suggestion that I first went to Busama. Before the month was over he made a tour of the coast south of Lae. I give in his own words the account of what he found.

'The census check shows that an abnormal percentage of effective males is absent with ANGAU, and close examination reveals recruiting of men with families of up to four children. Many aged people and orphans have no means of support. Percentage of effective males [1] absent is shown hereunder:

Labu Butu	49·1
Labu Miti	30·2
Labu Tali	32·3
Busama	60·3
Buakap	74·5
Wamasu'	50
Asini'	68·5

'I find it impossible to ascertain how the weekly quotas of thatch sheets were determined, as they show little relation to populations.

Village	Quota	Resident in Village	Effective Males in Village
Labu Butu	1,200	285	30
Labu Miti	1,000	180	30
Labu Tali	1,200	164	23
Busama	1,600	527	30
Buakap and Wamasu'	1,600	237	14
Asini'	1,200	247	17

'The results of continued production are the exhaustion of the material, damage and destruction of palms, and inability to devote

[1] 'Effective males' were able-bodied adults, exclusive of village officials and fathers with more than three young children living, between the apparent ages of sixteen and forty-five.

15

time to food cultivation. At Labu Butu and Labu Tali all good local supplies are now exhausted, and the natives are producing inferior thatch from wild sago which has already been cut once. At Labu Miti all sago supplies are exhausted, and in view of the alarming food situation work must cease immediately. Labourers sent from Lae to increase thatch production have ruined nine-tenths of all the Labu planted sago by reckless and continued cutting.

'At Busama all supplies from planted sago within reasonable distance are exhausted. The natives must at present walk for two hours to reach the sago area, and if production were to be continued at the present rate it would be necessary in three months to walk for three hours. The food situation here is serious, and I have ordered the immediate cessation of thatch production.

'The Buakap quota has been produced from planted sago, as there are no wild palms here. The people have just completed cutting their palms for the second time, and I have ordered them to cease production.

'The incessant demand for thatch has crippled these people and rendered impossible their rehabilitation after campaign dislocation. . . .

'Taro is the staple diet of these coastal people, supplemented by bananas, pawpaws, sugar cane, greens, and coconuts. Sago is a reserve food supply prepared for special occasions. The cultivation of taro depends on the availability of suckers. It is certain that the gardens were smaller than usual on our return in 1943, and there was a consequent diminution in the number of suckers for planting. The imposition of an inordinate quota of thatch in addition to forced labour has deprived the natives since that date of the opportunity to rehabilitate themselves. The cessation of thatch production will enable the people to devote time to food cultivation, but I stress the fact that the size of their gardens will for many months be limited by the small number of suckers at present available. . . .

'There are practically no domestic pigs or fowls in the area, hunting has been limited owing to the loss of nets, and fishing has suffered through the loss of tackle and canoes. . . .

'The Busama appear to be very much under-nourished, especially the children. Their own resources feed them for nine days each month, and Army rations for a little over twelve. For the remaining nine days they have nothing. . . .

16

'I spent four days in Busama observing life in what is possibly the most seriously affected village in the area. This has been described by Lieutenant-Colonel Hogbin as a tropical slum, and I cannot improve on the description.'

The vital statistics, together with details about the absentees—how many were married and the number of their children—are given in Appendix A. Fifty-one men were away on October 1, 1944 (60·3 per cent. of the total effective males), and twelve months

ACRES

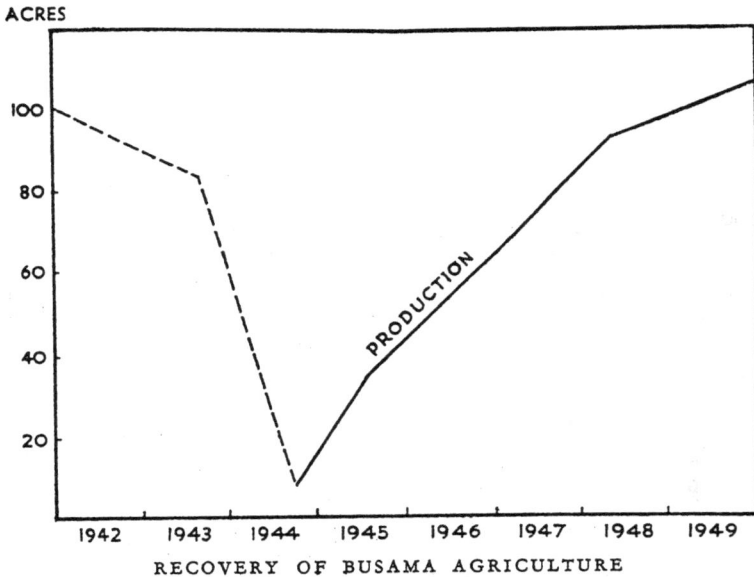

RECOVERY OF BUSAMA AGRICULTURE

Accurate figures are not available for the period up to September 1944, and the dotted section represents the assumed fall in production.

later the figure was still thirty-three (43 per cent. of the effective males). These numbers appear at first glance to compare favourably with those of more normal times: thus in February 1948 fifty-four were away (forty-two labourers and twelve Mission workers). At this date, however, the absentees also included eleven wives and twenty-three children, whose village kinsfolk had no further maintenance responsibilities. By 1948, too, rehabilitation was almost complete; moreover, the population, 578 on October 1, 1944, had increased to 617, and there were more effective males.

17

Rations had to be supplied till the beginning of 1946, but once thatch making was stopped the garden acreage began to increase. The 8·5 acres of 1944 went to 38 in 1945, to 65 in 1947, to 95 in 1948, and to 106 in 1950 (see Appendix B). Expansion would have been more rapid had there been enough taro suckers. During the first year reasonably satisfactory houses were erected in the bush

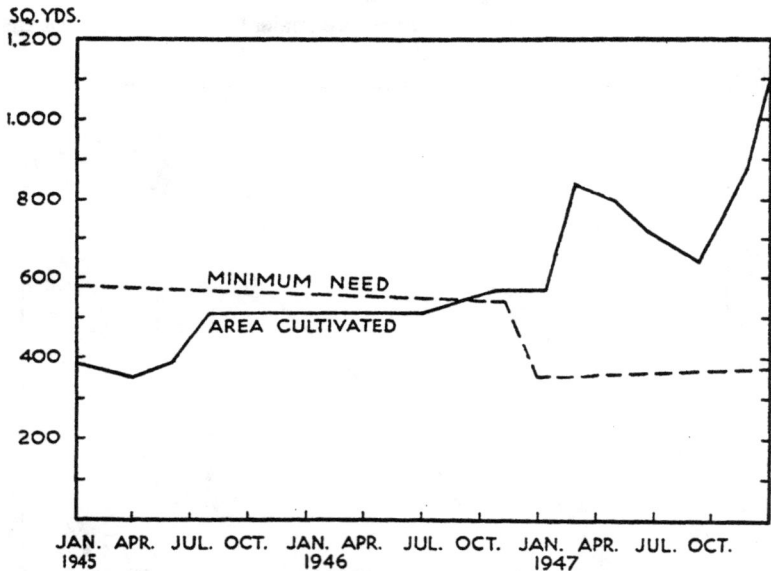

FAMILY GARDENS

Area cultivated by the household of three adults and two children 1945–1947 (see Appendix F, Household A).

Heavy line indicates area cultivated, dotted line minimum requirements to provide enough food. After January 1947 the crop could be left till fully mature, and the minimum area was therefore less.

clearing and thirty canoes constructed. A few fowls had also been obtained, but no pigs. Eighteen months later the settlement had been rebuilt on the old site (Plate 5) and ten more canoes made. Fowls were now available in plenty, and a couple of young sows had been ordered from a European who had established a piggery at Lae. By January 1948 the village had eighty-five dwellings (Plate 2a) and fourteen club houses, the majority with plank walls,

1. Wielding a digging stick in the garden

2a. New house built after the return of the conscripts

2b. Completing one of the new school buildings, January 1950

twenty-seven small canoes each about eighteen feet in length (Plate 9) and seventeen large canoes of thirty feet or longer, and nineteen pigs. These houses must have been adequate, for after two more years only three extra had been built. The increase in the number of canoes was also inconsiderable, three small and four large ones. Now, however, there were 180 pigs; and three seines made from camouflage netting, each sixty fathoms long, had been purchased (Plates 10*a* and 10*b*).

Compensation

The natives from Lae and other areas where large concentrations of troops were stationed were able to earn substantial sums by selling fruit and curios, but the Busama were not so fortunate.[1] The leave parties which came so frequently on picnics were prepared to take everything offering, but in the early days Bumbu maintained that he had the sole prerogative to engage in trade, the profits from which he kept for his own use, and afterwards all the food was needed and no time was left over for making grass skirts, fancy combs, and other souvenirs. Only a little extra money was therefore available at the end of the war to purchase new goods in place of those which had been destroyed.

The Australian Government agreed to accept the responsibility, and the Minister for External Territories invited J. V. Barry, Esq., K.C. (now Mr. Justice Barry of the Supreme Court of Victoria), Major J. L. Taylor, a senior District Officer of the New Guinea Administration, and myself to advise him on 'a just and practicable

[1] Many of the Solomon Islanders earned far more even than the residents of Lae. In the Solomons, as in New Guinea, the natives were forbidden to take in washing, but the officers of the military Administration were so few and the soldiers so numerous that the prohibition could not be enforced. In one village in Guadalcanal in 1943 I found all the men engaged in laundry work, for which they were receiving sixty dollars (£18) per week each plus rations for themselves and their families. The District Officer, on hearing this, ordered two-thirds of the population to go back to ordinary work, which had been badly neglected, and posted police to see that his command was obeyed. The American officer in charge of the camp nearby thereupon ran out a mile of power line to the village and installed two washing machines. It is unnecessary to add that the Solomons have had more post-war unrest than New Guinea.

plan for compensating the natives of Papua and New Guinea for loss or damage to land and property and death or injury arising from military operations or arising out of causes attributable to the existence of a state of war in the Territories.' Our Report was adopted shortly after the cessation of hostilities.[1]

A summary of the principal recommendations follows (paragraph 3):

'(I) All natives except those who have voluntarily assisted the enemy with a knowledge that it was wrong to do so should be eligible to receive compensation.

'(II) Compensation should be paid for deaths, injury and incapacity arising from causes directly or indirectly connected with the war.

'(III) Compensation should be paid for all damage or loss arising from causes directly or indirectly connected with the war.

'(IV) Simple machinery to enable compensation to be assessed promptly should be adopted.

'(V) Compensation should be paid in cash.

'(VI) Provision should be made for the immediate deposit of all sums in Savings Bank accounts.

'(VII) Adequate provision should be taken to protect natives from reckless expenditure and exploitation.

'(VIII) Stores for natives should be established by the Administration throughout the Territories as soon as possible.

'(IX) Stores should be stocked with approved goods of standard quality.

'(X) Store prices should be controlled.

'(XI) Government piggeries should be established to enable the natives to replace pigs which have been destroyed.

'(XII) Government nurseries should be established to permit the natives to acquire seeds and plants to improve their food supply.

'(XIII) Pools of building material should be established in areas where local materials are now unobtainable.

[Recommendation XIV deals only with the highland area.]

---

[1] *Compensation to the Natives of Papua and New Guinea for War Injuries and War Damage*, Department of External Territories, Commonwealth of Australia, Canberra, July 1945. The document includes a section (paragraphs 8-47) giving the general effects of the war on the native peoples.

'(XV) A trust fund should be established to be used for re-afforestation.
'(XVI) Independent arbitrators of known competence should be appointed to assess land claims.
'(XVII) In all but claims in respect of land, District Officers should be investigators and assessors.
[Recommendations XVIII, XIX, and XX deal only with procedure.]
'(XXI) Village Councils and Village Treasuries should be established. Compensation for property owned communally should be paid to the Village Treasuries and expenditure controlled by the Village Councils subject to the approval of the District Officers.'

I had already investigated the value of the losses of the Busama, and, as an example of the sort of payments which would have to be made, we included these (see Appendix C). The total sum involved was £3,398 10s., made up of claims for £420 in respect of seven natives killed (£60 each), for £319 2s. in respect of village property, for £300 in respect of property belonging to small groups, and for £2,259 8s. in respect of goods owned by individuals. The village property included the church (£99 12s.), the school (£34), the rest house (£16 10s.), a seine (£89), and a whale boat (£80); the property owned by groups of various club houses worth from £10 to £40 each. Individuals wanted money for houses, coconut palms, hunting dogs, livestock, bicycles, sewing-machines, trade boxes, spectacles, furniture, irons, lamps, gramophones, axes, knives, gardening tools, carpenter's tools, clothing, beds and bedding, books, cooking utensils, household crockery and cutlery, canoes, mats, woven bags, clay pots, and wooden bowls. One hundred and twenty-five separate claims were put forward for amounts averaging £18 (the biggest, £68 19s., was from a fully trained carpenter whose kit of tools had been destroyed).

The scheme was criticised by some on the grounds that honesty is not a conspicuous native virtue and that the claims would be too high. The District Officer of Morobe determined to make Busama a test case, and instead of paying out on my figures he waited for two years and sent one of his staff to collect new ones. Then, pretending that these had been lost, he had a third set compiled a year later again. He informs me that when the three were compared only one man's claim showed any considerable variation.

The exception was a youth by the name of Tawasi, who on the third occasion computed his losses at £242. Such items as an electric lighting plant, thirty sheets, fifteen shirts, and fourteen pairs of trousers were enumerated, with the cost of each. Consulted about what should be done, I advised that the claim be handed to the elders for their opinion. A meeting was summoned, and a teacher read the statement aloud. As he reached the total the man sitting next to me burst into a guffaw of laughter and ejaculated, 'Christ, Tawasi's the bloody Bank of New South Wales true!' The amount was quickly reduced to £9.

Money received for village property was devoted to the purchase of material for two school buildings, which were completed in January 1950 (Plate 2b). The floors were concrete, the walls fibro-cement sheeting, and the roofs corrugated iron.[1] The total cost, excluding the value of the iron, the local timber, and the labour, was £176.

These structures have a value for the community, but only a proportion of the money handed to individuals was invested so wisely. An analysis of the expenditure of twenty-five persons disclosed that although sixty per cent. of the total sum was spent on tools, lamps, pigs, and clothing, and five per cent. went into banking accounts, no less than thirty-five per cent. was squandered on food-stuffs, tobacco, and rubbishy cosmetics.

Several of the recommendations of the Compensation Committee proved to be unacceptable, and it is this fact no doubt which largely explains the waste. The setting up of Government stores was declared to be contrary to policy, the regulations controlling prices could not be enforced, and no Government piggeries were established (a number of European business men set up piggeries on a small scale and sold piglets at £7 and £8 each). Further, the Committee's suggestion of a means for preventing reckless spending and exploitation was rejected as impractical. We had thought that all money should be paid into banking accounts and that the District Officer's permission might be required for withdrawals in excess of £5 in any six months' period.

In the circumstances, it is gratifying to be able to record that on December 31, 1949, 33,000 native depositors in Papua and New

---

[1] Corrugated iron is not on sale to natives at present. This lot, second-hand, was a gift from the Government.

Guinea had between them £466,000 in the bank. Much of the money must have come from other sources, for at that time only about £1,000,000 had been paid in compensation. Pre-war figures are not available, but I am assured that bank deposits did not exceed £50,000.

Chapter Two

PEOPLE AND VILLAGE

'History books which contain no lies are extremely tedious.'—ANATOLE FRANCE, *Crime of Sylvestre Bonnard.*

EXCEPT for a few small communities of pygmies, numerically insignificant, New Guinea natives are all of the same racial stock. Like the other peoples of the south-west Pacific, such as the Solomon Islanders, the New Hebrideans, and the New Caledonians, they are Melanesians, a branch of the great Negroid group, their distinguishing features being dark skins, fuzzy hair, longish heads, a slight degree of prognathism (out-thrust jaw), fairly thick lips, and rather broad noses. Various local sub-types have developed, however, probably through isolation and inbreeding, and it is usually possible to tell at a glance from whence the labourers in the compounds have come. The special characteristics of the Huon Gulf are stature above the average, massive chest development, and rich brown colour.[1]

[1] At the end of the last century, when New Guinea was still unexplored, certain anthropologists, mainly German, suggested the separation of the natives of the south-west Pacific into two divisions, Papuan and Melanesian (cf. A. H. Keane, *Ethnology*, Cambridge, 1896). The classification won general acceptance after the investigations first of Dr. A. C. Haddon (*Races of Man*, London, 1909) and later of Professor C. G. Seligman (*Melanesians of British New Guinea*, Cambridge, 1910)—though they used the terms Papuasians and Papuo-Melanesians. The 'Papuans', Dr. Haddon thought, were probably confined to the centre and west of New Guinea, while the 'Melanesians' were spread over the New Guinea coast and the eastern islands. The physical anthropology

24

PEOPLE AND VILLAGE

The New Guinea area resembles Babel of old, and the scores of dialects so far recorded are but a fraction of the total. Two linguistic families are represented, Melanesian and Papuan—the first in most parts of the north-east coast of New Guinea, the south-east coast, and the bulk of the eastern islands; and the latter in central and western New Guinea, here and there on the north-east coast, and parts of New Britain, New Ireland, Bougainville, Vella Lavella, Savo, and the Russells (the last four in the Solomons).[1]

Eleven dialects are spoken around the Huon Gulf (see map, p. xiv). All are classified as Melanesian, but the differences between some of them are as marked as those of, say, English and German or French and Spanish. One, Gawa', is the mother tongue of about 7,000 persons, including the Busama, but the majority are understood in only three or four villages and one, Buasi', in a single settlement with a population of less than three hundred.

Such multiplicity presents difficulties to the Administration and, nowadays, to the natives themselves. A *lingua franca* is obviously essential, and the feeling of all, white and coloured, is that English will meet the need best. Progress in teaching a speech so alien

of the area still awaits full study, and without this evidence one must continue to guess; but in the past two decades I have travelled far more widely than would have been possible in Dr. Haddon's day—around the New Guinea coast, in the interior, from one end to the other of the Solomons, in the New Hebrides, and in New Caledonia—and I believe that the distinction is unwarranted. I suspect that he may have been influenced by seeing two strongly contrasted local sub-types, probably the Kiwai of the Papuan Gulf and the Hanuabada of Port Moresby. Inland peoples, such as those of the central Sepik, Mount Hagen, and Goroka, are unlike each other in minor details and unlike the Kiwai; and such coast peoples as those of the Huon Gulf, the Buangs, and Bougainville are again unlike each other in minor details and also unlike the Hanuabada.

[1] The term 'Melanesian', it is to be noted, is applied both to race and to language; 'Papuan', by me but not Dr. Haddon, to language only.

I should point out that I have found no connection between the families of dialects and the appearance of the speakers. The natives, whether they have a Melanesian or Papuan language, appear to be broadly similar, though development of the sub-types has gone on everywhere. At the same time there are plenty of examples of physically identical neighbours—for instance the peoples of New Georgia and Bougainville—speaking fundamentally different languages.

Information about language distribution is given by A. Capell, *Language Study for New Guinea Students, Oceania* Monograph 5: see also S. H. Ray, *Melanesian Island Languages*, Cambridge, 1926.

is necessarily slow, and for the present Pacific pidgin English has to suffice.[1] This is a compromise, a language with a Melanesian grammar and a vocabulary seventy per cent. English but pronounced in a Melanesian way. Yet considerable subtlety of thought can be expressed, and I have often had the experience of discussing international affairs and theology in pidgin for an evening with central-European missionaries unacquainted with the King's English.

The origin of pidgin English is a mystery—certainly it was not deliberately taught to the natives by Europeans. The first record of its use was in the latter part of the nineteenth century around Rabaul by labourers who had returned from the cane fields of Queensland. From here the spread was rapid, and, except in the newly discovered highland areas in the depths of the interior, 'tok boi' (i.e. talk boy), as pidgin is called, is now understood by every male over the age of sixteen and by many females.

Some of the Roman Catholic Missionary societies employ pidgin for translations,[2] but other denominations have preferred to make a selection from the vernaculars. The Lutherans, the only Mission working in the Morobe District, chose Yabim (Jabêm), the speech of the natives south of Finschhafen, the first church centre, for their Melanesian-speaking converts and Kate (Kâte), from the interior of the Huon Peninsula, for the Papuan speakers. Yabim, though it is the mother tongue of fewer persons than is Gawa', is now by the accident of history the one native language understood throughout the Gulf area.[3] The people prefer this if travelling locally, but it

[1] The most exhaustive studies of pidgin are J. J. Murphy, *The Book of Pidgin English*, Brisbane, 1947; R. A. Hall, G. Bateson, and J. M. W. Whiting, *Melanesian Pidgin English*, Linguistic Society of America, Baltimore, 1943; and S. W. Reed, *The Making of Modern New Guinea*, Philadelphia, 1943, pp. 267-291. Varieties of Pacific pidgin are spoken in the Territory of New Guinea, the Solomons, and the New Hebrides. In Papua its place is taken by Police Motu, a pidgin version of the language of the Hanubada of Port Moresby, and by broken English, an unsatisfactory medium in which each speaker follows his own rules.

[2] E.g. *Liklik Katolik Baibel* ('Little Catholic Bible'), Alexishafen, 1934.

[3] The widespread adoption of Yabim has led to the corruption of the other languages, and Gawa' speakers today use their own and Yabim forms almost indiscriminately (they even give their own speech its Yabim name and now refer to it as Kawa'). In the following pages I have tried to keep to the Gawa' terms, but Yabim has probably caught me unawares now and then, especially —and for obvious reasons—in matters relating to religion.

Both Gawa' and Yabim have seven vowels, the five Italian sounds common

26

is useless for dealings with the residents of other places, when pidgin is spoken.

History of Busama

The Gawa' group do not recall any original home in their songs and stories and are content to go back only to the parent settlement in the Gulf, Bu-Gawa' (nowadays always given its Yabim spelling, Bukawa') near the centre of the north coast. From here the people gradually spread westwards to the Markham and eastwards to the borders of the Yabim territory. The country had apparently not been occupied before, or, if it was, the earlier inhabitants were so swiftly overcome and absorbed that their existence could be forgotten.

During a bad drought, probably between 1750 and 1775, a handful crossed the sea and made a home at Lutu on the tip of the Salamaua peninsula. This spot was of great economic importance as the site of the only quarry in the whole region where stone could be obtained suitable for the manufacture of adzes and other tools.

The soil near Lutu proved to be so poor that the villagers were soon driven to take up a vacant belt of coast on the mainland nearby. They cultivated their gardens here and attended to their sago palms during the day, but in the first stages, fearing attacks from the Kila who lived on the seaboard immediately to the south, or from the Kai and Kaiwa of the hill country to the west, they always returned home towards nightfall.[1] Eventually, however, as their numbers increased, two permanent settlements were founded, one at Asini' on a hill directly opposite Lutu and the other a few miles to the north.

The latter site proved difficult to fortify, and some years later, in about 1835-40 as near as I can judge from genealogies (but see

to all Melanesian dialects plus two more, one midway between *i* and *e* and the other midway between *o* and *u*. These are written *ē* and *ō* respectively by the Mission, but as I am not here concerned with linguistics the distinction will be ignored. My symbols *i* and *u*, that is to say, stand for both closed and open versions. I also use *y* for the sound in the English word 'year' not the *j* of the Mission script, *ng* not *ŋ*, and an apostrophe not *c* for the glottal stop. Tones are of some importance in the language, but these also I do not indicate.

[1] Kila, Kai, and Kaiwa are Yabim forms. The Gawa' refer to Gela, Gai, and Gaiwa.

p. 102, footnote), the people moved further north again, this time to Busama. Schneider Point (Ho'tu in the local tongue) above, a second headland below, and a cliff behind rendered the place almost impregnable, and before long a dozen or so friendly Kaiwa householders who had been living on a hill close by at a place called Gaiwaku decided that they also would move in.

After a lapse of seventy years one more Lutu offshoot came across to the mainland, this time to Buakap, half-way between Asini' and Busama. The Lutheran Mission had shortly before set up a station at Mala'lo on a terrace immediately behind, and these folk, for the sake of the children's schooling, preferred to live close at hand.

Changes had in the meantime taken place at the mouth of the Markham. The warlike Laiwamba from higher up the river, following their usual practices, drove out a collection of Gawa' who had set up a village on the right bank and sent them into the foothills to the south, country claimed by the Labu from the swamps around Labu Lagoon and the Kaidemoe of the Buang Range to the west.[1] Pushed continually southwards, the group reached Awasa Hill, two miles south of Busama, in approximately 1830. Even here there was no respite, and for the next forty years the Awasa, as their neighbours now called them, were subjected to raid after raid from the Kai and the Busama. Finally, round about 1880 or perhaps a little before, the latter were moved to pity and invited the remaining families to make a home with them.

From 1840 onwards the Busama also received additions from such places as Labu, Lae, Bukawa', and various Kila and Kai settlements. These persons came in as single individuals, not as groups like the Gaiwaku and the Awasa. Several, perhaps the majority, were seeking refuge after their villages had been attacked by enemies and their relatives killed.

Reference must also be made to a further migration leading to the founding of the two villages closest to Busama. Under pressure from the Mission, two Kai settlements moved down from the foothills in 1910 to Wamasu', three miles to the south, and Gwado, two miles to the west. Both are said to have been at first fairly large, but now they have together a population of less than one hun-

[1] In Gawa' the Laiwamba are referred to as the Lahi-wapa, 'the inland Lahi (Lai)'; the Labu as the Apu'; and the Kaidemoe as the Gaidemoe.

dred. The explanation for the decline may well be the lack of immunity to malaria, which at lower levels in New Guinea is endemic. The astonishing thing about these people is that although they have lived near the sea for four decades—Wamasu' is not more than fifty yards from high-water mark—their Kai traditions have been so strong that they have not learned to swim, fish, or handle canoes.[1]

Traders were the first Europeans to visit the area, probably between 1895 and 1900. Today only a few of the older generation can recall the days when steel was unknown and implements were still being made from stone, when cotton loin-cloths and dresses were not worn and clothing consisted of a strip of bark cloth for the men and a grass skirt for the women. Contact with officers of the German Administration and with labour recruiters began soon afterwards, and by 1900 native warfare had been practically stamped out. Missionaries followed in 1906, when the station at Mala'lo was opened. Church schools were soon set up in the villages, and within a couple of decades the population was fully literate in Yabim.

Today the Busama and their neighbours have a better acquaintance with Western culture than most New Guinea natives. The European settlement, the District Office, and the Mission centre are within easy reach, and contact with all three is close and continuous.

Busama Village

The population is made up of two main elements, a group descended from the early Lutu settlers and another descended from those of Awasa. The rest are such a small minority that they generally ignore their separate origin and consider themselves to be members of one of the bigger divisions. Only six Gaiwaku families remain, of whom four claim to be 'the same as Lutu' and two 'the same as Awasa.' 'We don't think of our Kaiwa ancestors any more,' they

---

[1] Wakop, a little farther to the west, is still a third lowland Kai village. Due north of this is Buasi',where the language is unique, though it is said to be related to that spoken in the Watut area on the right bank of the middle Markham. These villages have occupied their present site for many years, but no one knows how or why they came to be there.

told me. 'Why should we? The light of their fires has long been dead, and we have forgotten their language. No, we go back to the persons whom they married from Lutu or Awasa and call ourselves after them.' The absorption of those descended from the migrants from Lae, Labu, and the other places is also complete. The 'foreign' ancestor at the time of his arrival had to put himself under the care of a protector, and the children in due course accepted this man's allegiances.

With 600 inhabitants, Busama is three times as large as most New Guinea villages, and in 1945 the officer then in charge of Morobe District came to the conclusion that the place ought to be split into its component parts, which he called Busama-Lutu and Busama-Awasa respectively. He had just granted permission for the people to leave the temporary settlement in the bush where they had been living for the past two years and rebuild on the old beach site, and this was therefore the appropriate time for the change to be made. He suggested that those who wished to be counted as Busama-Lutu might put up their houses on one side of Schneider Point and those wishing to be included in Busama-Awasa on the other side. No compulsion was exercised, and two-thirds chose the former and one-third the latter.[1]

Schneider Point proved to be an inconvenient boundary, but although a few Lutu houses went up on the wrong side, the spirit of the District Officer's intention was fulfilled. Each section has its own officials, its luluai and tultul, and runs many of its affairs separately, though the larger undertakings are handled jointly. Thus there is a single rest house for travelling Europeans, and only one church is to be erected.

On my earlier visits I lived in a hut in the bush clearing, but latterly this rest house has served my needs. It stands on a shoulder of the Point at the very heart of the village. The main thoroughfare runs alongside, and from the verandah the whole place is in full view, Lutu on the one side and Awasa on the other (Plate 5). The coast stretches away beyond, to Lae and the Rawlinson Mountains northwards and to Salamaua in the south, and all strangers entering by sea or by land can be seen coming.

[1] A number have for personal reasons since changed their grouping, though the proportions remain the same. A new District Officer has altered the names of the sections to Busama Nos. 1 and 2.

PEOPLE AND VILLAGE

The dwellings are not arranged in regular rows or streets but are scattered along the sandy shelf in groups. Each consists as a rule of a single room measuring about twenty-four feet by fourteen with a verandah either in front or along one side (Plate 2a). A few are much larger, but a wall then runs across the middle, making as it were a pair of semi-detached cottages, and each half is occupied by a separate family. Maternal uncle and nephew may choose to live as neighbours in this fashion, or, more rarely, father and son, or a pair of brothers or cousins.

The buildings stand on piles from three to five feet above the ground, and a notched log or a flight of steps leads up to the doorway. For flooring the outer covering of the trunk of a species of wild palm is used, and roofs continue to be thatched with sago leaf. The walls, however, are nowadays constructed from planks of sawn timber carefully planed smooth, and the verandah is often screened with blinds woven from canes. Most of the cooking is done on the ground in front, but there is always a fireplace inside for cold or wet weather. A sheet of iron is laid down first to protect the palmwood and a covering of earth placed on top.

In former times pandanus-leaf mats imported from the north coast served everyone both for beds and bedding, but most men and a few women today sleep on folding cots. The mats are still in demand as mattresses, though for covering there is a plentiful supply of blankets and a few sheets. Pillows are made of cloth stuffed with teased kapok obtained from local sources. Other household furniture includes tables, chairs, and boxes. Shelves line the upper parts of the walls to hold the various utensils—clay cooking pots, Europeans saucepans, carved wooden bowls, polished coconuts used for water-bottles, plates, cups, and baskets.

Alongside each house is a shed where the fowls are shut up at night, and at the back is the pit latrine, an innovation of fairly recent date.

Scattered amongst the dwellings are the clubs, scene of much of the social life. The male half of the population adjourns thither during the late afternoons to chat, smoke, and chew betel-nut or hold informal meetings, and it is there also that guests are entertained. The clubs serve as dormitories, too, for the youths from puberty till after their marriage. Prior to the bombings of 1943 the fourteen clubs were each built to the same distinctive design.

31

Unlike the dwellings, they were of two storeys, the lower consisting of a platform without walls, to give shelter from the hot sun with access to the cooling breezes, and the upper of the sleeping apartment. The posts, to support so much weight, were always of immense thickness, and in pagan times they used to be carved into representations of mythical heroes (Plate 16b). Since the war the people have had to forgo elaborate structures of this type, and the clubs of today, which serve the same sort of purposes as their predecessors, are practically indistinguishable from the residences.

Leading Informants

It will be well at this point to say a word or two about some of the men whose names appear in the following pages. At the head of the list is Ahipum, in his early forties on our initial meeting in 1944, when he was one of the most respected men in the village. Quiet, gentle, and unassuming, he was renowned for his steadfastness, wisdom, and sense of justice. His nomination as luluai for Busama-Lutu on the division of the settlement was a foregone conclusion, and no serious rival was suggested. Bumbu, the paramount luluai who had caused such trouble after our return to Salamaua, is the eldest brother of Ahipum's mother, now deceased, but the two men have not been on friendly terms for more than a decade.

Next comes Nga'gili', the tultul of Busama-Lutu, in his mid-thirties in 1944. We began addressing one another in fun at first as 'younger brother' and 'older brother', but the use of the terms soon became a habit, and relations between us have long been fraternal. Nga'gili' has great strength of character, is something of a wit, and has considerable charm; but if crossed he can be difficult and forthright to the point of rudeness.

Ida', the third of my closest friends, of approximately the same age as Nga'gili', has had long experience in the Lutheran Mission. For some years a teacher at the seminary near Bukawa', he took charge of the Busama school during 1945 and 1946 and is now headmaster of a college at Lae. Highly intelligent and serious minded, he will forgive me I hope for referring to his fiery temper. (At the present time he is the only person from the village able to read my publications.).

PEOPLE AND VILLAGE

My other intimate associates included Gwaleyam, the luluai of Busama-Awasa; Busilim, an elder notorious for his hot head and unbridled tongue; Nga'sele', one of the oldest men in the village, recognised as a muddled thinker and bore but useful because of his great interest in the past; and Gi'lahi, an intelligent youngster who was just-nineteen when we first met.

I shall have to quote the statements of other natives frequently, but no special reference is necessary here. Their identity, in any case, must often be disguised, sometimes to prevent their embarrassment, sometimes to avoid confusing the reader. The number of names in the village is so limited that many of them are shared by four and even five persons.

Chapter Three

DAILY ROUTINE

'No man has ever learned anything rightly until he knows that every day is Doomsday.'—RALPH WALDO EMERSON, *Works and Days*.

VILLAGE life in the pre-European era must have proceeded without any major social changes. A limited mastery over the physical environment had been achieved, and with the technical equipment available the standard of living could not be improved; moreover, there was no alien civilisation near at hand from which borrowings might have been made.

The passage of the years is unimportant when each one is the same as those which have gone before and seems likely to be identical with those which will follow. The members of the senior generation still cannot say how old they are, and although everyone is aware that the site on which the village now stands has been occupied for a comparatively short period, even the better-educated Mission teachers never speculate about when the move took place.

The months, too, are not distinguishable by native names. The counting of the moons was said to have been necessary in past times only in such places as the Buang Range, where agricultural work had to be planned ahead. The main crop there is the yam, which is planted at one particular time and harvested at another; but the Busama staple, taro (*Colocasia antiquorum*), grows throughout the year.

34

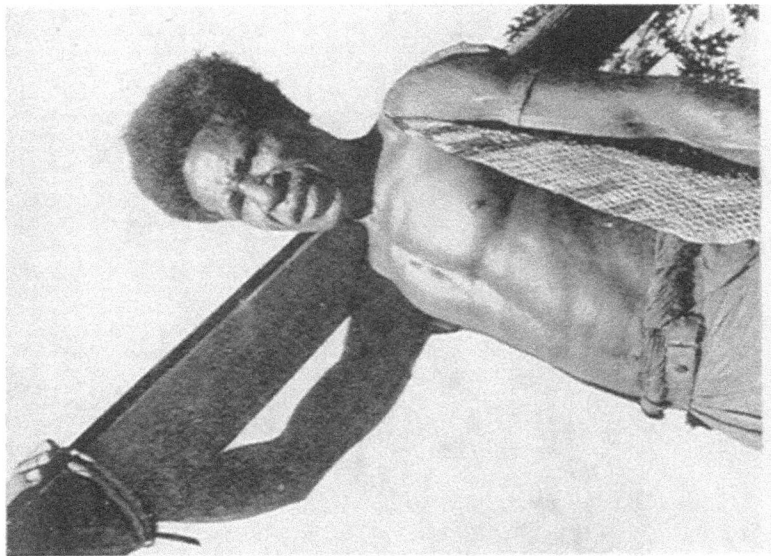

3b.   Flooring material for a new house

3a.   An expert builder sketching
      the plan for a house

4. Bumbu before dismissal. His white-topped cap is the
mark of a paramount luluai

DAILY ROUTINE

Our calendar has been introduced into the schools, but its use is for the most part restricted to the activities for which we are directly or indirectly responsible. The Mission leaders consult their diaries when making arrangements for church festivals, for instance, and youths under indenture to an employer reckon out their pay days and the length of time which their contract has still to run. Parents, it is true, now like to give the date on which their children were born when the census is taken, but, although many younger persons have some notion of their age, birthdays pass by without comment.

The phases of the moon, however, are of some significance: fishing with flares is possible only on dark nights and evening visiting and games only when there is adequate light. The waxing and the waning are therefore noted, though the successive nights have no names.

The seasonal rhythm is also not without its effects. The two contrasting periods are called respectively 'the wet' and 'the hot', *uho* from *u*='rain', and *a'sa* from *a'*='sun'. The first is dominated by the south-east trade wind (*mu'salu*), which blows fairly consistently from May to September, reaching gale force (when it is known as *mu'timwi*) in July and August, months in which the sun is rarely visible for more than half a day at a time. December to April, on the other hand, is the period of the monsoon (*mu'la*), a hot wind blowing out of the Markham valley. In January, February, and early March sudden storms, *mu'asa*, are likely to descend in the late afternoon without warning and bring trees and houses crashing down.

Exposure to heavy rain can have a chilling effect even in the tropics, and at one stage of the 1945 wet season I was treating twenty cases of pneumonia and an untold number of malaria victims, at least three times as many as usual. Fearful of being patients themselves, the remaining villagers kept indoors as much as possible, sometimes leaving essential work undone. The result was that they became bored, disgruntled, and on edge and were apt to see a slight where none was intended. It is acknowledged that more quarrels occur in July and August than throughout the rest of the year.

The appearance of the Pleiades on the eastern horizon immediately before dawn at the end of August is welcomed as a harbinger of

35

Month	Stars	Wind	Rainfall	Fishing	Gardens	Agricultural Work
January						
February	Pleiades disappear	Monsoon	Hot season (Heavy thunderstorms March and April)	Best time for offshore fishing	Gardens in low-lying areas	Some families short of taro
March						
April						
May		Calms and variable winds				Extensive areas cleared before wet season begins
June						
July		Trade wind	Wet season		Gardens on hillsides or in sandy soil	No clearing done and less planting than usual
August	Pleiades appear					
September						
October		Calms and variable winds		Best time for tuna fishing		
November		Monsoon	Hot season		Gardens in low-lying areas	
December						

better times on the way. The constellation is said to represent six sky maidens, the *dam-awi*, setting out for the gardens. In olden times the first man who saw it woke the rest of the village with a loud yell, and the population tumbled out of bed in a hurry to pay their respects. They rushed into the sea 'to wash away the sickness and bad temper' and then marched up and down the beach singing songs and beating the hulls of the canoes with sticks. The sunrise was carefully observed on the next few mornings, for a clear sky was the sign of good fortune.

The approach of the Pleiades to the western mountains gives a warning that the monsoon will soon be passing. At this time there are frequent thunderstorms, which the natives still describe as the disturbance caused by the *dam-ngga'* (Orion's belt), the menfolk who accompany the maidens, preparing a canoe for the return voyage to the east. The vessel is ready by early April, giving the party a chance to take advantage of the now failing westerly wind. February and March are the best months for certain kinds of offshore fish, which are playfully spoken of as the chips hacked off by the sky men as they work away at the dug-out.

The major pagan festivals used to take place in November. Large open-air gatherings were out of the question during the preceding months even if it had been possible to cross the flooded rivers. Invitations were sent out long before for 'the time when the Pleiades had risen high enough to be encircled', and as the weeks went by the commencement was fixed for so many days ahead. The count was marked by a cord with a series of knots, one of which was untied each morning.

Other recurrent events are regulated by the flowering of certain plants or by some of the trees shedding their leaves. Thus the tuna (bonito) lures are prepared when one of the forest creepers is covered with brilliant red blossoms in about the middle of September. Shoals of the fish are already to be seen cruising along the coast, but, 'dazzled by the colour of blood', they refuse to take the hooks till the last petal has withered.

Taro is ideally suited to the wet climate, and crops planted during the continuous downpour of July and August do just as well as those planted in the less rainy months. Yet the alternation of seasons demands that the gardens shall be located in different areas. From the time when the leaves of a species of tree (it grows close to the

37

coast, but I do not know its botanical name) start turning yellow, in the first week of October, till the flowering of a certain bush shrub at the end of March cultivation is restricted to low-lying ill-drained plots where the soil is likely to be permanently damp, whereas at other periods hillsides or patches of sandy soil close to the rivers are chosen.[1]

Again, clearing is usually avoided during the wettest months on account of the difficulty of burning the rubbish. Householders like

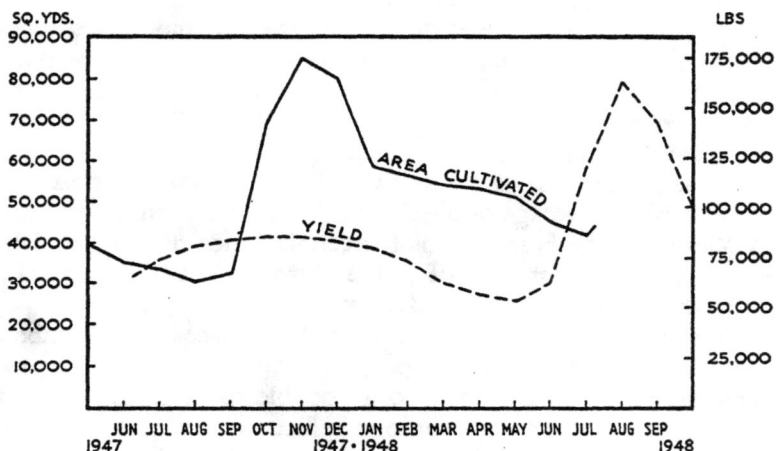

BUSAMA AGRICULTURE 1947–1948

Heavy line indicates area cultivated, dotted line yield. Note the time lag between planting and harvest, the small area cultivated during the wet season, the low yield eight months later, and the rapid recovery after the rain cease.

to be ready for the rains of late June, July, and August, and in March and April, after the Pleiades have disappeared and the *Saccharum robustum* is in flower, days on end are spent cutting down an immense area of forest, through which the owners put a fire during early June. The problem then is that a luxuriant growth of weeds has

[1] The rains continued in 1947 right through what should have been the dry season, and the flats were so waterlogged, and in consequence so infested with insects, that the natives continued planting hillside gardens. They went farther afield than usual, however, and chose areas which had been lying fallow for a generation.

always to be removed before planting can begin, a task which may be onerous if constant rain confines everyone to his dwelling. It follows that the July and August gardens are often somewhat smaller than those begun at other times and that as a result a few families are a little short in February, March, and April.

The Average Day[1]

The village is so close to the Equator that there is no appreciable variation in the hours of daylight all the year round, and sunrise occurs regularly at about 6 a.m. The women make a move first, in fine weather usually a quarter of an hour before the sun appears over the horizon. The children soon follow, but the men do not bestir themselves for another ten or fifteen minutes. The fire is lit at once—the mornings can be quite cool—and the house is then swept and the bedding put out to air.

By this time the bell is ringing for prayers, and everyone troops along to church. The service lasts for fifteen minutes, but the men who have no pressing engagements often stand around afterwards discussing how they intend to spend the day. The women, on the contrary, make their way home as speedily as possible to feed the children. If the adults eat at all they have only cold left-overs from the evening before.

Fridays are often devoted to what is called 'Government work,' which consists of cleaning the village, setting the latrines in order, cutting the grass on the track leading around the coast, and repairing the bridges over the many streams; and on Sundays all but necessary tasks are forbidden, and the whole countryside attends church at the Mission station. During the rest of the week, however, the people look after their own concerns. They begin to drift away soon after seven, and an hour or so later only those who intend spending the day at home remain.

The women generally go to the cultivations, but each carries a circular net on her head ready to stop by the rivers and freshwater lagoons to try her hand at taking small fish or shrimps (Plate 12). Hanging down her back she also has a couple of string bags in which she will bring home vegetables and firewood (Plate 6*b*). Her small

[1] See Appendices D, E.

baby is, if need be, carried in a bag of this kind slung either back or front according to which side is more protected from the rays of the sun (Plate 6a).

The men proceed either to the gardens or, if they are on the lookout for timber for house building or a new canoe, to the forest; or they may spend the day fishing. They disappear along the road carrying an axe or bush knife in their hands or else board their craft with paddles and tackle.

The school pupils form the largest group left in the village. Lessons begin at seven or shortly before and continue till noon, when the older children join their parents.[1] The younger ones, on the other hand, go off with the boys and girls of pre-school age and play games. Busama must be one of the most delightful spots in the world for growing up. There is a shelving beach with clean white sand, smooth seas and many streams for swimming, waterfalls under which to sit for a shower bath, a dense forest for hide-and-seek, and sandhills nearby for rolling and sliding.

Other stay-at-homes include the aged and the invalids, the women with babies too tiny as yet to be taken out, and the older women and girls in charge of the children. There are also a few women who have no gardening to do. These either sit on the verandah or choose a shady spot on the beach and net string bags.

A number of the men may also wish to spend a day in the village either because something demands attention there or because they have toiled hard at clearing or other heavy work for a time and are determined to potter around by way of a change. One of their kinsmen may need help with a new house, or someone's thatch may want repairing, or possibly a seine has been torn, an axe handle broken, or the outrigger boom of a canoe smashed. Odd jobs are always accumulating, and few can afford to be idle.

The women begin to leave the cultivations soon after two o'clock but often proceed only as far as the nearest beach. They have a bathe first—this is never omitted—and then congregate in twos and threes to chat and do the vegetables. The taro is peeled, the greens washed, and if young taro leaves are to be on the menu the stringy parts are removed. No move is made until shortly before four, when a breeze has usually sprung up, and if the other work is completed

---

[1] Morning and afternoon classes were held in 1945 and 1946 to make up for the two previous years when the schools were closed.

first they may devote half an hour or so to netting a few rows for a string bag. Burdens are then shouldered once more, and each woman sets off for home.

The men who have been absent return at about the same hour. Before entering the village they too have a bathe in the nearest stream, often their second since the morning. The remaining hours of daylight are occupied with such tasks as making fishing spears, sharpening axes, and mending the lashings of canoes; but if there is nothing else to do they may play cards, or mind the babies, or even set out along the beach to try their hand at fishing.

The late afternoon is the busiest part of the day for the housewife. She first calls up the children to find out what they have been doing and after attending to them fills the water-bottles, sweeps the house once more, and prepares dinner. The blue smoke of many fires curling upwards makes a pleasant sight against the long shadows.

Everyone is present for the evening meal, which is eaten soon after dusk. The children may wish to take their portions back to where they have been playing but are usually told to sit down and behave. Father has not seen them all day long and wants to know what they have been learning at school and how they have occupied themselves since the teacher dismissed them.

A platter of food is always carried across to anyone who has helped the household during the day—youths who have assisted the man with his clearing, neighbours who have spent an hour or two chipping the inside of his new canoe, women who have taken care of the youngsters, girls who have worked with the wife at her weeding, and so forth.

Visits to neighbours follow until the bell gives the summons for evening prayers at about eight o'clock. There is sometimes a village meeting lasting for an hour or two afterwards, and when the moon is shining organised games and more visiting may take place. On dark nights, however, the women and children soon retire to bed, though many of the men take their spears and fish by torchlight till the early hours of the morning.

Rain brings about certain changes. If it follows a week of sun it may not be unwelcome, for all sorts of tasks can be carried out at home. The men have hibiscus fibre ready for twisting into fishing lines and the women rolls of dried pandanus leaves stored away for sewing into mats. But the striking thing about wet weather is the way in which it results in the night being expanded and the day compressed. Everyone remains in bed in the morning till eight or nine o'clock and retires immediately on finishing his dinner. Unlike ourselves, the natives are not enslaved by the clock—instead, they make time suit their convenience.

European residents of New Guinea sometimes urge that natives benefit from employment by learning the virtue of regular habits of industry. The large commercial concerns to which we are accustomed obviously have to keep fixed hours and start work and finish off at set times irrespective of the weather or other considerations. But as in the village everyone is his own master there is no reason why he should not follow an independent course. On some occasions, when need dictates, he toils all day long and half the night; and on other occasions, when the job is not so pressing, he stays at home. In the end he does at least as much as the employee—probably, indeed, a good deal more.

Food Resources

Taro, the staple, is eaten every day, by itself in the mornings, often at midday, and again with garnishings in the evening. A host who for some reason has to offer his guests a substitute suffers acute embarrassment and hangs his head in shame.

Other root crops are sweet potatoes, yams, and tapioca. The first two are grown with some success by a few householders but are not generally popular, except as an occasional change. Every family, however, has a tapioca patch alongside the dwelling as a reserve.

The standby in prolonged emergencies is sago, and if for some reason disaster overtakes the gardens groups of men and girls set off for the swamps to cut down a palm and prepare a stock of flour (Plates 11a and 11b).

The other starchy food is the plantain or cooking banana. It is never eaten alone but is frequently used either to eke out the taro or give variety to a meal. It is regarded by most persons as somewhat inferior, and many elders turn up their noses at it in scorn.

Several extra vegetables are available, including such greens as cultivated spinaches and grasses, the leaves of certain creepers and ferns, bamboo shoots, and the immature flower tassel of the wild sugar cane, as well as pumpkins, tomatoes, cucumbers, and maize, which have been introduced by Europeans.

The chief food eaten raw is the coconut. The green nut, besides providing a pleasant drink, has a palatable jelly-like flesh; the meat of the ripe nut, when grated and squeezed, yields a thick white cream forming an excellent base for sauces;[1] and inside when a shoot has appeared a delicious snowy sponge forms. In addition, there is a wealth of fruits, such as bananas, pawpaws, pineapples, South-Seas apples, mangoes, sour-sops, oranges, and pomeloes. The sugar cane may also be included, though it supplies a beverage rather than a food. The stalks are chewed for their juice, and the fibrous residue is afterwards discarded.

The roots, greens, nuts, and fruit are supplemented as often as possible with pork, chicken, and fish. Domestic pigs and fowls are killed only on the occasion of feasts, nevertheless, and game is not plentiful. Again, fishing rarely brings a good return except in the short tuna season, lasting a couple of months, when teams of four men sometimes have catches of between one hundred and two hundred pounds. Hen eggs, shrimps, bandicoots, turtle, turtle eggs, and the tails of young crocodiles are also eaten, but the total amount of high-grade protein is still small (see Appendix B). The people are in fact so starved for meat that they often dream of feasting on it and in the morning regale their companions with the details. They even eat pork after it has begun to go bad. A man came to my house one afternoon for a dose of Epsom salts and explained that he knew he had been foolish to join some bushmen in a meal. 'I thought I might have pains later,' he said, 'but I couldn't refuse. You see, I hadn't had pork for so long.'

The desire for fish is equally keen, and my good fortune in being able to secure a new seine in 1945 created much excitement. The old nets had been lost when the village was bombed, and everyone now crowded round to handle the meshing and examine the ropes. 'My stomach turned over, and I was so moved that I nearly vomited when I heard what you'd done,' one old man told me afterwards. 'Could this be a seine for us at last? Were we really to have fish again?'

[1] Coconut cream is eaten from one side of the Pacific to the other, but the Busama are the only natives I have ever heard of who squeeze the grated meat with their bare hands. Other peoples use either a small bag or a bundle of hibiscus fibres and are able to extract far more.

43

It is significant that the sounds which infants babble before they begin to talk are identified as *tata*, 'fish'. 'The child has begun asking for fish already,' the parents proudly boast. (Little pieces of fresh-water fish, masticated first by the mother, are thrust into the mouth of the baby when it is only a few months old.)

Physiology and Nutrition

Food and drink are rightly regarded as necessary to sustain life, but the natives maintain that the stomach alone is responsible for the extraction of the useful elements. From here the goodness is supposed to pass to the flesh and blood direct. The waste products alone, it is said, go on into the intestines, from whence they reach the lower bowel and the bladder. Blood is held to give the heart its strength, which necessarily fails when the intake of food stops. The red colour comes from a dye in the liver, and when this organ ceases to function properly in illness the patient's face grows increasingly pallid.

The importance of air is also stressed, this being essential to keep the blood fresh. Just as water sealed in a bottle becomes stale and smelly, so the body begins to decompose soon after the last breath is drawn.

The views about diet are equally crude, and the main assumption is that taro is the source of energy. Without taro a heavy day's work, it is claimed, would be out of the question, and I have several times heard men attributing their temporary laziness to having confined themselves at the previous meal to other foods.[1]

Yet on one point the natives are astonishingly accurate. The consumption by a lactating woman of food cooked in salt water, or of salt-water fish, is held to be injurious to the infant, causing it to

---

[1] In the central highlands, where the sweet potato is the staple, this is looked upon as the vital food. While I was on a visit to this area in 1944 the officer in charge of one of the compounds received a deputation of labourers who complained that they could do no more work until given 'something to eat'. Mystified, he pointed out that rice had been served daily. Yes, there was plenty of rice, was the reply, but everyone was wasting away for lack of sweet potatoes. Many Australians deprived of their customary meat when visiting England after the war behaved in somewhat the same manner.

DAILY ROUTINE

'shrivel and die'. Salt-water fish are also withheld from the child for the same reason until all four of the incisors have been cut. The vital fact here is that babies are given no water to drink until such time as they can hold the heavy coconut water-bottles. I am informed by Dr. F. W. Clements, Director of the Institute of Anatomy at Canberra, that in such circumstances they would be able to excrete salt only by absorbing fluid from their tissues. (Dr. Clements is at present conducting experiments to test whether any of the salt which the mother eats passes into her milk, as he surmises is the case.)[1]

To counterbalance this there is a wrong-headed theory that abundance of meat or fish is injurious to all save adults and likely to bring about premature senility. The doctrine almost certainly goes back to the time when the authority of the elders was maintained by their control of the tastiest foods, which were mainly reserved for themselves; but, although a few men are today notoriously greedy, the majority are inspired by real solicitude for the welfare of the rising generation. Those whom I know best have genuine sympathy for the children's cravings and dislike having to hold back supplies. The biggest joints of pork are always by custom taken to the clubs, into which the youngsters seldom penetrate, but many fond fathers smuggle fragments into their handbags for presentation later to a favourite son or daughter. The women also ignore the warnings to put their helping on a high shelf until the brood is out playing or asleep, and they too give away as much as they dare. Then time and time again I have heard men returned from a good day's fishing express regret at being unable to take the full catch to their families. 'It wouldn't be safe,' they used to tell me. 'That fish there must go to the club, that to so and so, and that to someone else. We don't want our sons to have white hair before we have any ourselves.'

One other nutritional theory demands a mention. Most persons believe that illness would follow if they were to eat any of the pork from a pig which they had themselves fed. This means that when a household slaughters an animal the meat is always given away.

---

[1] I was unaware of the danger of an infant being given salt without water when I was in Wogeo in 1934. It is probable that the milk taboos of the inhabitants, mentioned in my paper, 'A New Guinea Infancy', *Oceania*, Vol. XIII, pp. 294–296 , are as soundly based as those of the Busama.

Cooking

Three meals are normally eaten during the day, breakfast soon after sunrise, a snack round about midday, and dinner during the evening, generally when darkness has set in. Supper is not a regular meal, but men who have been out fishing during the night sometimes cook a portion of the catch immediately on their return, at one or two o'clock. The women may be awakened if the haul is a good one, but they mostly receive their share the following day.

Adults do not regard going without the morning repast or lunch as a hardship, and a party leaving on a fishing expedition before dawn seldom partake of food till their homecoming late in the afternoon. Children, on the contrary, can have food whenever they ask, often four or five times during a single morning. The aunts and uncles, seeing them at play close by, may each in turn call them over for a special titbit, such as a few ripe bananas or a platter of spinach. Never on any occasion have I heard youngsters refused on the ground that they would ruin their appetite for dinner, nor have I known them to be told to clear their plates on pain of being given nothing later. Regularity is at no time consciously inculcated, and many of them do not learn to control their hunger till attendance at school begins, when they may be as much as ten years old.

The men carry out a fair share of the work before a feast (Plate 8), but the women cook the everyday meals. Dinner alone requires preparations on anything like an elaborate scale, and if the housewife wishes to avoid complaints then she must have a starchy food as a foundation with some kind of relish, greens if neither fish nor meat is available, as well as a sauce.

The first job is to do the vegetables. The taro corms are scraped with a shell or a piece of sharpened hoop iron, and the stalks and other stringy parts are removed from the greens. The fire is then lighted, usually on the ground outside. A shallow depression is scooped out, and around this a triangular framework of small sticks is built. A dry leaf is then dropped in the middle and hot ashes scattered on top. The pot, which is conical in shape, is placed firmly in the centre with the point resting in the hole as soon as the sticks have caught.

The commonest methods of preparing taro are boiling and steaming. If the first is to be followed the pot is lined with either banana or palm leaves to prevent the food from sticking to the sides, and it is then partly filled with a mixture of fresh and salt water in the proportion of three to one. The corms, which are now sliced into chunks, are dropped in immediately, more water being if necessary added. Finally, the top of the pot is neatly sealed with a thick pad of taro leaves. For steaming less water is used, occasionally with the addition of a little coconut cream, and the corms are cut into smaller pieces. If plantains figure on the menu the woman peels them and mixes them in with the taro. A few squares of pumpkin may also be added for variety.

Where the household includes a woman with a child still at the breast her meal has to be cooked in a separate pot by itself with fresh water only.

If the taro is being boiled, the greens are tied into bundles and popped in at the top after an interval, but if it is being steamed they go in at the bottom. Water in which food has been boiled is always thrown away, but before the taro is served coconut cream mixed with a little fresh water and salt water may be poured on. Water from steamed taro, however, with the greens left in, is served as soup.

The pudding known as *blom*, consisting of taro mash and thick coconut cream, is a treat for special occasions. The taro has to be carefully selected as many types are too coarse to make a smooth paste. The pieces are first boiled and then pounded in a dish by one of the men with a heavy wooden spoon. He adds the cream last, stirring the mixture thoroughly till it resembles a stiff custard.

There are three recipes also for sago. In the first the cook fills the pot with fresh and salt water, this time in the proportion of seven to one, and, having brought it to the boil, she drops in lumps of sago starch wrapped in leaves. The finished dumplings are afterwards tossed in a shallow dish of shredded coconut, which sticks to the gluey surface.

The second recipe is for sago gruel, a thin porridge of fresh and salt water, coconut cream, and starch (Plate 8). The cream and water are brought to the boil, and the powdered starch is added gradually while the pot is continuously stirred.

For sago cakes powdered starch and cold coconut cream are worked into a dough, which is cut into lumps, tied firmly in leaves, and then steamed for about an hour.

47

The sago palm also provides the material for the soup given to invalids. This dish is made not from the starch but from the shoots at the crown, which are boiled in a broth of coconut cream and fresh water.

Yams and sweet potatoes are cooked in the same manner as taro, but all save two of the other vegetables are steamed. The exceptions are maize and bamboo-grass shoots, which are roasted on the open fire. Rice, which is sometimes obtained from the trade stores, is always boiled, though in petrol drums or saucepans rather than in clay pots, which are more difficult to clean.

Fish is sometimes roasted on the hot embers but is more often steamed, pork and other meats steamed, and hen and turtle eggs boiled.

Breakfast, in contrast with dinner, requires little forethought, as it consists of remains left over from the night before. The adults usually eat their odds and ends cold, but the mother almost always warms up something for the young children. Lumps of taro, fish, and perhaps a bundle of spinach are either put in a saucepan for a few minutes with some hot water or else tied in leaves and placed on the glowing coals.

The older folk, women as well as men, have plain taro also for the luncheon snack. Most housewives prepare sufficient the previous evening, though if the family is large they sometimes cook a small pot specially. The vessel may even be carried to the gardens if the group expects to be working there throughout the day. The children and young people, however, much prefer to make their meal of fresh fruit washed down with coconut water or the juice of sugar canes.[1]

The Evening Meal

Breakfast and lunch are eaten without ceremony, and adults as well as children often stroll about with the food in their hands. But dinner is generally a formal repast, and most persons prefer to be seated. The men and youths may stay in the club, but on three or four days of every week the family sits down together under one roof.

[1] The fruit lunch is a fairly recent innovation—several of the fruits have been imported only during the last thirty or forty years—and I gathered that the elders are too conservative to appreciate it.

DAILY ROUTINE

Hurricane lamps and burning sticks held aloft shed inadequate illumination for close work, and the women like to have the cooking well under way before the sun has begun its final descent to the horizon. Should everyone be near at hand waiting they dish up as soon as the food is done, but if the men have not yet come back from the cultivations and the children are happy at their play the fire is allowed to die down, leaving the pot resting in the hot sand. There may even be a delay of a couple of hours, though such a long period is unusual, and most households have dinner over by about seven-thirty. Anyone still absent has then to be content with helpings set aside for him. The fact that the food may be cold is not regarded as a disaster—certainly there would never be reproaches on this account—but it remains true that one hot meal during the day is looked upon as desirable.

The prerogative of serving rests with the housewife, and she delegates the task only if she is ill or otherwise occupied. She is regarded as the controller of supplies by virtue of the care which she gives to the growing crop.

If the men are at the club, or have expressed the wish to have their food sent thither, the woman piles a somewhat lavish portion, rather more than they actually need, into a bowl and sends it across. They do not eat alone but invite all who are present to gather round and help themselves. Later, when these men receive their dishes in turn, the invitation is reciprocated. A club dinner may thus go on, with intervals between identical courses, for upwards of two hours. I have sometimes seen a man whose meal did not arrive till nine o'clock—usually because his wife had been expecting him to come home—arouse his now sleeping companions.

When the members of the family are eating as a group they arrange themselves on the verandah or inside the house, depending on the weather. The elders have recognised places, the men in one circle or half circle and the women in another a yard or two away, but precedence is not important, and nobody objects if his accustomed spot is already occupied. In earlier times cross-cousins and relatives-by-marriage, who had to hide their mouths from one another with a mat 'out of respect' while eating, took care to go to opposite sides, but this custom has been in abeyance for many years.

The adults and older boys and girls share communal bowls or

49

platters, which are arranged in pairs, one containing the taro or sago and the other the relish. Two pairs, a men and boys' and a women and girls', normally suffice, but more are provided for a large family or when there are guests. A nursing mother also has a set to herself containing her special diet cooked without salt.

If the starch food is in lumps each person takes a piece in his right hand and a small bit of relish, enough for a couple of mouthfuls only, in his left. After the solids have been finished the bowl with the liquid is passed round, first to the guests and seniors. Everyone has his own spoon, which he produces from his handbag. These spoons appear at once when mashed taro or sago gruel has been prepared, and the diners dig into the mess from the sides. If anything is left the dish is given to a child to scrape.

The only local drinks are plain water and the fluid from green coconuts, but the natives have now acquired a taste for syrupy tea and coffee. These when available are not brewed till after dinner as any kind of drinking with meals is frowned upon.

The youngest children do not eat from the common dishes but are given their helpings on individual plates purchased from the trade stores. It is explained that if they were allowed to dip in with the elders there might be some difficulty in preventing them from seizing more than their share of the relish. As it is, they often finish the tasty morsels first and cry for more. 'No, that's all you may have,' I once heard Mu'alimawi, the wife of my friend Ahipum, tell her young son Kamaya as he began to yell. 'This here is for us. You're a greedy boy, and you haven't eaten one bit of taro yet. No, I mean it. Not one more piece of fish do you get.' At this point his grandmother came to the rescue and handed over a fragment. 'Oh, you make me cross, both of you,' Mu'alimawi continued. 'Go on, eat it quickly before I take it from you. Now that is really the end. Sit down and finish your taro.'

Only small quantities of meat and fish are given to the children, as has been mentioned. If a pig has been killed or a good catch obtained the men consume most of their portion in the club and the women the bulk of what they receive in private. When dinner is eaten at home it is accordingly possible to divide the amount equally, or even to permit the young sons and daughters to have more than their elders. A man who has caught only a couple of fish, too, may go without so that each of his offspring can have a little.

DAILY ROUTINE

Gluttony in grown-ups is deplored, but no one seems to mind if youngsters over-eat. 'They'll learn the size of their stomachs in time,' the parents remark tolerantly. On another occasion the lad Kamaya was allowed to have a large ripe pawpaw on top of a meal, after which he drank the full amount of fluid from a coconut.' You're going to be sick, I tell you,' his father warned, though without attempting to stop him. Within an hour the boy began to complain, and a little later he had a violent attack of vomiting. Despite the fact that he was himself to blame his mother soothed his forehead. Her only rebuke was a gentle reminder that his father had been right and that in future he would do well not to make such a pig of himself.

It is also not considered to be a matter for scolding if a child pecks at his food instead of having a hearty meal. Provided he is in apparent good health and neither listless nor inclined to be fretful, he is sent outside to join his friends and allowed to come back later.

From the age of six or seven onwards, nevertheless, the child is given careful instruction in good manners. Observance of the rule that taro should be held in the right hand and relish in the left, for instance, is now expected, and warnings are issued against putting back portions which have been half eaten. One must never take more than one is sure of consuming, the parents reiterate, and if a lump of taro is too big it must be broken in halves and the rejected piece restored to the dish. Again, food has to be treated with proper respect, the children are told, and when a portion is laid aside temporarily it should be placed on a plate or mat, never on the bare ground.

Eating too rapidly is deprecated lest any guest present should gain the impression that there is some anxiety that he may take the better pieces; but, on the other hand, extreme slowness is disliked as implying that the meal is unpalatable. Smacking the lips and belching are also considered to be out of place, especially before strangers. An amusing incident took place while another guest and myself were being entertained by a neighbour. A small girl belched loudly and was brusquely informed that the place for vomiting was outside, not in the dwelling, where people were still having dinner. 'What's wrong, father?' she asked innocently. 'You often make that noise when we're alone.'

Estimating Quantities

Though the average daily consumption of taro for the ordinary adult is several pounds,[1] the actual intake in any given twenty-four hours may vary considerably. The more appetising the relish, the greater the amount eaten is likely to be, and if meat or fish is served everyone goes on till his belly is considerably distended. Men in their early twenties sometimes have half a pound of fish and five pounds of taro at a sitting. 'This is the right way to be,' they used to tell me. 'We like to be so full that we can't eat another bite. The food stops with us then for a long time.'

. It follows that the good housekeeper always cooks more when she has a tasty relish. Long practice has taught her that a pot of certain size may be adequate if there is only spinach but that when meat is to be offered she must fill a bigger one. During the earlier months of my stay, when Ahipum's wife Mu'alimawi had only four adults and five children to consider, she alternated between a medium pot and a big one according to what else was to be had.[2]

The remarks of this woman over the preparation of dinner on the first afternoon after the return of two of her husband's nephews to the village from Army employment are worth recording. The girl who was doing the cooking—Mu'alimawi was busy with a new baby—reached for the medium pot as usual but was at once told that this would not do. 'Don't forget the two young men,' Mu'alimawi reminded her. 'Take the largest we have.' Then, on examining it, she changed her mind and asked for two medium pots. 'The large one for tomorrow,' she continued, 'but today we'd better have these full. There's been no taro at Lae, and the men may want to eat a great deal.'

Extra taro is also cooked if a platter has to be sent to another villager, perhaps because his wife is ill or temporarily absent or because he has been helping with some of the work of the household.

Visitors who arrive early are easily catered for—more taro is

[1] But cf. Appendix B.
[2] At that period the people had no domestic pigs, but in normal times taro has to be cooked for them to eat. Left-overs are always kept for the pigs, and there is in consequence no waste. When too much has been prepared for the family—and this more usual than too little—a smaller amount is put into the pot for the pigs.

brought from the garden and an extra quantity cooked. The appearance of a party late in the day, however, may lead to some embarrassment. Two or three can be satisfied by using what was originally intended for the family breakfast, but if a large number come the host has to call upon his kinsmen. He beats the hull of a canoe with a stick, yelling out as he does so that the vessel must be hollow to give out such a loud noise. Various households then come to the rescue with as much as they can spare.

Chapter Four

WORK

'There is no ancient gentlemen but gardeners, ditchers, and gravemakers; they hold up Adam's profession.'—HAMLET, Act V, Scene 1.

THE view of many European residents is that New Guinea is a man's paradise, with women occupying the position of drudges. One reason for this assumption is undoubtedly the fact that the females do most of the carrying. When a party enters a town to dispose of fruit at the market the wives are to be seen with loads of seventy or eighty pounds trudging along behind their unencumbered menfolk. Yet the most casual acquaintance with a native village reveals that the various tasks are evenly divided and that neither sex sponges on the other. Some duties are, indeed, carried out by the women; but others are performed exclusively by men. The wives who are so laden in the towns, for example, may have been sleeping soundly for hours as passengers while their husbands were toiling hard at the paddles of the canoe to bring them from some distant settlement.

In this chapter we shall be concerned first with the allocation of work on the basis of sex and then with various activities in order of their importance. Agriculture, which normally takes up nearly half the working time, heads the list, with fishing next, and canoe and house construction in third place.

Division of Labour

The men's superior muscular strength provides the initial basis of allotment. They are better equipped to bear the heavier burdens, to fell timber, to dig, to fence, to haul logs from the forest, and to erect the dwellings and other buildings. They also look after the tools used, and in the past they chipped out the rock and shaped the stone adzes. Men do the hunting, too, which often demands a great burst of speed to overtake the flying quarry, and in ancient days they made the weapons, defended the village in time of war, and carried the attack to enemy settlements.

The women, on the other hand, as the providers of nourishment, necessarily take charge of the infants and children. Again, because wandering far afield with a young baby would be unwise if not impossible, they also attend to most of the occupations radiating from the hearth. They keep the dwelling and its surroundings clean, stitch the mats, net the string bags, fill the water containers, fetch the firewood, prepare and cook the family meals, wash the dirty utensils and dishes, and feed the animals. The men have to be called upon, nevertheless, to operate the old-fashioned fire sticks, to kill the pigs and fowls, and, when the menu requires it, to mash taro and squeeze grated coconut to extract the cream. Further, the members of each sex wash their own clothes, air their own blankets, and make their own beds. Feasts also involve a good deal of separate effort, and the women mainly cook the vegetables and the men the meat.

Men, not being tied down with youngsters to mind, are able to perform the tasks involving absences from the village. Overseas voyages, most inland journeys, and fishing on the high seas accordingly fall to them, together with the manufacture and care of the canoes, nets, hooks, lines, and other tackle. They have to be able to handle the vessels from an early age, and navigation is always in their charge. Yet most women are able to paddle and steer, and there is nothing to prevent them from taking out a craft for a short journey of a mile or two. The women also take small nets to the streams in search of freshwater fish and shrimps, and they often gather mussels and other shellfish from the reefs.

The main duties of men in agriculture are clearing, burning off,

WORK

ALLOCATION OF TASKS

Activity	Men	Women
(1) Daily duties.	——— ———	Cleaning the house. Sweeping house surroundings.
	Digging rubbish pits. Airing own bedding.	Burying rubbish. Airing own and children's bedding.
	Making own beds.	Making own and children's beds.
	Washing own clothing.	Washing own and children's clothing.
	——— ———	Filling water containers. Chopping firewood and bringing it home.
	May help to bring bananas from garden. Lighting fire if no matches available. Carrying all heavy loads. Sharpening axes and knives. May help to mind children.	Carrying fruit and vegetables from garden. ——— ——— ——— Caring for babies and young children.
(2) Agriculture.	Felling trees and cutting shrubs. Burning rubbish. Marking boundaries. Final clearing of ground.	——— ——— ——— Helping in final_clearing of ground.
	May help to carry banana suckers to garden. Making holes for taro and banana suckers. May help to plant taro suckers. Planting banana suckers, yams, and sweet potatoes. Staking yams. Tying up sugar canes. Erecting fences.	Carrying taro and banana suckers to garden. May help to make holes for banana suckers. Planting taro suckers. Planting greens, sugar canes, tapioca, etc. ——— ———
	——— Digging yams	——— Weeding. Digging taro, sweet potatoes, and tapioca.
	Cutting bananas. Planting coconuts, areca nuts, betel pepper and, tobacco.	May cut bananas. May plant coconuts.

WORK

Activity	Men	Women
(2) Agriculture—cont.	Collecting green coconuts (usually done by small boys). Collecting dry coconuts. Collecting areca nuts, betel pepper, and tobacco. Curing tobacco.	——— Collecting dry coconuts. ——— May cure tobacco.
(3) Fishing and hunting.	All offshore and deep-sea fishing (with hooks and lures). Spearing fish. Seining. Poisoning fish. Manufacturing hooks and lures (most hooks are purchased, but lures are still made). Preparing bamboo rods. Manufacturing fish lines (often purchased). Preparing fishing spears. Repairing seines. Hunting wild pigs (specialists only). Hunting bandicoots. Hunting young crocodiles (very occasionally). Hunting turtle. Collecting turtle eggs.	All freshwater fishing (with small net). Collecting shellfish. ——— Weaving cord for small nets. Manufacturing and repairing small nets. ——— ——— ——— ——— ——— ———
(4) Collecting.	Climbing trees for fruit. ———	Collecting most forest foods. Bringing forest foods to village.
(5) Domestic animals.	Erecting pig sties. Erecting chicken houses.	Feeding animals. ———
(6) Food preparation.	——— Occasional cooking if no woman available. Making taro pudding. Making coconut cream. Killing and carving pigs. Cooking pork. Killing and cleaning fowls.	Preparing food for household meals. Everyday domestic cooking. Serving family meals. May make coconut cream. ——— ——— ———

Activity	Men	Women
(6) Food preparation—cont.	Cooking big hauls of fish. ——— Cooking for feasts. Arranging and distributing food at feasts. Felling sago palms. Pounding sago pith. Setting up washing troughs. Washing sago. Preparing sago for storage. ———	——— Care of cooking utensils. Washing up. Cooking for feasts. ——— ——— Carrying pith to trough. ——— Preparing sago for storage. Bringing sago to village.
(7) Building.	Felling timber, bringing all materials to village, erecting frame, lashing flooring to joists (mostly done by youths), shaping planks for walls, securing planks, making thatch, attaching thatch. Building latrines and excavating pit.	Removing leaflets from sago fronds and taking out central rib. ———
(8) Crafts.	Felling log for canoe dugout, hauling log to village and all stages of canoe manufacture. Making canoe sails (mats or canvas). Making all objects of wood (furniture, drums, handles for tools, coffins, etc.). Burning shells for lime. ——— ——— ——— ——— Sewing clothing (a few men only). Making crude baskets of coconut leaf. Collecting pandanus leaves.	——— ——— ——— ——— Collecting, preparing and dying material for weaving bags. Weaving bags. Collecting material for grass skirts. Making grass skirts. May sew clothing (a few women only). May make baskets of coconut leaf. Preparing pandanus leaves and making mats.

WORK

Activity	Men	Women
(8) Crafts—*cont.*	Preparing coconut water-bottles. (Formerly beating bark cloth). (Formerly making weapons.) (Formerly making stone tools.)	—— —— —— ——
(9) Voyages and trade.	Navigating, paddling, sailing, and steering canoe. Exchanging gifts and trading. Buying goods in trade stores. Boiling sea water to make salt for trading. May mind cash.	May paddle and steer canoe, but women never steer if craft is under sail. . May occasionally undertake gift exchanges. May occasionally buy goods. —— Minding cash.
(10) Medicine.	Administering first aid. Administering European drugs. Administering some native drugs. —— —— Massaging.	Nursing the sick. —— Administering some native drugs. Midwifery. Bleeding. Massaging.
(11) Funerals	Carrying corpse to cemetery. Digging and filling in grave.	Preparing corpse for burial. ——
(12) Festivals.	(Formerly preparing ornaments.) (Formerly dancing.) (Formerly singing dance songs and playing musical instruments.	(Formerly preparing ornaments.) (Formerly dancing.) ——
(13) Fighting.	Fighting with fists. (Formerly fighting with weapons.)	—— (Formerly women sometimes followed the warriors carrying extra spears.)
(14) Law and Government	Sitting as members of the village assembly. Maintaining public roads and bridges.	May speak as witnesses in the village assembly. Cleaning village and public roads.

Activity	Men	Women
(14) Law and Government —cont.	Building and maintaining Government rest house. All village officials are men.	—— ——
(15) Missions and Religion	All Mission officials (including teachers) are men. Conducting informal prayer meetings. Speaking at special Mission gatherings. (Formerly conducting most pagan ceremonies.) (Formerly carrying out most magical rites.)	—— —— —— (Formerly conducting a few pagan ceremonies.) (Formerly carrying out some health magic.)

marking the boundaries, fencing, and digging the holes for the taro suckers. They also look after the banana trees, which have to be set deep, and the yams and sweet potatoes, both recently introduced. Again, as the betel chewers and more constant smokers, they plant the areca palms, betel pepper, and tobacco. (The curing of the tobacco, in addition, is usually left to them, as well as the burning of lime for the betel-nut mixture.) The main food crops, taro and greens, are, however, planted, weeded, and harvested by the women. The men are capable of carrying out all three operations, of course, but too much of their time is occupied by fishing.

Facilities for training in medical work are available only to men, and they accordingly practise first aid and administer all European drugs. But nursing the sick and carrying out the traditional operation of blood-letting are still left for the women, who also act as the midwives. It is their job, too, to prepare the corpse for burial if a death occurs, though the men fashion the coffin, carry the body to the cemetery, and dig the grave.

Other occupations are the preparation of sago flour, the collection of forest products, and the stripping of palm leaves for thatch. There is no reason why any of these should be the responsibility of one sex rather than the other, and in New Guinea generally it is impossible to say beforehand which will be involved. The Busama custom, however, is for the men to pound and wash the sago and pick most of the fruit, and for the women to bring the fruit to the village and gather the wild vegetables and palm leaves.

WORK

Detailed schedules taken with a watch reveal that in the average household where there are two or three children the husband's duties take him about nine hours daily and the wife's rather more than ten (see Appendix D). The difference is to be explained in part by the fact that many of the men's tasks call for such a great expenditure of energy that a period of rest is from time to time essential. The wet-bulb thermometer is often over the seventy-five-degree mark during the daytime, and at this temperature such work as cutting down trees, hauling logs, and digging reduces the labourer to a state of exhaustion. The women's tasks, though arduous enough, are less severe, and pauses to recover breath are not so necessary. Then, in addition, as many wives have been at pains to point out to me, domestic problems are always urgent. A little delay in making a new garden or in building a house or canoe does not matter much to anyone, but housework cannot be postponed. Children are always hungry, firewood and water never last long, and dwellings have to be swept continually. 'It's the everlasting eating which breaks our backs,' a mother one day told me with a sigh as she gazed at her five children.

Female vanity furnishes consolation, and women take great pride in their indifference to pain and fatigue. They parade their importance as they hurry to and fro when a child is born and openly snigger that if the men had to suffer labour pains the village would long since have ceased to exist.

This attitude is reflected by the men, who refer to themselves in self-pity as a tidal creek (*buka saung*), in comparison with the women, who are like a broad river (*buka atu*). Women are so constructed that weariness and disease flow away from them with the same speed as a flooded stream empties itself of driftwood. (This is not a reference to menstruation.)

Taro Cultivation

The season of the year in part determines the choice of site for new gardens. Marshy flats (*gameng pi'*) are preferred during the relatively dry months of the monsoon, hillsides and the banks of streams in the wetter period, adequate drainage being then essential. Either of two types of soil may be picked on the flats, *nom dumbwi* (literally 'ground black', that is, dark clay loam) or *nom dulu* (sandy loam),

61

and either of two in the hills, *nom pu* ('ground white', that is, a light loam) or *nom ho'* (gravelly).

Most types of taro will grow anywhere—about twelve are recognised—but some are better adapted than others to certain soils. The main identification marks are the colouring, size, and toughness of the leaves and the texture of the corms.

The gardens on the flats are so swampy that I found myself at each step sinking in the slush to the tops of my boots. Unseasonable rain can be a danger to the crop here, for if a stream nearby is flooded the area may be covered with silt. The gardens on the hillsides are equally difficult to work, though the problem is now not mud but the extreme steepness, which demands the attributes of a human fly. Terracing is not carried out, and the only attempt made to reduce erosion is the placing of lateral balks of timber. The natives fix the logs in position firmly with heavy stakes and pile up heaps of rubbish behind them. Even then the sudden deluge which sometimes accompanies a hot-season thunderstorm can cause a landslide and sweep away an acre or more. A week of continuous sun may also prove disastrous as the plants shrivel up when the soil has no moisture.

Another concern is the interval during which the ground has been lying fallow. Leguminous food crops are unknown in this part of New Guinea, and rotation is therefore not at present possible. After the taro has been harvested the jungle advances once more, and the area is not considered to be fit for replanting till certain trees, whose botanical name I do not know, have reached a diameter of about eight inches.[1] The natives have no notion of the exact period of time required, but I judge it to be at least seven years, and probably longer. Only if labour is for some reason scarce do they take a risk earlier, and it is then fully realised that the hope of a fair return may not be justified.

The different valleys are selected more or less in order. In 1945 that of the Buim River was chosen; in 1947 that of the Ibimata' and of the Buli; and in 1948 that of the Budu, the Buaki, and of the Bukebele. Some of these are close to the village, but others are several miles away, and the journey to and from the garden may thus occupy a good deal of the working day (see Appendix D).

[1] The soil is said to be to some extent exhausted after a single crop, but an additional reason for abandoning the garden is the impossibility at this stage of keeping the secondary growth in check.

WORK

The group of men who exercise their land rights together generally collaborate in carrying out the preliminary clearing. Informal discussion takes place, and after some debate a decision is reached about which of the suitable areas should be cultivated next. Matters affecting the choice are whether any other group has already made a garden close by and how well the crop is progressing. Anyone who disagrees can with perfect propriety go somewhere else, but working in company is so much pleasanter than being alone that all are usually prepared to accept the plan. 'When there are several of us the task seems to be finished quickly,' one of the men explained. 'We gossip and laugh and joke and then by sunset look around and find that everything has been completed. But if someone sets out by himself he keeps thinking that he'll never finish. So he becomes lazy and goes home at noon and then has to return day after day. Felling the bush alone is like trying to empty the sea with a canoe bailer—it never ends.'

Each person in the land-holding group is accompanied by one or two of his other kinsmen (see below pp. 105–107). These men make no claim to the ground but when the trees have been cut down are rewarded for their services by being given the use of a plot, which after the harvest reverts back to the original owners. It often happens that the basic group, consisting of perhaps five or six members, has its ranks swelled to as many as sixteen or more.

On the flats each tree has to be felled individually, but if a sloping site has been chosen the workers chop only half-way through the trunk. Beginning at the bottom of the hill, they work upwards till the ridge is reached, and then the cutting of the topmost line brings the whole forest crashing down together. The youths finally go through the area severing the creepers and hacking the bushes.

On one occasion I accompanied a party of sixteen men, three youths, and three young boys who were setting out to prepare a new garden near the Buang River. We left the village at 6 a.m. and reached our destination two hours later. All went to work at once, and, although the lunch-time pause lasted for less than an hour, by 4.30 p.m. not much more than three acres had been finished. The next day we were two men and two youths short, but by continuing for an hour longer the area was doubled.

Clearing is particularly exhausting, for energy is used up both by chopping and by having to climb over the fallen branches. The

WORK

natives feel the heat keenly if the breeze is unable to penetrate the surrounding forest; moreover, they are as subject as Europeans to the attacks of leeches and bush mites, which often cause intense irritation.[1] Ahipum, whom I had accompanied to the Buang garden, was in bed on the second day within an hour of our return. While eating his dinner he asked his wife anxiously was she likely to have enough taro suckers to plant the whole garden at once. Her stocks turned out to be rather limited, and on learning this he breathed a sigh of relief. 'No more clearing for two months: I am content,' he murmured.

The timber is now left to dry. At the end of about a month it is examined, and any poles which may afterwards prove useful for marking out the plots or constructing the fences are pulled to one side. To prevent deterioration some men are in the habit of constructing special frames. The remaining rubbish, if ready, is then disposed of by burning.

The next task is to divide the clearing into allotments. Another meeting takes place, and each member of the group gives an indication of how much ground he and the relatives who have accompanied him require. There is no unit for the measurement of length or area, and such descriptive terms as 'very big', 'fairly big', or 'not big and not small', have to suffice. If a man has a large number of suckers available or is contemplating holding a feast, this is the occasion for making the appropriate demand. Should he be short of suckers he may fall back on his kinsmen, or he may make purchases from the villagers of Wakop or Buasi' a few miles inland. The regular price is goods from the trade stores worth 2s. for a small bundle containing from twenty-five to thirty or goods worth 5s. for a large one of about seventy.

When allocating the shares of ground the senior man of the group walks slowly across the clearing from one side with pauses at appropriate intervals, usually thirty or forty paces apart. The piece on the right, he announces, is to go to so and so, and that on the

[1] The mites burrow under the skin, and some species if infected give rise to a form of typhus which was responsible for heavy casualties amongst the troops. It is not known whether natives have any immunity to the disease, but those living near the coast take care to rid themselves of the pests by bathing in the sea for about ten minutes after work. The salt water is sufficient in itself, and no probing is necessary.

left to such and such. Persons who have many suckers receive two or even four allotments. The owners mark the furthest limits with a stake, on which nowadays they frequently write their names, and then proceed to run a line of poles along the boundaries.

Fencing, which is postponed for the present, involves general collaboration once more, but otherwise the different households work separately from now on.

The first task is to complete the clearing. Although the trees and bushes have already been burnt, a good deal of decaying vegetation remains to be tidied up. The allotment is gone over carefully and a bonfire made of all the sticks, creepers, and stumps. The corms will only grow to a large size, it is said, if the ashes are scattered over the soil, and this is now done. If the quantity available is insufficient to cover all the surface a few saplings from the surrounding bush may be dragged in and fired to make an extra supply.

Once the ground is ready for planting logs are laid across to break it into small plots each ten paces wide. Most of these are distributed amongst the householder's immediate dependants—his wife, his unmarried daughters, and possibly his unmarried sons and uterine nephews—but in carrying out the different tasks the divisions are usually ignored, and the household works together as a team. One or two plots, in addition, are made available to other kinsfolk, possibly the man's mother, his married daughters, his sisters or his sisters-in-law. These women may choose to join in with the rest or to keep to themselves, but in any case they always provide their own suckers.

The soil is not turned over, and even prior to the war, when all sorts of tools were available for purchase, the natives were never attracted to spades or hoes. They select a stout stick from six to eight feet long from the bush, sharpen one end, and make a series of holes by driving it in the ground to a depth of about ten inches (Plate I). (The average is twenty-four holes to every nine square yards.) A sucker, or sometimes two or three if they happen to be small, is planted in each. The base is thrust firmly into the soil at the bottom, and a handful of earth which has been scraped from the sides is pressed round to cover the end to a depth of an inch.

The men and older youths generally wield the digging stick, though women take their turn. Planting, however, is left for the women and children. The steam rising from the damp earth makes the atmosphere oppressive, and both jobs are in consequence somewhat tiring. In the middle of the day it is customary to take an hour off for a rest under the trees, when a drink of coconut fluid or a couple of sugar canes and a few pieces of fruit or cold taro are most acceptable (see Appendix B).

The suckers begin to take root almost at once, and within ten days or so new shoots begin to make their appearance. But the weeds are just as hardy, and for the first three or four months the women have to go over the ground systematically at regular intervals to prevent the young plants from being choked. By harvest time the large heart-shaped leaves, which are now upwards of two feet high, may be partially hidden by a dense mass of coarse grasses.

Every plot also has a couple of patches of the three varieties of cultivated greens (*Abeloschonus manihot*, *Amarathus* sp., and an unidentified grass), a few clumps of sugar canes (*Saccharum officinarum*) and of plants known as 'pit', and banana trees (*Musa sapientis*) here and there. Lengths of sugar cane are pushed into the earth in bundles of half a dozen wherever there is a slight mound: on reaching a height of a couple of feet they can be tied together to prevent the wind from blowing them over. 'Pit' is a related species (*Saccharum robustum*) of which the immature flower tassel is edible—when cooked it somewhat resembles asparagus. The bananas are mainly of the type which requires cooking, for those eaten raw are planted in groves close to the village. The young trees are carried across from abandoned cultivations.

Other plants include tobacco (*Nicotiana tabacum*) and European vegetables. Some men cultivate a few yams (*Dioscorea esculenta*), but these are not a traditional crop and are generally unpopular—the reasons given are that the creeper has to be provided with long stakes for climbing and that care is necessary when the tubers are dug up.[1] There are also objections to sweet potatoes (*Ipomoea*

---

[1] The men who grow yams choose light sandy soil, which they heap up in small mounds. The tubers are harvested when the rosewood tree sheds its leaves in April.

Many of the yams of today are the progeny of one which I brought from the Trobriands in 1945. This was a huge specimen, nine feet long, presented to me by Mitakata, the present chief, when he learnt from the District Officer that I had been a pupil of Malinowski.

5. Busama rebuilt. The view looking southwards from Schneider Point

6a. Mother and child

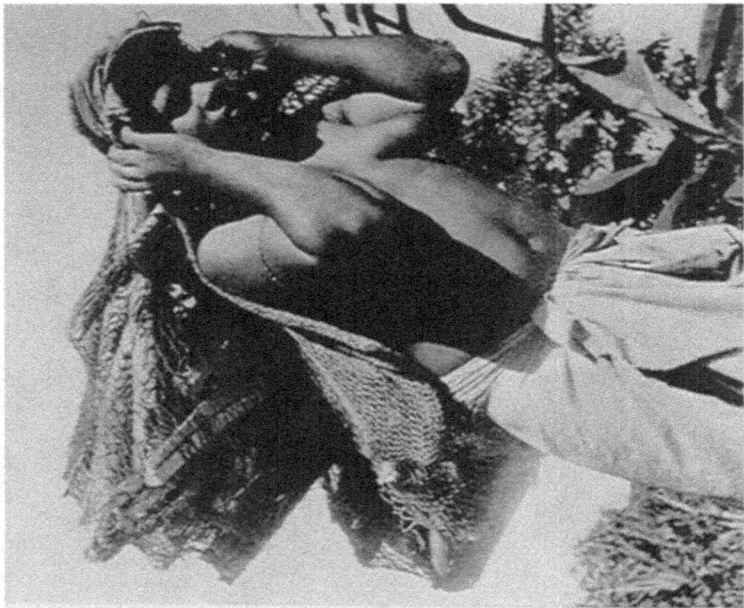

6b. Housewife with a load of firewood

batatas), which grow remarkably well—they have far too great an attraction for wild pigs.

The pigs are not indifferent to taro, but this is a second choice, and they can often be kept away from the garden for several weeks if the owners clear an extra patch of bush or light a few bonfires. Sooner or later, however, a fence has to be erected. The job is postponed to the last moment as in this climate timber rots so quickly that the posts are unserviceable at the end of three or four months.

Fencing is detested because the workers have to go so far afield to find suitable material. Everyone with an interest in the garden comes along to help, nevertheless, and the job can usually be completed in a few days. Yet I have frequently heard men argue that, as the pigs had come from one side only, the other three could be left without protection. Pairs of stakes five or six feet long are first driven into the ground to a depth of a foot, and poles are then lashed in place horizontally between them to almost their full height. Rough stiles are afterwards constructed at convenient points to provide ingress.

Visiting the gardens of others is regarded as improper especially if the owners are not at work. Rather than trespass, most men prefer to go round the fence at the expense of several minutes' walk. Should a passer-by be thirsty and catch sight of a succulent sugar cane in the cultivation of a close kinsman he is permitted to help himself, but that night he gives a full explanation lest there should be any suspicion of theft.

It is easy to tell whether the corms are ready from the appearance of the leaves, but the school teachers, who conduct experiments at the Mission College as part of their training, are the only persons who can state definitely how many months must elapse after planting. Digging can proceed at the end of half a year if food is scarce, I was told, but the harvest is better after seven months and larger still at eight months. By the ninth month a few of the corms may have begun to rot, and after the tenth the crop is ruined. This information I checked by my own observations. The yield was approximately 5,200 pounds per acre (2·3 tons) at six months and 8,875 pounds (4 tons) at seven or eight. A large garden run by the Army a few miles inland from Lae on the Markham River flats in 1944 and 1945 was said to have produced 9 tons to the acre, but I have never seen anything comparable to this figure in a native village.

WORK

Women collect the corms. They push a stout stick underneath and gently lever it up and down until the plant can be pulled out with the hands. If it has been growing for more than six months two or three suckers will have appeared at the sides. These are cut off with a single blow from a large ·bush knife when the head is being removed and, like it, carefully laid to one side. The earth is then rubbed off the corm, which is placed inside the net bag, along with others, for carrying to the village. Most women like to take home sufficient to last the family for two days, perhaps as much as forty or fifty pounds. (I have at times seen them carrying sixty pounds of taro and twenty pounds of firewood (Plate 6*b*).) It is useless to bring much more as decay is so rapid—by the fifth or sixth day taro is unfit for use.

If a new garden has not as yet been prepared the head and suckers are pushed back in the earth and left. The area is not used again for a second crop, but the suckers put down roots at once and are thus alive and healthy when required a few weeks later. Had they been brought to the village they would by that time have died. If the fresh cultivation is already available, however, the woman either goes over at once with as many heads and suckers as are needed or else carries them to her house to wait till the next day.

With heads and suckers capable of producing a new crop, it follows that the cultivations could in the course of a few years be increased tenfold. In normal times such expansion is unnecessary, and the acreage used is fairly constant. The householders are therefore in a position to make a continuous selection of the best stock, and it has become the regular practice to look the corms over with a critical eye and pick out the heads and suckers from the largest. Some inferior types may have to be used if a feast is planned, or if a pig has destroyed a garden, or if a relative is in need, but they are ordinarily abandoned.

Conditions throughout the period of my study have so far been abnormal on account of the dislocation brought about by the war, and I cannot say for certain what area is necessary to support the villagers in the manner to which they are accustomed. In January 1948 they informed me that the ninety-five acres then planted were inadequate, and they were not satisfied till two years later, when the figure had increased to one hundred and six.

At this time most men had five gardens, though several had six (see Appendix F). There was a set of plots which had either recently been made ready or was in process of being prepared, a set newly planted, a set in which the taro was from two to three months old, a set in which it was from four to five months old, perhaps a set in which it was practically fit to be harvested and a set where digging had already begun. The size varied according to the number in the household, and the men with large families always had bigger gardens than those with only a few dependants. Men who had thought of enlarging their dwelling or making a new canoe, work involving feasts to entertain the helpers, had at least one plot which was of very considerable extent.

Village Needs

I estimated that the ninety-five acres in cultivation early in 1948 would give an average yield of about forty tons for each of the next nine months. As the village required only about twenty-eight tons monthly, this meant an apparent surplus of twelve tons.[1] Why was it, I wanted to know, that everyone persisted in regarding the gardens as too small?

To this question the natives had a ready answer. I had taken no account of the fact that there would normally be domestic pigs to feed, they pointed out, nor had I remembered the possibility of destruction by landslides, floods, droughts, wild pigs, and insects; further, large quantities of taro are in normal times exported to the villages of Laukanu, Lababia, Buso, and Siboma in the south.

Many New Guinea natives give their pigs coconuts to eat, but in Busama these are considered to be too valuable, and taro mash is supplied. As the pre-war pig population ran into several hundreds, it seems probable that three or four tons may have been used up every month for this purpose alone.

The wisdom of being forearmed against losses caused by storms

---

[1] Requirements were based on the assumption that the diet of the average adult is 4 lb. 8 oz. daily and that children and elderly persons consume three-quarters of this amount. (Cf. H. I. Hogbin, 'Tillage and Collection', *Oceania*, Vol. IX, p. 290; and F. W. Clements, 'Tropical Ulcer with Special Reference to Aetiology', *Medical Journal of Australia*, No. 7, 1936, p. 615.) This figure greatly exceeds that given in the report of the nutrition survey (see Appendix B).

and other calamities is obvious to anyone who has spent any time in the village. On one occasion I saw a hillside garden an acre in extent slide down the slope into the creek below leaving not more than three dozen plants standing, on another the floodwaters of the Budu Lagoon ruined half an acre of garden by covering it with silt to a depth of nearly a foot, and a few weeks later the suckers planted three months before on a hill exposed to the north-west monsoon and the afternoon sun had to be transferred to a more protected area. Again, householders who delay too long with their fencing or neglect to replace defective timbers often find that pigs have rooted up several hundred pounds of taro in a single night (two acres were destroyed on January 21–22, 1950). The taro beetle has fortunately caused no serious trouble in this part of the country for some time, but in 1944 a plague practically wiped out the crops of two villages respectively five and ten miles distant. In the following year, too, another neighbouring community lost every one of its riverside gardens through flooding.

The export of taro to the southern villages from Laukanu to Siboma is based on trade exchanges to acquire pots (see Chapter V). I took part in the first trading voyage organised after the war, in November 1945, but could gain little knowledge of the taro which would normally have changed hands. We ourselves had so little to spare—indeed, we were unable to feed ourselves—and not more than a gross of pots had as yet been manufactured. The probability is, however, that Busama exports upwards of five tons monthly. (Every Sunday during January 1950 the women carried a bag full for southern friends when they visited the Mission station for church. I actually saw three-quarters of a ton taken away each time, and there may have been more, for I could not inspect all the bags. Canoes were also passing to and fro, but, busy with other things, I was unable to look at many of the cargoes.)

When in 1950 the cultivated area had reached 106 acres, the surplus to cover pig food, accidents, and exports was about twenty-one tons monthly (see Appendix B). This the people said was at last sufficient. If they were right, as they probably were, it follows that, provided the birth and death rates in the different villages were constant, and no new wants were to arise, about twelve acres would have to be planted each month, a total of 144 annually. The ground has to lie fallow for about seven years, so that there would be a need for

1,152 acres of arable land—nearly two square miles. I cannot tell how much is available—the investigation would require the co-operation of the anthropologist with the surveyor and the agri-culturalist—but it is relevant to mention that only a fraction of the country is suitable. Swamps occupy much of the lowlands, and the mountains are too steep.

But the population, far from remaining stationary, went up by over 9 per cent. between 1944 and 1950, and wants are changing every year. The introduction of new crops, either for local use or for sale, would, of course, be an additional complication.

The problem arises of how the householder knows when he has enough gardens if there is no unit of measurement. Regular routine is part of the explanation: it is the custom to choose a new piece of land every couple of months, and by the time one area is on the point of being abandoned, another is already available. The division into separate sections for each member of the household is also of assistance. The plots are always of approximately the same size, and if it is discovered that insufficient ground has been cleared an extra strip of bush is immediately cut. Special care is only necessary when an enterprise requiring the provision of a feast is contemplated, and on such occasions a garden is planted for the purpose. In 1946, when the villagers began returning to their old site, many of them had to delay the erection of new dwellings because they had no taro as yet for entertaining the workers. But even when there is ample notice of a great occasion the hosts may be somewhat worried. So although it had been agreed six months before that guests from all over the Huon Gulf should be invited to the church ceremonies at Christmas 1947, several persons expressed concern lest there should not be enough to eat.

Sago

Everyone likes an occasional dish of sago but regards it as un-suitable for regular consumption. The chief uses therefore are as part of a feast or for tiding over temporary shortages of taro. Co-operation is necessary to fell the palm and extract the starch, but the owner can depend upon his kinsmen for assistance. If he is holding a celebration they receive a share then, but when no entertainment is to take place he presents each of them with a lump of the starch.

WORK

The sago palm (*Metroxylon rumphii*) produces seeds only once, after which it dies, when it may be anything from ten to twenty years old, twenty-five to thirty-five feet high, and eighteen to twenty inches in diameter at the base. In preparation for this event starch is stored in the trunk. The appearance of the flower spike is the sign that the maximum has been reached.

The workers sever the trunk some distance from the ground and afterwards cut off the two ends, leaving about twenty feet. They remove the top of the outer covering lengthwise and then sit down alongside and pound the fibrous mass, which has the consistency of stale bread. Each one works with a mallet shaped like an adze handle shod with a piece of iron piping or a heavy stone (Plate 11a).

While this is being done other men set up a series of half a dozen washing troughs at the edge of the nearest stream. These consist of the central rib of a sago leaf, which is fixed firmly on supporting cross sticks so that the narrow end is a few inches above the ground. A collecting pan made from the sheath of a wild palm with upturned ends is placed underneath. Finally, a piece of fibrous sheath from the base of a coconut leaf is fastened across the head of the wide part of the sago-leaf rib to serve as a screen.

Women now carry the pith to the troughs. Three baskets at a time are tipped into the broad end and a few quarts of water poured on top from a bailer made of a loop of wild-palm spathe attached to a long handle. Youths or young men then pull and knead the mass to separate the starch from the fibre (Plate 11b). The former, suspended in the water, passes down the rib into the pan below, where it falls to the bottom. They pour more and more water till only the fibre remains. This is then tipped out to make way for another pile of pith.

Washing methods are very careless, and a good deal of the starch is wasted. I can well believe the statement of my personal servant, who came from the Sepik River, where this work is undertaken by the women, that his mother would have wept with annoyance at the sight of such inefficiency. On the Sepik as much as 700 pounds can be secured from a fair-sized palm, but in Busama 400–500 pounds seems to be the limit. A single worker here can without assistance wash upwards of forty-five pounds per day, but I feel sure that a Sepik woman can produce a great deal more. The job is hated nearly as much as fencing: it causes backache, stiff neck, and sore wrists.

The finished starch, which is either greyish white or dull pink, depending on the variety of the palm, is pressed into lumps weighing thirty pounds each which are then wrapped up tightly in leaves. These may be baked immediately on an open fire before storage or carried back to the house and smoked for several days on a shelf erected over the hearth. They will keep for about a month without becoming mouldy.

Other Foods

The coconut (*Cocos nucifera*) is the most important of the subsidiary items of native diet. The palms are all owned either by single individuals or by matrilineal kin groups, but there are plenty to spare as they grow in great profusion along all the beaches and on the river flats, and more are always being planted. The green nut, besides providing a pleasant drink, has a soft pappy flesh which is much enjoyed on hot days. The meat of the ripe nut, on the other hand, is seldom eaten plain: it is first made into coconut cream.

Tapioca (*Manihot utilissima*) is in times of plenty regarded as fit only for pigs, and the pot-making peoples, whose staple it is, are sometimes referred to contemptuously as 'tapioca eaters'.

The chief of the fruits eaten raw is the banana. The people are keen judges of flavour and on their trips to other places are always looking out for new kinds, which if possible they bring home with them to plant. The principal banana groves are located on the banks of the smaller streams within half a mile of the village.

Pineapples, imported within the last thirty or forty years, are also popular. The natives plant them in clumps on the lower slopes of the hills behind the houses.

Other fruits include the native South-Seas apple (*Eugenia malaccensis*), the native mango (*Mangifera* sp.), the native pandanus (*Lerum* sp.), the pawpaw (*Carica papaya*—introduced during the nineteenth century), and the recently introduced orange (*Citrus sinensis*), lime (*Citrus histerix*), pomelo (*Citrus grandis*), and sour-sop (*Anona muricata*). The breadfruit (*Artocarpus incisa*) flourishes also, but only the seeds are eaten, and these are always boiled. A few of the fruit trees

73

are individually owned, but the vast majority are looked upon as common property.

The menu is supplemented also by the leaves and shoots of one or two bush trees, ferns, and creepers (including *Ficus* sp., *Gnetum* sp., and *Pteris* sp.), which are served as greens, by the shoots of bamboo grass (*Bambusa* sp.),[1] and by two fungi (*Polyhorous* and *Auricularia*).

Drug Plants

The men are heavy smokers, and though they now buy most of their tobacco from the trade stores, a certain amount is still grown. They cure the leaves over the household fire and do them up in bundles till required.

Betel is also popular with the men, and every householder has his groves of areca palms (*Areca catechu*), which he periodically extends, often with nuts brought in from other areas. He plants betel-pepper vines (*Piper betle*), the fruit of which is an essential ingredient of the mixture, at the base of the areca palms or other trees growing near the village and trains the shoots around the trunks. (Lime, the third ingredient, is manufactured at home by burning shells or obtained by trading from the natives of Labu.)

Fishing

The simplest method of seeking fish is with a bamboo spear armed at the end with barbs of wire or slivers of palmwood (Plate 9). Men when walking along the beach in the daytime usually carry a spear to aim at anything which catches their attention, and at night they organise expeditions for garfish. Each party sets off in a canoe with one man paddling and a second waving a coconut-leaf flare while the rest stand poised to hurl their spears. The garfish, attracted by the light, leap out of the water and are taken on the surface or in mid-air.

Hooks and lures are also used. The former are purchased nowadays from the trade stores, but the latter, reserved solely for tuna, are still made from pearl shell and turtle shell. Those who can

[1] Ready in the pigeons' mating season.

afford the expense buy their lines, but many are compelled to stick to the home-made article, which is twisted out of local fibres.

Fishing with hooks is carried out within a few miles of the shore in small canoes for two or three. In the tuna season, however, during October and November, large and small craft are engaged, and the shoals may be followed for long distances. Good hauls are likely to be obtained, and intense excitement reigns on the beach as the parties arrive back. Some men make a habit of indicating their good luck by singing, others by hoisting a piece of cloth at the masthead. The watchers rush forward if congratulations are in order and joyfully assist in pulling the vessel out of the water. A fine catch is remembered for months, especially by the fortunate crew, who boast of their skill at the slightest encouragement.[1] Tuna are not as plentiful as they were before Europeans began using dynamite to secure cheap rations for their employees, but enough are obtained to permit of a quantity being kept for later consumption.[2] The fish are cleaned and afterwards smoked over a fire of green wood for two or three days.

Three types of net are employed, of which the largest and most important is the seine, often as much as sixty fathoms long by a depth of over a fathom. Floats of balsa wood or cork are fastened along the top, weights of clam shell or lead along the bottom, the whole being lashed to two stout ropes. A large group is necessary to operate such an appliance, some men to handle the canoes taking it out, some to remain on the shore and in due course drag it in (Plate 10*b*).

Smaller nets, requiring half a dozen men, are kept for reef fishing. A section of the coral is encircled, and pieces of pounded derris root are then pushed into the interstices between the growths. The fish become stunned after a few minutes, float to the surface, and can then be removed by hand.

The small round hand-net is the prerogative of the women. They seldom stir far without it and if unencumbered with an infant generally wear it on the head when setting out for the gardens

---

[1] The canoe remains on the reef to give everyone in the village time to assemble, and the crew then paddle to the shore at full speed, shouting as they come.

[2] Dynamite has recently been forbidden, but the regulation is honoured more in the breach than the observance.

(Plate 12). A trial may be made at any stream, but the catch is never large, two or three small fry a few inches long and possibly half a dozen shrimps at most.

The women also bring in shellfish from the reefs but seldom secure enough for a meal.

Acquiring Nets

The men of earlier generations all understood how to make the netting used in a seine, and large teams collaborated for each new one. A leader had to co-ordinate their efforts, nevertheless, and tell them how the work was to be arranged. This office was filled by a man who had inherited a knowledge of the magical rites performed at different stages of the undertaking. He subsequently claimed the seine as his own, a privilege which involved not only the right to superintend its use but also the responsibility of maintaining its upkeep. The village always had four or five of these experts, each with a private following of fishermen, men to whom he was related, eager to do his bidding and share in the hauls.

Like so many traditional skills, seine manufacture is a thing of the past, and the nets have nowadays to be obtained from one of the more conservative southern villages, where the old crafts are still carried out, or from a trade store. The cost in either case is high, as much as £90 before the war. No one man can afford so great a sum, and a joint effort is necessary to achieve it. The head of a club house puts up a fairly large contribution, perhaps £12, and calls upon his kinsmen to give what they can spare, from a few shillings to a couple of pounds. He arranges the purchase as soon as the desired figure has been reached and thus becomes the owner, fulfilling the same sort of functions as his predecessor of olden days. He gives the word for the seine to be taken out and says where it is to go, who is to work the canoes and who the ropes, and who is to have a part of the haul; and he also sees that the net is properly dried and put away, aired in the sun, and mended when torn.

The seines of the pre-war years were destroyed in the 1943 bombardment, and the first replacement did not take place till late 1945, when I was able to secure a net from the Army Fisheries Unit at Salamaua. The vital need of a single owner was clearly brought out by the reaction of several of my friends when I announced my intention of making a gift to the people at large. A presentation on those terms, they assured me, would be the height of folly, an invitation to disharmony and waste. With no one in particular having the title, how could quarrels be composed?—or repairs affected? Each person would say to himself that the net was not his and that he accordingly saw no reason for taking any trouble with it. If it was put outside to dry by someone else he would leave it there when the rain came on, and if it was inside he would not bother himself to spread it out for airing in the hot sun. 'Give it to your brother Nga'gili',' I was advised. 'We'll all fish with it just the same, and if it's his he'll see that it will last.'

The smaller nets, used with derris root, are less expensive, and enough money can generally be accumulated without trouble by a small group of householders. The man who gives the biggest amount becomes the owner.

Canoes

The craft are still of the traditional type, a hollowed-out log with sharpened ends to which an outrigger is attached by a set of booms (Plate 9). The main divergence is in the shape of the ends of the log, for some curve upwards into a beak, some lie blunt and square, and some push outwards in a graceful arc. The last design gives the best speed but has the disadvantage of cutting through the waves rather than riding them, necessitating constant use of a bailer. The large vessels, which accommodate upwards of eight persons, are fitted with a stout platform on the booms and twin masts each capable of holding a square sail of light canvas or pandanus-leaf matting.

Many trees are available for dugouts, but the best specimens grow in the remoter valleys a few miles inland, and the job of bringing them to a workshop on the beach calls for ingenuity and great effort. A route has first to be roughly surveyed, the undergrowth cleared, and dozens of rollers prepared for the more difficult sections. Even then a large party is necessary to pull on the ropes.

Relatives come along to drag the log and later to help in the construction of the canoe, but an expert supervises their work and himself carries out the more difficult tasks, such as carving the prow and stern.

WORK

To achieve the best results the length of the dugout, of the float, and of the booms must stand in a definite proportion to one another. I had many conversations with all seven of the skilled shipwrights in an endeavour to have them explain to me exactly what this was. They could all say how the craft would behave if any part was too long or too short, but the exposition of principles seemed to be beyond them. 'We decide on the float and the booms after examining the dugout well,' was the usual reply to my questions. 'Then if on its trials the canoe is heavy or unstable or veers to one side we make an alteration.' Long practice must have developed their knowledge, for not one new craft of the forty odd which I have seen made called for adjustment.

The man who arranges for the canoe to be cut becomes the owner and decides when and how it shall be used. Certain obligations to his relatives have to be respected, but in the event of conflict—as, for example, when two claims are put forward for the same seat—he has the final say. As usual, responsibility goes hand in hand with privilege, and the persons who habitually use the vessel expect him to maintain it properly, with their assistance if need be, and keep it in good repair.

'The biggest canoe, large enough for twenty people, always belongs to somebody, and it's he who is in charge of it,' the villagers explained. 'True, such a craft, or a smaller one, couldn't be taken out without a crew; but if they all owned it there'd be bound to be quarrels about using it, and each would be sure to leave the repairs for the rest. You know what would happen then—nothing at all would be done, and the lashings would fall apart. That's why the canoe which the District Officer gave us is now derelict. He presented it to the village, not to one man, and the village doesn't take care of things. If it had come to Ahipum, or to Salingbo, or to someone else, everybody would have gone out in it just the same, but the owner would have looked after it.' The vessel referred to had been ordered immediately before the officer's transfer to a new station. As he had no facilities for taking it with him, he donated it to the community.

A further duty of the owner is the division of the catch irrespective of whether he was on board during the expedition. One fish is always put aside for the expert who superintended the work of construction—even if years have elapsed—and the bulk goes back to the

78

crew. They receive no credit, however, for any other presentations which may be made, and the honour for these accrues solely to the owner.

House Building

Architecture has not changed to any marked degree, though sawn planks are now substituted for the plates of wild palm which formerly served as walls, and nails have replaced the old rope lashings (Plate 2a). Studs and stumps are of hardwood; bearers, joists, beams, ridge, purlins, braces, rafters, and battens of various softwoods, each specially chosen in relation to the purpose which it has to serve; flooring of strips of palmwood; and thatch of sago leaf. Decay is fairly rapid, and despite constant repairs, the life of a dwelling rarely exceeds a decade. At the same time, the plank walls are often used twice, and the hardwood posts may last a lifetime.

Materials have to be brought from the bush, often for a distance of several miles. The lighter timbers are floated down the rivers and along the beach, but the hardwood and palm flooring are not sufficiently buoyant and must be carried, an onerous task (Plate 3b). A specialist is called upon to supervise the construction, together with a team of labourers (Plate 3a). From eight to a dozen men, not always the same ones, are kept fully occupied for at least three weeks, and when the hauling and thatching are being carried out the number may rise to twenty or thirty (see Appendix G).

The owner of the house is expected to furnish a meal for his helpers on every working day. This is in itself an undertaking and necessitates still further assistance. Various relatives come along bringing contributions of taro, fish, coconuts, and greens.

The specialists of today are all carpenters trained in one of the Mission schools, and each has his kit containing rule, square, plumb-bob, and so forth. In former times such tools were unknown, and the experts had to depend solely upon their eyes. Yet they are said to have attained such skill by long practice that their guesses at a right angle never varied by more than a degree. An ingenious method was adopted to ensure that the sides of the house should be parallel. Three corner posts were placed in position first and a rope stretching round on the outside fastened to the two farthest apart. This was then pulled over the top of the middle post towards the fourth corner, and the proper position of the last post was then ascertained by marking off the lengths of the two sides.

Economic Co-operation

Each person, it will now be clear, is dependent on his fellows. The individual Busama carries out his various tasks as a member of a group—a domestic unit, a gardening unit, a canoe unit, or one of several others. Such collaboration is arranged according to definite principles, to which in due course we shall have to give some consideration. But it will be convenient to deal first with another branch of native economics—the exchanges of goods which take place between the peoples of neighbouring communities.

Chapter Five

TRADE

'So that the more she gave away,
The more, y-wis. she had alway.'
GEOFFREY CHAUCER, *Romaunt of the Rose*, I, 1159.

THE natural resources of the Gulf villages differ considerably, and a good deal of local specialisation has developed. Busama, for example, has more agricultural land than is required to meet immediate needs, and the people produce quantities of taro for export; and Buakap, Asini', and Kila, a little to the south, possess big areas of swamp where surplus sago is grown. Beyond the Salamaua Peninsula, on the other hand, cultivation can be carried out only with difficulty, and the natives from the villages of Laukanu, Lababia, Buso, and Siboma have to depend partly on food obtained from outside. Laukanu is even short of trees from which canoes are made, and since 1949 they have had to be supplied by Busama. The southern group is amply compensated, however, in having easy access to a deposit of clay on a small island nearby. A flourishing pottery industry has been built up, and as in this region suitable material can be obtained in only one other spot—the central Markham valley—the pots travel far afield to the remote highlands of the Huon Peninsula and New Britain.[1]

The three villages of Labu Lagoon also have specialities: the

[1] Cf. W. C. Groves, 'Natives of Sio Island', *Oceania*, Vol. V, pp. 43–62.

81

TRADE

grasses from the muddy flats at the lakeside are woven into baskets, handbags, and purses, for all of which there is a keen demand.

Again, the north-coast peoples make mats and string bags (Plates 6a, 6b). The mats, used for bedding and rain capes, consist of dried pandanus leaves sewn together lengthwise. They appear to be the same as those prepared practically everywhere but are in fact of superior quality and more durable. The explanation is probably a slight difference in the mineral composition of the soil, resulting in a toughening of the leaves. Some of the women from the other villages, including Busama, have recently learnt the art of netting the bags, but these are all so fragile that there is still a market for extra ones from the north. Fibres obtained from the inner bark of a bush shrub are twisted into the string, which is then dyed a variety of colours with vegetable stains. New designs, often of great intricacy, are worked out while the netting is in progress.

The Tami Islands, a group lying close to the south-eastern corner of the Gulf not far from Finschhafen, also come into the picture. The soil here is poor, and, as in the pottery region, much of the food has to be imported. The islanders, compelled to have something for exchange, have developed great skill in carving wooden bowls (Plate 13). A range of sizes is available, some vessels holding only a couple of quarts and others enough for an army of visitors, but all are of the same graceful shallow oval shape. The sides have delicate carvings of human figures, animals, or birds, which on festive occasions are picked out in lime.

In earlier times two other places were of importance, Lutu on the Salamaua Peninsula and the Siassi Islands in the strait between New Guinea and western New Britain. Lutu is located alongside the quarry where the stone for the adze blades was obtained, and the Siassi natives used to bring volcanic glass for knives from Talasea on the north coast of New Britain.

Each coast village also has connections with the peoples of the hinterland. The inland folk nowadays come along with tobacco and such foodstuffs as yams and sweet potatoes, which grow better in the hills than at sea level, and return with native manufactured goods, pigs, fish, and salt.

7. Group of men at a house-building feast. The palmwood flooring in the background

8. Cooking sago gruel for a feast

Gift Exchange and Barter

The coast dwellers, as in many other parts of the Pacific, carry on their relations on the basis of gift exchanges.[1] Each item has its recognised equivalent, and a pot of certain size, for instance, is worth so many taro or so many mats (see Table of Equivalents, p. 90). Pigs' teeth were formerly given in return for a carved bowl, but for a bowl only. The use of these has been given up in favour of money, but the value remains unaltered. Only the canines were saved, and two units of four, each known as a 'dog', have been replaced by a shilling piece. Cash is felt to be an inappropriate offering for anything else, though very occasionally, when a man is temporarily without anything else, he may have to give it. He considers himself to be something of a defaulter and is careful to make an apology.

Villages situated at a distance from one another do not have direct dealings but depend upon neighbours in between to act as middlemen. The latter make no profit, and in one instance, at least, suffer a loss. Each community needs the products of all the rest, and the natives freely admit their willingness to sacrifice economic gain in order to keep within the exchange ring. In addition, though visits are made ostensibly for the sake of trade, the motive of sociability is probably of equal importance.

The dealings of the coast people with those of the interior present a marked contrast, for barter is here usual. The parties seem slightly ashamed, however, and conclude their arrangements outside the village. Commerce, it is considered, should be carried on away from where people live, preferably alongside the road or on the beach (the native-owned store at Busama is located fifty yards from the nearest dwelling).[2]

The Busama sum up the situation by saying that the maritime peoples give one another presents but insist on a proper return from

---

[1] *Vide* B. Malinowski, *Argonauts of the Western Pacific*, London, 1922; and R. Firth, *Primitive Economics of the New Zealand Maori*, London, 1929, Chap. XII, and *Primitive Polynesian Economy*, London, 1939, Chap. IX.

[2] The man who runs the store says that it is his own, but the villagers are convinced that he is acting for a European. The stock is never large, and he told me that he keeps no books and is thus unaware of what his profits amount to. Prices are fifty per cent. higher than in Lae.

the bushmen. The basis of the distinction is that on the coast activities are confined to relatives, but so few of the beach folk have kinsmen in the hill country that most transactions take place of necessity between comparative strangers.

A certain amount of migration and intermarriage has taken place around the seaboard, and every coast native has kinsmen in some of the other shore villages, especially those close at hand. When trading by sea it is with these, and these only, that he makes exchanges. Kinship ties and bargaining are considered to be incompatible, and all goods are handed over as free gifts offered from motives of sentiment. Discussion of values is avoided, and the donor does the best he can to convey the impression that no thought of a counter gift has entered his head.[1]

Yet at a later stage, when a convenient opportunity arises, hints are dropped of what is expected, whether pots, mats, baskets, or food. When a canoe carrying a cargo of mats arrived in Busama from a north-coast village towards the end of 1945 I heard one of the visitors comment during a meal with his host on the excellent flavour of the taro. 'It's nonsense to say, as some do, that iron saucepans are as good as the vessels from Laukanu,' he went on. 'I was remarking to my wife the other day what a pity it was that our last clay pot had been smashed. You know, we once had four, a large one, two like that there, and a small one.' On the day before his departure, as no doubt he had hoped, four pots similar to those described were handed to him.

Most of the visitors thus go home with items at least as valuable as those with which they came. Indeed, the closer the kinship bond, the greater the host's generosity is, and some of them return a good deal richer. A careful count is kept, however, and the score is afterwards made even.

The difference between the native method of doing business and our own was made plain by an exchange which took place early in 1947. The Salamaua area had suffered more damage than the northern settlements, most of which still had their pigs. On the resumption

---

[1] From my own observation this is still true, but the Busama told me in 1950 that the population of Laukanu has increased so greatly, and the people are in consequence so short of food, that for the past year they had been unable to make sufficient pots to pay their debts. Some of them were saying, so far to deaf ears, that prices would have to be raised (more taro per pot).

of voyages after the Japanese defeat a man from Bukawa' had the notion of bringing a young sow to a Busama kinsman named Boya. The animal was worth about £2, but hints indicated that pots would be more acceptable than money. A collection of ten was required for a reasonable equivalent, and as Boya had only five to spare he informed his relatives that anyone prepared to assist would in due course receive a piglet. This invitation was accepted, and twenty-two pots were contributed, making a total of twenty-seven. All were handed to the visitor, rather to his surprise, as he confessed to me in private. Yet such generosity was not as absurd as it may appear: by giving so much Boya imposed an obligation on his guest to bring across another sow.

Although etiquette prevents argument, I was interested to observe when accompanying some Busama on a trading journey southwards how the Buso villagers kept exaggerating the labour involved in pot making. 'We toil all day long at it from sunrise to sunset,' one man told us over and over again. 'Extracting the clay is worse than goldmining. How my back aches! There's always the chance, too, that in the end the pot will develop a crack.' The members of our party murmured polite agreement but subsequently brought the conversation round to the inferior quality of present-day pots. They confined themselves to generalities, accusing no one in particular, but it was apparent that here was an attempt at retaliation. 'I remember in my childhood knocking one of my mother's pots off a high shelf,' our leader told me in front of a group of the Buso. 'But do you think it broke? Of course not. The people of those times knew how to make things to last. It's not like that now. If you push a pot with your little finger it's likely to break.'

There are two reasons why, despite the absence of compulsion, all obligations incurred should be faithfully discharged. In the first place, a man who is dissatisfied with his bargain can always change over to another kinsman and in future take his gifts to him, leaving the former partner without a direct source of supply. But of even greater importance is the fear of acquiring notoriety as a person who is mean. The natives are sensitive to criticism, and, as generosity is universally acknowledged to be one of the chief virtues, only fools are prepared to run the risk of the gossips whispering about them. It is significant that when a Busama acquired a string bag from a fellow villager, as has recently become possible, he always gives twice what he would pay to a more distant relative on the north coast. A Bukawa' would be content with goods worth 1*s*. 6*d*., but a Busama receives 3*s*. 'One is ashamed,' the people explain, 'to treat those with whom one is familiar like tradesmen.'[1]

Men who are related to families living in the interior carry on exchanges on the same principle of gift and counter gift, but where no kinship bond exists—and this applies to the vast majority—the arrangements are more business-like. Yet haggling is uncommon, and arguments only develop on the rare occasions when the supply of fish outruns the demand, perhaps because several men have had a good haul, or when the demand for vegetables outruns the supply owing to a drought or some other calamity. During the war when many coast communities lost all their gardens, the value of foodstuffs increased enormously. The bush people living behind Lae, a group known as the Wain, who were formerly in the habit of giving twenty-five taro suckers in exchange for goods worth 2*s*., were for a time asking 1*s*. for a single sucker.

Speech differences today present no problems as all Gulf natives are fluent in Yabim and pidgin English. In the past reliance was placed mainly on the odd handful of persons who for one reason or another—perhaps their mixed parentage—were bilingual, though some groups were able to understand but not speak the langauge of their neighbours. The southern villagers spoke in Gela to the Busama, for example, who replied in Gawa'.

The final point to be mentioned is that trading is carried out exclusively by men. The women are responsible for many of the objects—the pots, the baskets, the mats, and the string bags—and nowadays may accompany their husbands or brothers on canoe voyages and on journeys to and from the interior, but they neither exchange gifts nor play any part in bartering. This is no doubt because few of them in earlier times ever left home.

[1] Once I had gained the villagers' confidence I found that they preferred to conduct their relations with me along similar lines. Men who had received fishhooks or tobacco made a point a few days later of bringing me fish or fruit the value of which exceeded that of my gift to them. As when trading, too, they liked to suggest what they wanted rather than ask for it outright.

Canoe Voyages

Journeys around the coast are made by canoe, though since 1949 the Busama have begun taking advantage of the regular Sunday gatherings for church at the Mission station to take taro for the Laukanu villagers.

Water traffic is suspended in July and August, the height of the trade-wind season, and in January and February, when the monsoon sometimes whips up sudden squalls, but during the rest of the year no serious difficulties present themselves, and canoes of medium size set off alone or in pairs. A large party was formerly essential, however, and the biggest vessels sailed together as a fleet under an expert possessed of special magic which helped to guarantee safety. A welcome could be counted on only in villages where relatives were living, and if a group too small to put up an adequate defence had the misfortune to be driven ashore in a strange place hostilities were inevitable. A canoe load of Busama who had been separated from their companions were on one occasion wiped out by the people of Apo, near Lae, and a year or two later the kinsmen of the murdered men slew the occupants of a northern craft which had been compelled to seek shelter when struck by an unseasonable blow on the way to Kila.

The Busama have long since given up building the old-style trading canoes, which have a tall gunwale and two decks, though one may still see them occasionally in northern waters, and in 1950 some men from Laukanu decided to construct a couple. An immense load of cargo is carried, but practically no headway can be made in anything less than a stiff breeze.

The natives are thoroughly at home on the sea and handle their craft with such skill that voyages from places as far apart as Siboma in the south and the Siassi Islands of the east would present no insuperable problems of navigation. Marriages into distant communities do not occur, however, and kinsfolk are thus confined to the villages close at hand. The members of each settlement accordingly have to restrict their voyages to one section of the Gulf. The pot makers of Siboma, Buso, Lababia, and Laukanu stop short at Busama; the Tami Islanders never go past Lae;[1] the Busama,

[1] The pot makers and the Tami Islanders sail southwards and northwards respectively out of the Gulf. But of these further activities I have no details.

Buakap, Lutu, Asini', and Kila sail southwards to Siboma and eastwards to Tamigidu about two-thirds of the way along the north coast; and the people of the north coast keep to an arc bounded by Tami at one end and the Salamaua Peninsula at the other. Even within these limits certain places are avoided. The Busama have close ties with Bukawa' but none with Apo, and the Kila have links with Apo but none with Bukawa'.

The Pottery Trade

The initial task when making pots is to obtain clay. The men set off by canoe with empty petrol drums and spades, taking enough food to last for a couple of days. Despite the insistence that the work is hard, I found that everyone behaved as though he were on a picnic and that less energy is demanded than in clearing the ground for a new garden.

The clay deposits are in the Fly Islands, a few miles off Siboma. Three different kinds are available, one grey-green in colour, one red-brown, and the third dark chocolate. To my inexperienced fingers the texture seemed to be identical, but the party indicated that previous attempts to work with a mixture had always resulted in the appearance of cracks during the baking process.

Years of digging have resulted in a series of deep holes, which have to be bailed out. The clay is then shovelled into heaps and turned over by hand. Any pieces of shale are tossed to one side.

On the return of the party the drums are tipped out, and the clay which is to be kept for future use is rolled into big balls for storage under the house.

From now on the women take over. First they select a lump of clay, break it in pieces, and soak it overnight in an old wooden bowl. In the morning, after the water has been poured away, the sticky mass is closely examined to make certain that every fragment of stone, no matter now small, has been removed. It is then made into long thin rolls, which are nipped off into six-inch lengths (Plate 13). These strongly resemble sticks of plasticine and have much the same consistency.

Each potter now seats herself on the ground, and, taking a roll into her left palm, makes the base with the fingers of her right hand.

TRADE

When the vessel is about three inches high she places it on a leaf on the ground and builds up the sides, turning with her left hand as she adds the rolls and smoothes them into shape, again with the fingers of the right hand (Plate 13). Disaster most often occurs at this stage—either the sides collapse or cracks appear—and she has to begin again. The finished pot is a symmetrical cone with a slightly turned in lip, on which each maker leaves her trade mark, perhaps a scroll design, a group of spirals traced with a stick, the imprint of a small bamboo, or even a pair of animal heads. Some of the vessels are tiny and others very large, twenty inches high and eighteen inches across. The most popular size is somewhere between the two, about sixteen inches by twelve.

The pots are left in the sun for a few hours and are afterwards transferred to a rack over the fireplace for some days. Finally, they are taken down and baked inside and out on an open fire, from which they emerge a dull, sooty black.

The next step is to test them. Taro peelings are boiled, and if the water becomes discoloured the pot is at once smashed. Vessels which are approved are used by the household for a week or more to make certain that there are no undiscovered flaws, and they are then stacked in the loft of the house to await disposal.

When the family becomes short of food they load a canoe and sail northwards to one of the villages where the members have relatives —Kila, Asini', Lutu, Buakap, or Busama. On arrival the craft is beached, and the crew make their way to the dwelling of their host. The cargo is left on board till the following morning, when it is laid out and formally presented.

The travellers generally remain for two or three days and receive their return gift of food on the last evening. A bag of taro weighing approximately fifty pounds is recognised as equal in value to a small pot, two to a medium pot, and three to a large pot. If sago is given instead the amounts are respectively one lump of twenty pounds, two lumps, and three lumps. A host who is short can easily borrow supplies from some of his kinsmen.

Persons unrelated to the visitors never deal with them direct no matter how urgent the need: they wait till the party has departed and then approach the host.

The Busama and the villagers from nearby conduct their voyages to the south in the same manner. They take a cargo of taro or

89

sago as a present and come back later in the week laden with pots.

The Laukanu, as was mentioned, are now in need of canoes. During 1949 they asked Busama friends for four small ones like that illustrated in Plate 9. Twenty-four to thirty pots were given in return for each.

Gift Exchanges

TABLE OF EQUIVALENTS

The Busama group gives:

For a large pot	about 150 lb. taro or 60 lb. sago, or for 24–30 pots a small canoe.
small pot	about 50 lb. taro or 20 lb. sago.
string bag	large pot for 4 string bags (or rarely 1s. 6d.)
mat	small pot, or large pot for 3 mats (or rarely 2s.).
woven purse	small pot for 4 purses (or rarely 1s. for 2).
woven basket	2 large bowls (or rarely £1).
carved bowl (popular size)	10s. to 12s. (more for bigger sizes).

The north-coast group gives:

For a large pot	4 string bags, or 3 mats (or rarely 6s. to 8s.).
small pot	mat (or rarely 2s.).
woven purse	mat for 4 purses (or rarely 1s. for 2).
woven basket	10 mats (or rarely £1).
carved bowl	food—quantity not known.

The Labu group gives:

For a large pot	woven basket for 2 large pots (or rarely 6s. to 8s.).
small pot	4 purses (or rarely 2s.).
string bag	3 purses (or rarely 1s. 6d.).
mat	4 purses (or rarely 2s.).
carved bowl	10s. to 12s.

The pot-making group gives:

For taro	large pot for 150 lb., or small pot for 50 lb.
sago	large pot for 60 lb., or small pot for 20 lb.
string bag	large pot for 4 string bags
mat	small pot, or large pot for 3 mats.
woven purse	small pot for 4 purses.
woven basket	2 large pots.
carved bowl	8s.
small canoe	24–30 pots.

Trade in other Goods

Exchanges similar to those described took place prior to 1941 between the peoples of the north coast and the Tami Islanders: the former supplied food and the latter wooden bowls. The Tami natives lost their tools during the war, however, and when I last visited Finschhafen had still not been able to replace them. I am unable to say whether their supplies are at the present time deficient.

The Busama and their neighbours keep sufficient pots for their own needs and set the rest aside for the natives of the north coast and elsewhere; and the natives of the north coast keep some bowls for themselves and put the rest by for the Busama and other villagers. But the northern peoples are more fortunate in that mats and bags are also available for giving away. Following the practice of former times, they exchange these last items for the pots, a single mat for a small one, two mats or a mat and a bag for one of medium size, and three mats or four bags for a large one. Money is considered to be inappropriate, but on rare occasions a man may offer 2s. as a fair return for a mat, 1s. 6d. for a bag, 2s. for a small pot, and from 5s. to 8s. for a large pot.

A gift of a bowl, on the other hand, is invariably followed by a counter gift of cash. This also is in line with what happened in the past, except that our coinage has replaced the dogs' teeth of the old native currency. A bowl two feet long, nine inches wide, and five inches deep is considered to be worth from 10s. to 12s.

The Labu villagers receive their pots from the Busama, Buakap, Lutu, Asini', or Kila and their mats, bags, and bowls from the north coast. They always give money for the bowls, but purses and baskets woven by themselves are preferred for everything else. Two purses nine inches wide by six deep are valued at 1s. and a basket three or four feet square at about £1. A man who has received a small pot or mat thus gives four purses, and if he has been presented with a couple of large pots or a pile of ten mats, he offers a basket.

The pot makers depend on the Busama-Kila group for their bowls, mats, bags, purses, and baskets but never receive any of these items on their journeys north: always and invariably there is a delay until their kinsmen come southwards. The Busama-Kila charge nothing for their trouble or for transport and actually give away the bowls for less than cost. They are happy to present a bowl for which they have paid 10*s*. in exchange for a pot worth only 8*s*.; further, they refrain from making derogatory remarks about the man afterwards, something they would not do if a fellow villager had been involved. 'We're sorry for the potters,' one of my friends remarked. 'They live in such hungry country. Besides, we want pots for use ourselves and to exchange for mats and other things.'

The Tami Islanders are similarly beholden to the northern villages but I believe pay a fair price—possibly because surplus pots are traded northwards and eastwards.[1]

Barter between Coast and Interior

The Busama exchange goods with the Kai from the immediate hinterland and with a second group, the Kaidemoe, living high up in the mountains more than a day's walk away.

A few have relatives amongst the Kai and carry on dealings with them by means of gifts. They journey inland on visits bearing objects to offer to their hosts, and at a later date the bushmen come down with presents for their former guests. Arrangements are sometimes made, too, for a Kai to take charge of one of his Busama kinsman's sows. Word is sent when the animal farrows, and the two divide the litter, each cutting the ears of his piglets with his private mark.

Where kinship ties do not exist, however—and no Busama has ever married a Kaidemoe—trading is by means of barter.

The most constant demands of the Kai are for the usual items of native manufacture, such as pots and mats, and for tuna fish. The use of stone and volcanic glass for tools has been abandoned, but the need has been replaced by another. Lacking canoes, these natives find visits to the stores in Lae and Salamaua burdensome, and they therefore look to the Busama for their trade goods.

The Kai have only agricultural products to offer, but their tobacco is of high quality, and the ample stocks of yams and sweet potatoes are a change from taro.

[1] I have not visited Tami since the earlier years of the war before beginning my Busama study. At that time I knew nothing about the trade which was carried on and, in any case, was occupied with other problems.

TRADE

Regular markets are not held, and a bushman wanting a pot or a mat chooses a time convenient to himself for a journey to the beach with his tobacco and vegetables. He sits outside the village or on the beach and makes his wants known, and before long someone always agrees to make a deal. Correspondingly, a Busama needing tobacco or foodstuffs takes his catch of tuna, or possibly a pot, a length of calico, an axe, or a knife to the interior. Arguments are of rare occurrence, and the bargain is generally made within half an hour. I several times saw a seven-pound tuna exchanged for a bag of about fifty pounds of sweet potatoes.

The Kaidemoe are by native standards comparatively wealthy. The goldfields are within easy walking distance, and many of them enter employment as labourers. They have a certain amount of tobacco for exchange, but most of the goods which they obtain from the Busama are bought for cash. Frequent expeditions are made to acquire pots and salt, which the coast villagers prepare by boiling down drums of sea water, and when feasts are to be held parties set out, or they did before the war, to purchase extra pigs. Pups are occasionally in demand, too, for training as hunters. Pigs are valued at from £1 10s. to £2 and upwards, and for a likely pup as much as £1 10s. may be paid. The Busama again seek no margin of profit on the pots and charge the set prices of from 2s. to 8s.

The Kaidemoe were converted to Christianity by Busama native missionaries, and when making a visit to the coast nowadays they go straight to the house of a retired church worker. They tell him of their wants in expectation that he will spread the news, and on the following morning adjourn to the edge of the village to await an offer from someone willing to sell. If a pig or a dog is desired those available are examined and the best selected.

In former times, when travel was fraught with risk, upwards of forty or fifty persons made the trip from the mountains together. They camped at the mouth of the Buang River, and it was here that goods were bartered. In addition to pots, salt water, and pigs, they were eager to have stone tools and shell ornaments, in return for which they gave carved spears, bird-of-paradise plumes, cockatoo feathers, and dogs' teeth.

Importance of Trade

The speed with which exchange relations were reopened after the upheaval of war is indicative of their place in the native economy. Without trade, indeed, the southern peoples could not long survive in their present environment. The mountains here are so precipitous that improved methods of cultivation would probably still not produce sufficient food.

The fact that so many of the goods are used by women, who in New Guinea are always the more conservative members of the family, was undoubtedly of some influence. Unlike the men, they have little opportunity for learning new ways in European employment (see below p. 183), and, although lads always have at least six years of schooling, two of them spent in a boarding establishment, the formal education of girls ends after four years (see p. 237). In the circumstances it is not surprising that the average housewife should prefer clay pots to the iron saucepans sold in the stores, wooden bowls to enamel basins, string bags to canvas rucksacks, and pandanus-leaf mats to woollen blankets.

But if the men were indifferent—and the remark quoted expressing appreciation of taro cooked in a clay pot suggests that this is not always so—it is doubtful whether in normal times there would be sufficient cash available for the purchase of large quantities of European goods.

Judicious encouragement might succeed in developing the trade still further, thereby improving the people's diet and fostering their advancement. The Huon Gulf has a number of fishing grounds—Army Fisheries Units discovered some of them in 1944 and 1945—and if a simple means of preservation was taught many tons of good food would be available for wide distribution. The villages of the interior, too, could be induced to grow a variety of new crops.

The increasing industrialism of the town of Lae also presents possibilities. The Europeans, already over two thousand in number, are eager to obtain fish, fruit, and vegetables, and the time is not far distant when the natives living in the vicinity will also wish to purchase many of their supplies. Several of them have already abandoned gardening in favour of running motor-transport businesses, and the recent setting up of a Mission high school where English is taught will be followed by the young men offering themselves as clerks for high wages.

A first step in development must be to persuade the natives to meet at regular intervals in market places where the goods can be selected as required. Gift exchanges were satisfactory in the past but are too cumbersome for the world of today. Barter may suffice at first, but within a few years money will probably be used on all occasions.

Chapter Six

SOCIAL GROUPING

'The truth has never been of real value to any human being—it is a symbol for mathematicians and philosophers to pursue. In human relations kindness and lies are worth a thousand truths.'—GRAHAM GREENE, *The Heart of the Matter*.

T HE net of kinship is throughout Melanesia cast wide, and every Busama counts between two hundred and three hundred persons as relatives. Each relationship term is applied not to two or three individuals alone but to a number: there are many 'fathers', many 'father's sisters', many 'mothers', many 'mother's brothers', and so forth. Close kinsfolk, with a grandparent in common, are, however, distinguished from the rest—they are *da-tigeng*, 'one blood', while those linked by a more remote ancestor are *hu-tigeng*, 'one stem' (*hu*='stem', 'trunk of a tree', and hence 'foundation', 'cause', 'origin').[1]

Each term has an appropriate type of conduct associated with it; so men classed with the father, for example, are treated in one way and those classed with the mother's brothers in another. The divergencies will be dealt with in the later publication: what concerns us here is that all kinship behaviour is characterised by mutual helpfulness, loyalty, and trust. The ties serve in fact to create a body of individuals who can be depended on more or less absolutely for

[1] Relatives in other villages to whom the ties cannot be accurately traced are known as *nga'leng*. Strangers are *laudung*.

SOCIAL GROUPING

assistance and sympathy. Scold and nag as some of them may—any save cross-cousins,[1] who have to show formal courtesy—they forget their ill-feeling, or regard it as irrelevant, in the face of real need. The kindred is too big, nevertheless, to be required to function all the time in its entirety, and on many occasions a segment suffices. Different groupings, such as the household, the matrilineal lineage, and the club, have come into being to cope with particular activities. Each of these units retains all, or almost all, its former significance. European goods and the suppression of raiding may have made life easier and safer than it used to be, but such fundamentals as housing and the basic foods are not much altered. It follows that the people still combine on the old pattern.

In many parts of the colonial world this is not so: in West and East Africa, for example, the larger groups are disintegrating. The main cause is to be sought in export crops. Where cocoa, coffee, or cotton has been introduced on a major scale the old co-operative methods are not required—or are not at present practised—and the householders who have done the work and received the money for the harvest lack the compulsion of future needs to preserve the good-will of the wider circle of their kinsfolk.[2]

[1] The word 'cross-cousin' is used for the children of the father's sisters and of the mother's brothers: the children of the father's brothers and of the mother's sisters are known as 'parallel-cousins'. Parallel cousins, though not cross-cousins, are classified with the brothers and sisters and called by the same kinship terms.

[2] Economists and agricultural experts are urging that collective farming could in many cases be more efficient than family cultivation (see Sir Alan Pim, *Colonial Agricultural Production*, Oxford, 1946; Sir Philip Mitchell, 'General Aspects of the Agrarian Situation in Kenya', Despatch No. 44 of 1946 to the Secretary of State for the Colonies; and E. B. Worthington, 'A Development Plan for Uganda', *Colonial Review*, 1948—reprinted in *South Pacific*, 1948, pp. 147–152). There is a moral here for those concerned with the development of New Guinea. Groups like the Busama lineage and club can be utilised while they still exist: resuscitating them after they have been allowed to perish might be difficult. New crops, in other words, should be started off on a collective basis, for it may be too late to change later after peasant methods have proved a failure (see D. M. Fienberg, 'It Could Happen in New Guinea', *Monthly Notes*, 1947, No. 10).

97

The Household

An individual family—a man, his wife, and their young children—forms the core of the household, but other persons may be counted as members. The sons of the man's sisters are the most frequent additions, and other possibilities are the sons of his deceased brothers, his aged parents or parents-in-law, his unmarried or widowed sisters or sisters-in-law, and even odd hangers on with no close affiliations.

The more important the man is in village affairs the larger his group is likely to be. The most numerous today is that of Ahipum, made up of himself, his wife, their eight children, his sister's son, his mother-in-law, his wife's orphaned niece, a son of one of his wife's sisters and this man's newly acquired spouse, and an ex-indentured labourer from Madang who many years ago elected to make Busama his home.

The household is the everyday working unit, performing jobs connected with the satisfaction of immediate needs. In gardening, for example, although preliminary clearing involves extensive collaboration, the actual cultivation—planting, weeding, and harvesting—are household matters (see above pp. 63–65). The various household heads receive an allotment each, which they divide into small plots, one for every dependant, but the boundaries between these latter—though not those between the main allotments—have little importance. The menfolk of the group combine to dig the holes, and the women labour side by side, finishing one plot before beginning the next, when setting the suckers in the ground, removing the grass, and taking out the corms. In fishing, too, the men of the household generally act together and either man a small canoe by themselves or join in as a separate section of a large party.

Personal property is also in the main a household concern. Owners of pigs always consult their group before selling the animals or killing them, and each person regularly hands a large proportion of his earnings to the head for expenditure on tools and clothing for all. Once purchased the various items are allocated to particular individuals, but a good deal of borrowing still takes place.[1]

---

[1] The average household in 1944 owned £7 10s., mainly in shilling pieces (notes, being perishable, are disliked). The woman usually looked after the

Finally, the members of the household are responsible for one another's conduct. The head almost always sues for damages in the village assembly if a follower has been injured or insulted and may himself be sued on account of misconduct of which one of them has been guilty.[1]

The Lineage

This group is made up of five or six householders who trace their descent in the maternal line through about four generations from a single ancestor or a set of brothers.[2] There is a noticeable tendency—though one finds several exceptions—for them to occupy adjoining dwellings.

The lineage is today of importance as the land-holding unit. In the past it was also a religious body, and the members stood in a ritual relation to a special colony of spirits and owned much of their magic in common (see below pp. 207–209).

When the earliest settlers came from Lutu each man selected such areas as he fancied—two or three strips near the beach for planting coconuts, a couple of sections in the swamps for growing stands of sago palms, fifteen to twenty large plots in the river valleys and on the surrounding hillsides for cultivating taro and other vegetable crops, and extensive tracts in the remote bush as a source of timber for houses and canoes. The Awasa also picked out areas for themselves in the vicinity of their hill and on the neighbouring beach, and unclaimed land was still available for the first of the late-comers from Lae, Labu, and other villages. The last immigrants, finding nothing left, had to seek incorporation in existing households, most of which had far in excess of what they needed.

Busama inheritance is unusual for the Pacific (though many examples have been recorded from other parts of the world) in that real estate passes in the female line and personal property in

money, and as all the boxes with locks had been destroyed she either buried it beneath a corner of the house or carried it about with her. Each household had lost goods to the mean value of £18 and at this time possessed others to the value of £7.

[1] Discussion of the rôle of the household in the upbringing of the young must for the present be postponed.

[2] The lineage as here defined consists solely of males. The exclusion of women, both sisters and spouses, is explained in the next section.

the male line.[1] The natives give the rule in a sentence: 'What a man has received from his forbears must be transmitted to his sisters' sons, but what he has acquired by his own efforts may go to his sons.' The phrase 'acquired by his own efforts' is taken to include any trees or palms which the person has planted, and his sons in consequence often inherit a flourishing grove located on land which now belongs to their cross-cousins, the sisters' sons of the father. No one seems to be inconvenienced, probably because the life of most of the cultivated trees—they are used mainly for canoe dugouts—and of all the palms is comparatively short (a coconut ceases to bear fruit after seventy years).

The first squatters were allowed to entrust the ground to their sons, but these men had the legal obligation of transmitting it to their sisters' sons, and the latter in turn had to give it to the sons of their sisters. The man of the senior generation who is looked upon by his contemporaries as 'elder brother' acts as head of the group.

An interesting situation arose when in 1949 some of the Kaidemoe sought permission to found a lowland village on Busama land in the inner valley of the Buang River. The Busama were all aware that the ancestors had had gardens in the area and established rights for their heirs—I was told so explicitly three years before—but it was now realised that the boundaries had been forgotten. The distance from the settlement is so great—eight miles and upwards—that no one now living had ever made a garden there. A public meeting was accordingly summoned to determine what ought to be done. A site was first allocated to the Kaidemoe, with limits clearly defined, and the remaining territory declared to be unoccupied. The soil proved to be excellent, and within a few months practically every man in the village had chosen several sections, for himself and his sons in the first instance but ultimately for his daughters' sons (several pairs of brothers acted together). Claims were established by cutting down a few trees, sometimes without the immediate intention of planting taro, invariably in the vicinity of an obvious landmark, such as a bend in the river, a side creek, or a large ficus tree. By January 1950 a strip a mile deep and several hundred yards wide had been taken up.

Figure 1 shows a lineage which may be regarded as typical

[1] The only other Melanesian example of which I am aware is that of the Siwai of Bougainville (see D. L. Oliver, *Papers of the Peabody Museum, Harvard University*, Vol. XXIX, No. 4, p. 45).

FIGURE 1

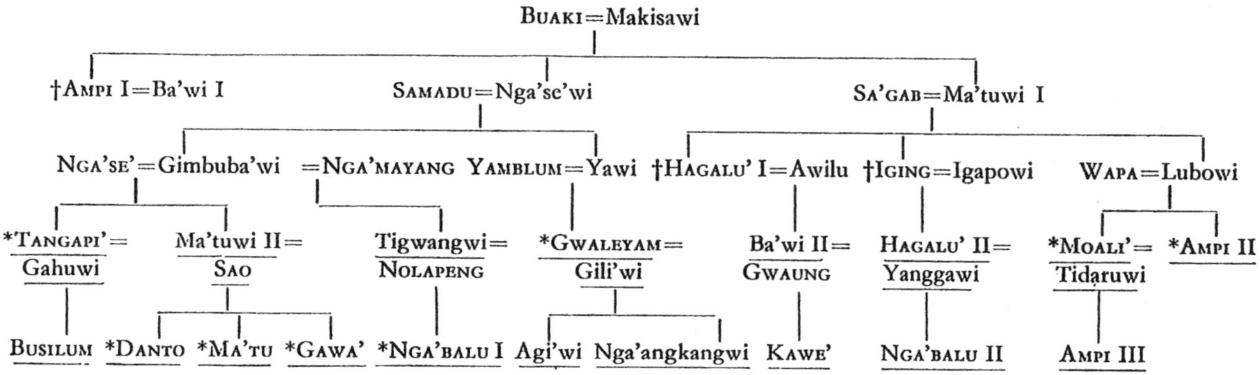

Buaki=Makisawi

†Ampi I=Ba'wi I   Samadu=Nga'se'wi   Sa'gab=Ma'tuwi I

Nga'se'=Gimbuba'wi =Nga'mayang Yamblum=Yawi †Hagalu' I=Awilu †Iging=Igapowi Wapa=Lubowi

*Tangapi'= Ma'tuwi II= Tigwangwi= *Gwaleyam= Ba'wi II= Hagalu' II= *Moali'= *Ampi II
Gahuwi   Sao   Nolapeng   Gili'wi   Gwaung   Yanggawi   Tidaruwi

Busilum *Danto *Ma'tu *Gawa' *Nga'balu I Agi'wi Nga'angkangwi Kawe' Nga'balu II Ampi III

Names of males arc in small capitals, of females in lower case.
Living persons are underlined.
* Living members of the land-holding group.
† Deceased members of the land-holding group.

(certain members, especially those of the older generations, have for convenience been omitted). The present leader is Tangapi', who will be succeeded first by Gwaleyam, then by Moali', then by Ampi II.[1] The native language has no word for the lineage, probably because the group does not operate in isolation. When land is cleared each member is accompanied by kinsmen or connections from outside —sometimes the sons, sometimes the brothers' sons, sometimes remote blood relatives, sometimes the father-in-law, sometimes the brothers-in-law, sometimes the sons-in-law. The nucleus is the same, but the accretions change from garden to garden.

A word about building sites will not be out of place as the rights relating to their use are different from those concerned with agricultural land. The village area is looked upon as common property, and houses may be erected anywhere provided no inconvenience is likely to be caused. There is a slight feeling of resentment if a man builds in a spot close to where someone else's ancestors are supposed to have been buried—until the Government insisted on land being set apart as a cemetery the dead were interred among the dwellings—but he is unlikely to be asked to move.

Hunting may be carried out all over the countryside, though those taking part are expected to keep clear of standing crops.

Women's Property

A woman's goods are at her death divided among the daughters. The reason why no mention is made of this in the inheritance rule may well be that her possessions are of such slight value.

[1] The genealogies, though accepted by the people as authentic, may be a legal fiction giving authenticity to the land tenure system. (Cf. M. Fortes, *Dynamics of Clanship among the Tallensi*, Oxford, 1945, p. 65: 'Genealogies are significant to [the Tallensi] as one of the principal instruments for organising their present social relations. They are kept alive only in so far as they serve this end, and have no value, therefore, as a measure of time during which a clan or lineage has been in existence.') If this is so, the dates for the founding of Lutu and Busama given in Chapter II are incorrect. It must be admitted that the residents of Lutu remember only the same number of generations of forbears as the Busama villagers: on the other hand, they do not regard the earliest of these ancestors as the original settlers from Bukawa'; and their land-holding groups, as is to be expected if the place was established half a century earlier, are often larger than those of Busama.

Land and houses are held exclusively by men, and though a few women have a small stock of cash, either gifts from kinsfolk or personal earnings from the sale of fruit and vegetables to Europeans, and one or two are said in the past to have owned a pig, the property of the majority is confined to items of clothing and household utensils actually in use. (Clay pots and wooden bowls held in reserve for re-export are looked upon as the man's.)

Yet women are in no sense at a disadvantage. Thus they can demand that gardens shall be prepared for their use both by the husband and by the brothers. Spouses normally stick together, but if a man has a prolonged illness, or if he seeks employment and leaves his wife at home, as occasionally happens, she can always turn for help to the family into which she was born. Again, the men are under the obligation of providing the womenfolk with adequate shelter, with supplies of pork, and with clothing and utensils. In practice a husband always consults his spouse when the residence has to be renewed, when a pig has to be killed, sold, or presented to a neighbour, and when goods have to be purchased at the stores. He is also the real loser if he tears her dress or smashes her pots in a brawl, for he not she has to make the replacement.

Father and Mother's Brother

The discussion of inheritance will have made it clear why so many households include the sons of the head's sisters. These lads are his chief heirs, the persons who will keep his memory green and carry his name on into the future. What could be better for him than having them as his constant companions? Correspondingly, what could be better for them than working at the side of their uncle? By this means they learn the location of the different areas which they are to acquire and the type of soil to be found in each. Even youths who remain with the father throughout adolescence usually erect their dwellings after marriage close to that of the maternal uncle.

But a switch to the mother's brother does not mean that the father and the relatives on that side are forgotten. The strength of the filial tie is obvious to the outsider, and informants stated over and over again that far more affection normally exists between the children and their father than between them and their maternal uncle. To ram the point home Nga'gili' held two fingers of his left hand close together, saying, 'There, that is sister's son and mother's brother.' Then, bringing up his right hand, he entwined the first and second fingers and added, 'But that is the son and his father.' It is also pointed out that one of the purposes of the old initiation ceremonies was to wean the boy from his father forcibly and emphasise his relation with his uncle.

Paternal devotion is equally strong and is given as the reason why personal property goes to the sons. Matrilineal inheritance for everything was once the practice, so it is claimed, but the fathers long ago revolted and insisted on leaving their livestock, chattels, and currency within the family. I discovered no evidence of such a change, though whether or not it occurred is in a sense irrelevant to the issue: the significant point, so far as we are concerned at present, is the belief in its having taken place.

Further indications of the strength of the attachment are furnished by the theory of conception. Patrilineal societies normally exaggerate the physiological rôle of the father, matrilineal societies the rôle of the mother. A society in which patriliny and matriliny are balanced might then be expected to attribute responsibility to both. The Busama, however, ignore the mother almost entirely—and this after half a century of European contact. It is admitted that the embryo has need of a womb in which to develop; but the organ is looked upon as a container, 'a vessel where seed planted by the man can begin to grow.' The natives even deny that the mother supplies nourishment and cite the cessation of her menses as proof. Menstruation is considered to be the outward sign that a woman is capable of conceiving. What else is to be expected than that the flow should cease after she has in fact conceived? And if there is no blood, how can the foetus be fed?

I countered statements of this kind with a query as to why so many children grow up to resemble the mother and her kindred. The answer was invariably that babies are at birth all alike and only later take on the features of those with whom they live. Half-castes begin by being white and develop dark skins through being left with the native mother, several men informed me. If snatched away at once and brought up in the father's household they would be practically indistinguishable in appearance from Europeans.

SOCIAL GROUPING

With father and sons so determinedly united it is scarcely surprising that the boys should continue to help in his gardens whenever they can spare the time. The members of the man's lineage are his main collaborators, but if much clearing has to be done the children often go along for at least a day or two, a service for which they are rewarded with an allotment. The area does not become their property but reverts back to the group after the harvest has been gathered.

Hagalu' II, who appears in Figure 1, to quote a particular case, although inheriting land from his mother's brothers, made a practice of sometimes working with his father Iging and the latter's heirs, Tangapi', Gwaleyam, and Moali'. Iging is now dead, but a friendship between the younger men persists, and at intervals one may still see them cutting the bush together and later planting a crop in adjoining allotments. Inquiries in 1947 revealed that Hagalu' then had three gardens with his own lineage and two more, both rather smaller, with the members of his father's lineage.

The same sort of attachment may linger into the following generation. Tangapi' explained that Nga'balu II, the young son of Hagalu', would probably have an odd garden now and then with Danto, Ma'tu, and Gawa', the ultimate successors of Iging. 'The ground is ours,' Tangapi' added, 'and if Nga'balu' wants to grow his taro with us he'll have to seek our permission or else wait till we ask him. But we won't refuse. How can we? Aren't we all of us *hu-tigeng?*'

The maintenance of the link with the different branches of the male line depends on a variety of factors, including whether the paternal grandfather is still alive and whether the young man has stayed near his father or has moved across to the part of the village where his mother's brothers' residences are situated. Tangapi' can barely remember his father's father and never developed any special sympathies for the men who now represent the extended family to which the old man belonged. The father of Tangapi', Nga'se', on the other hand, was still living when his grandson Busilim first reached years of discretion. Today Busilim, though concentrating mainly on his own group, co-operates at times with that of Tangapi' and even to a slight extent with that of Nga'se' (Figures 1, 2).

Other persons belonging to different lineages who may be given occasional help in clearing and fencing are the sons of the father's brothers, the sisters' husbands, the wife's father, the wife's brothers, the daughters' husbands, and remote kinsmen held in high regard. Kawe', in Figure 1, usually works with the members of his own group, but once or twice I saw him assisting Hagalu' II and also

FIGURE 2

Matrilineal Groupings and Patrilineal Relationships

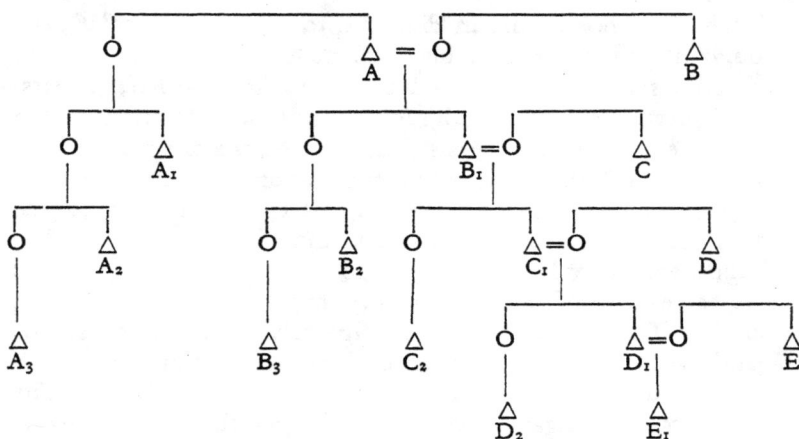

The symbol $\triangle$ represents males, O females.

C_1 makes the bulk of his gardens in collaboration with his maternal uncle C and the other members of their lineage. But C_1 has an attachment to his father B_1, and through him to the latter's sister's son B_2. He therefore joins them sometimes and is allowed the temporary use of a plot. There is also a tie with the paternal grandfather A, and with his sister's son A_1, and with this man's sister's son A_2 (C_1's second cousin). Occasional collaboration with these persons may take place.

D_1, the son of C_1, joins his maternal uncle D, has a strong link with C_1 and C_2, and a slight one with B_1, B_2, and B_3. The relationship with A_2 and A_3 has by now become so tenuous that D_1 is not likely to make gardens in their company.

Moali', the sons of his maternal grandfather's brother and sister respectively.

It is taken for granted that after such efforts an allotment will be acceptable, but the offer may be declined if for the time being the man has other plans. Tangapi' on one occasion went out to clear an area with some of his distant kinsmen and later explained to them that he would be grateful if in the course of the following week they would come with him to cut down the bush on his ground half a mile or so away. It was agreed that this was reasonable, and a couple of them, together with a few lads, appeared on the day appointed with their axes.

From time to time, too, a man may ask one of his kinsmen for a plot when he has taken no part in felling the timber, either because he was ill or was otherwise engaged. Such requests are always granted, though there is a tacit understanding that adequate return will be made at some date in the future.

A few details relating to the gardens of Tangapi', Gwaleyam, and Moali' during September 1945 will be of interest. Four of their areas were planted, in each of which all three had an allotment. Other men represented included Busilim, the son of Tangapi' (plots in two areas); Madulu, the brother of the wife of Tangapi' (a plot in one area); Ho'giling, a close relative of Gwaleyam (plots in two areas); Nga'lu a remote relative of Gwaleyam (plots in two areas); Anggu, another remote relative of Gwaleyam (a plot in one area); Hagalu' II, the son of the brother of the mother of Moali' (plots in two areas); Kawe', the son of the daughter of another brother of the mother of Moali' (a plot in one area); and Sa'gab, a remote relative of Moali' (a plot in one area). Tangapi' also had two plots on ground belonging to lineages of which he was not a member and Gwaleyam and Moali' one each.

One might be pardoned for coming to the same conclusion as the first agricultural officer of the Administration to pay a long visit to the village—that the natives do not take their land rights seriously and make gardens almost anywhere they please. Yet disputes occur if persons who are not members of the lineage attempt without first asking permission to cultivate areas to which it lays claim. The plants are torn out of the ground as soon as the offence is discovered, and that evening the matter is discussed by the village elders. The trespassers are severely castigated and told to go to the places where their maternal uncles were accustomed to grow crops (see below pp. 177–178).

Irregular Descent

A small minority, about a dozen in all, have flouted established custom and remained with the father for life. Common explanations are that he was especially devoted or that the maternal uncle had died young or neglected his obligations.

The members of the father's lineage raise no objections to such persons sharing their land. The cross-cousins, who have to behave with the utmost politeness, would in any event refrain from making complaints, but the rest when asked insist that, as there is enough ground for all, any kinsman, a *da-tigeng* or a *hu-tigeng*, is always welcome. The only limitation on a man's participation in the rights of his father's group is that he can never become the head and superintend the work.

The maternal kinsfolk, especially any of the mother's own brothers who are still alive, may express some indignation amongst themselves, but they avoid airing their grievance in public. It would be regarded as undignified and silly to insist that all those who are entitled to do so should join in with them for agricultural activities.

The community at large does not interfere, but several of the older men told me of their misgivings lest the bad example might be imitated. I have referred to the initiation ceremonies, when the youths were separated from their parents and given instruction in duties to the wider circle of kinsmen. The old religion has been abandoned, however, with a consequent change of standards, and the elders point out that there is a chance that inheritance of land rights through the father may come to be accepted as normal. I am prepared to agree, from what I know of other matrilineal societies, that this fear is probably well founded, but the evidence at present available gives no hint of increasing stress on patriliny.

The irregularity passes into the next generation if the nephews choose to go to their true maternal uncle and work with him and his father's kin. But most of them adopt the other alternative of forming an attachment to one of the men classified as a mother's brother who has joined the normal group.

Wagang will serve as a convenient example (Figure 3). He ought to have united with his mother's brother Hagili but instead kept with his father and now says he is linked to his father's sister's son Kamsili. Hagili, he told me—and other informants confirmed the statement—was of surly disposition and always in trouble with the neighbours. Yet Gi'sali', Wagang's mother's sister's son, has been cultivating their uncle's ground for years.

Kamsili fully agreed that he and Wagang were 'the same as brothers' and indicated that most of their gardens were made in collaboration. I learnt from other sources of a difference of opinion between them some years before about the choice of a bridegroom for one of their young kinswomen, but no open breach occurred, and the basic friendship was not impaired.

Wagang's son Alumba has already gone to live with his uncle Ho'nung; but it is a moot point which man the uterine nephew, the boy Lahi, will join. He may elect to work with his mother's real brother, or he may choose Gi'sali', a man classified as her brother. Should he select Wagang he can never become the head of the group—the title will go in due course to Kamsili's heir, Haku. But if instead he prefers Gi'sali' he will automatically succeed. At the same time, the link with Haku will still persist, and whatever happens the two will probably make some of their gardens together (cf. Figure 2).

Ankong, who died in about 1935, provides another example of a man remaining with his father's group (Figure 4). His case is the more remarkable as the younger brother Luya associated himself with their maternal uncle Nga'sele'. Isaka, the eldest son of their only sister, is today recognised as a team mate by Laugwi', Buaki, and Apilum, the proper successors of Angkong's father, but Bonggi, Isaka's brother, who is twelve years his junior, recently moved into the house of Tuuli', the eldest surviving heir of Nga'sele'. Their father Topia had died in 1940, after Isaka's marriage, leaving Bonggi, then aged fourteen, and the mother to be cared for by Luya. The latter till his death four years later worked mainly in company with Tuuli', who then took over the guardianship of Bonggi. The two brothers Isaka and Bonggi are often together, and, though each clears the ground chiefly with the group which he regards as his own, it seems likely that they may share many gardens. Apim, the only son left by their sister, is at present a small boy, and one cannot predict to which he will go.

FIGURE 3

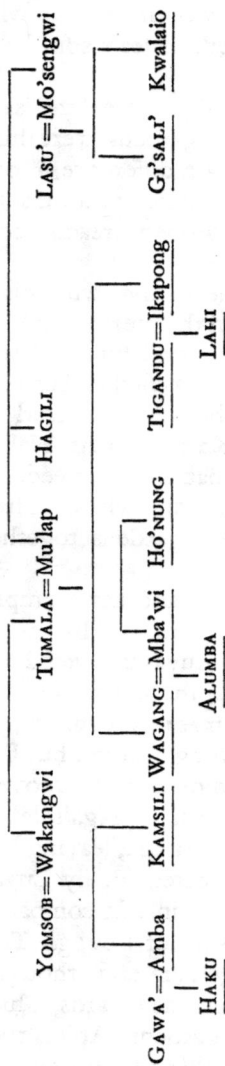

FIGURE 4

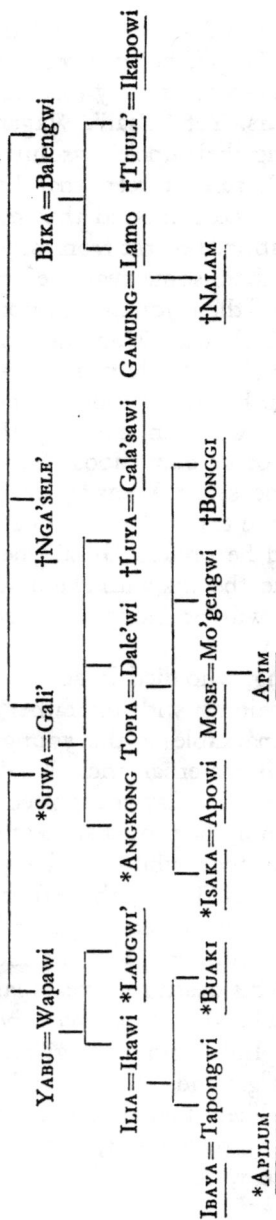

* The lineage into which Angkong was improperly incorporated.
† The lineage to which he really belonged.

Land Rights of Immigrants

The incorporation of a male stranger from another village presents no difficulties. His protector gives him plots to cultivate, and
if a wife is found for him the children are provided for by her
brothers, whose heirs they become. In earlier times there were
apparently sufficient women to spare, and most of the refugees who
came in before 1900 seem to have married and had families. Conditions have now changed, however, and the surplus of males is
creating serious problems all over New Guinea.[1] Only one of the
three recent arrivals has been furnished with a wife, and he had
seduced the girl before the parents agreed to the match.[2]

The entry of a foreign wife, on the other hand, creates awkward-
ness—not for her but for her children, who cannot legally inherit
any land in the village. One of the daughters is usually sent back to
the place from whence the mother came as a means of compensating
her kinsmen for their loss, and the rest of the offspring are incorporated in their father's lineage.

FIGURE 5

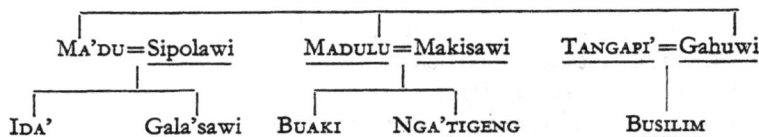

MA'DU=Sipolawi	MADULU=Makisawi	TANGAPI'=Gahuwi
IDA' Gala'sawi	BUAKI NGA'TIGENG	BUSILIM

A recent marriage of this type was that of Ma'du to Sipolawi, a
woman from Labu (Figure 5). He died in 1944, committing her and
their two children, a boy of four named Ida' and a baby daughter,
to the care of his brother Madulu. There is little doubt that when the
time comes Ida' will be accepted into the lineage of his father's
sister's son Busilim, though it is perhaps just possible that Madulu's
two sons will insist on the boy's continuing his association with
them. They call him 'elder brother' and will no doubt continue to
treat him as such.

[1] Vide H. I. Hogbin, 'Sex and Marriage in Busama', Oceania, Vol. XVII,
p. 138.
[2] Ibid., pp. 228–229.

Sentimental Attachment to Land

The fact that even twelve of the natives do not cultivate the areas which are rightfully theirs suggests that the Busama lack that passion for the soil which characterises so many agricultural peoples. In Wogeo, another New Guinea community with which I am familiar, the people regard the use of ground handed down from their fore-fathers as a sacred duty, and men with large families encourage the adoption of some of their children by less fortunate relatives in order that all areas shall be directly inherited and cared for.[1] Aged men, too, when on the point of death sometimes request that they be carried on a bier to the places where in the past they have made gardens. Weeping, they take a cermonial farewell of each and entrust it to their heirs. Far from being moved by my accounts of such prac-tices, the Busama treated them as absurd, and when I went on to say that these folk also adorn their allotments with borders of flowers and ornamental shrubs my statements were ridiculed. The garden is a place to work in, was the general verdict, not something to be looked at.

It is possible that the collapse of the old religion may have led to a change of attitude, for in former times each lineage had a close ritual bond with a colony of spirits which were supposed to look after the different areas (see below pp. 207–209). The short period of settlement may also be significant. The first crops were not planted till after 1830, and a century or so. is perhaps not long enough for the development of an overwhelming attachment. But I believe that the real explanation is the natives' conviction that they are sailormen rather than gardeners. So much of their love is taken up by the sea that little is left over for the land.

During my early days in the village, in 1944 and 1945, when the people were living in the bush clearing five hundred yards from the shore, the exile was so much deplored that scarcely a month passed without a deputation being sent to the District Officer for permission to return. The sound of the waves was distinctly audible on windy days, but it was urged that this was not enough. 'We want to be able

---

[1] *Vide* H. I. Hogbin, 'Tillage and Collection', *Oceania*, Vol. IX, p. 303; 'Native Land Tenure in New Guinea', *Oceania*, Vol. X, p. 164; and 'Adoption in Wogeo', *Journal of the Polynesian Society*, Vol. XLIV, pp. 212–214.

to look at the sea,' my friends insisted. 'We don't belong to the hills, nor do we trap our food in the forest. No, we're fishermen. And who ever heard of a coast people with their houses surrounded by trees?' Despite a positive prohibition, men who became ill cajoled their relatives into building them a temporary hut on the shore. 'We couldn't get better if we remained where we were,' they said. 'It's the smell of the sea we want to put us right.'

The Club

Each of the fourteen club houses has an associated social group, and the same word, *lum*, is used for both. New clubs come into being occasionally, but the majority have a long history behind them and traditional names with counterparts in Lutu and Bukawa'. Membership is determined in part by descent and in part by choice. Most persons like to consider themselves as belonging to two, that of the mother's brothers and that of the father. But, although visits may be paid to both, they commonly spend the bulk of their time in one. If they become attached to a maternal uncle then it is in his club that they are usually to be found; and if the bond with the father has been kept up to the full, then they keep in the main to his. A small number join neither but instead follow a distant kinsman, either because of a special fondness for him or because of his outstanding place in village affairs. A census revealed that, if secondary allegiances are disregarded, considerably more than half the men are members of the mother's brothers' club, rather more than a quarter members of the father's, and approximately one-eighth members of that of another relative. The title of club head is bestowed on the man who accepts the responsibility for the re-erection and repair of the building.

Women never set foot in a club house—it is said that in pagan days, when various sacred objects were stored there, the death penalty would have been exacted had they ventured to approach. Yet they are always included in the group. 'A woman belongs to the club to which she brings food and firewood,' it is explained— that of her father or guardian before her marriage, that of her husband afterwards.

Like the lineage, the club forms a nuclear group for certain types of communal work, notably house building and canoe construction, tasks which require more workers than agriculture.

A man putting up a new dwelling has at some stages to call upon both distant and near kinsfolk (see Appendix G). Bringing in the materials from the forest, in particular, demands an army of workers. These men have to be given a meal at the end of the day, and, in addition, the completion of each stage of the undertaking is the occasion for a feast (see below pp. 126–128.). The householder furnishes most of the food himself but receives handsome contributions from his fellow clubmen, who also look after a good deal of the cooking, leaving him free to superintend the labours of the other helpers. Further, the clubmen take over many of the smaller jobs for which only about a dozen men are needed, such as sawing and planing the wall boards and fixing the thatch. The head usually owns the pit saws and other expensive tools, though each man will have contributed a few shillings to help him buy them.

The construction of a canoe proceeds in much the same sort of way. The main body of relatives cuts down the tree, drags or floats it to the workshop, and removes a portion of the centre, while the club members occupy themselves preparing the daily meals and the feast.

The club is also concerned with certain types of fishing. The members generally combine to obtain a small reef net, and though the head, as the organiser of the purchase, is looked upon as the owner, everyone is entitled to use it and have a share in the haul. Again, most club heads are the nominal owners of a large canoe which is at the disposal of their followers.

Marriage, too, is a club matter, and the young people have to accept the mate approved by the elders of their group. A general discussion usually takes place to investigate the virtues and vices of possible candidates and their families, and the immediate kin then make the final choice. Club exogamy and brother-sister exchange are the rule, youths who have no sister of their own being paired with one of the girls so classified from their club. In the past, when the traditional wedding ceremonies were still performed, the club members also paid the bride price.[1]

Finally, contributions to important inter-village feasts are usually

[1] The subject is fully discussed in my paper 'Sex and Marriage in Busama', *op. cit.*, pp. 234–287.

made in the name not of individuals but of clubs, and the members
lump their gifts together as a joint offering. The host also divides
the food among the different clubs taking part, leaving the principal
men of each to distribute the portions to their respective followers.
Army rations during the war were always allocated first to the clubs.

Lutu and Awasa

Kinsfolk, whether or not they are members of the household,
lineage or club, are knit together by their mutual dependence as
much as by their blood ties. Quarrels between them are rare, partly
because of the ethical responsibility of loyalty and trust but possibly
still more because of the risk of losing an indispensable helper afterwards.

In the average New Guinea community, where the population is
only two hundred or so, everyone is a kinsman, and the village acts
as a single unit. But Busama has snowballed to 600. Nobody counts
much more than half this number as relatives or has need of assistance from the remainder. Each person, that is to say, divides his
fellows into categories, associates and outsiders; moreover, because
intermarriage between Lutu and Awasa, though never forbidden,
is somewhat rare, the categories have come to be largely identified
with these two divisions. Either the Lutu are mainly kinsmen and
the Awasa mainly outsiders, or the Awasa are kinsmen and the Lutu
outsiders.

Irritation with outsiders, unlike irritation with a relative, need not
be suppressed—their goodwill and animosity are alike immaterial,
especially now that fighting is prohibited and the village never has
to be defended from attack. The result has been a growth of bad
relations, and it is on this account that the District Officer gave
orders for the settlement to be split into two.

The decision was precipitated by a series of open disagreements.
Several Awasa had brought trivial charges against men of Lutu to
the District Court for settlement when there appeared to be no
reason why the matters in dispute could not have been adjusted by
the native officials. At this period only one pair had been appointed,
a luluai from Awasa and a tultul from Lutu, each of whom was
supposed to have a measure of authority. But they repeatedly

complained that orders given to the other section were flagrantly disobeyed.

In fairness to the Lutu it must be said at once that the Awasa were responsible for most of the trouble. The bulk of the criminals, too, were Awasa—they supplied the sexual offenders and the thieves for a period of over ten years. I do not wish to give the impression that all are bad citizens—that is not so—but it is undeniable that many anti-social qualities are an Awasa monopoly. This is perhaps to be accounted for by the people's history. Fugitives for many years, they were harried in turn by the Laiwamba, by the Labu and Kaidemoe, and by the Kai and Busama; and even after admission to their present home they must have felt that they were guests and did not quite belong. Today they are suffering from wounded vanity because the break has made it plain that they are the minority, and several approaches have taken place to persuade unsuspecting Administrative officials new to the area to cancel the separation. Many elders are convinced that there will be no peace till Awasa Hill is resettled and the Lutu again have sole possession of the beach. Capital investments in the form of houses and palm trees, however, put withdrawal out of the question.[1]

It is to be noted that conditions in the last century at the time of the amalgamation were in no way comparable. The population, to begin with, was smaller; but, more important, general collaboration had to take place then both for defence and for the purpose of carrying out the tasks involving the use of the inefficient stone tools. Felling a tree which can be done today by one man in an hour took the labours of several for the full day.

The majority of the villagers chose the section to which they properly belonged, though there were one or two surprises. Nga'lu and Ma'du, for instance, both of whose forbears had been exclusively Lutu, went over to Awasa, the first on account of a friendship with an elder there and the second because he had recently had a disagreement with the men whom it had been decided should be appointed as the Lutu office-bearers. These latter, Ahipum and Nga'gili', happen to be descended from Labu immigrants, who had arrived two generations before, and Ma'du gave as his reason that he, a

[1] There is an obvious parallel with the dual division of certain communities in the eastern parts of Melanesia, such as New Ireland, Guadalcanal, and the Banks Islands. But no other Gawa' village near Busama has such an organisation.

'pure' Lutu, had no wish to accept orders from 'foreign riffraff.' His brothers chided him for his foolishness, but he remained firm and left them. Other brothers who separated were Bu'da' and Muengpop and also Isom and Sa'gwi'. The first pair were of Gaiwaku descent, but Bu'da' had for years been particularly attached to one or two of the Awasa and Muengpop to some of the Lutu. Isom had been born into Awasa but was so filled with resentment at the shabby treatment which he had received from the old luluai Bumbu, who was also Awasa, that he took the opportunity to sever the connection.

The remark of Mabiyeng is of some interest. He picked Awasa but with the reservation that he might later change over to Lutu. 'I am feeling the Awasa leaders to see whether they are good,' he told me. 'If they're ripe I'll eat them; if rotten I'll throw them away.'

Busama Groups

The household, the lineage, the club, and the full kindred each forms a co-operative unit with recognised duties. The household is concerned with such matters as planting, harvesting, certain types of fishing, and the accumulation and expenditure of money; the lineage organises clearing the ground for new gardens; the club is called upon when feasts are arranged or marriages planned; and the kindred looks after the biggest enterprises of all, such as bringing in timber for new houses. Ties of blood bind all these groups into a separate division, either Lutu or Awasa.

The two sections have at present few points of contact, and they are in consequence drifting apart. But if in the future some common aim emerges requiring a band of workers 600 strong for its achievement the differences may come to be forgotten. The names of Lutu and Awasa will then sink into the background, and Busama will again be one.

Chapter Seven

STATUS AND LEADERSHIP

'Liberty is not a crowned goddess in a spotless garment : liberty is the man in the street, bloody, brutal, rampant.'

FRANK NORRIS.

THE major office holders in the village today, apart from the luluai and tultul appointed by the Government, are the club heads. In former times there were also two or three headmen who wielded influence in a small circle of club groups outside their own. The early writers speak of these latter as chiefs, but the word is a misnomer, implying grandeur and power quite foreign to most Melanesian societies.[1]

Birth and seniority are not entirely ignored, but the prime qualification for a title has always been wealth. This wealth, too, is not inherited but accumulated by personal initiative and enterprise. The club head is the richest man in the group, and the headman of olden days was the richest of half a dozen related club heads.

The main item of wealth, now as in the past, is food, and the marks of a rich man are the extent of his taro gardens, the number of his palms, and the size of his pig herd. Dogs' teeth were also of importance once, but extra supplies of these could only be obtained by exporting stocks of food; further, their use was largely restricted to ceremonial payments such as bride price. The introduction of

---

[1] The Trobriand Islanders, described in the works of Professor Malinowski, are in this and certain other respects unique.

money has led to certain complications, especially as the principal
—though not the sole—source of income is wage labour. Yet the
sums earned are so small that expensive luxuries are out of reach;
and capital goods, apart from simple tools, would be of little use
without a higher standard of education.

The attitude towards food may be gathered from the way in which
it is constantly displayed.[1] The women when returning from work
dump their loads on the verandah for all to see, and the preparation of the meal at the end of the day is carried out in public. 'This
is Busama fashion,' I was informed. 'We like to show what we have,
not hide it. No one can then say there isn't enough.' It is also significant that persons arrived back from a journey always speak at
length about what they had to eat, how it was prepared, and whether
the flavour was equal to that of local products.

To be short of food is looked upon as disgraceful, and the hardships of the war were a real humiliation. Having nothing to eat,
Ahipum told me sadly, was the worst experience possible. Hunger,
naturally, was unpleasant, but he was not referring to that—the
pain of an empty belly was no worse than a headache. The dreadful
thing was that other places knew Busama was unable to feed itself
and had to depend on Army rations. 'We are ashamed,' the people
used to lament. 'Our village is the home of taro, and now we have
so little that we take what food the soldiers give us. We don't like
being talked about. It is dreadful that this should happen.' When
on one occasion news came that the residents of a more fortunate
settlement where the nets had been saved were bringing a gift of
fish most persons disappeared into the bush for the day. Shame had

[1] Cf. D. L. Oliver, *Papers of the Peabody Museum, Harvard University*, Vol.
XXIX, No. 2, p. 14: 'Eating is considered first and foremost a social event
and only secondarily a means of satisfying hunger and restoring energy. To
eat with a stranger is to show confidence in him, to demonstrate that one does
not fear his sorcery. Staple food is an integral part of every ritual and is
used to seal every pact. `. . . Food is exchanged when a young couple is
betrothed. It is shared by bride and groom as a sign of marriage. The critical
aspect of mother-in-law avoidance is the taboo against exchanging food. . . .
Sorrow is most poignantly expressed by voluntary food restrictions. Cessation
of hostilities used to be signalised by food exchanges; and today, whenever a
serious quarrel is settled there must be a feast of forgiveness.' Dr. Oliver is
speaking of the Siwai of Bougainville, but his remarks apply equally to the
Busama—and, indeed, to the Melanesian peoples generally.

overwhelmed them, they said afterwards, at their inability to prepare even a picnic meal for the visitors.

Consternation reigned also when a letter was received announcing the arrival of a group of itinerant Mission leaders. They were coming to discuss arrangements for the baptism of the children born during the Japanese invasion, a matter of genuine concern to the parents, all of whom, nevertheless, were gravely annoyed. Most of the criticism was turned on the native pastor, who was indirectly responsible. 'It doesn't matter to you; you've only one child to consider and have food to spare,' one man told him tartly. 'But what about me? My wife and I have four children and a mother and mother-in-law to feed, and if we give away a bowl of taro we'll not have enough for ourselves. And who ever heard of receiving important guests without killing a pig for them to eat? Where's that to come from? You know quite well there's not a pig in the place. When these men go home and are asked what there was to eat, they'll reply that all we gave them was just a little taro and rice without pork. Their kinsmen will laugh at us—or else they'll say they're sorry for us, and that would be as bad. Anyway, we'll have to hang our heads.'

The lack of pigs was given as the explanation of why the rebuilt club houses were of only one storey instead of two. The erection of the usual structure would have involved feasts, and without animals to kill no meat could be provided. Each club leader therefore put up a simple building.

A revealing incident took place at a much later stage when I was paying an evening visit to Ahipum. Another man arrived shortly before dinner and as is usual was invited to join in. All through the meal he spoke of the enormous amount which he had already eaten in his own home, and after his departure I commented on his appetite, for he seemed to me to have consumed as much as anyone else. 'What he said was all lies,' my hostess said bluntly. 'A wild pig has destroyed his garden, and his wife has nothing to cook.' 'Listen to me,' Ahipum interposed. 'When a man comes to your house at this time of night and starts talking about how full he is, it's certain that he's really hungry. He wants you to give him something but covers up his shame by pretending that he's already fed.'

Another of my friends, Ida', suffered permanent injury as a child because of his reluctance to ask for food. He had not long before lost both his parents and was being cared for by an uncle, his mother's only brother. This man was remarkably kind, but the wife resented the boy's intrusion and did her best to make his life miserable. One day she went visiting and, although not intending to return till the moon rose very late in the evening, made no provision for his dinner. Instead of seeking out another relative, he preferred to climb a palm for a coconut. Missing his hold in the darkness, he fell and twisted his spine.

Perhaps the most serious discourtesy which one person can offer to another is refusal to accept a gift of food. A quarrel is inevitable, and all social relations may be suspended afterwards for many months. Thus when the Awasa luluai Gwaleyam spurned the gift of a man called Boya only my presence in the village prevented a brawl, and a year later the two of them were still ignoring one another. They had disagreed about the choice of a husband for a girl who was related to them both, and Gwaleyam was indignant that Boya's word should have carried greater weight than his own. He deliberately absented himself from the wedding and on returning to the village threw his share of the feast which had followed it off his verandah into the village street. The adults are not in general given to weeping, but the young bridegroom when informed of what had occurred burst into tears and assured me that he would never live down the insult.

Gifts and Reciprocity

Despite all this concentration on plentiful supplies, a super-abundance is of little immediate benefit. The amount which anyone can eat is strictly limited, and methods of preservation and storage are unknown. Pork can be left for only a day or two, taro rots within a week, and sago starch is mouldy in a month. The natives have therefore to distribute their resources or see them deteriorate. Everyone likes to be able to send presents to relatives and friends; and the richer a man becomes, the larger and more numerous are his gifts.

The virtues of generosity are impressed upon the children from their earliest years. If an aunt gives a toddler some bananas he is instructed to divide the bunch and see that no one goes without. The parents of the other youngsters may protest that he should be allowed to keep all the gift for himself, but his own insist on the order being obeyed, if necessary by the use of force.

Later, when social responsibilities are appreciated, portions are handed to the boys and girls for presentation. 'Heblawi wasn't at work today, so I expect she's ill,' I heard a mother remark to her ten-year-old daughter. 'That means that her husband Nga'lai won't have anything prepared for his dinner. Here, child, take these taro over to the house for them.' 'The pigs have been at Ongwi's garden again,' another woman announced to her family. 'This is bad news for her, because I know she's no more taro ready. Both her sisters are away, too, and can't send anything. Never mind, we have plenty now. Come, Mangwi, carry this dish across and tell her to come with us tomorrow and help herself in some of our plots.' The mother watched the little girl down the road, calling out as a last reminder, 'Don't forget now; ask her for tomorrow.'

Invitations of this kind always follow a misfortune, and the woman is allowed to take away as much as she can carry. Food taken to her house, however, is cooked beforehand.

Now the keynote of Busama social life is reciprocity, and a person who accepts help of any kind has to be prepared to offer his services when the assistant is engaged in a similar undertaking. Even marriage is arranged on a reciprocal basis: a group seeking a wife for one of its young men always agrees to hand over a girl later as a spouse for the bride's brother. It follows that every gift imposes an obligation on the recipient to make a counter gift. Assets and liabilities are carefully remembered and in the event of death are taken over by the heir as part of the inheritance.

The man who is generous over a long period thus has many persons in his debt. No problem arises when these are of the same status as himself—the poor give one another insignificant presents, and the rich exchange sumptuous offerings. But if his resources are greater than theirs they may find repayment impossible and have to default. Acutely conscious of their position, they express their humility in terms of deference and respect. Their conduct brings to mind the words of Milton: 'grateful minds, by owing they owe not, at once indebted and discharged.'

The relation of debtors and creditor forms the basis of the system of leadership. The clubman who is the creditor of his fellow members becomes their head, looked up to by them all. The old village headmen acquired their honours in similar fashion and were each the creditor of several club groups as well as their own. The club head has no special name and is referred to simply as *nga'atu*, 'a big man'. The headman, on the contrary, had a title, *apumtau*, a contraction of *wapum-ngatau*, literally 'generous principal man' (*ngatau* is as a rule only used in combinations, e.g. *ngatau-wangga*, 'captain of the canoe', and *ngatau-wasangga*, 'leader of the netting party'). Headmen are also described as *nga'tiwai*, 'men widespread' (that is, whose reputation is known far and wide) or, alternatively, as 'the men who ate bones and chewed lime'—they presented the best meat to others, leaving only scraps for themselves, and were so free with areca nuts and pepper that they had no betel mixture left.[1] Folk-tales about legendary headmen of the past relate that, although these men had 'more pigs than anyone could count and bigger gardens than are made now', they gave everything away.

The words applied to a man notorious for his meanness are also worth noting—*bangkong*, *gewe'boa*, and *tita'gaming*. *Bangkong* is to bolt food greedily like a dog without proper mastication; *gewe'boa* is to take no notice of those who are hungry (*gewe'*='to sit with head bowed', and *boa*='always'); and *tita'gaming* is 'his belly holds him back', 'he is constipated', 'he is stingy'.

Importance of Feasts

A convenient opportunity for giving the food away is provided by feasts, which take place with great frequency. But although the host always endeavours to make as fine a showing as possible, the amount which he himself can provide is necessarily limited by the fact that pork, taro, and sago are all so perishable. Even if he has fattened a few pigs in readiness and enlisted the aid of other workers to plant a large garden some months beforehand—and these are elementary precautions—his immediate resources are still somewhat meagre. The difficulty is overcome by dropping a hint that a squaring of accounts will now be welcome. Some of his kinsmen can be depended upon to take heed and come along with counter gifts;

[1] The word *konigi* has also gained currency. This is obviously derived from the German 'könig' and must have been introduced by missionaries. It would be difficult to find any expression less appropriate.

and there are others who will wish to make new offerings as a means of piling up assets for future use. If in the preceding years he has presented, say, four cousins with a pig apiece and twenty more each with two hundredweights of taro, he can be sure of receiving at least two pigs and a ton of taro back at once. Perhaps another pig and a further half ton of taro will come in from other sources, making a lavish repast a certainty.

The notion of interest is in this particular context unknown, but it seems that there are sufficient grounds for arguing that giving goods away is in Busama a form of investment. The native by this means stores up the fruits of his labour and after an interval reaps an accumulated benefit.

The common Melanesian convention obtains in respect of the pigs. A presentation from a close relative imposes the usual obligation to return an animal of equivalent size on some future occasion, but no money changes hands either when the original gift is made or later. A similar obligation exists between distant kinsmen, but in this case each pig has also to be paid for at its full market price. The transaction is in line with earlier practice, except that dogs' teeth then served as payment. The members of the purchaser's group help him out nowadays with a few shillings, just as formerly they would have given him a string or two of teeth.

Many persons thus find themselves owing pigs for which they will not be paid, pigs for which they will be paid, and several small sums of money; and some of them are also owed pigs for which they will not have to pay, pigs for which they will have to pay, as well as again, various sums of money. Gwe'tam, to take an example, produced for my inspection a notebook recording that he is indebted to two men for pigs worth £1 10s. each for which he will receive nothing, to one man for a pig worth £2 for which he will be paid, to two men for 6s. each, and to three men for 5s. each. These items are in part balanced by credit entries of a pig worth £1 10s. for which he will not have to pay, a second worth £1 10s. for which he will have to pay, and one amount of 10s. and two of 3s.[1]

The feasts at which I have been present, both during and since

---

[1] Because of war-time losses no pig has ever been killed during my stays in the village. I cannot say for certain therefore whether any attempt is made to earn a profit by presenting an animal to a distant kinsman rather than to a near one; but I am inclined to believe not.

the war, were of necessity only a shadow of the real thing; but even for such tiny celebrations those responsible went to the trouble of reckoning up how much they could hope to provide. I reproduce here a fragment of a conversation between Nga'gili' and his father-in-law Gilingu' reconstructed from notes which I made at the time, in 1945.

'Over there in the corner you can see that I have saved up more than a drum of Army rice and a dozen tins of meat,' Gilingu' began. 'Then we have a little taro from the garden at Mala'guku'. There's not much, mind you, but it will fill several cooking pots.'

'You can count on me for some rice and ten tins of meat,' Nga'gili' told him, 'but I haven't any taro, not a bit.'

'What are Kaneng's gardens like?' Gilingu' went on. 'I know he's got some along the Buim River. Then there are those on the Matangyang—but I don't think they're ready. I gave him a pig just before the Japanese landing, and he ought to help me now. See what you can find out.'

'Don't think of Kaneng,' was the reply. 'He has rice set aside and I think taro. But remember Ida' will be giving a feast soon. It's he that Kaneng is thinking of at present. He can't assist you both at once.'

'Yes, that's true,' Gilingu' sighed. 'We'll have to forget him, I suppose. But what about Nga'sele'? He'll help. Speak of my plan to him one evening so that he's aware of it early and can save up some of his Army rations.'

'There's Buaki, too,' Nga'gili' reminded him. 'You gave him a pig.'

'No, that's no good; I've thought of him,' came the answer. 'The children in that house are like the sandflies on the beach when there's no wind. Buaki hasn't enough to feed them, and if that's so I can't expect anything.'

The discussion continued for an hour or more, during which consideration was given to the resources of between thirty and forty persons. Several were eliminated at once, like Kaneng and Buaki, because of liabilities to more immediate kinsmen or to their families, but a number were noted down for further investigation. Nga'gili' was instructed to prepare the debtors by making casual references to the projected celebration in their hearing, but I was informed that no demand for a settlement could be countenanced. An oblique reminder, yes, that was permitted, but anything more would be unthinkable. 'I've told you before, and I now say it again,' Nga'gili' scolded me;

'no Busama asks for food.' Gilingu' interrupted at this stage, however, with a recollection from his youth, when the last of the headmen still flourished. These men, he said, were much given to issuing
orders to their followers, calling for particular pigs. But they had
the excuse of heavy responsibilities and having to provide feasts of
gigantic proportions. Even in those days lesser individuals would
not have had the effrontery to copy them and request that all debts
owing be paid on a certain date.

No effort of imagination is required to appreciate the complicated
calculations which must have preceded a big feast in the past. The
natives were without notebooks then, and memory alone had to
suffice. Days and days must have been spent in spying out the land,
finding out exactly how many pigs each household possessed and
how big the gardens were. But even this was insufficient: it was also
necessary to have information about which villagers had feasts of
their own in mind and who were aiming to give them contributions—there was no point in counting on persons who had prior
claims on their generosity. I am inclined to agree with a remark
which Nga'gili' made on another occasion when we were discussing
the Pacific war. Planning a military campaign and making certain
that the infantry, the artillery, the air force, and the supply and
medical units were all in their right places at the proper time, he
said, must be as difficult as getting ready for a feast.

We have seen already that the natives' anxiety about their reputation is usually sufficient to make them pay their debts without extra
pressure. A man who is prepared to take advantage of others is
despised, and sooner or later further assistance is withheld from
him. He sinks to the bottom of the social ladder, and, though his
gardens may be adequate for the support of his family, he is considered to be of no account. The one or two individuals of this type
today usually receive courtesy to their faces but are spoken of behind
their backs with contempt. They are the rubbish men, the dirt of
the village sullying its good name.

Arranging a Feast

Preparations begin a couple of days beforehand. If it is to be a
small affair, with no major contributions from outsiders, only the

immediate kinsmen of the host are in the beginning involved. But for the great occasions each prominent householder who is sending gifts forms the focal point of a separate working group. The men and the women both take part, at first carrying out their own tasks but later toiling side by side. The sago is washed, the taro brought from the gardens, and numbers of coconuts collected, some green for drinking, others ripe for grating. Finally, when all else is ready, great stacks of firewood are built up.

On the day itself the men's initial job is to catch and kill the pigs. The carcases are then singed over a fire and cut into joints small enough to go into the clay cooking pots. Meantime, the women peel and slice the taro. A series of long fireplaces is next built, each sufficient for a row of from six to a dozen pots (Plate 8). Fresh and salt water are brought, and the cooking proceeds, pork, taro, and sago each going into separate vessels. Some persons remain close at hand to tend the fires, but the rest set to work breaking the ripe coconuts, grating the meat, and straining out the cream into wooden bowls. A variety of dishes is prepared, including plain steamed taro, taro mashed with coconut cream, sago gruel, and sago dumplings tossed in shredded coconut.

At length, when the host is sure that everyone is ready, usually in the middle of the afternoon, he gives the word for the members of his own group to carry the food which he is supplying to the front of his dwelling. Mats and coconut leaves are spread on the ground and the various pots, baskets, and bowls set out in neat rows. The drinking nuts are then heaped in a pile at one side. Each of the principal contributors now adds his gifts separately. The host watches carefully so that he can afterwards make a record of the different amounts. Those who are expecting payment for their pigs receive the money at this point. The shillings are counted out before the assembly with much ceremony.

Some minutes elapse while the people crowd round and admire the display, but the distribution is not long delayed. A share is first marked off to be eaten immediately and carried to a shelter nearby. Next the name of any guest who is to be specially honoured is called out, perhaps a man to whom the host is under a particular obligation or a distinguished visitor from another place. This person receives a a goodly portion, and the baskets and pots are borne off to a convenient verandah by his supporters. The remainder is then divided

127

among the different club groups. Precautions are taken to see that no one receives back anything which he has himself given. This is partly a matter of courtesy, but there is also the rule that a man may not eat the flesh of an animal which he has reared. To do so is thought likely to bring on a severe attack of vomiting.

The guests now fall to on the portion first set aside, stuffing themselves till they can barely move. They sit in parties, some of men, some of women, beneath the trees or under coconut-leaf awnings erected for the purpose, with a set of bowls for each half a dozen persons (Plate 7). The host and hostess rarely have so much as a mouthful, as it is their responsibility to see that nothing is lacking. At a later stage they go round with cigarettes, areca nut, and betel pepper, chatting with each group in turn.

The crowd begins to disperse at about sunset, and before dark the recipient of the special share and the club heads allot their food among their kinsmen and followers. If enough meat has been provided each family receives a small portion, which some of them divide with friends who have not attended. Pork is so highly valued that a gift of a few ounces is welcome.

Occasions of Feasts

Such celebrations do not take place haphazard but are reserved for particular events, such as the erection of a house, the construction of a canoe, or the union of a young couple in marriage. The average villager on these occasions provides from one to four pigs, a ton or two of taro, and a few hundredweights of sago, but persons who are already looked up to as leaders, or who are determined to be so accepted, often give a dozen pigs and proportionately larger quantities of other foods.

For a new house three feasts are essential in addition to the daily meals for the workers, a minor one as soon as the posts are in position, another on the completion of the flooring, and a third, much larger and often delayed, after the structure is ready for occupation. The hardwood trees and palms supplying the building material grow deep in the forest where the wild pigs rub themselves on the trunks, and the view is that pork must be presented to those whose shoulders have been chafed by carrying the heavy loads.

For a small canoe a single celebration suffices; for a large one two are necessary. The first follows on the arrival of the log at the beach where it will be shaped, and the second takes place after the trial run.

Modern weddings are quite simple. The couple shake hands in front of all their kinsfolk, and afterwards pigs and other foods are presented to the bride's relatives by the relatives of the bridegroom. One, or occasionally two, animals come from his father, one or two from his mother's eldest brother, and taro, sago, and perhaps a little fish from his other uncles and his cousins. A general distribution concludes the ceremony, and all save the contributors receive a share.

Matters were arranged differently in the past.[1] To begin with, the girl was taken to her new home with great ceremony by her kinsfolk, who were there entertained by the bridegroom's relatives at a small breakfast. After a few days the young man's kinsmen returned the visit, taking with them as bride-price from five to twenty pigs, taro, sago, and hundreds of dogs' teeth. The husband's father and eldest maternal uncle supplied several animals each, but the remainder were donations from his other uncles and such persons as the head of his club and his headman, who also gave many of the dogs' teeth.

Custom decreed that for the first daughter in the family the bride-price should go to the men who had helped the father to secure his wife, or to their heirs (the aim was 'to even things up'). The father himself received nothing, for he had not put in a subsidy. For the second daughter all the gifts went to the mother's relatives; and for those younger still there was an even distribution to the two sides.

Birth feasts have been abandoned, but it was only the leaders who made much of a show, and even they confined their attention for the most part to the first-born. The maximum number of pigs was about five.

Funeral feasts still take place but are no longer impressive as never more than two or three pigs are slaughtered. It was formerly the practice for the heirs to kill off at least half the dead man's herd and to give presents of dogs' teeth to all who came to pay their respects.

[1] *Vide* 'Sex and Marriage in Busama', *op. cit.*, pp. 234–235.

A girl's coming-of-age is nowadays unmarked, but in the past this, too, was an event. She remained in seclusion until such time as her father had enough supplies to re-introduce her to the village as now old enough to be married. He had to have a minimum of three pigs, and to these her kinsmen always added more.

Club-house Feasts

The host who caters for his guests more handsomely than convention demands is rewarded with enhanced prestige. Before he can be accepted as a community leader, however, he has to organise the renewal of a club house and shoulder the responsibility of furnishing the biggest share of the food for the associated feasts. He may if he has sufficient support begin a unit of his own, but the more usual procedure is to take over the one to which he already belongs.

Club houses are more solidly built than the majority of dwellings and not only take longer to build but require a greater number of labourers. It follows that supplies for the feasts have to be correspondingly increased: the sponsor, in other words, must be a man of substance.

The posts are donated by the different club groups in which the head has kinsmen, and a series of feasts is held to reward each in turn. When Busilim erected a club house in 1938 he had to supply seven pigs, five tons of taro, and rice, bread, and tinned meat for which he paid £4 in a trade store. His followers helped out with four more pigs, five more tons of taro, and European food costing £3.

The clubs of olden days were still more elaborate structures, with posts cut into atlantides, nude male figures with the chin sunk into the chest, often to the navel, to indicate the weight of the structure above, and plank walls adorned with carvings of men, crocodiles, fish, and birds, all painted with lime, charcoal, red and yellow ochre, and blue and green vegetable dyes (Plates 16a, 16b). The sculptors were honoured with special feasts held during the night on the theory that their handiwork appeared to greater advantage by torchlight. An elderly informant gave me an account of the erection of a club house during his early manhood when fifty pigs were given to a single artist.

Leadership and Ambition

The problem of why anyone should agree to become a club head still remains for investigation. In point of fact only a small minority wish to hold office, and the rest accept it either from a sense of duty or as a result of persuasion. This reluctance is to be accounted for in part by the nature of the reward. The club leader has high social status but little else besides. Thus he may be in a position to dispense pork often, but he himself receives less than other persons; and his clothing, ornaments, and household furniture are no different from those of the humblest villager. Again, he has to work harder than anyone else to keep up his stocks of food. The aspirant for honours cannot rest on his laurels but must go on holding large feasts and piling up credits. It is acknowledged that he has to toil early and late—'His hands are never free from earth, and his forehead continually drips with sweat,' the people explain. 'He isn't like a foreman on a plantation strolling around with a stick and directing others what to do; he carries out the jobs himself.' Only when a leader has looked after the affairs of his followers for years and grown old in their service is he allowed to turn over the bulk of the physical work to younger men.

Sensitivity to gossip and adverse criticism is a further curb on ambition. The natives detest the thought that someone may be sneering at them and are terrified lest they should have cause to feel ashamed of themselves. Asked the reason for a particular line of conduct, they invariably reply that they would have had *maya*, embarrassment, had they given the neighbours a chance to deride their failure to achieve the customary standard or to poke fun at their arrogance. The result is a tendency for everyone to cluster round the average and avoid not only sinking too low but also rising too high.[1]

[1] *Vide* H. I. Hogbin, 'Shame', *Oceania*, Vol. XVII, pp. 273–288.
Maya was given by two natives as the reason for their abandonment of the intention to open village stores. Each claimed that he could obtain sufficient credit from a European and was deterred only by the thought that his fellows might think him presumptuous.
The fear of gossip was well founded, and the one man who at length opened a shop, though never interfered with, is the subject of constant talk. 'The idea of one of us conducting his own business! Yakob is behaving as though he were a white man,' is the general verdict.

STATUS AND LEADERSHIP

Aggressiveness, at least within the Lutu or the Awasa section, is also not a local characteristic, and rivalry is reserved for dealings with the opposite section or with neighbouring villages. The absence of competition in everyday life is indeed remarkable. The children have no competitive games of any kind—no trials of strength against strength or skill against skill—never race one another on land or in the water, and never issue challenges for wrestling contests. What passes for football has been taken up with enthusiasm, but teams are not picked, and play consists of aimless kicking and running about. Further, attempts are never made to put any child—or any adult—on his mettle by urging him to do better than someone else or by making comparisons to his credit or discredit, and school examinations are dispensed with, pupils being rated simply as satisfactory or unsatisfactory. With such a background it is scarcely surprising that the man who kills four pigs for a house-building feast when three would have sufficed should not be concerned with scoring off his fellows. That he can only acquire merit at their expense is to him perhaps scarcely a misfortune, but it is emphatically not a matter for boasting.

Ahipum's assumption of headship is typical of what frequently happens. Some years before he was faced with a decision. The club house to which he belonged was falling into disrepair, and he had to make up his mind whether or not to set about arranging for the construction of a new one. The old head had died, and nobody else appeared to be making a move. 'If I didn't take on the job, it looked as though the club would disappear,' he said. 'Well, the club was not going to disappear: I couldn't have that. We'd had a house called Sawatu since Busama was founded, and it would be unpleasant to let the name be forgotten if I could save it. Besides, our young men deserve a club of their own. Why should they have to scatter and go elsewhere? So in the end I resolved to go ahead. Mind, I didn't want to. I have many children to feed, and growing extra taro and feeding extra pigs meant that I'd have to work very hard.'

I know Ahipum so well that I had no hesitation in accepting this statement. I had convincing evidence of his initial dislike of office when the Lutu group elected him as their luluai after the village was divided. He strenuously resisted nomination for several days and was only prevailed upon to accept when urged by a mass deputation of elders. His popularity was to some extent the result of his industry, but this was not the whole story; he was also held to be wise, loyal, and tolerant; and though his own morals were above reproach, his judgments of others were never unduly harsh. Everyone listened with attention when he spoke, for his common sense was outstanding, and, despite a lack of brilliance in debate, he always had something to contribute.[1]

Salingbo is a further example of conscientiousness. Unlike Ahipum, he has no large family to support, but a wife who was blinded soon after her marriage is an even greater handicap. An early escapade with the wife of a distant kinsman, though not forgotten, has long since been forgiven, and he is now revered as one of the foremost personalities of the village. When the old head died there was no thought of his failing to step into the breach, but I believe he spoke the truth when he said that he would have preferred to play a less exacting rôle.

A club group without an obvious successor to a dead leader is sometimes forced to bring pressure to bear on one of their number. A series of informal discussions takes place, and the best man is selected. Nga'gili' was explicit on the qualities which are demanded. Generosity, he said, is, of course, the first essential, and only persons who make a practice of inviting callers to meals, of contributing lavishly to the feasts of their kinsmen, and of sending delicacies to the sick can be considered. Good temper is also necessary, as well as pleasant manners. It is no use giving authority to men who fly into rages easily or whose moods are unpredictable. What is wanted is amiability—deference for elders, joviality for contemporaries, and firmness tempered with consideration for juniors. At the same time, there are occasions when a display of wrath is called for, as, for example, when a serious offence has been committed; though then the ideal leader should be prepared to forget any reproof which he has administered and later on treat the wrongdoer as though nothing untoward had occurred. Loyalty is another requirement, but this, too, is subject to qualifications. Much trouble has been caused by men who always support the members of their immediate family irrespective of the rights and wrongs of their conduct. When a brother has been publicly rebuked at a village meeting it is proper to point out the extenuating circumstances but only after an admission that the complainant may have a legitimate cause for annoyance.

[1] See, however, p. 161, footnote.

133

STATUS AND LEADERSHIP

To these qualifications I would add courage, self-assurance, organising ability, tact in personal relations, a fair degree of eloquence in public speaking, and perhaps a disinclination to commit breaches of the moral code. Salingbo has a stain on his record, but this adultery took place many years ago and may be dismissed as youthful folly. Technical skill is probably a help, and it may be no accident that over half the present club heads are specialists of some sort, either canoe carvers, house builders, or carpenters.

Tangalaung is numbered among those who had to be thrust into leadership. He agreed only after long argument, and to prevent him from withdrawing at the last moment his fellow clubmen rallied round and put a huge garden into cultivation. 'We wanted to have his fame properly established,' one of them related, 'and to do this we decided that the feasts at the rebuilding of the club should be very big; they were to be not just ordinary feasts, but feasts to be remembered for a very long time. So his fame was spread about.' When the house was renewed a second time, however, eight or nine years later, the celebrations were in no way exceptional. But by then Tangalaung had become resigned to his prominence.

In sharp contrast are Gwaleyam and Busilim, almost the only two of the present heads who are inspired by ambition. They have a thirst for advancement and were determined to push their way to the top. Gwaleyam systematically outgave everyone else and recently organised the reconstruction of the club without consulting the man hitherto acknowledged as leader of the group. This latter, an elder named Mabiyeng, thus finds himself in the background. Never assertive, he has accepted his position with equanimity, not unmixed I fancy with relief. Busilim's moral scruples are more in evidence —he waited for death to claim his predecessor—and there is greater subtlety in his approach, but underneath he is equally unfaltering.

The natives are well aware of the peculiarities of Gwaleyam and Busilim but have no explanation to offer. Both were past forty when I first made their acquaintance, and though they proved excellent informants I could not discover whether their upbringing had been irregular. My only clue is that each was left fatherless in infancy and had been reared by his mother's second husband, a situation which may have led to frustrations and consequently psychological disturbances. This supposition is partly confirmed by the fact that two contemporaries who were also orphaned at an early age are equally

unusual, though their aberration expresses itself in criminal tenden-
cies. Several of the more ambitious youths, too, as well as a couple
of ne'er-do-wells, are also the sons of widows who have remarried.
It should not be concluded, however, that children who lose one
of their parents inevitably turn out to be oddities: on the contrary,
many are indistinguishable from anyone else.

Elevation to Headmanship

In olden days a club head who was prepared to advance to still
greater heights undertook the sponsoring of the feasts which formed
an essential part of the cycle of *sam* ceremonies carried out during
the initiation of the youths to the male cult (see below pp. 213–219).
To do this he had to provide over one hundred pigs himself, as
well as the thousands of dogs' teeth paid for those supplied by his
various guests. Only two or three men at any time were rich enough
to launch on such an enterprise, and these had to spend years building up their capital.

The old rites were abandoned when the people accepted Christianity, and the last initiation took place round about 1906. Since
that time no occasion for a really mighty feast has presented itself,
and the institution of headmanship has in consequence disappeared.
'The headmen had their origin in initiation,' the natives relate.
'There is now no initiation, so there cannot be any headmen,'[1]

The first task was the laying of a taboo on minor feasts. The pro-
spective headman consulted the leaders of the villages round about,
and all who agreed to co-operate were invited to send two official
representatives for the opening ceremony, which involved the erection of the model of a shark. The men later returned home and set

[1] Pacific missionaries have almost always taken a stand against feasting, even
when religion was not involved, on the score of waste and interruption of routine.
A statement by the Reverend Father Ross in 1937 is characteristic (quoted by
A. L. Gitlow, *Economics of the Mt. Hagen Tribes*, New York, 1947, p. 51). 'After
the big triumph . . . tribesmen went strutting about the area, decorated in
all their finery. They were living on their glory. We could scarcely get food
for the station. I asked one young chief how long all this humbug was going to
last. He replied that it would be a month before the people felt normal again.
Meanwhile they made a nuisance of themselves around the station, hampering
our work, carrying on horseplay, singing through the night.'

up similar carvings in their settlements. From now on till the main figure was destroyed, on the day of the final feast, the people were expected to imitate its rigidity and refrain from stooping to kill pigs, distribute taro, or pick up ripe coconuts—everything had to be left for the forthcoming festivities. Disobedience was followed by illness induced by the sorcery of the irate headman. Quarrelling and fighting were also prohibited, and it is said that anyone found guilty of murder, adultery, or any other major offence was likely to be killed by his own kinsfolk.

The inhabitants of every village which had agreed to take part now began planting large gardens and fattening their pigs.

Initiation involved a long period of seclusion for the youths, and it was not until their isolation was drawing to a close that the biggest feasts took place. The only two men left who can remember in detail what occurred state that over five hundred carcases were sometimes displayed on the long platform erected for the purpose, with taro close by in tall cylindrical containers made from poles and bark cloth. Some hours were occupied by the crowds admiring the food, and the host then handed over the dogs' teeth in payment to all the headmen who had brought donations. The distribution followed, and, so my informants stated, everyone ate himself into a coma.

It was also incumbent on the headmen to arrange dances, which again demanded a large feast. They sent out invitations from time to time to the residents of each of the neighbouring settlements in turn to come along and give a performance. The host community took no part, except to form an audience, but kept the guests supplied with refreshments and at the end sent them home with the usual gifts of pork, taro, sago, and coconuts. By this means, it is said, 'they paid for being amused.' After an interval the guests reciprocated and themselves acted as hosts.

Some of the dances were worked out locally, others purchased from distant places, notably the settlements on the far side of the Gulf. The villagers here had often obtained them from somewhere else, and it is claimed that one came by devious routes from Talasea, on the north coast of New Britian, and another over a distance of hundreds of miles from Madang. Buyers were sometimes content to acquire the performing rights only, which left the sellers free to continue peddling their wares; but the copyright was often disposed of for a higher fee, and any further sale was then a matter for the purchasers to determine. Payments were made in pigs' and dogs' teeth, the bulk of which were furnished by a headman.

None of the dances was religious in origin or content, but the Mission authorities looked upon them with disfavour, in my opinion without adequate reason, on the grounds that they served as an encouragement to sexual immorality. In the end the people decided to give them up, though a revival took place during the last years of the Pacific war, and I thus had the good fortune to witness a performance by the residents of Buakap in Busama and another by the residents of Busama in Buakap. Food was distributed on each occasion, but, for reasons already explained, only a small amount was available.

The Buakap began to congregate on the beach near the outskirts of our village during the latter part of the morning and there proceeded to decorate themselves in readiness, a task which occupied them for a couple of hours. Both men and women smeared themselves with a coating of oil and then applied powdered paint, mainly red and yellow, with touches of brilliant blue. Some covered themselves completely, but the majority preferred intricate designs which emphasised the eyes, nose, and nipples. A few of the men put on the old-fashioned strip of bark cloth, but red cotton loincloths were more popular. The women retained their dresses, to which they have now been accustomed for thirty years, and added on top skirts of dyed sago-leaf fibres. All had a variety of ornaments, including breast plates of dogs' teeth and boars' tusks, necklaces of cowrie shells, coloured bags decorated with dogs' teeth, bracelets of shells, and anklets of dried seed pods to serve as rattles. The men also wore white conical hats, some of them over two feet tall, with flat projections back and front, and many added giant plumes made from the skins of birds of paradise, cockatoo feathers, and phalanger fur.

The dancers entered the village in the mid afternoon. The men formed a single line, each carrying a hand-drum of the typical hourglass shape, and, turning to left and right, they advanced step by step beating out a steady rhythm. The women joined in at the sides with linked arms shuffling rather than walking. Arrived at the dancing area, the men fell into place in four columns with the women in a row at each side facing inwards. The first figure, which was repeated at the end of each of the more complicated ballets, consisted of a sort of jog-trot with knees bent. The party advanced, retreated, stepped now to the right, now to the left, gyrated and turned, all in strict time to the complicated rhythms of a song emphasised by drum beats.

Some ballets called for only a dozen main dancers, others for the whole of the men, but always the women kept up their shuffling, thus forming a sort of background or chorus. Each separate dance was based on some incident—the robbing of a nest by some youths and the return of the mother bird, the spearing of a wallaby, a fight between two cockerels, and so forth. Every step and gesture was highly conventionalised and closely followed the beating of the drums, but it was obvious that the animals and birds which were being imitated had been observed with loving care, and there was no mistaking what was supposed to be happening.

Refreshments were brought at the end of a couple of hours, and at about eight o'clock a full meal of sago, rice, and tinned meat was produced. Except for short pauses of this kind the show continued by torchlight and bonfire till dawn. The spectacle was at its best under the leaping flames, for the tawdriness of some of the decorations was then hidden, and the paint looked even more vivid against the surrounding blackness. Here was a show which could never be parallelled in a European theatre no matter how expert the stage-craft.

The last dance finished as the sun began to show over the horizon. Baskets of taro and other foods were brought out, and the visitors took them up and departed.

The Busama's performance in Buakap was similar, though there were differences of detail. Instead of white dunces' caps, for instance, the headdresses were of shells and feathers, and, in addition, everyone thrust bunches of brightly coloured croton leaves in his belt (Plate 15). The ceremonial entry was also arranged in a new way, with a pair of men and of women alternately (seventy-six pairs took part, thirty-eight of each). They went around the dance area twice and then took up positions in a series of concentric circles, one of women outside and two of men within. These began to revolve, men and women in opposite directions, in a gigantic rainbow maypole (Plate 14).

The basic steps of this dance were the same as those which I had witnessed earlier, but the songs were quite unlike, and the rhythms showed a corresponding variation. The ballets were also different even when inspired by the same incidents.

Our arrival had been timed for three o'clock, and we were given snacks at six, at midnight, and at four. The final distribution took place soon after sunrise, when we received rather more than a ton of taro, three hundred pounds of sago, three crates of biscuits, and three cases of meat. In the course of the night our party, dancers and spectators, had managed to consume over two thousand coconuts, and we set off home with a thousand more. I was told that in former times the procedure would have been much the same but that we could have counted on between fifty and one hundred pigs.

The best informed natives are firmly of the opinion that the headmen did not require pushing forward, as so often happens with the club heads, but were eager to have distinction. The view is well summed up by a statement of the school-teacher Ida'. 'We can't be sure of what took place: true, some of our elders were born while the village still had a headman or two, but no one now living saw their rise—that happened too long ago,' he said. 'Yet surely men who disliked fame wouldn't have worked so hard to make all those gardens and feed all those pigs. No, I don't think it's possible.'

The assumption is supported by another piece of evidence. It is frequently insisted that the headmen were so jealous of their reputation that they went to the trouble of inventing excuses for giving food away. This was amusingly illustrated when on one occasion I was paying a call on a club head at Buakap. The steps of the house were still wet from a recent scrubbing, and I slipped and fell headlong. He immediately sent his son to catch a fowl for me, at the same time apologising that no pig was available, 'to wipe out the disgrace' of his rudeness in causing the tumble. My Busama companions, though full of sympathy till reassured that I was unhurt, were the reverse of impressed at this ostentation. The action would have been reasonable, if unexpected, had the man been a headman, they laughed, but in a mere club leader it was rather silly.

The probability is that the Gwaleyams and Busilims of today had their parallels in the past, psychological rarities though they may have been, and that it was these men rather than the counterparts of Ahipum, Salingbo, and Tangalaung who reached the topmost rungs of the social ladder.[1]

Duties of Club Heads

The club head exercises the same degree of authority now as formerly. His followers, less wealthy than he, are unable to return his gifts with counter gifts of equal value and feel compelled in consequence to defer to his wishes and carry out his orders. The young people fear his displeasure, in addition, lest his influence should result in their marriages being delayed. The rebuke administered to Mingkwa when he had neglected some task is typical. 'So you sat gossiping instead of fetching your uncle's taro from Wakop,' the club head scolded. 'Lad, your eyes are in the back of your head. You don't see, do you, that it's to him and to me that you'll have to come when you're big enough to marry. If you lounge about now, do you think we'll trouble to find you a wife? We'll be the ones sitting over our gossip then.'[2]

Yet the club head's power is by no means without limit, and high-handed methods bring ruin in their train. The leader may work harder than the humbler persons in the group but is still dependent upon their assistance, which they continue to give only so long as he retains their goodwill. The unit of which the tultul Mayeng was the head, to give an example, declined from twenty at the time of my arrival to six a year later, and twelve months later again it had no one at all. He had always been unpopular, but as long as the Administration accepted him as its representative, there were advantages in remaining. With his dismissal from office this motive no longer existed.

Obligations go hand in hand with prerogatives, and the leader has to undertake the duty of organising the enterprises with which the group is concerned. He looks after the repair and renewal of the meeting house, the construction and operation of the larger canoes, and the purchase, maintenance, and use of such expensive equipment as reef-fishing nets and pit saws.

[1] It was impossible to discover whether any of the famous headmen of the past had, like Gwaleyam and Busilim, been orphaned in childhood.

[2] Cf. the almost identical statement quoted in 'Sex and Marriage in Busama', *op. cit.*, p. 238.

The club head is also expected to bring his influence to bear on his followers to prevent them from quarrelling. Conflicts are rare, however, and he seldom has to interfere. I pointed out earlier that the members of the group depend upon one another to such an extent that they cannot afford to give or take offence: each puts up with the rest, that is to say, for his own good. He helps his neighbours to build their new houses, drag their canoe logs from the forest, and make fine showings at their feasts because at a later stage he will have to look to them for the same kind of assistance. But if a clash seems imminent the leader at once steps in and urges the parties to talk the matter over calmly. Adjustment follows as a rule without further discord.

Order in Earlier Times

Responsibility for the well-being of the village as a whole used to rest on the headmen, whose job it was to preserve harmony between the different club groups and arrange for all the most important undertakings. But the wise headman kept in touch with the elders before reaching a decision. He called them together when any urgent matter required attention and announced what must be done in the light of their deliberations.

Primitive Melanesian society, in the words of a District Officer of my acquaintance, was living proof that anarchy can work. In so far as personal retaliation was the recognised method of settling disputes he is right. The injured party, supported by his kinsmen, set off to exact punishment on the wrongdoer, or to insist that he hand over compensation. If the fault was admitted and the proposed penalty reasonably appropriate no more was heard of the matter. The point which must always be borne in mind, however, is that a higher authority, one or other of the headmen, could step in should a brawl develop, either because the accused was innocent or because the accusers were expecting too much. Disinterested persons were sent to the scene with orders to stop the argument, and the assembly of elders then made a thorough examination. The headman responsible for the intervention acted as president or chairman, and it was he who in the end pronounced judgment.

The two most heinous offences were murder and adultery, both of which were held to merit death. The culprit sometimes ran away to another village, but if, unaware of his discovery and impending doom, he remained where he was, the avengers waited for a favourable opportunity and slew him. His relatives, when convinced of his guilt, acquiesced in the killing and made no attempt to shed more blood by way of retaliation.

Murder was taken to include unjustified killings not only by violence but also by sorcery. Magical rites which had death as their object were generally reserved for use against persons living in other places, but informants state that from time to time a sorcerer so far forgot himself as to bewitch some of his fellow villagers. His removal was then held to be desirable, partly to pay him back, partly to prevent further trouble.

The only case remembered is one which occurred in 1905, when the alleged culprit was a man named Sa'gwi'. One cannot now be certain of any of the details, but the constant references to his bad temper and unco-operative disposition suggest that he may already have been unpopular. If so, it is easy to understand why he should have been suspected. Experience in other areas where the native culture is still flourishing has convinced me that the integrity of ordinary citizens who fulfil their obligations with care is seldom doubted. Villagers who are living together in amity attribute their serious misfortunes to strangers: someone from within is blamed only when he has aroused enmity by continued bad behaviour. Such a man is particularly embarrassing to his immediate kin, who tend to look upon his death with relief rather than with anger.

The woman Gimbubawi died suddenly, and as she had not long before quarrelled with Sa'gwi', her brothers feared that he might have been responsible. This was only a suspicion—he had not threatened her—and as yet there was no proof. A specialist was called in to conduct a magical inquest, and the upshot was that their view was confirmed. Taking weapons, they surrounded the house where Sa'gwi' was living and caught him as he was emerging through the door early in the morning. He escaped in the scuffle but was later found dead from his wounds in the jungle. 'We were glad to know that he was finished,' an old man who was present told me. 'He'd bought his magic from some hill people and had previously killed his mother and sister to try it out.'

The natives have always had a great respect for the marriage tie, and the elders state that not more than ten adulteries took place during the couple of decades prior to the arrival of the first Europeans. In most instances the lover was slain, though the woman escaped with a beating, but a few saved themselves by flight. On one occasion, after the adulterer had run away, the husband sought to avenge himself by attacking the man's brother. A headman interposed and had the pair disarmed.

The seduction of a single girl was a less serious matter, and her relatives were only permitted to spear the youth in the fleshy part of the arm or thigh. Further, they were expected to indicate that their wrath was now appeased by binding up the wound and presenting him with a bowl of soup made from the shoots of a sago palm, the food always served to invalids. If they were reluctant to forgive, the headman administered a public scolding and reminded them that the village could not function properly unless its members were willing to wipe out all memory of grievances which had been expiated. 'The elders always warned us in my childhood against allowing our anger to flicker on like the light of a firefly.' one of the old men told me. 'Anger should burn itself out quickly and vanish.'

Other wrongs, such as theft and slander, were adjusted by payment of compensation. It was with these cases that the assembly of elders had most often to deal, for offenders sometimes refused to pay on the ground that the claim was out of all proportion to the crime. The headman who had taken charge opened the proceedings by outlining such of the facts as were known to him. Various seniors followed, and younger men were called on if need be for extra information. Once the evidence had been sifted and guilt established, consideration was given to the appropriate course of action. Argument continued till those not directly involved had reached agreement or else were irreconcilable. In the latter event the meeting was adjourned for several days, by which time there was some hope that the passions aroused would have subsided and that the opinions of all might be more objective. The presiding headman gave the verdict. If no property had as yet changed hands the defendant was ordered to hand over a certain quantity of valuables, if he had given too little he was told to present more, and if too much the recipients had to hand some back. It is possible that justice was sometimes tempered by expediency when the parties were of unequal status;

but the Melanesians were not alone in regarding public order as of greater consequence than individual right.

Disputes arising out of marriage payments, land claims, and the depredations of village pigs were settled in the same sort of way. The chairman of the meeting called the witnesses as usual and later gave a summary of the debate.

' Pigs caused most of the conflicts, for fences were always falling into disrepair. The rule was—and still is—that the gardener whose cultivation had been damaged must inform the owner of the animal and ask him for assistance to renew the timber and lashings. If the pig did further damage the gardener could now kill it, though he had to hand the carcase over to the owner as soon as possible. The latter might if he wished give back a portion of the meat as compensation for any vegetables which had been eaten. The difficulty was that gardeners were often so angry that they killed the pig on first discovering it and sometimes ate the whole animal without telling anyone. At times, too, the owner of the beast which had made itself a nuisance failed to go along when the fence was being repaired.

The villagers accepted the verdicts of the headman for a variety of reasons. In the first place, he stood in the relationship of creditor to all and was on that account entitled to deference. Then, in addition, his office carried great prestige. It is clear, too, that he represented public opinion: he was the mouthpiece of the elders, and his judgments were as much theirs as his own. Finally, there was always the fear that those who incurred his displeasure might be bewitched. Most headmen were thought to be acquainted with the black arts, and if this was not so they had wealth enough to employ someone who was. The rites were generally reserved for use against outsiders, as has been stated, but a fellow villager who failed to conform ran a grave risk. Some informants were of the opinion that the headmen actually owed it to their people to rid them of such an encumbrance. 'Sorcery kept the ancestors honest,' one man explained. 'It was like prison today. Many persons obey the law now because they may be sent to gaol. In earlier times the ancestors followed custom because they were afraid a headman might use black magic against them. If they went on ignoring custom, it was only proper that they should have been killed.'

Apart from rare lapses, when an erring kinsman received support to which he was not entitled, most headmen appear to have used their powers with fairness and discretion. One or two, however, are said to have become filled with their own importance 'and behaved as though they were masters of their people. Yomsa', for example, committed adultery a number of times, was always demanding pigs, and carried out sorcery against all who opposed him. A conspiracy was ultimately formed against leaders of this sort, and they were removed. The story goes that the family of Yomsa' enticed him to a lonely part of the beach and there stabbed him in the throat. With such close kinsmen involved, reprisals were out of the question, and the man who had actually handled the knife lived in honour for many years. Matap, a headman from Lae, was put out of the way in similar fashion, though this time the whole village took part.

Warfare

Activities which concerned everyone in the community included dances, initiations, trading expeditions, and warfare. The headmen invited the elders to say what they thought of the proposals and the steps which should be taken to implement them, but the wishes of the leaders, especially if any feasting was involved, carried the greatest weight. If they were anxious for a move to be made the likelihood of anyone opposing them was remote. At the same time, the details of initiation rites, of voyages, and of campaigns had to be left to the care of an expert, a man with special knowledge handed down from earlier generations. Where several were available, the assembly picked out the right one for the particular job in hand.

Dances, initiation, and trading are dealt with elsewhere, but this is the most appropriate place for a short discussion of warfare. As each community was independent, friction tended to arise when a dispute occurred with someone from outside. Raids were especially likely if the guilty party belonged to Kila or Buasi', for the inhabitants of both were looked upon by the Busama as hereditary enemies. But if he came from Lutu, Asini', or Labu, villages which were normally friendly, the headmen often tried to pacify those who had been injured and induce them to forget the incident. Efforts to secure redress, it was argued, might arouse general animosity and prejudice future alliances.

Why the Kila and Buasi' should have been treated as foes is not clear, though differences of language may have had some influence. The Kila people, probably migrants from the south, where the same dialect is spoken, almost certainly settled in their present home before the Busama; and the Buasi', whose tongue is unique, came in either slightly before or at the same period. The friendliness for the others is easily explained. Busama and Asini' are both offshoots from Lutu; and although the Labu have a different language, the Busama constantly gave them refuge when the Laiwamba of the Markham valley were on the warpath.

Sorcery, or rather the suspicion of it, seems to have been the major cause of war. The natives' view was that death was brought about by black magic—men should go on living, it was claimed, till they became senile, and if anyone perished in his prime this was proof in itself that he must have been bewitched. There was seldom any reason for supposing that a fellow villager was responsible, and in most instances the survivors concluded that someone from another place was to blame. If the dead man was at all prominent they at once set about the task of identifying this 'killer'. Evidence which would have satisfied a European court of enquiry was seldom, if ever, forthcoming—often sorcery had never been performed at all, and where rites were carried out the utmost secrecy was observed. But the people overcame the difficulty by an appeal to the supernatural. A specialist was invited to secure the information by an appeal to the spirits, and after a good deal of mumbo-jumbo the name of a man known to have a grudge against the victim was announced as the culprit (see below pp. 222–226).

Other offences held to justify an attack were adultery, seduction, and passing remarks which could be interpreted as a reflection on the honour of the village or any of its headmen.

Most of the able-bodied men took part in the foray, and after a short period of preparation, when they were subjected to various taboos and strengthened by the performance of several rites, they all set forth. Each took four or five spears made from palmwood, a light club, and a wooden shield. The women sometimes accompanied the expedition with a few extra spears, but this was not usual.

The village was if possible taken by surprise round about dawn and the chief offender and his family despatched as they came out in the morning. It often happened, however, that some of the attackers sent warnings to friends urging them to avoid all danger by making an extended visit elsewhere. These men spread the news to their neighbours, thus giving them a chance to take defence measures. Allies were called in, ditches dug, palisades erected, and sentries posted in watch towers.

The bodies of the slain were carried back in triumph and treated with great indignity, though cannibalism was indulged in only during the wars with Kila and Buasi'. The underlying notion seems to have been not so much a desire to acquire the dead man's strength as a determination to humiliate him to the greatest possible degree. Homicides were given special honours and permitted to wear the beaks of hornbills in their headdress as a mark of distinction, one for each kill.[1]

A successful campaign often led to retaliation. A feud then developed, and raid was succeeded by counter raid. At such times the people took the precaution of going about fully armed and in large parties, and each village repaired its fortifications. A special form of sorcery was carried out, too, this time in public, to bring about the annihilation of the opponents (see below pp. 223–224). Peace was finally restored either by one side defeating the other utterly, burning the dwellings, and dispersing such as survived to other settlements; or by the headmen coming together and agreeing to collaborate in a joint initiation ceremony, a decision which involved the outlawing of violence for a period of many months.

The last disturbance, at the turn of the century, occurred as a result of the insulting remark of a man from Buasi'. The Busama were holding a feast and had invited guests from Buasi' and other places, including Labu and Wakop, a bush settlement some miles inland. During the late afternoon, when everyone was enjoying the sea breeze on the beach, smoke was observed coming from a distant headland in Labu territory. 'That's the spot where our ancestors fought and wiped out the inhabitants,' a Buasi' elder said in an aside to a companion. A Labu who understood the language overheard, however, and later told his fellows. Most indignant, they made an excuse for returning the next day in order to lay an ambush for the Buasi' visitors, several of whom they killed.

[1] If a warrior came to the rescue of another, thereby saving his life, the two were afterwards bond friends and could refuse one another nothing. The expression used was *nengga'*, which is also the kinship term for the wife's sister's husband.

The Buasi' who had remained at home now accused the Busama of complicity, saying that the incident had been deliberately planned. The Wakop, too, were enraged, for a kinsman of theirs was amongst the slain. The two villages therefore joined forces and shortly afterwards murdered three Busama who had gone to Wakop to trade. A combined attack by Busama and Labu followed, and this time three Wakop were butchered. The bodies were disembowelled before being carried away and the intestines draped over the garden fence. The countryside was rent asunder by the resulting vendetta for the next couple of years. Certain inland villages supported Wakop and Buasi', and Lutu and Asini' came forward to assist Busama and Labu. In the end the Buasi' split into small groups and built themselves shelters deep in the forest. They returned to their old site only when the coast peoples embraced Christianity and renounced fighting.

The final struggle with Kila had taken place a couple of decades earlier. A marriage was arranged between a Busama youth and a girl from Lutu, but a man from Kila persuaded her to elope with him. The Busama determined to kill them both, but in the skirmish the husband escaped. A chance of retaliation presented itself to the Kila a few weeks later when a Busama fleet set out on a voyage to the south. The party had taken shelter for the night in one of the intermediate villages and was able to beat off the attack, but in the morning they found all their craft smashed. An expedition against Kila was now planned, but this was foiled and a Busama speared.

So far the Busama had come off badly, and they now decided to enlist help from Lutu and Labu. A full-scale expedition was arranged and the Kila settlement burnt to the ground. Half a dozen persons were killed, including two women, and a good haul of native valuables secured.

Several of those who fled were given shelter in Asini', which is only two miles away. This village has close ties with Busama, but for reasons which are now forgotten the sympathy on this occasion was for Kila. The Busama made an early morning attack in an endeavour to exterminate the refugees but were met with fierce opposition and driven off without inflicting any casualties.

From this point onwards the original quarrel seems to have lapsed, and the Busama's wrath was turned against the Awasa, who at that time were still living in their own settlement. Trouble arose over a gloating reference by an Awasa headman to the success of the Asini'.

An attack was decided upon, though with some reluctance, for several Busama had Awasa relatives and not only refused to kill them but tried to persuade their fellows to be merciful. The way out of the impasse finally decided on was to send several women ahead to sit on the steps of the houses of those who were to be saved. This action required great fortitude, for the Awasa, taken by surprise in the morning gloom, could not easily distinguish friend from foe. Not long afterwards the invitation was sent bidding the survivors abandon their hill site and link up with the Busama.

Chapter Eight

NATIVE ADMINISTRATIVE OFFICIALS

'When that the general is not like the hive
To whom the foragers shall all repair,
What honey is expected?'
Troilus and Cressida, Act I, Scene 3.

ONE of the chronic colonial problems is shortage of European staff, and everywhere some form of Government has had to be devised in which the natives play a part. To the Germans who first brought the coast of New Guinea under control this presented no apparent difficulty. Chieftainship was at that period taken for granted—it was presumed that there was invariably someone who was respected on account of his noble birth with dominion, if not over a wide area, at least over a village; and the obvious procedure was to take advantage of his hereditary power. The possible existence of a system of political organisation such as the Busama possessed does not seem to have crossed anyone's mind, much less the notion that this might be typical of Melanesia. The plan adopted was to confer upon the leading headman an official title, 'luluai', the word meaning 'village leader' in Rabaul dialect, and hold him responsible for the settlement of minor disputes and the discipline of petty transgressors. Customary penalties were regarded as sufficient, and the Government reserved for District Officers the right of sentencing offenders to imprisonment.

The first luluais were usually of advanced years and thus ignorant of pidgin English. A younger official, the 'tultul' (another Rabaul word), was therefore chosen to act as interpreter and spokesman. This man had always served a term in European employment and knew a little of the white man's ways. The mark of office was a navy-blue peaked cap with a broad red band for a luluai and two narrow red bands for a tultul.

The system probably worked reasonably well so long as the luluai had risen to his position of supremacy by traditional means. If the people already accepted him as a headman any further honour coming from outside was irrelevant: his directions were no more assiduously followed on account of it, nor were his rebukes listened to with greater attention.

By 1920, however, the last of the headmen had died, and the rungs of the ladder of social advancement had rotted away. Initiation and dance feasts were only a memory, and the practice of sorcery was now an offence. Yet the new Australian Administration tried to perpetuate the German form of control. Reports reveal the same misapprehensions in the senior branches of the service about native authorities and complete ignorance of any changes of custom. Documents submitted to the Permanent Mandates Commission, for example, refer to the development of self-government by 'the encouragement of the native chiefs'. A new title was even created, that of paramount luluai. Men on whom it was conferred had the task of supervising the ordinary luluais in a dozen or more neighbouring settlements, where the languages were often different. They wore a cap with a white cover and carried a silver-topped staff. The duties of the tultul were also somewhat modified, for the spread of pidgin English eliminated the need for an interpreter, and he became a sort of luluai's assistant.

An Instruction stated that the villagers were to be allowed to nominate their local officers, but the usual procedure was for the District Officer to pick out the men who impressed him most. Some proved to be conscientious and eager to do their best, but the majority were either nonentities or else arrant rogues seeking personal aggrandisement.

Busama at the time of my arrival had a paramount luluai, the man Bumbu referred to in the first chapter (Plate 4). The story of his doings illustrates what can happen when a knave is in control. I shall tell it here, for although he represents a somewhat extreme case, parallel examples have occurred in other areas. By manipulating Europeans to his advantage he set up a despotism which in earlier days could not have existed. In this he was assisted by the tuĩtul, his son Mayeng, who had succeeded the 'pro-Japanese' Isom.

Bumbu was dismissed from office while I was still new to the village. His successor, Gwaleyam, though not as dominating a personality, also proved to be unsatisfactory. An account of his behaviour will reveal further faults in the system.

First Impressions

Bumbu was already a prominent New Guinea character before I made his acquaintance. In the early years of the Wau goldfields he had endeared himself to many of the mining community by supplying porters. Air transport was not developed for some time, and at first everything had to be laboriously carried inland over a high mountain range. He received handsome payment for each man produced, and his earnings ran into several hundred pounds. Then during the first part of the war he was supposed to have resisted the enemy, an achievement which was rewarded by a Loyal Service Medal. The tale as related in the Australian Army publication *Jungle Green*—a collection of sketches by the troops—tells how he was marched to Salamaua and ordered to proclaim his detestation of the former Administration. This he steadfastly refused to do, and the Japanese military police accordingly tortured him and threw him into prison, where he remained till an air raid enabled him to escape.

During the first week of my stay Bumbu selected Mayeng, Gwaleyam, and Ho'giling as my assistants. All three were related to him and appeared to be intelligent; at the same time, I was not satisfied, for anthropological work requires that the observer make his own friends and choose informants for himself. For a month, however, no one else would have anything to do with me, and repeated invitations to visit the house resulted in not a single guest. Men to whom I spoke answered my questions but showed no desire to volunteer information or linger in my company.

At this stage Mayeng presented the District Officer, who had been placed in charge only a few weeks before, with the sum of £37 'as a gift from the Busama to restore their good name with the Government.' The officer did not accept the money but left it in the village for the time being in Mayeng's custody. I assumed that the action might be an expression of shame at having aided the Japanese and concluded that feelings of guilt were responsible for the treatment which I was receiving.

Soon afterwards, in my fifth week, an accident occurred which was to prove of value. The youth Gi'lahi was bitten by a snake, and his kinsman Nga'gili', whom I did not as yet know, came to me for assistance. Whether the reptile was poisonous is perhaps doubtful, but the victim recovered, and I was given the credit. Nga'gili' called one evening to express his gratitude but begged me not to single him out for any familiarity afterwards 'lest Bumbu should be angry'; moreover, he cautioned me to keep his visit secret.

This sounded mysterious, but my suspicions had already been aroused, and from now on I kept a close watch on Bumbu's activities. The first point to strike me as odd was the retinue of six elaborately dressed girls in his house who did no work. Not one of them had lent a hand with the Army thatch making—neither, indeed, had Bumbu and Mayeng—and they now sat about the village all day depending on women with families to bring them firewood and water. A pack of dogs was also maintained and fed twice daily with taro when many persons were hungry. Every morning, too, half a dozen girls were detailed to collect fresh fruit, all of which found its way to Bumbu or Mayeng, who sold it to the picnic parties of troops from Lae. The two had a monopoly of the trade; they punished a young man who attempted to sell pawpaws on his own behalf. Again, an official instruction that no house was to be rebuilt till the area under cultivation had been considerably extended was being ignored. Bumbu had ordered that his dwelling, the best in the village, be pulled down and re-erected on a new site, and far from sending the people out to clear new ground, he kept them rehearsing for a dance every afternoon and half the night. Each day defaulters were called upon to give an account of themselves, and those whose explanations were unsatisfactory were publicly reprimanded. Finally, Bumbu, Mayeng, and Ho'giling seemed to be claiming far more of the Army rations than was their due.

Knowing how Melanesians detest a lazy women, I made enquiries about the retinue first. The two informants Mayeng and Ho'giling said lamely that Bumbu was an old man and had to be constantly nursed, a statement which was manifestly ridiculous, but the third, Gwaleyam, at first hedged and then under pressure suddenly whispered, 'Don't say any more now. Tomorrow come for a long walk, and I'll ask someone to join us who'll tell you all about it.'

This was the turning point, and I at last began to discover the truth. The earliest details came from Ahipum, to whom Gwaleyam introduced me on the walk, but that evening Nga'gili', on the pretext of asking for some aspirin, hurriedly made a request that I should meet him in a deserted hut half a mile along the beach, and in the course of the following week no less than seven more men came separately to my house at the dead of night.

The Real Story

While still a young man Bumbu had been notorious for an ugly temper, and his appointment as luluai in 1926 caused consternation. As expected, his brutality was soon felt by all, men, women, and children, for he went round with a cane belabouring those who incurred his displeasure. One women, the wife of Salingbo (see above p. 133), he struck over the face and permanently blinded—she is a pathetic figure and has to be led everywhere by a small child. Isom, at that time tultul, and other villagers gave accounts of this behaviour to successive District Officers, but nothing was done.

Two seductions followed, first of one of the village girls, who bore a bastard, and second, a few years later, of a niece. The latter was pregnant when the affair became public, but Bumbu, as her guardian, married her off in haste to a crony, who, already somewhat elderly, was prepared to father the child in return for a young wife. Isom reported the first incident and Ahipum, supported by the whole village, whose moral sense was outraged by the incestuous relationship, the second. Bumbu so terrified the women with threats, however, that they denied that he was responsible, and the charges were dismissed.

One may well be astonished that the officer in charge of the district did not make a more thorough examination of the witnesses, especially as the Mission held an investigation each time, found Bumbu guilty, and on the second occasion suspended him for many months from Church membership. But administrative officials are

NATIVE ADMINISTRATIVE OFFICIALS

constantly changed from station to station and so have little chance to acquire an intimate knowledge of the details of village life. They are forced to rely a good deal on the luluais, and there is a tendency not unwarranted, to attribute any charge made against them to malice. Of this Bumbu was well aware, and his usual defence was that the people made a habit of concocting lies about him because their minds had been poisoned against the Australian Government by the Lutheran missionaries, who wished for a return of the Germans. The story was untrue but was acceptable during the years 1930 to 1939, for the Mission was largely staffed by German nationals. It is possible that suspension from the Church may have allowed Bumbu to pose as something of a martyr. A further point in his favour was the marriage of his younger daughter to the sergeant-major of police, who made it his duty to keep the District Officer informed on local gossip.[1] (This man, Tape, whose name will crop up again shortly, retired from the police force in 1938 and settled in Busama; in 1944, however, he re-enlisted and is now sergeant-major at the Wewak Government Station.)

The villagers made one further attempt to secure justice. On this occasion they complained that for refusal to work in his gardens Bumbu had ordered them to stand for hours holding a heavy weight with one finger. His explanation, that the Busama were liars, was accepted as sufficient answer, so they maintain, to a charge brought by nearly one hundred persons.

Hope was now abandoned. The Administration, it was felt, was determined to accept Bumbu's word in the face of the evidence, and the people resigned themselves to the inevitable and made no effort to check his career of oppression. Thus they submitted when told to contribute towards the purchase of a boat which cost £80, and not only allowed him to keep the profits from charters to Europeans but gave him even higher rates when they themselves had occasion to use it. His vindictiveness was hardest to bear. He harboured grudges for years and forced all who obstructed him sooner or later to pay the penalty. Isom and Ahipum, as ringleaders of the opposition, became his special butt, and he once framed a charged of sorcery

---

[1] The senior members of the police are seldom moved about. If the District Officer listens to their stories, as, new to the area, he frequently finds himself compelled to do, they acquire enormous power, which many of them use for their own advantage and enrichment.

155

against them. It is significant that the figure for men absent during the war, when labour was conscripted, was not greatly in excess of the average for the four or five years preceding, though in the neighbouring villages the number was often more than doubled. Life in Busama was so unpleasant that all who were able to do so went away.

Then came the war and the withdrawal of the Administration. Bumbu fled to the jungle not from motives of loyalty but because he feared that the people would seize the chance to make reprisals.

Shortly after the landing at Salamaua a party of Japanese went on a tour announcing that all the natives must assemble there on a given day. As Bumbu did not attend Isom was appointed over his head as the new luluai. The villagers were told that orders for food and labour would be given through him and must be obeyed, and he himself was instructed to send Bumbu in to explain his absence.

Isom soon found Bumbu's hiding place and made several attempts to persuade him to comply. For two or three weeks he refused but eventually made his way to Salamaua in secret with a gift of fresh fruit. The Japanese, however, were determined to use him as an example. They tied him to the trunk of a coconut palm for several hours first and then imprisoned him. Isom asked many times for his release and after about a month was told to bring along some of the senior men to take him away. On arrival they were informed that the same punishment would be meted out to them if orders were ignored.

His removal from office and subsequent disgrace rankled in Bumbu's mind, and, although he attributed blame to most of the villagers, he looked upon Isom as his worst enemy. His next move therefore was to try and bring about the rival's downfall. The daughter married to Tape, ex-policeman, provided the means. According to informants, who included Tape himself, her morals were as loose as her father's. She was carrying on an intrigue with a 'foreign' native temporarily resident in Busama, and Bumbu now suggested that she and her lover should elope to the Australian base at Wau and there lay information. The officer in charge accepted the tissue of falsehoods, which are now on the files, and shortly afterwards a police raid took place. This was a fiasco, as has been mentioned. Three villagers were slain, but Isom made his escape.

By the time our troops captured Salamaua in the following year Bumbu had added circumstantial details to his story. He speedily poured these into the ear of the then District Officer and within a few months received his decoration for distinguished service to the Allied cause. The natives, after long experience of administrative gullibility, were not surprised: this sort of thing had happened so often before.

Re-establishment of the Administration

Debauched with power, Bumbu determined that the village should be utterly humiliated and the people if possible starved.

The first step was to take revenge on the Mission for its action in passing sentence of suspension years before on account of the sexual irregularities. The European missionaries had been evacuated to Australia, and Bumbu now forbade all services, personally thrashing those who came together for private prayer meetings. School lessons, too, he prohibited and burned many of the books.

The order to make thatch for the Army played into his hands. The task occupied three days each week, during which he and his henchmen sat about in idleness or slept, refusing to prepare a single sheet. When the rations arrived, on the other hand, they became most active. At two distributions when, unobserved, I kept an accurate record, I saw them set aside three-sevenths for themselves. The total strength of their household was only thirty, and the remaining villagers were even worse off than I had thought. Rations not needed for personal consumption were sold, and subsequent enquiry established that eighty natives had between them paid over £20 for rice and meat.

The parading of the village, necessary for the allocation of duties on the days when thatch was made, was continued throughout the rest of the week. Bumbu abused the natives for half an hour and then picked out a certain number to gather food and firewood or to perform other work for himself and his satellites. During the tirades he used to state that the Administration was in his control, and when I arrived solemn warnings were given that no one was to approach me or to give any hint of what was taking place.

The gardens had suffered during the bombing raids, and the food shortage became steadily worse after the conscription of manpower and the setting of the weekly thatch quota. But for Bumbu this was not enough—he determined that agriculture should cease. To

157

achieve this end he organised a continuous series of dances, and on the days not taken up with preparing thatch rehearsals began at three o'clock in the afternoon and continued till well into the night. Three hours of daylight which might have been devoted to cultivation were thus lost. Further, for fear of being late, no one dared go far away to where the better lands are located. The penalty for not being on time was sitting for several hours with hands in one of the village latrines.

A pole was erected alongside the dance area, and beneath a flag presented by an Army officer from Lae, Bumbu watched and criticised. He used his stick on dancers who were not doing their best and on spectators who fell asleep. Visitors from other places were invited from time to time, and to entertain them he ordered the few remaining pigs to be killed.

This order for dancing, bad enough in itself considering the circumstances, appeared even worse to the participants, for the Mission had preached for years that such entertainments are of the devil. The view is in my opinion regrettable, but it is accepted as an integral part of the Christian religion.

There remained a further affront to the villagers, the retinue of idle girls, all kinswomen who had been ordered to join the household. A certain amount of evidence suggests that they were used for the entertainment of visiting troops and that Bumbu enriched himself in the process: and I also had it on good authority that he himself had had relations with two of them.

My presence in the village was an embarrassment, for thrashings had to cease and no longer was it possible to sentence offenders to sit with their hands in a latrine. Yet so confident was Bumbu of his power that the parades and the dancing continued, with consequent loss of time for garden work.

Court Proceedings

Once sure of the facts, I visited Salamaua for discussion with the newly appointed District Officer. He came to the conclusion that a public enquiry was called for, but we agreed that witnesses might be afraid to come forward. A day was fixed, however, and I returned to the village to try and convince my informants that at last the time

NATIVE ADMINISTRATIVE OFFICIALS

had arrived when they might secure redress. I was willing to give evidence but explained that I could only tell of what I had seen myself: they, too, would have to play their part. Eight of the nine volunteered to speak, Gwaleyam alone proving a coward, and together we prepared our case.

Word had not leaked out to either Bumbu or Mayeng that their careers might be approaching an end, and the District Officer was greeted with the usual honours. He summoned the people to the centre of the village, and, after a concourse of native police had taken up their position behind the Bench, the Court opened.

The District Officer's first words were an order to the police corporal to search Bumbu's house. The man returned, his eyes popping, ejaculating in pidgin English, 'Master, master, house belong Bumbu he full up all same store.' The dwellings of Mayeng, Ho'giling, and the other henchmen were then searched. When distributed the food proved to be sufficient to feed the village for nearly six weeks.

The information received at the District Office was then outlined, and I was called into the box. After my statement was finished the eight men who had said they would come forward followed one by one. Fortified by what they heard, various others spoke, and the case against Bumbu closed with eighteen Crown witnesses. He and Mayeng were asked for an explanation, but, instead of replying, they began to quarrel. They were promptly stopped, but Bumbu had nothing further to say, though Mayeng continued to protest that he had been an unwilling victim.

The District Officer dismissed them both and took their caps away to be burned. He informed Bumbu that only age had saved him from a long term in gaol.[1]

[1] The statement in the Village Book runs as follows:

'9.xi.1944. Visited village and investigated complaints about malpractice by officials. Thatch production ceased 1.x.1944, and some progress in rehabilitation should have been made.

'(1) Bumbu, paramount luluai, and his son Mayeng, tultul, have deliberately disobeyed my instructions and prevented the people from making new gardens.

'(2) Supplementary rations have been sent to this village, and officials have taken three-sevenths of the supplies for their own use.

'(3) Religious observances and attendance at school have been forbidden by Bumbu.

159

The following morning, when new officials were appointed, Mayeng was called upon to produce the £37 which he had been holding. The District Officer stated that a good reputation could not be bought but must be earned and that he proposed to return the money to the donors. An exact record of what each had given was available, and the distribution raised no difficulties. It was then disclosed that neither Bumbu nor Mayeng had contributed—the 'gift' was in fact a levy, the purpose of which had been to convince the Administration that the villagers were aware of their guilt, thus giving confirmation of the lies which had been spread about them.

Further Troubles

Gwaleyam was chosen for the post of luluai, Ahipum for that of tultul. The latter had at that time a real sense of public responsibility, but Gwaleyam's weakness in refusing to give evidence at the enquiry indicated that he might not be satisfactory. A week or two later I learnt that some of the villagers also had misgivings. On being pressed for their reason for not making a statement earlier, they pointed out that his familiarity with the white man's idiosyncrasies was a potential advantage. He had been employed for many years in a store at Salamaua and had there developed an easy manner which many Europeans were known to appreciate.

The events of the next twelve months proved that the fears were justified. The village was then divided into the two sections, Lutu and Awasa, each with its own officials, Ahipum and Nga'gili' for one part, Gwaleyam and Ma'du for the other. A brief reference is called for here as a further indictment of the luluai system. Gwaleyam was without Bumbu's genius for advancing himself;

'(4) Compulsory dancing has been introduced by Bumbu, and failure to dance was punished.

'(5) Essential repairs to dwellings have been forbidden, but Bumbu has ordered the construction of a new house for himself.

'(6) Rations intended for Busama have been sold by Bumbu to Buang villages.

'For above and other reasons I have suspended Bumbu from office and have dismissed Mayeng. I am recommending the dismissal of Bumbu.

'A./D.O. Morobe.'

at the same time, he was not ideal as a Government representative.[1]

At first everything was satisfactory, and, as though freed from a millstone—the expression anchor-stone was used locally—the people set about their rehabilitation with vigour and enthusiasm. A large area was put under cultivation, and the village was a hive of activity from before sunrise till after dark. Then, after three months of self-effacement, Gwaleyam began to make his presence felt. At this stage he and a kinsman who had been living together determined to separate and put up dwellings for themselves. House construction, as was mentioned, demands communal effort, and all the workers have to be fed. The pigs were destroyed or ran away during the air raids, but most persons managed to make some sort of a showing with Army rations. Gwaleyam, however, expected assistance without giving any form of return, arguing that the erection of the luluai's house should be regarded as work done for the Administration. The order was obeyed, but with much unwillingness and private criticism. This was the beginning, several men complained, and soon all sorts of other services would be demanded.

Another common failing of unscrupulous luluais is contracting alliances which in native eyes are illegal. Running true to type, Gwaleyam before long made advances to one of the young girls. She immediately ran to her uncle, who told the story at a public meeting, but after some argument it was agreed to let the matter drop. The elders decided that the village had already received sufficient notoriety over Bumbu, and they thought that the District Officer would hardly welcome news of still further misconduct.

Two more scandals followed within the space of six months, but, although there was little doubt of Gwaleyam's guilt, no public protest took place. Both women were married, and it was felt that if the husbands, who were at the time absent, were debarred from taking action the rest of the community ought to keep silent. One man would have almost certainly demanded vengeance had not his wife died as a result of a sudden illness within a fortnight of his

[1] Four years later, in 1950, some of the villagers had become critical also of Ahipum, who they said was now overbearing and prone to use influence for the benefit of his kinsmen. The charges were to some extent justified, though no serious offence had been committed. I mention them only as a possible hint of future developments. *Corruptio optimi pessima.*

return. Gwaleyam's spouse could also have brought a case against him, but she is by nature colourless and weak and took no action beyond confiding in friends.

Several charges were made at the District station, nevertheless, but it is characteristic that the plaintiffs should have been mainly inspired by personal grudges. Maye' reported that he had had his ears boxed, for instance, but investigation revealed that some years before he had been proved wrong by Gwaleyam in a dispute over a pig. Ho'nung's complaint was equally frivolous. He objected to being ordered to repair a bridge which had been destroyed as a result of his wife's carelessness but was really annoyed over a disagreement concerning the choice of a husband for one of the girls.

Material gathered today obviously cannot give a definite answer to the question whether Bumbu and Gwaleyam would in earlier times have gratified their ambition along traditional lines, but it seems likely that this is so. If the village were closer still to a European town they might, instead of abusing their powers, have been satisfied to turn their attention to business. Butibam, on the fringe of Lae, is perhaps saved from oppression by having a small group of successful truck owners (the hire of truck and driver cost £8 per day in January 1950). On the other hand, if the Busama had had less contact with the Western world these two luluais could well have founded a new religion (p. 284). Such cults are always developing in outlying areas, and the information available suggests that in several instances, if not all, the leader is a potential headman frustrated in his efforts to give secular expression to his talents.

Unhappy as Busama has been in its luluais, the village has been spared an internal feud between Government and Mission representatives. This affliction is not uncommon, especially in places some distance from European settlement. The Church officers, with several years of training in leadership at the colleges behind them, sometimes become impatient with the ignorance of the luluais, who may not be able to read or write and have often had no experience outside their own district. Struggles for power then take place, with each side marshalling its forces to the best of its ability.

The problem is aggravated by the fact that most of the Mission bodies have separate zones of influence—within each area one only is carrying out the work of conversion. The result is that its representatives, natives as well as whites, tend to have the same sort of

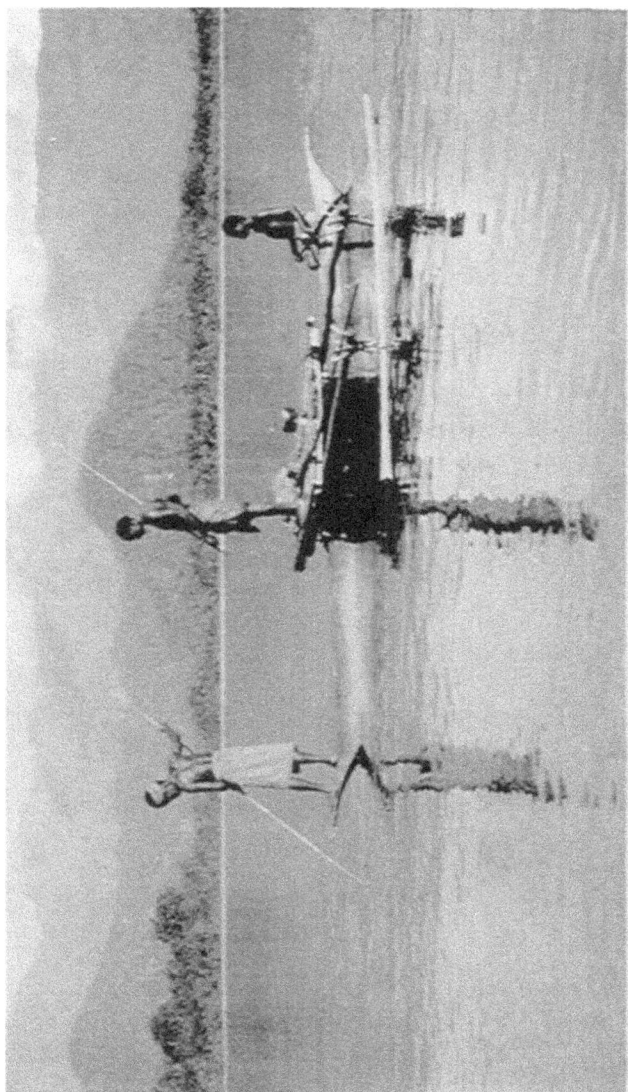

9. Fishing with spear.   The Buang Range in the background

10a. Repairing the seine

10b. Hauling in the seine

authority as the clergy of mediæval Europe, and every difference of opinion between village teacher and luluai is apt ultimately to assume the proportions of a quarrel between Church and State. Details of arguments in the Solomon Islands between Mission leaders and officers of the Government will be found in some of my other publications, but as in that territory most villages have representatives of three or four Missions, the rivalries are of less consequence.[1] If one set of elders, perhaps the converts of the South Seas Evangelical Mission, have a difference with the District Headman, the local equivalent of the paramount luluai, he can usually depend for support upon the remainder—a combination possibly of pagans, Anglicans, and Seventh Day Adventists or possibly of Catholics and Methodists—who fear that if he loses the fight they may have to suffer religious discrimination.

A statement by Voltaire points the situation. 'If there were one religion in England its despotism would be a menace,' he wrote; 'and if there were two they would be at each other's throats. But there are thirty, and the people live together and are at peace.'

[1] E.g. 'Native Councils and Native Courts in the Solomon Islands', *Oceania*, Vol. XIV, pp. 267–269.

Chapter Nine

COUNCILS AND COURTS

'It is always wonderful when something altogether wrong ends right without the help of either religion or the police.'—LUDWIG BEMELMANS, *Life Class.*

THE failure of the luluais is now generally acknowledged,[1] and early in 1947 the Administrator called a series of conferences to advise him on what changes should be made. The heads of Departments directly concerned with native welfare attended, and I was also present as a guest. The majority agreed that the best course was to revive the old assembly of elders and give it the necessary legal sanction to act both as council and court. The natives had become increasingly dependent on outside authority, we argued, and a form of local government was indispensable to restore their self-reliance; moreover, such developments were now a commonplace in other colonies.[2] We urged that the scheme finally adopted, however,

---

[1] J. K. Murray, *The Provisional Administration of the Territory of Papua–New Guinea*, Brisbane, 1949, pp. 60–61.

[2] Cf. Lord Hailey, *African Survey*, Oxford, 1945, Chap. IX; H. I. Hogbin, 'Native Councils and Native Courts in the Solomon Islands', *op. cit.*; and C. S. Belshaw, 'Native Politics in the Solomon Islands', *Pacific Affairs*, June 1947, and *Island Administrations in the South West Pacific*, London, 1950, pp. 118–129.

A scheme was put into operation at Busama during 1947 by the then Assistant District Officer of Morobe. It failed, partly because the legal authority was lacking, partly because the natives received neither advice nor guidance.

164

should in its early stages be carefully watched and guided and, with this end in view, suggested that only a limited number of communities be selected for trials.

The proposal was accepted, and the conference was then asked to frame appropriate legislation. The judiciary and officers of the Crown Law Department at first looked askance at the notion of native magistracies but were eventually won over and gave much helpful criticism. By October 1947 the completed drafts of a Village Councils Ordinance and a Village Courts Ordinance were ready for submission to the Minister for External Territories for promulgation.

Their adoption was foreshadowed in the Australian Parliament early in 1949, but so far the councils alone have been approved (on December 9, 1949). A Local Government branch of the Native Affairs Department was set up immediately, and the three officers appointed to it have begun their preliminary arrangements.[1]

When the plan is put into operation Busama will be one of the first villages to benefit. I shall now consider the later history of the elders' assembly and the adaptations which will have to be made.

Mission Assemblies

Meetings continued to be held while Bumbu was in power but had lost their democratic character. Tyrant that he was, he used them solely as a means of announcing what he wished to be done, and the only persons permitted to open their mouths were followers who could be depended upon to reinforce his arguments. A man who had ventured to express disagreement shortly before my arrival was still in bed a month later recovering from a beating.

The Mission kept up the old tradition, nevertheless, and under its aegis assemblies were from time to time called at Mala'lo, headquarters for the district. Matters relating to Church work were discussed, such as the erection and dedication of places of worship, the opening of new schools, the modification of ancient customs, and the despatch of 'black missionaries' and teachers to other places. All the

---

[1] The funds available even to a settlement the size of Busama will necessarily be small, and the village councils and courts must ultimately become regional bodies with authority over a small district (see K. E. Read, 'Notes on Some Problems of Political Confederation', *South Pacific*, Vols. III, IV).

local congregations attended, each headed by its leaders, who gave most of the addresses.

Use was also made of the judicial functions of the assembly, and infringements of Mission doctrine were brought up for investigation. As the Christian code is at many points identical with the code of law, this meant that some of the charges related to actions which were offences also in the eyes of the Government. Stealing and certain sexual irregularities, to give examples, are forbidden not only by the Commandments but also by the Statutes. The Church has two penalties, public reproof and suspension from membership. Only if the injured party thought these insufficient was the culprit handed over to the civil authorities.

Even Bumbu was not immune from the proceedings. After the seduction of his niece it was decided that imprisonment would be most fitting, but when the District Officer of the day dismissed the case the assembly sentenced him to a long term of suspension.

The people are wholehearted in their adoption of Christianity, and there can be no doubt that being put outside the fellowship of the Church was a severe penalty. Most offenders withdrew from community life and lived alone in the bush till the wrong had been expiated.

Not all religious offences, of course, are crimes: the Government has no interest in bringing to book those who fail to put in an appearance at services or show disrespect for their parents. Correspondingly, certain crimes are not religious offences: the Mission feels no concern about the maintenance of roads or the payment of taxes. Further, really serious breaches of the law, such as murder, though forbidden by the Commandments, were held to be too grave for the assembly to deal with.

Village Assemblies Today

With the Mission example before them, the people lost no time after Bumbu's disgrace in resuscitating the secular meetings, and within a month most of the old features had been restored.

The earliest of the assemblies were held for the purpose of deciding on matters of village policy, such as determining which day should be set aside for public work—cleaning the village, erecting and repairing the latrines, weeding the main roads, and maintaining the bridges. Friday had been fixed in the past, but many claimed that this had unpleasant associations on account of Bumbu. After some debate it was agreed, nevertheless, that no other time was so suitable. The new luluai and tultul were accordingly left to decide what should be done each week and to allocate the tasks.

Other matters dealt with were the selection of a site for a new school, the erection of a house for the native pastor, the entertainment of two parties of visiting Mission elders, and the conduct of returned labourers. A meeting called to remind these young men of their responsibilities was of special interest. A large number who had been absent for two years had just arrived back, and the elders were concerned lest the standards of conduct taught in childhood should have been forgotten. It was the duty of the younger generation, speakers warned, to carry out orders, not to strut about. Food was a major consideration in the village, and there was no white man to make weekly issues of rations. Gardens must accordingly be attended to with diligence and fishing expeditions undertaken at every opportunity—idleness might be very well for indentured labourers, but it meant empty bellies when indulged in at home. Liaisons must also be avoided till the time came for marriage, when wives would be found for all who had behaved themselves. The indolent, on the other hand, could expect no sympathy and would have to remain bachelors. Finally, it must be remembered that in the village one lived with one's own people, and quarrelling and stealing must be at all costs avoided.

From this the step to judging wrongdoing was easy. As with the Mission assembly, the offences dealt with included certain crimes for which legal penalties are provided, such as adultery and theft, together with others which the Government ignores—casual affairs before marriage, laziness, and disregarding the claims of a parent or guardian. At first a few men preferred to go to the District Office with their complaints, but by the end of a year this practice had almost ceased, at least for minor troubles.

The elders took no further action as a rule than administering a severe rebuke, though from time to time they came to the conclusion that this was insufficient punishment and that the case must be heard at Salamaua. The community is so small that a convincing demonstration of public disapproval served to make most culprits feel properly ashamed. They kept out of sight and for a time either visited friends in other villages or remained behind closed doors when not actually at work. If addressed they gave brief answers but were mainly silent.

Failure occurred, however, with the rare offender who proved to be impervious to the opinions of his fellows. The most conspicuous example was a young man named Biyaweng, who in the space of fifteen months was four times found guilty of theft, twice of prostituting his wife, and once of adultery. He avoided church services, certainly, but conducted himself otherwise as though welcome everywhere. Thus at most public functions he was well to the front. 'What's the use of scolding such a person?' Ahipum lamented. 'We've told him so many times already that we think him abominable; there's no point in doing it again. He's thrown shame overboard, and if I reproached him for stealing today he'd probably be found taking something else tomorrow.' Such persons can only be dealt with by imprisonment, and it is on their account that the Administration must give the assembly legal powers.

Many civil disputes were also brought along for settlement. Discussion continued till the elders present had reached agreement about the rival claims, and if the party against whom the judgment was given accepted the ruling, as usually happened, all was well. Yet no means of forcing him to do so was available, and when convinced that the right was on his side he sometimes took the law into his own hands. After an argument had developed between two men over the ownership of some trees, for instance, one of them took his axe and felled the grove. He declared that if he was not to be allowed to gather the fruit nobody else should have it. This was clearly another case requiring punishment with the utmost rigour of the law.

An elder always took charge of the proceedings. The luluai or tultul, at that stage Gwaleyam and Ahipum, acted in this capacity more frequently than anyone else but were emphatic that they had no special right by virtue of their office. All the elders were eligible, they said, and resentment at the choice of a particular person was out of the question. 'The assembly of elders belongs to the village,' Ahipum assured me. 'It's not like the court at Salamaua—that's the Government's affair—and it's not like the meeting at Mala'lo—that's the Mission's business. This is different: it's ours, the people of Busama. We come together now as we did in olden days, and any one of us can have a say about what's happened and what he thinks ought to be done. Building the new school, cleaning the roads, adultery, thieving; that's what we talk about. But there's got to be someone to start the business off, and at times Gwaleyam is chosen, at times I am, and at times another man. Anybody who has some sense will do.'

It is to be noted that only traditional matters were dealt with and that the responsibility for policing new rules of conduct was left to the Government. Thus no one was ever hauled up before the elders for having a dirty dwelling or a dilapidated latrine. In general the luluai or tultul had to report offences of this kind. Other persons once or twice took it upon themselves to complain, it is true, but their inspiration was provided not by a sense of duty but by malice. Although Bonggi's latrine had been on the point of collapse for a month, it was not till a disagreement over an areca palm that La'ku went to the Government station with the story; and Maria refrained from reporting her neighbour Tangapi' for dynamiting fish till he quarrelled with her over one of the children three months later.

Procedure

Persons with a grievance usually talked things over first with an elder known for his balance and common sense. Gwaleyam and Ahipum were often chosen, as has been mentioned, but several others, including the Church leaders and teachers, were also popular. If after hearing the story the elder decided that a meeting was justified, he gave instructions to one of the youths that a conch shell was to be blown at sunset in the centre of the village as an indication that after prayers everyone would be expected to assemble.

The people began to arrive in twos and threes shortly after seven o'clock, the men seating themselves on one side and the women on the other, and half an hour later there was usually a full attendance. The elder then rose to his feet to relate what he knew of the case. His speech lasted five or six minutes, when he gave place to the plaintiff, who elaborated any points requiring special emphasis. The defendant followed with his version of the affair, and the witnesses were then called to make their contribution. Proceedings were always informal, and the chairman refrained from interfering unless a speaker appeared to be growing unduly angry or had become diffuse and was clouding the issue with irrelevant details. He also entreated those who were reluctant to come forward, begging them to state whether they had been correctly reported or felt that they had any additional information which might throw light on the discussion.

Once all the facts available had been set forth, the other elders rose to give their opinions. They sifted the evidence and related what they knew of the past actions of the principal parties concerned in order to give some guidance as to which of them could be accepted as trustworthy. The debate went on for at least half an hour, when it was usually obvious that there was general agreement that the accused was innocent or guilty. The first elder then summed up the case. If the man was held to be blameless a statement was made that the complainant had obviously been mistaken and the matter had better be forgotten. If, on the other hand, the man was guilty attention was directed to the need for deciding on a proper penalty, a matter which occupied the meeting for half an hour longer. They stressed how wrong his conduct had been and told him that he ought to hide his head in shame.

Opinion was occasionally divided, however, with some elders convinced of the innocence of the accused and some of his guilt. If after an hour or so the chairman came to the conclusion that unanimity was unlikely to be achieved he broke up the meeting. 'Let's go to bed,' he suggested. 'Some of us say "yes" and some "no", and if we stay here talking till morning we'll not change. I stand up among you now and tell you to depart. Our talk cannot be straightened, and we must break it.'

In the event of serious trouble, a second meeting was called a week or two later, often with success. The emotions aroused had simmered down, and the incident could be observed in proper perspective. At times, nevertheless, even a third meeting resulted in a deadlock, and an appeal for a decision had to be made to the District Officer.

Minor differences which could not be settled at once were allowed to lapse. One of my friends no doubt spoke the truth when he stated that after an interval nothing seems to be quite so serious. 'A wrong which makes you shake with rage when you first hear about it isn't worth bothering with a month later,' he said, 'and after a year you forget it.'

COUNCILS AND COURTS

Women seldom made complaints directly but acted through the husband or a brother. Female defendants, too, were usually, though not always, represented by a male.

The persons not involved in the cases, including the younger men and the womenfolk, remained in the background during the deliberations. Silence was not expected of them, and the elders' speeches were punctuated by such remarks as, 'True, true'; 'Indeed, he was wrong'; 'Lies, all lies'; and 'It's not the custom, not the custom of the Busama.'

On the occasions when the case for which the meeting was called was capable of settlement within a reasonable time, the opportunity was taken afterwards to bring up minor matters which did not in themselves justify a special gathering.

Busama oratory is somewhat flamboyant, and there is much use of gesture. Speakers paraded up and down, pausing now and then with clenched fists or waving arms to ask a rhetorical question. The plaintiffs made no attempt to restrain themselves, and seldom have I witnessed such demonstrations of passion. Some of the performances were remarkable, the most striking being that of a man who, screaming at the top of his voice, literally danced with rage. My personal servant, a man from the Sepik who in fifteen years of employment by white men had travelled the length and breadth of New Guinea, confessed himself astonished at such lack of control, which he said was in his experience without parallel. 'Whenever there's a village meeting,' he concluded, 'I go to bed with my head aching.'

It is of interest to compare these goings on with the behaviour of the children. In most New Guinea communities efforts are made to prevent small boys and girls from crying, but in Busama, although if hurt they are comforted, no one seems to mind how much they howl. I took the trouble once to put a stop-watch on a little boy who was yelling because his father had slapped his hand for some minor fault, a common occurrence, and found that sixty-five minutes had passed before he ceased, when he went outside and, in an ecstasy of misery, threw himself into a puddle. At this stage I took a photograph of him, much to the amusement of everyone, including his parents, who made no attempt to pick him up. 'He's rather irritable today,' was his father's only comment.

Details of Cases

One of the first offences to be dealt with was that of the youth Laugwi' after his attempt to seduce Homkiwi, the unmarried daughter of Isom.[1]

Busilim was asked to preside and made the opening address. Everyone knew what had happened, he began, but the story had better be told to make certain that none of the facts was forgotten. Isom had been awakened the previous night by a great commotion in the corner of the house where he and Homkiwi slept. She was screaming and seemed to be fighting an intruder. He accordingly ran to her assistance and found that she was clutching someone by the hair. Not waiting to make enquiries, he had plunged into the fray and managed to deliver a few well placed punches before the man made his escape. Homkiwi then explained that she had been roused by a hand lifting her dress and that when she had sat up a voice, which she recognised as that of young Laugwi', had urged her to submit to an embrace. After daybreak Isom had gone to Gwaleyam, who had agreed that a meeting must be held but was himself unwilling to take the lead as Laugwi' was closely related to him. He therefore recommended that another elder be approached.

'We know that this isn't a tale of what someone thinks took place,' Busilim concluded. 'Many of you heard the noise, and I've insisted that Laugwi' should be here so that you could be sure that he was the culprit. If you look at him in the light you'll see the marks of Isom's fists.'

At this point the boy's eldest brother, Gingmamboa, arose. 'Yes, it's true,' he said. 'Laugwi' was caught in the house. But Homkiwi had been accepting his presents—last week he gave her a blanket—and he thought she'd be willing to receive him. If she didn't want to, why, then, did she take the blanket?'

The next speaker was a senior man named Gase'. Was it marriage or seduction that Laugwi' was after? he asked. If the boy wanted Homkiwi for his wife, this was not the way to set about securing her—he should have told his relatives in the hope that they would approach Isom. But he ought to have known that a wedding was

[1] This case, along with several others, is referred to at length in 'Sex and Marriage in Busama', *op. cit.*, p. 130.

impossible. Had not Gingmamboa already taken one of Isom's daughters to wife, and was it to be expected that anyone would allow two of his girls to marry into the same family? No, the intention of Laugwi' must clearly have been dishonourable. There was too much of this bad behaviour in the village, and for his part, said Gase' he would advise Isom to take the matter up with the District Officer and have the boy imprisoned.

Mabiyeng then arose and, in great distress, urged that there be no further talk of gaoling anyone. The village should deal with the case, he urged, and administer suitable punishment. He had had a talk with Laugwi' and was sure that the lad was sorry for what had occurred. The fact that he was now being shamed in public would make him mend his ways and behave better in future. But if this was considered to be insufficient, he could be put outside the Church.

Talk of this kind was all very well coming from Mabiyeng, Nga'gili' interposed; he was the boy's uncle. It was only to be expected that kinsmen would stand side by side. But what of those without blood ties? They would not want to condone evil. He himself agreed with Gase' that imprisonment was the best way to stop such conduct.

Isom, who had in the meantime been holding himself in with difficulty, now stepped into the centre to have his turn. In the beginning his throat was choked with sobs, and as he continued his fury increased. Busama had fallen upon evil days, he lamented, and nowadays girls as young as Homkiwi were not safe. The men were becoming a pack of ruffians who gloried in seduction and rape, and unless action was taken against them all the customs of the past would vanish. But, old as he was, he was determined to give his daughter protection. 'You, Laugwi', are no better than a dog, and I intend to thrash you,' he threatened. 'You came to our house hungry, and after we'd fed you, you treated us like this. Marriage! Let me hear no more of it. If you were the only man left in the place Homkiwi should never go to you. I tell you that you are filth and excrement.' By this time his voice had risen to a squeak, and he stood in front of the boy brandishing a stout digging stick. The threat would probably have been carried out had his brother not led him back to his seat.

Madulu followed, addressing most of his remarks to Mabiyeng. Why had not more care been taken with the boy's upbringing? he asked. Why was it not insisted that he spend his nights in the club house, where his comings and goings could be watched? It was the business of the older men to see that their young kinsmen conducted themselves properly, and lapses were only to be expected when this duty was neglected.

An argument then developed between the two men, and for the next five minutes insults passed back and forth. It appeared that Madulu resented the fact that Mabiyeng had a few days before borrowed his canoe without first asking permission and was moved more by this than by his disapproval of the methods adopted in the education of Laugwi'. Busilim finally interrupted with a restatement of the case. 'What are we to do?' he finished. 'Is Laugwi' to go to prison? He did not seduce the girl, and I am inclined to think that we've now shamed him enough.'

There was a chorus of agreement, but four or five more insisted on having their say. Laugwi' was a disgrace to the village, they reiterated, but, as this was his first offence, perhaps he might be forgiven. The discussion then closed with Busilim dismissing him. He slunk away, and for several days we did not see him. In normal times he would probably have made a contract with a European employer and absented himself for three or four years, but in 1944, when the war was at its height, this was not possible.

Rather more than an hour had so far been occupied, but, as no one was making a move to go home, Hungmpi seized the chance of enlisting help to reprove his orphaned nephew Ngaganda for laziness. In a short speech he told how the young man was never to be found when garden work was in progress—that day he had spent visiting friends in a neighbouring village, the day before he was playing cards, the day before that he had slept, and the day before that again he went skylarking in the forest with some friends. Scolding seemed to have no effect upon him, and on more than one occasion he had rudely turned his back on his uncle. What would become of such a person? Although nearly old enough to marry, he still carried on like a child. Five speakers arose in turn, three of them relatives of Hungmpi. They confirmed what had been said and reminded the offender that there would be an easy way of punishing him. If he failed to assist his uncle, who did he think would find him a wife?

Once this matter was disposed of, the woman Tapongwi arose

and complained that her husband had beaten her a few days before without cause. She had no close kinsmen to take up her case, she said, and it was therefore fitting that the elders should intervene and order the man to keep the peace within the home. Gwaleyam, who had been silent hitherto, called him to the front to give some explanation. He had been hungry, was the reply, and, although the evening was far far spent, supper was not yet cooked. This did not justify ill-treatment, Gwaleyam stated, and a further complaint would necessitate a visit to the District Officer. The only other speaker was Madulu, who, besides talking at length in the early part of the evening, had also supported Hungmpi. I found that this was his usual practice and that no meeting took place without his making a ponderous statement. My servant called him derisively 'the village policeman', a name so apt that it was soon in general use.

The crowd had by this time begun to diminish, and it seemed as though there would be no further business. After five or ten minutes, however, Yakwageng stepped forward and announced that he wished it to be known that he was no longer angry with his two kinsmen Gaposawa and Yapa. His wrath had been kindled against them, he explained, because they had arranged for his nephew's marriage when in his opinion the man was not old enough to undertake the responsibilities involved. But the wedding had now taken place, and no useful purpose would be served by harbouring the grievance. Gaposawa did not come to the front but called out from where he was sitting, 'Yapa and I were not angry with you: we didn't wish to quarrel. Come, let us smoke together and forget the incident.'

There was now a general move, and although one or two groups remained chatting around small fires for a short time longer, the majority departed to bed.

Another meeting dealt with the case of a youth found in possession of stolen property. Gwaleyam was in charge and gave an account of how his neighbour Tabi' had missed a knife bought a few days before at the store. He searched in vain and then made enquiries next door. Everyone there denied borrowing it, but one of the children mentioned that she had seen the youth Ki'dolo' hanging about. He was known to have stolen a number of things in the past, and Tabi' accordingly went to the house where the lad lived with his mother's brother. After a brief search the knife was discovered at the back of a shelf. 'Ki'dolo' now says that it's his and that he bought it last Friday,' Gwaleyam went on, 'but his uncle Buasi' knows nothing about any buying. You will hear what he has got to say. If afterwards you think the boy's a thief, then tell Tabi' what to do with him.'

Buasi' admitted at once that he had never seen the knife before and that he had no information to offer about how it was obtained. But it was a fact that Ki'dolo' had been to the store the previous week, he said, for he had mentioned the price of some new calico which was for sale.

One of the women, an aunt, then spoke from her seat. 'Why pick on Ki'dolo'?' she wanted to know. 'No one saw him go into the house. If the door was left open, how do you know the neighbours are speaking the truth? Besides, there are other knives like this one. Why, then, is Ki'dolo' the only person asked for an explanation?'

Nga'gili' spoke next. Ki'dolo' had been accused, he pointed out, because so many thefts had been traced to him in the past. The boy was notorious, and it was no use his relatives pretending that he was above suspicion. Who had stolen Ninggis's torch? Ki'dolo'. Who had taken Selep's blanket? Ki'dolo'. Who had burgled Nga'mung's house and been found afterwards with eight shillings? Ki'dolo'. Who had made away with Gi'lahi's bottle of peroxide? Ki'dolo'. Here was a person who obviously was born stealing, and no doubt Tabi' was right to blame him for the missing knife.

Biyaweng, the eldest brother of Ki'dolo', arose in his defence but had proceeded no further than to ask Tabi' to produce his witnesses when Dahungmboa ran up yelling, 'He did it, Ki'dolo' did it.' After a pause to regain his breath he explained that that afternoon he had missed a wallet containing two pound notes. Having no idea at the time who the thief could be, he had kept silent, but, on hearing Gwaleyam's remarks a few minutes before, suddenly recalled that Ki'dolo' had been in the house for a short time during the morning. He had slipped away in the darkness to visit the house where the lad slept—it was then empty as everyone was attending the meeting—and searched the bed, the most likely hiding place. Concealed in the kapok pillow was the missing money. 'And if Ki'dolo' took my cash,' the recital concluded, 'then he must have taken the knife.'

This supposition seemed to be reasonable, and there was a roar of approval. Gwaleyam ordered the lad to stand and asked him to tell the truth. Had he or had he not stolen the knife? There was no reply, but so shamefaced was he that no one now doubted his guilt. A debate then followed as to whether the uncle should be allowed to carry out punishment or whether the case should be referred to the District Officer. Buasi' and Biyaweng pleaded and even offered two shillings each as compensation but were overborne by those who pointed out that thrashings had been ineffective in the past. 'What Ki'dolo' needs,' said Andi', is a few weeks in prison with a policeman behind him all the time to make certain that he works hard. He's a boy without shame, and our beatings are useless. I tell you all that, if you want to keep your things in future, you must take him to Salamaua.' The last word was left to Tabi', who announced his intention of visiting the Government station the next day.

The villagers now began to move about and chat. Before many minutes had passed, however, Ahipum called them to order and stated that he also had a matter which he wished them to consider. He had intended to have the conch blown that afternoon, he said, but Gwaleyam made his move earlier. There was trouble over a garden. Samasam had that day come to him to say that when on his way to clear a patch of bush he had noticed Kawa'wi, the wife of Tangabi', planting taro shoots in a plot above the beach alongside the mouth of the Buim River. This area, Samasam claimed, had originally been cultivated by his mother's brother and therefore belonged by rights to him and his nephews. He wished to know who had given Tangabi' permission to make a garden there and why this person had not consulted him, as the principal owner. 'Tangabi',' Ahipum called, 'what have you to say about it?'

'The land is ours,' Tangabi' answered. 'Samasam's boundary lies alongside the big ficus tree farther down the beach. I made a garden here when I was first married, as my mother's brothers did before me. This land isn't Samasam's; it's mine. I know I'm right. I remember going there when I was a little boy with my uncle Apilum. He left me playing in the water and I was nearly killed when the tree which he was chopping fell into the river instead of into the bush.'

'Nonsense,' replied Samasam. 'My land goes right to the river. Your plot is on the other side of the path higher upstream. Isn't that so, Salingbo? You know. You worked there in times past with my mother's brother Ngada'pu.'

Salingbo confirmed this statement and said that Ngada'pu had to his certain knowledge at different times made three or four gardens in the area. Further, he stated that Apilum had always worked higher up the river and that Tangabi' must have been in error about the spot where he was playing when the tree fell.

Mabiyeng, who is a distant relative of Tangabi', denied this. When he was a young man it was always understood, he maintained, that Apilum's land extended along the river bank and that Ngada'pu's was behind it on the farther side of the ficus tree.

Five others also spoke, three in support of Samasam's claim and two in support of Tangabi'. There appeared to be no reason why any of them should have been personally interested in the ground, and the conclusion was that one side was making an honest mistake. The difficulty was in deciding which, and when it became clear that several persons, including the two disputants, were beginning to lose their temper, Ahipum thought that the wisest course was to cut the discussion short. 'Finish talking,' he ordered. 'Enough, I say. Go to your dwellings.'

The subject was brought up again three weeks later, but, as everyone held to his opinions, there was a further postponement, this time for over a month. The two men were now able to face each other calmly, and Ahipum had little difficulty in persuading them to divide the land. This was a more satisfactory arrangement, they agreed, than putting the case in the District Officer's hands and having him make a decision which of necessity would be arbitrary.

One more meeting deserves a few details. Ida', the head teacher of the school, on this occasion called the people together to find out what support he would have for the dismissal of a member of his staff. The man in the case, Kamundong, already disliked on account of his bad temper, had some days previously quarrelled with his mother, beaten her soundly, and thrown her out of the house, nearly breaking her arm.[1]

'We have summoned you, Kamundong, to hear your explanation,' Ida' told him. 'Tell us why you hit your mother. Was there a reason? Had she sworn at you? Come, we want to know.'

[1] This was in October 1945. When in January 1950 Kamundong's young daughter died it was said that God had intervened to punish him.

178

11a.   Pounding sago pith

11b.   Washing sago

12. Girl with net for catching freshwater fish

'Yes,' the talkative Madulu interrupted, 'we want to straighten this thing out. We can't have a man who tries to kill his mother teaching our children.'

'You called me here, and I'll listen to you,' Kamundong replied. 'It's up to you to speak, not me. What goes on in my house is my affair. I don't have to explain what I do.'

'That's where you're wrong, you swine,' said Sale, the woman's brother. 'I don't allow my sister to be hit by anyone, not even her son, my own nephew. I can't believe, though, that you are my nephew. No kinsman of mine would call his mother a bastard and refer to her as excrement. You, Kamundong, must be the offspring of a tree—certainly, nobody born of woman would speak like that. Men, real men, remember the pains their mother suffered and recall that she suckled them and looked after them as children. They show her respect. As for you, you are a monster.'

'Sale, my uncle,' was the sneering rejoinder; 'go, find your mother and copulate with her.'

A fight would have taken place at this point had not the native pastor seized Sale by the arm. 'Enough,' he said. 'We want no more blows struck. You are an old man.' Turning to Kamundong, he then asked him why he had abandoned the law of God. Did he not know of the Commandment bidding us to honour our parents? And had not the ancestors, too, always stressed the importance of respect for the father and mother? Could he offer any excuse for abandoning such teachings and making a new set of customs for himself?

Bu'da' interposed before this address could be finished and gave it as his opinion that an enquiry into the reason for Kamundong's conduct could wait; the present speakers should confine themselves to the question of whether they considered him a fit person to teach the children. 'For myself, I'm sure he's not,' Bu'da' finished. 'How can a man who doesn't obey the Commandments himself instruct others to do so?'

Kamundong, now beside himself, picked up the flour drum on which he had been sitting and, screaming filth, hurled it into the middle of the elders. By good luck no one was hurt, and Bu'da' flung it back, hitting him on the thigh. 'There, your talk is like your drum; it turns aside from us,' he shouted. 'But our talk hits you because what we say is true.'

This time a fight actually began, with the attack led by Hagatu', one of Kamundong's cousins. Ida' called him off, however, and after calm had been restored declared that enough had taken place to indicate that such a man was a menace to the school. 'Go, leave us,' he declared. 'Busama has finished with you. We don't want you with us.'

Several other matters were raised before the meeting closed. The most serious was a complaint by one of the women that her husband had sworn at her. The enquiry revealed that she had given provocation by criticising him for assisting a relative to collect flooring material, and it was she in consequence who was reproved. An elder also took up some time by pointing out that he was horrified to see that several young women were adopting the 'disgraceful' Rabaul habit of putting peroxide on their hair and that a number of young men were sleeping in their parents' dwelling instead of in the club houses. This was all most unsatisfactory and must cease forthwith. Two or three others supported him, one of them adding that he also saw much to condemn in the behaviour of Ibaya and his brothers. These boys not only continued to sleep in the family dwelling but were remiss in bringing fish to their sick father.

Local Government in the Future

In spite of the absence of formal procedure or of anyone empowered to pronounce sentence—in spite, too, of the elements of a slanging match—it is clear that the elders reach some consensus of opinion about what is the right thing to do, and on lines which would probably commend themselves to the white man; moreover, the idea of taking advantage of having the village gathered together to discuss other business is not new. Creating a formally recognised council-cum-court therefore will not be in any sense a revolutionary action.

Little change will be necessary in the conduct of the gatherings, and there is no need at this stage to complicate matters with instructions about counting votes when opinion is divided. It is to be hoped that the natives will learn to appreciate the wisdom of accepting the view of the majority once they begin to realise that immediate decisions are sometimes called for.

COUNCILS AND COURTS

The presiding elder will probably always have to be the representative of Government, but I foresee no objections to the successor to the luluai and tultul acting in this capacity. The limits of his powers will, of course, have to be carefully defined and made clear to him and to the villagers. He must understand that a continuation of the present system is wanted, not a return to the era of Bumbu.

In their rôle as a council the elders must first of all be given experience in handling public funds. This can be arranged by allowing them to fix the amount of tax and entrusting them with the task of its collection. The cash may have to be handed over to the Administration, but a proportion of it can go back for expenditure, subject to the approval of the District Officer, on capital goods which will be of value to all—perhaps simple gardening implements in the early stages but later, as educational standards improve, a cutter maybe, or a sawmill, or a lighting plant. Difficulties regarding maintenance will have to be faced and overcome, for each person is certain to treat village property as someone else's responsibility (cf. pp. 77–78). One possibility would be to have ownership vested in the chairman of the council and for rules to be worked out governing the use of all equipment.

The court requires more preparation. One obvious need is a digest of the legal code, setting out the offences with which the elders can deal and the maximum penalties to be imposed. This should be written in form of simple rules, a line or two to each.[1] Pidgin English would suffice, though Yabim is preferable. Fines should be handed over to an official and paid direct to the council treasury. Gaol sentences will normally be served in the District gaol, though in special circumstances, especially if a woman has been convicted, it may be possible to have the criminal kept busy carrying out work of public benefit at home. Sentences are likely to be somewhat severe till the court finds its feet, but injustice can be prevented by allowing an appeal.

A code of customary law will also be required to deal with purely native offences not recognised by the Government, and framing the rules should be one of the first tasks undertaken by the council. The major concern will probably be fixing the damages to be paid to the parent of a single girl when she has been seduced, but

[1] Cf. 'Notes and Instructions to Native Administrations in the British Solomon Islands', *Oceania*, Vol. XVI, pp. 61–69.

consideration will have to be given also to such things as the proper procedure when a pig has destroyed a crop and when gardens have been made on another person's plot without permission.

A clerk will have to be appointed to make a record of the cases, but as the whole population is literate in Yabim the selection should not be difficult. A few young men are also able to read and write in pidgin, and it may be argued that if this were used the reports could be readily understood by the District Officer. But if the people are to continue to treat the court as a village concern they must be allowed to retain their own language. A verbal translation when the District Officer is on patrol should suffice for purposes of inspection. Should it be considered advisable to give the clerk a small salary, he could be paid out of the village treasury.

Throughout the experiment the watchword must be persuasion rather than coercion, and for this reason it will be advisable to have an officer at hand who already has the people's confidence. But while nursing will often be called for, coddling must be avoided. Self-confidence cannot be achieved without a measure of freedom, and, though precautions to guard against big mistakes may be admirable, it is only by making little ones that the natives can progress. Like ourselves, the peoples of New Guinea have the unfortunate characteristic of profiting only from their own experience.

Chapter Ten

WAGE LABOUR

'Take but degree away, untune that string,
And, hark, what discord follows! each thing meets
In mere oppugnancy: the bounded waters
Should lift their bosoms higher than the shores
And make a sop of all this solid globe:
Strength should be lord of imbecility,
And the rude son should strike his father dead:
Force should be right; or, rather, right and wrong,
Between whose endless jar justice resides,
Should lose their names, and so should justice too.'
Troilus and Cressida, Act I, Scene 3.

EMPLOYMENT by Europeans has come to be accepted as normal routine, and till the Pacific war began the bulk of the youths offered themselves for service at about the age of sixteen. The average period of absence was six years, but those who became interested in their jobs often remained away for longer.[1] The majority were still bachelors, but the older men sometimes took their spouses to the labour compound, where a small section was set aside as married quarters. One or two single women worked as nursemaids, but the Administration discouraged the engagement of females.

A number of men also elected to become 'black missionaries'

[1] Two only have today been away for so long that their return seems doubtful. Both are believed to have married women from villages close to their place of employment (in New Ireland).

183

or school teachers and after a period of training in a college were sent to the more remote areas. These mission workers spent their vacations at home but did not come back permanently till middle age. Their wives accompanied them—the Lutheran authorities wisely insisted that all helpers should be married—and the children grew up amongst comparative strangers.

It follows that the village lost a large proportion of its able-bodied males and several of its females. In the period between the years 1920 and 1940 few single men would have been found there, and absences would also have been noted in the ranks of the married men with young families (see Appendix A).

Busama was in this respect like other parts of Melanesia. Except in the remote highlands of New Guinea, which white men were only just beginning to penetrate, the story was everywhere the same.

The effect of wage labour on native societies has already attracted a good deal of attention, and a mounting body of research is available concerning the dependent territories of Africa.[1] Many problems there are acute: one reads, for example, of the slums in which workers live on the outskirts of the towns, of the very long—and increasing—period for which the men are absent from the reservations, of the plight of wives who have been taken to the centres of employment and then widowed or deserted, of the immorality of children reared in ignorance of the tribal background, and of the starvation of the old people at home. Similar trends can be observed in the Pacific, but still as trends only: the most significant features here so far are, first, that the village is coming to be despised and, second, that the relations between the generations have been disturbed.[2] In former times the old men were able to maintain their authority because, among other reasons, they owned all the objects of value: nowadays, on the contrary, the most prized item of all, money, flows into the

[1] It is impossible to refer to them all here, but the following may be mentioned: G. St. J. Orde Brown, *The African Labourer*, Oxford, 1933; M. Hunter, *Reaction to Conquest*, Oxford, 1936; G. Wilson, *Economics of Detribalization*, Rhodes-Livingstone Papers 5 and 6, 1941; Lord Hailey, *African Survey*, Oxford, 1945; and I. Schapera, *Migrant Labour and Tribal Life*, Oxford, 1947. See also numerous papers in the journal *Africa*.

[2] For a general account of labour in New Guinea see L. P. Mair, *Australia in New Guinea*, op. cit., Chap. VII; S. W. Reed, *The Making of Modern New Guinea*, op. cit., pp. 178–184, 216–234; and J. A. Decker, *Labour Problems in the Pacific Mandates*, Shanghai, 1940.

village mainly through the efforts of the young. Busama is something of an exception in that here the seniors still command respect. But the forces which operate, as we shall see, are practically unique. After giving the historical and legal background of employment, I shall consider the reasons for its popularity. Then, following on a short account of life in the compounds, I shall proceed to the subjects which concern us most in the present study, the deserted village and the labourer after he returns home. A final section deals with post-war changes.

The Indenture System

The first natives left their homes in about 1900. The only work then available was on the coconut estates, and for twenty-five years an increasingly large number was transported to the Madang District, where the copra industry had its earliest start. But in 1926, when gold was discovered in the range behind Salamaua, a change took place. From the beginning, before air freighting was developed, the Busama were much in demand as carriers. This established a connection with the goldfields, where wages were higher than elsewhere, and plantation work was thenceforward refused. Service in ships also became popular, and every year several young men signed on as deckhands. In addition, some acted as cooks, laundrymen, and personal servants, a few with skill in writing pidgin English were storemen, and there were half a dozen trained carpenters and mechanics.

The job of seeking out labourers was entrusted to professional recruiters, who received so much per head on delivery (the amount varied according to the demand). Gifts to a village leader as an inducement for him to bring pressure to bear on any eligible youths was at first the usual method—the practice was not declared illegal till 1933—and, as was pointed out, the foundation of Bumbu's fortune was laid by payments of this kind. In the beginning the natives were also lured away with all sorts of false promises, though later, with increasing experience, they became aware of their rights and would only go to employers who had a good reputation.

The recruiters also looked after the repatriation of the labourers. Travel was by schooner, and if the natives lived on the coast, like the Busama, there was no cause for complaint. Those who came from the interior, however, had sometimes to face a journey lasting several days. This frequently resulted in their arriving home without their new possessions, which had been stolen or abandoned on the way.

An indenture system was in force carrying penal sanctions against desertion or neglect of duty. The initial contract was for three years, though the period could be extended. The worker received a minimum wage of five shillings per month if he remained on the coast, ten shillings if he went to the highland goldfields. Living quarters were also provided, together with a regular issue of rations; and the hours of work were limited to fifty per week. Employers guilty of a breach of the regulations were fined, but, despite annual inspections by Government officers, the housing compared unfavourably with that considered desirable in most colonies. The barrack-like structures were sometimes infested with vermin, the hygiene was so neglected that outbreaks of dysentery were common. The standard diet was unsatisfactory, too, and beriberi was from time to time reported from some of the compounds.

Reasons for Seeking Employment

Even in ancient times the natives were not content to spend all their time in the village. They sailed up and down the coast on trading voyages and would probably have ventured farther afield had they been certain of receiving a friendly welcome. It is therefore not surprising that one of the strongest motives prompting the youths to go away to work should have been the desire to see something of new places. They regaled those who could be persuaded to listen with their experiences afterwards and boasted proudly of seeing places which no one else had visited. A lad whom I took with me on a tour of eastern Papua was overjoyed with all the new names, which he recorded in a diary so as to be able to impress those less fortunate than himself. His fondest dream was to become a member of the crew of a steamer from Australia, partly to see for himself the marvels of a large city, partly to be able to claim that he had been out of the islands. The engagement of native crews for overseas vessels has always been forbidden, but if the Ordinance were ever revoked I have no doubt there would be far more appplicants than could be accommodated.

WAGE LABOUR

The need for money was another important consideration. The Busama had for years been more favourably situated than the majority of New Guinea villagers in that, with a town at a convenient distance, they had regular opportunities for acquiring cash by disposing of surplus fruit, vegetables, fowls, and eggs; but the profits from such transactions were small, a few shillings at most, and the only way to earn a fair sized sum, say three or four pounds, was to make a contract with an employer.[1]

The planters used to argue that the native is self-supporting and that the fact that he left home to work for wages was proof of his satisfaction with the conditions offered. The peoples of New Guinea ceased to be independent, however, from the moment when they first began to appreciate the worth of steel. The technique of manufacturing stone axes and obsidian knives was quickly forgotten, and if the natives of today were deprived of money to buy tools they would starve. The Busama have even lost the art of making fish hooks and nets and buy these items also from the stores. Again, they now needs saws, planes, hammers, and nails for building; lamps, kerosene, and electric torches for illuminating their dwellings at night; and household crockery and cutlery for serving and eating their meals. A certain amount of clothing is also looked upon as essential both for warmth and decency as well as for prestige.[2] The members of the congregation at the Sunday services are invariably

[1] Unfortunately I could not discover the average annual profit from casual sales.

[2] Natives who have little acquaintance with Euorpean ways often present a grotesque spectacle in ill-fitting garments selected without any notion of what is appropriate or seemly. Their health may be seriously impaired, for they seldom have soap and also do not realise the danger of sitting about in wet clothing. For these reasons many well intentioned Europeans think that they should be forbidden to cover the upper parts of their bodies. (An Ordinance was introduced for the purpose but has never been enforced.) But the Busama, through long experience, are as much at home with their wardrobe as any white man, and there is no good reason why they should be deprived of it. Indeed, they might with advantage be encouraged to wear sandals as a protection against foot injuries and hookworm. My objection is to the blue serge tunics of the native police—wool at sea level in the tropics!—and to the mother-hubbards worn by the women. Such Victorian relics are an anachronism, and the Administration might well give attention to the introduction of a hygienic uniform. Perhaps the Missions might then set the fashion by designing a new type of woman's dress.

187

resplendent in newly washed and ironed garments (those who have nothing clean to wear prefer to remain at home). Other goods for which there is a demand include foodstuffs, tea and coffee, tobacco, soap, furniture, bedding, sewing-machines, and bicycles.[1] Finally, cash is indispensable for the payment of tax.[2]

The collecting of family budgets proved to be impossible—expenditure is so haphazard and irregular—but the war damage claims illustrate how much the natives have come to depend upon European goods. Of the total amount of £2,259 8s. claimed for individual losses (see p. 21), £413 18s. (18 per cent.) was for articles bought in stores and £127 17s. (5·8 per cent.) for sums of money.

Many young men also sought employment as an escape from boredom. The Lutheran Mission disapproves of dancing and bodily decoration, and the result was an early ban on the old festivals which were the focal points of village life, giving it zest and flavour. The eternal round of work with only prayer meetings to relieve the monotony was felt by the high-spirited youngsters to be too dull. 'Back here there's only toil and church,' one of them who had not long completed a contract remarked to me in disgust. 'But in the labour compound we had our dances after knocking-off time. We painted our faces, put on ornaments, played the hand-drum, and enjoyed ourselves.'

The puritanical sexual code meant, too, that indulgence in the village was both difficult and dangerous. Morals in the centres of employment, on the contrary, were lax or non-existent, though the number of women was usually limited. The only opportunity which the majority of the labourers had for casual alliances was with prostitutes who had come to the compounds ostensibly as the wives of workers. The few men whose jobs involved travel, such as schooner crews and personal servants of recruiters, were, of course, in a different category, especially if visits were made to the Sepik or

[1] Goods exposed for sale in the small stores located around the coast include tea, coffee, cocoa, lemonade, sugar, butter, dripping, bread (once every fortnight), rice, flour, kerosene, soap, powder, perfume, tooth paste and brushes, razors, mirrors, calico, cotton, towels, fish lines, hooks, fly sprays, tobacco, cigarettes, axes, knives, crockery, and table cutlery.

[2] Till 1942 a head tax of ten shillings per annum was levied on all unindentured fit males between the apparent ages of sixteen and forty. Labourers were not liable to payment, and, in addition, exemption was granted to village officials, Mission workers, and fathers of large families.

Waria River areas, where the looseness of the women was notorious.

A further factor was the excess of males over females, a feature of practically all New Guinea villages. Young men who found that, for lack of an eligible girl, their marriage had to be postponed beyond the due time usually preferred to spend the period of waiting as labourers.

Again, I have often been informed by ex-labourers that the effort called for by employers was usually less than is required in carrying out family tasks, a statement which I can well believe. The work done for a European master was often tedious, imagination and ingenuity being alike out of place, but it was rarely as exhausting as felling timber to make a new garden, digging holes to plant taro suckers, or dragging logs from the remoter valleys to fashion canoes or build houses. With every departure, too, the responsibilities of those left behind increased.[1] The ration issue, though open to criticism by dietitians on the score of vitamin deficiencies, was also held in high favour by the natives. Meat was the attraction, as this is a luxury in the village. There was always a bigger exodus than usual after a drought or flood, when food was short.

Finally, going away to work was a means of avoiding village discipline. Those discovered in an offence generally took the easy way out and made a contract.

The Compound

Life on the labour line was crude and unsavoury. The men were young, and, detached as they were from home influences, the majority threw off moral restraints and became socially irresponsible. Services comparable to the education and amenities units of the war-time armies, which had similar problems to face, might have proved effective in maintaining a standard of citizenship and possibly also in fostering intellectual growth; further, in such areas as the gold-fields where some thousands of native labourers were concentrated,

[1] In some villages, notably those along the Sepik River, the few natives who had no desire to leave were at times forced into doing so in self-defence. The old folk, the women, and the children were left to fend for themselves in tumble-down houses and neglected gardens which they could not extend.

the setting up of welfare bodies and night schools would have presented no insuperable difficulties. The employers were, however, indifferent, and the Missions of the mainland never took the initiative.[1]

The chief pastime for the hours of idleness was gambling. I have known of labourers who collected several pounds after a single night of the card game 'Lucky' and others who were not only penniless but had mortgaged their earnings for some months ahead. The police made periodic raids on the workers' quarters but were powerless to stop the play. Thieving was naturally an everyday occurrence, though the Labour Ordinance provided that all employees must be issued with a box capable of being locked.

Every group had its traditional enemies—the Markham valley natives, for example, hold those of the Sepik River in the greatest contempt—and although the men from each place had their own houses, fighting was always going on. It was an offence for any native to consume alcohol, but the hatreds were sometimes inflamed by drink. Bottles were apt to disappear from liquor stores, and the manufacture of home-brew was not unknown.

It was hardly to be expected that men in their late teens and early twenties would be able to subdue their sexual impulses. Few of the compounds were located near a village, however, and a still smaller number had a resident prostitute. Precautions had therefore to be taken to avoid the rape of white women. A native found in the European section of the towns after a certain hour was imprisoned, and all bedrooms were protected by bolts and strong wire netting, 'boy-proofing', as it was called. (White women on outlying plantations with villages at a distance of a stone's throw were quite safe, and here such measures were unnecessary.)

In the circumstances homosexuality was inevitable, and the men of more mature years made a practice of taking a youth of sixteen or seventeen as a lover. He was first attracted by gifts of tobacco, sweets, and gaily coloured clothing and then seduced. Resistance was countered with the threat of sorcery, of which many are still in deadly fear. Bitter rivalries developed if young lads were in short supply or if one of them attempted to transfer his allegiance. Blows were

---

[1] The Administration sponsored one night school only, at Rabaul. The Methodist Mission whose activities were confined to New Britain and New Ireland, supplied a teacher to any plantation manager with accommodation available, but the offer was rarely accepted.

struck, and there have been occasions when the men, mad with jealousy, have resorted to knives. The most popular dance by far was the Bagana, in which each main performer paraded openly with his sleeping partner of the moment. Certain of the movements, which were carried out by separate couples, were unmistakably imitative of sexual congress.

'Unnatural vice'—which in this instance was 'natural' enough—if detected was severely punished. Those who were without a paramour, either through inclination or temporary loss, were thus able to levy blackmail on their more fortunate companions, an advantage which they were not slow to seize upon. I have heard of native foremen, themselves married and with a wife on the spot, who made a habit of threatening exposure to anyone who refused to renew his contract of indenture. Each recruit earned the foreman a bonus.

The Returned Labourer

Busama labourers who had reached the age of twenty-three or twenty-four when their contracts were completed usually found a bride awaiting them. It is not the custom of this village, as has been mentioned, to allow a young man to choose his partner, and all the arrangements are in the hands of the elders. His wishes were sometimes consulted by letter as his time drew to a close, and he occasionally rejected the first name put forward and suggested another, but in general the plans were accepted without comment. Sexual relations with the wife began soon after marriage, and the irregular activities of the compound were abandoned.

Those for whom no such provision was made were in a less favourable position. Most of these were men considered to be too young as yet to enter the married state, though there were sometimes a few in their late twenties for whom wives for one reason or another could not be found, perhaps because they were lazy or physically repulsive or because the number of girls was for the time being inadequate to go round. They did their best to make assignations in the village, usually with single girls but occasionally with married women. Such advances were not invariably successful, but scandals blazed up periodically when an alliance became public, especially if pregnancy had resulted. Administrative officers refused to take

191

action against offending couples who were still unmarried, but adultery was punished by a term of imprisonment.

Earlier perversion did not lead to permanent maladjustment, and only an odd case or two of indecent assault on a village schoolboy occurred. Such acts were strongly disapproved of, and the offender was roundly abused; yet the lad's parents never reported the incident at the District station. It appears that they did not consider that tampering with a son was a serious personal affront: unlike his sister's, his chances of a favourable marriage were not impaired.

Returned labourers were at first somewhat lazy and devoted much of their time to sleeping or paying visits to relatives and friends. Fathers of families have to spend between eight and nine hours at work each day, but a group of young men who came back in 1944 were after two weeks occupied for an average of only three hours daily (see Appendix E). Their behaviour was characterised, too, by bumptiousness and insolence. The villagers called them 'big heads', a term taken over from pidgin English. This exactly described them, for they swaggered around with lordly airs claiming to know every-thing and replying to criticism with a snigger and a stare. When the luluai scolded them for disobeying his order to help the other men in repairing a bridge they laughed in his face. What did he know about Government authority? they wanted to know. On what date was he last in conference with the District Officer? His instructions must only apply to raw bushmen and stay-at-homes, not to men of the world like themselves.

The news which arrived early in my acquaintance with the village that twenty-three finished-time labourers could be expected back in the following week aroused a good deal of trepidation. 'We're glad to know they'll soon be with us again—yes, that's true—but you see they'll all be "big heads" to begin with, and we're bound to have trouble with them,' one old man lamented. 'They'll be lounging about in the village all day or else sleeping. Garden work? Oh, no: that'll be too hard. For the next month there'll be seduction after seduction and rudeness on top of rudeness.'

The absorption of such a big group was not easy, and for a few weeks it appeared that authority might not prevail. The youths flagrantly disobeyed orders, and a visit to any club house at high noon was bound to reveal some of them still sleeping soundly. Despite a most careful watch on the girls, too, it was whispered that several

WAGE LABOUR

were having affairs. 'I wish we still carried out initiation ceremonies,' remarked Nga'sele', one of the older men, to a crowd of his contemporaries. 'I've told Obin [the name by which I was known] how in the past the boys who were brought forward to be swallowed by the spirit monsters were seized and soundly beaten. Their kinsmen fell upon them with nettles, with sticks, and with knives and gave them a trouncing. If we could only do this now we'd be listened to when we spoke. There'd be no telling us to shut up and mind our own business.' 'Things weren't like this in olden days, as you say,' somebody added. 'At that time the club houses were schools of behaviour. Instead of the youths going away, they lived there in the care of an old man, who taught them how they must conduct themselves. They learnt to be diligent and respectful and not to make advances to the girls.'

A slow improvement was soon noticeable, nevertheless, and after about a month I found that instead of only three hours being gainfully occupied the time had increased to seven, nearly as much as the figure for men with a household to support. By now, too, many of the labourers were beginning to distribute their earnings amongst their relatives. About half usually went to the guardian, either the father or an uncle, a quarter to one of the other uncles, and an eighth, divided into shares, to other persons. Two examples will suffice for illustration, Mamang and Gawa'. The first had £5, and after setting aside 15s. for himself he gave £2 10s. to his father, £1 to his mother's elder brother, 5s. to her second brother, 4s. to his own brother, and 3s. each to his two sisters. Gawa', with £6, kept £1 and presented £3 to his father, £1 to his mother's only brother, 10s. to his father's elder brother, 5s. to his own brother, and 5s. to his sister.

As the young men began to settle down a marked change was evident in their relations with the elders. Insults became less common, and an admonition was listened to with some show of politeness. At village meetings the new arrivals sat quietly on the outskirts, leaving the discussions to take place without interruption. 'They'll be all right,' Nga'sele' informed me. 'They know at last where they belong and that the manners of the compound won't do here. The answering back of the last month is finished, and we'll get along properly from now on.' A few days later when returning with a party from the gardens I saw one of the labourers insisting that his father should hand over the main part of a heavy load of canoe lashings, and on the

193

following morning two others tried to persuade their aged uncle to rest rather than take a hand with them in renewing the thatch of the house.

The conduct of this group of labourers was typical, and the old standards were in most instances accepted after a short initial delay. Some of the older men made a habit of grumbling amongst themselves, however, with accusations of consistent laziness, ignorance, and lack of decorum. 'The young people of today aren't a bit like we were,' they used to tell me. 'No, they're an idle lot thinking only of eating and sleeping. They can't do this, and they won't do that. Why don't they toil hard as we did? Why aren't they in awe of us? Why don't they do as they're bidden and keep silent? We were as subservient as children long after we'd grown up.'

The aged everywhere are inclined to be impatient with those who will follow after, and these charges are not to be taken too seriously. It is a fact that the young men, absent for so long, failed to master some of the traditional skills—seine netting, for example, once practised by everyone, is now almost a lost art—but after the month of unrest was over the majority appeared to me to be on the whole industrious, gracious, and properly reverent. There may have been times when they found authority irksome, and undue pretensions on the part of a father or uncle certainly irritated them on occasions, but they usually kept their opinions secret or uttered them only to a friend. Each generation accordingly retained a natural dignity, and village affairs progressed with a minimum of discord.

This is not to say that misfits are lacking. In 1944 there were, amongst other, the feckless charming Ilia, the bullying Kamundong and Kundu—two brothers who threw their mother out of the house —the trouble-making Yomsop, the adulterous Biyaweng, the lazy Tawasi, and the thieving Ko'dolo'. But ten or a dozen are a small proportion in a population of six hundred.

The easy pleasantness of Busama presents a marked contrast with the majority of island communities. Friction between young and old is the rule elsewhere; the former are discourteous and uncivil not merely for a few weeks but all the time, and the latter, trying in vain to assert themselves, are permanently querulous and petulant. The account of Malaita in my book *Experiments in Civilization* (pp. 162–171) gives the normal picture. I pointed out there that the word *ara'i*, which originally meant 'elder' or 'person of importance', was degraded from an expression of respect to a term of abuse and applied to everyone who complained; and that the proverb, 'The sun always rises in the same place', implying that temperament, in the broadest sense, does not change—the verse about the leopard and his spots (Jeremiah xiii, 23) is our equivalent—had been narrowed down till it signified only that the old fogeys would go on criticising no matter what occurred. Lawlessness was also on the increase, and such offences as theft, brawling, and adultery were more common than in primitive conditions.[1]

European contact has everywhere had the effects of reducing the old men's power. They can no longer threaten offenders with sorcery, for example, or with refusal to contribute to the bride price. But in Busama, although wedding payments have been abandoned, the elders have retained the right to arrange marriages. It is still possible for an unruly youth to be brought to his senses by a reminder that he may find himself condemned to a permanent state of bachelordom (see above p. 140).

The proximity to a town has also been a source of strength. The villagers had a chance to become acquainted with European ways from childhood, and labourers could not assume an arrogant demeanour on the assumption that they alone knew all about the white man. A single visit to Salamaua, indeed, was likely to furnish more information than three years spent on a remote goldmine or plantation. It was amusing to note the different reactions of the Malaita and Busama villagers to the weird jargon brought back by the young men who had been employed by the Army during the war. The Malaita concluded that this was proper English and were impressed; the Busama dismissed it for what it was, pidgin with a greatly enlarged but much mangled vocabulary used for the purpose

---

[1] A more general description is given in H. I. Hogbin and C. H. Wedgwood, *Development and Welfare in the Western Pacific*, Sydney, 1943, pp. 5–12, (London edition, 1944, pp. 8–15).

One or two officials from Lae with whom I have discussed the matter are of the opinion that Busama is no different from other villages and that here also the young men are resentful of all discipline. The misconception, along with certain others, is, I believe, due to greater acquaintance with the misfits, especially, Yomsop, Biyaweng, and Tawasi, than with the village as a whole. These three are conspicuously talkative and make constant visits to the District Office with complaints. But at home they are held in disrepute by their contemporaries as well as by their elders.

of showing off. 'If you want to speak pidgin, well and good; we can all follow,' an elder curtly informed one lad. 'Or if you prefer English, Obin here will translate for you. But this new rubbish is understood by nobody, and you'd better reserve it in case you want to talk in your sleep.'

Salamaua, too, provided the Busama elders with opportunities for earning small sums of money, thus rendering them to some extent independent of the young men's wages. They had no need to beg for shillings from their sons and nephews, and if an axe, knife, or pair of trousers was required they could always dispose of a basket of fruit or some eggs. The elders of the remoter villages were deprived of such chances and had to depend on the ex-labourers to supply all the European goods.

The more rigorous system of home education adopted by the Busama may also have been a factor in achieving conformity. Most island parents are able to secure obedience from their children by a verbal expression of disapproval. The villages are usually tiny, and the small boy, having few companions of his own age, spends much of his time in the family circle. Busama however, is quite large, and gangs play an important part in the child's life. Here then on occasion the parents are compelled to resort to force, even to the extent of tying a naughty youngster to a post. It is possible that habits inculcated harshly are less readily given up than those learnt without undue pain.

A last point is that the Busama labourers, unlike the majority, almost, never lost touch with their kinsfolk. The village school was opened as early as 1906, and during the next decade letter writing became a normal accomplishment.[1] Most parts of New Guinea had to wait longer for education, and some have no teachers yet.

Village Economics

Many records were lost during the war, but it is possible to gather some notion of the financial profit to the community from wage labour.

---

[1] The frequency with which letters are now exchanged is astonishing. Since 1947 never less than half a dozen Busama have been employed at Port Moresby, and on my way back to Sydney after visiting the village I always make a point of seeking them out to give them the latest news. I have never found them more than a month out of date. In 1950 some of them had even been informed from home of the probable date of my arrival and were looking for me before I had time to begin searching for them.

WAGE LABOUR

The population during 1937, a normal year, was approximately 565, of whom 125 were males over the age of sixteen. Of these 35 (28 per cent. of the adult males, 6·2 per cent. of the total population) were in employment. The average wage was probably 10s. per month.

I took a random sample in 1948 of 18 labourers who had recently returned home and found that although two had arrived empty handed and one with the full amount of his pay, the average was goods or cash to the value of 58 per cent. of the wages earned. I therefore conclude that before the war the various kinship groups were each richer by £3 10s. annually for every young man absent. In 1937, that is to say, the village received £122 10s. (But at least £25 was collected in head tax.)

The price of goods exposed for sale in the stores at Salamaua and Lae during 1937 is set out below. The figure in brackets represents the price in January 1950. I have added this for comparison: but wages have also increased (see below p. 200).

Bicycle	£7 (from £15).
Sewing-machine	£5 to £8 (£16 to £25).
Pressure lamp	£2 10s. (£4 to £5).
Lantern	6s. (15s.).
Petrol iron	£1 5s. (£2 10s.)
Coconut-shell iron	10s. (£1).
Axe	6s. (£1).
Tomahawk	5s. (16s.).
Bush knife	5s. (12s.).
Plane	from 10s. (from £2 10s.).
Plane blade	2s. (5s.).
Corrugated iron	3s. per 6-ft. sheet (unobtainable
Enamel basin	3s. (7s.).
Blanket	2s. 6d. to 15s. (£1 to £4).
Box with lock	8s. to £2 (£2 to £4).
File	2s. (5s.).
Frying-pan	3s. (5s.).
Boiler	5s. (15s.).
Hammer	1s. 6d. (4s.).
Kerosene	2s. per gallon (4s. 9d.).
Fish line	1s. to 5s. (3s. to 7s.).

Mosquito net	5s. (15s.).
Plate	1s. (3s.).
Mug	1s. (2s.).
Nails	4d. per lb. (7d.).
Saucepan	from 2s. (from 10s.).
Saw	from 10s. (from £1 8s.).
Level	6s. (15s.).
Square	5s. (10s.).
Rule	5s. (12s.).
Belt	1s. to 4s. (2s. 6d. to 6s.).
Cotton material	6d. to 2s. 6d. per yard (2s. to 7s.).
Shirt	2s. 6d. to 5s. (8s. to 18s.).
Trousers	2s. 6d. to 5s. (£1 to £1 5s.).
Dress	from 2s. 6d. (from 8s. 6d.).
Meat	1s. per 12-oz. tin (2s. 6d.).
Rice	16s. per cwt. (£3 10s.).
Tobacco	4d. per stick (8d.).
Matches	1s. per packet (1s. 6d.).
Sugar	3d. per lb. (8d.).
Tea	2s. 6d. per lb. (7s. 6d.).
Coffee	2s. 6d. per lb. (6s.).
Soap	1s. per bar (3s. 3d.).
Flour	10s. per 25-lb. tin (£1 10s.).[1]

Wage labour brought economic loss as well as gain. Had the men stayed behind they could have devoted themselves to gardening, house building, fishing, and other tasks. Assuming that each would have worked for 6 days during 50 weeks of the year, the absence of 35 reduced villages resources by 10,500 man days. In this period over 1,500 acres could have been cleared (see p. 63); or 50 houses built (see Appendix G); or many tons of fish caught.

Everyone would certainly have derived benefit from extra fish, and it is probable that individual groups which had lost several men were in need of new houses and increased supplies of vegetables (I have observed that this was so elsewhere). Yet there is no evidence to suggest that the Busama of the pre-war years were in general

---

[1] The natives cannot understand why prices are today so high. Those with a grievance against a particular white man are apt to regard the increase as a European plot.

worse off than their ancestors of the nineteenth century.[1] The coming of the white man meant the introduction of superior tools and the cessation of fighting, and workers who previously were indispensable could in consequence be spared.

Till now, however, the standard of living has been low; and there is some doubt whether it can be raised while 28 per cent. of the fittest young males are away in employment. Education will require extra time, and new crops may demand more labour than taro cultivation.

Changes in the Labour Code

Towards the end of 1944, when the restoration of the Civil Government was being considered, the Minister for External Territories invited representatives of the planting and mining interests, missionaries, administrative officers, and anthropologists to meet him for the purpose of discussing the replacement or modification of the pre-war indenture system.

Two opposite points of view emerged from the discussions. On the one hand, the planters, the miners, half the missionaries, and one or two of the administrative officers urged that the old system be retained in its entirety, including the long-term contract with penal clauses; and on the other, the remainder of the missionaries and administrative officers and the anthropologists supported the abolition of indentures or, if this was still impracticable, the shortening of the contract and scrapping of the penal sanctions. The division of the missionaries was interesting. Those who were against change belonged without exception to societies which supplemented their revenue by conducting planting and trading concerns in the islands. Such enterprises are largely maintained by cheap native labour.

The old arguments which had been appearing for half a century were advanced by those who wished things to remain as they were —the contract was a means of introducing the native to European civilisation and teaching him industry and regular hours, he would have been a nuisance in his village, at the end of his term he was in better health than if he had remained at home, the time could not be

[1] It is well to repeat that Busama was fortunate. In some villages the percentage of absentees was higher, and the persons who remained could not house or feed themselves properly.

shortened because he took so long to train, and imprisonment for breaches was the only practicable method of bringing home his liabilities to him. Every statement met with rebuttal from the other side, but it was admitted that free labour could not be a success unless better and cheaper transport were available. The main point made by the advocates of reform, however, was that employment with a European for a short or a long term was a dead end, and the advancement of the people, to which the Australian Government was committed, depended upon teaching them to develop the country themselves.[1] I quote the following remark of my own from the transcript. of the proceedings. 'Wiping out the indenture system with a stroke of the pen will get us nowhere. It is true that spending some years on a plantation or goldmine is part of the young man's life nowadays; and it will go on being like that until the villages are made more attractive. . . . In any considered scheme for the future it must always be borne in mind that hand in hand with changes in the labour system must come changes in village life to make it fuller, richer, and financially rewarding. Adequate education, including instruction in agriculture and technical matters, is essential.'

When the Civil Government was at length re-established, in October 1945, the Minister announced the inauguration of a Labour Department and major changes in the Labour Code. The indenture system was to be discarded in five years, and in the meantime the contract was to be limited to twelve months, wages to be increased to a minimum of 15s. per month, hours reduced to forty-four per week, and each employer was to be responsible for recruiting his own workers.[2] Since that date all general labourers engaged by the

[1] This view is confirmed by a recent statement of the Administrator (J. K. Murray, *The Provisional Administration of the Territory of Papua—New Guinea*, Brisbane, 1949, pp. 50–51.). 'The plantation economy was dependent upon the indigenous population for its labour supply. The amount of labour that could be recruited in an under-populated country was barely sufficient for existing needs and placed a limit upon further development along these lines. No more than the fringes of the country's resources could be developed. The natives meanwhile gained little in the process. If the European or Asiatic-owned plantation is to be the only form of agricultural production for export, the native is doomed to remain a hewer of wood and a drawer of water for the benefit of aliens in his own land.'

[2] A revised scale of wages for natives employed by the Administration became effective on January 1, 1950. General labourers during their first year

Government have been set up and the Department of Public Health and Agriculture much expanded (the last has become the Department of Agriculture, Stock, and Fisheries).[1]

Reaction to the Changes

The new policy created resentment in commercial circles, and there was agitation to have the three-year contract restored. The indenture system must go in the end, it was agreed, but the natives were not yet ready. The late Sir Hubert Murray, Lieutenant-Governor of Papua till 1940, became a sort of patron saint of the movement because of his frequent statements on the expediency of indentures as a temporary measure and his advocacy of the principle of *festina lente*.[2] Such views had an obvious appeal to those who wished to put the clock back, but the fact that the war has made New Guinea a different place was conveniently forgotten.

The complaints were taken up by the Opposition in the House of Representatives at Canberra, and a statement made by one member is worth quoting as indicative of the widespread ignorance in Australia both of world opinion on colonial matters and of conditions in New Guinea. Urging a longer contract, he said that 'the natives should be given the same opportunities as Australians for entering continuing employment' (*Sydney Morning Herald*, July 11, 1948).[3]

of employment now receive £1 per month, during their second year £1 10*s*. and after their second year £2. The Labour Department estimates that this will increase costs by 66·6 per cent. Nearly a quarter of the native labourers in Papua and New Guinea are employees of the Administration (10,502 in a total of 41,171 on December 31, 1949), and a general increase is therefore to be expected.

[1] J. K. Murray, *op. cit.*, pp. 29–55. Many villages, Busama included, have since 1949 had a clinic with a fair supply of drugs. The Native Medical Assistants in charge are trained for eighteen months before appointment. They receive a salary of £5 per month but no rations or quarters.

[2] Sir Hubert Murray disapproved of the indenture system and retained it only because the conditions of the pre-war colonial world forced him to do so. He once wrote: 'The indenture system may be defended on the plea of necessity, but it is really like slavery in many of its incidents, and it is not an institution that anyone would care to perpetuate.' (*Studies in Australian Affairs*, Institute of Pacific Relations, N.S.W. Branch, p. 252).

[3] The officer who had been in charge of ANGAU also opposed the changes. In an article contributed to the *Pacific Islands Monthly* of June 1948 he enquired, 'Of what use are a few extra shillings a month to a native of New Guinea who,

WAGE LABOUR

The Minister retained his stand, pointing out that many tropical products, especially copra, were in such demand that profits were higher than for twenty years. One must admit, nevertheless, that planters face many difficulties, some, though not all, the result of post-war problems which are world wide. The worst troubles are transport, which is still behind the standard even of 1939, and the diminishing efficiency of labour.[1]

It is too soon to say what the effects will be on the native community. The Education Department has concerned itself to date mainly with policy matters and the establishment of a few central schools, and the new agricultural officers are as yet too busy learning their jobs to impart much information. The villages remain therefore for the most part as they used to be, with wage labour as the main, and often the sole, source of income. On my last visit to Busama the proportion of young men absent was a high as formerly. Yet certain trends were apparent.

Indenture, it seemed, was already a thing of the past, and only casual employment was acceptable. On December 31, 1949, there were 9,057 indentured labourers in the Territory of New Guinea and 18,728 non-indentured labourers (of the latter 6,640 were Government employees). The figure for several years before the war was about 40,000 indentured labourers and a few hundred non-indentured labourers.

after finishing a three-year period of engagement, expends the whole of his deferred pay on fireworks?' He failed to give statistics of how many labourers squandered all their wage: in a somewhat extensive experience I have not met many. If the man came from the interior, and thus had little chance of taking any purchases home safely, such behaviour would not have been unreasonable.

The party which had been the Opposition since 1941 moved over to the Treasury benches after the election of December 1949. On June 1, 1950, when the MS. of this book was already in the hands of the publishers, the new Minister for External Territories announced certain changes. The main points were that a 'Native Employees' Agreement' will replace the old contract. The period of engagement is to be for eighteen months, renewable for a further six months. The period of absence may thus be doubled. No penal clauses will be included, and the Agreement can be terminated by either party at a month's notice.

[1] Planters have informed me that they now require 140 labourers to do the work which before the war would have been carried out by 100. The Labour Department confirms the statements. Some of the extra numbers are to be accounted for by the shortening of the working week by 12 per cent.; but the labourers are not working as hard.

WAGE LABOUR

The most popular firms were those which had taken the trouble to develop good relations with the staff, and two of these with headquarters in Lae were able to make an arrangement whereby anyone wishing to leave, after three or six months, always found a substitute. Four natives whom I knew well told me that they had only worked until they had enough money to buy a particular object (three wanted pressure lamps worth £5 each and a fourth a sewing-machine costing £16). Once this was in their possession they had come home.

But the most significant development was the job contract, which has great possibilities for extension. Despite a general shortage of labour, an ample supply was available for tasks which could be completed in a short period, perhaps a week or a fortnight. The Administration, which handles stevedoring, was able to allocate each ship as it arrived at a port to one or other of the neighbouring villages, and several plantations were being worked by settlements located close by on the understanding that payment would be at a fixed rate for every ton of copra produced.

Chapter Eleven

PAGAN RELIGION

'She became a legend in her old age; but of that I have nothing to say, for we did not meet, and except for a few broken letters, did not write; but she never was old to me.'—G. B. SHAW, Introduction to the volume of letters to Ellen Terry.

THE establishment of the Mission station at Mala'lo was quickly followed by the abandonment of the old rites, and today not even a mangled spell remains. The villagers have a clear picture, nevertheless, of what they claim was the religion of their ancestors. This we can with advantage examine as a background for our study of contemporary beliefs and practices. Tricks of memory may have falsified some of the details, but for the immediate purpose the additions and omissions are of little importance: in reaching an understanding of the present what the past is supposed to have been is probably of greater concern than what it actually was.[1]

[1] It may be said at once that there is little doubt about the main outline, so closely does this follow the pattern for the rest of New Guinea. The beings which I shall refer to as the land spirits and the monster of the male cult are so general that pidgin English has terms for them, the 'masalai' and the 'tambaran' respectively.

The religion of the Bukawa', probably identical with that of the Busama, is discussed in the following: R. Neuhauss, *Deutsch Neu Guinea*, Bd. III, Berlin, 1911, pp. 307–485; S. Lehner, 'Geister und Seelenglaub eder Bukaua', *Mitteilungen aus dem Museum für Völkerkunde*, Hamburg, 1930; and S. Lehner, 'Balum Cult of Bukaua', *Oceania*, Vol. V. pp. 338–345.

Accounts of the religion of other New Guinea peoples will be found in M.

PAGAN RELIGION

First it will be observed that the religion served to validate the social organisations: the lineage, the club, and the sex groups, male and female, were each allotted a special place. Then the golden age, instead of being advanced into the future, was relegated to a time long gone by. Goodness consisted in following ancient customs as faithfully as possible, and it was thought that if everyone could be persuaded to do this the world would return to its former state of perfect order.

Faith in the efficacy of tradition will be appreciated when it is recalled that conditions can have changed only slightly if at all in the course of centuries. There is no evidence of any contact with the outside world much before 1900, and the natives must long before that time have come to terms, within the limits of their knowledge and experience, with the physical environment. Their houses are still the most suitable for the climate, there is nothing which we can teach them about hunting and fishing—they are not permitted to use firearms—and until new crops and artificial manures are introduced there will be little for them to learn about agriculture. In the circumstances there were no unfamiliar problems to solve, and harking back to precedents was practical wisdom.[1]

Mead, *Sex Temperament in three New Guinea Societies*, New York, 1933; M. Mead, 'The Marsalai Cult among the Arapesh', *Oceania*, Vol. IV, pp. 37–53; G. Bateson, *Naven*, Cambridge, 1936; H. I. Hogbin, 'Native Culture of Wogeo', *Oceania*, Vol. V, pp. 308–337; P. M. Kaberry, 'The Abelam Tribe', *Oceania*, Vol. XI, pp. 223–258, 345–367; and the various writings of F. E. Williams.

[1] It was probably no accident that the first people to place the golden age in the future, the Jews, occupied the natural corridor, between East and West. Changes occurred in this area with each passing generation, and too literal adherence to tradition would have been an illusion.

Anthropologists have recently been insisting that native societies in pre-European times were not as static as I have suggested. Professor Malinowski, for example, has criticised those who, when setting out to examine culture contact, presume what he calls a zero point, the moment when changes began with the arrival of the first Europeans. I cannot speak for Africa, where migrations are known to have taken place, but there seems to be no reason for adopting any other approach in the south-west Pacific (cf. the slight effect of casual Malay contacts on the peoples of northern Australia; W. L. Warner, 'Malay Influence on the Cultures of North-Eastern Arnhem Land', *Oceania*, Vol. II, pp. 476–495). *Vide* B. Malinowski, 'Anthropology of Changing African Cultures', *Methods of Study of Culture Contact*, Institute of African Languages and Cultures, Memorandum XV; and *Dynamics of Culture Change*, New Haven, 1945.

Sky Spirits

Several different kinds of supernatural beings were distinguished, and, although the natives used the words *ngalau* and *balum* indiscriminately, it will be convenient to give them separate names. I shall accordingly refer to the sky spirits, the spirits of the land, the spirits of the dead, the lonely female spirits, the spooks, and the monsters of the male cult.

The beings who dwelt in the sky were supposed to look like humans but to carry torches always. The two brightest lights, representing the sun and the moon, were borne by the headmen, and the common people were content with stars.

These spirits, particularly the sun and the moon, were looked upon as culture heroes or high gods, and to them were attributed all the characteristics of the various peoples around the Huon Gulf. They were believed to be responsible for everything—the annual rhythm of work resulting from the seasonal cycle, the distribution of resources, the technical skills, the languages, the social organisation, even the marriage rules.

A myth related that in the remote past mankind lived in chaos. Each person had his own private speech and dwelt alone, and there were no households, no villages, no groups speaking a common tongue. But by and by the sun and the moon sent some of their followers down as instructors in the proper way to behave. These men gave the people their languages, showed them how to build houses, told them about marriage, the family, and group life, and taught them how to cultivate the soil and catch fish. It was at this time, too, that the natural resources were allocated and trade began. One area received pottery clay, another stone for manufacturing implements, a third grasses for weaving baskets, and so forth. In the end the culture of the earth duplicated that of the sky.

The sun, the moon, and their followers, having completed their task, forgot all about their handiwork, or at least displayed no further interest in it. This is in line with the beliefs about culture heroes and high gods in other parts of the world. Their presence was felt only in the wet season—the rain was ascribed to the displeasure of the spirit men at the behaviour of the spirit women—and when the ground was shaken by earthquakes as a result of sky wars. The natives considered that a debt was owed, however, and as an acknowledgment always set aside baskets of food at ceremonial distributions. Such offerings, like the sacrifices made to the spirits who were more directly concerned with human welfare, were left for some hours in a special place in the club houses to allow the essence of the food to be consumed, after which the elders ate its corporeal substance.

Spirits of the Land

Every set of areas cultivated by a lineage somewhere included a spot which was unusual because of its gloom, chill atmosphere, or danger—a cave with a fern-covered entrance, a waterfall drenched with cold spray, a lonely pool where a stray crocodile might be lurking, or a slippery precipice. Each of these places was formerly considered to be the abode of a colony of beings to which I have given the name spirits of the land.

Normally invisible, land spirits occasionally took the form of an eel, snake, or lizard but were then easily recognisable by their bright and varied colouring. Their breath was of the same radiant hues and was to be seen from time to time in the sky, where it formed the rainbow. Tempests, thunderstorms, and heavy downpours were attributed to them, especially when out of season, and they were thought to have the power also to cause a variety of diseases and even madness. They particularly disliked women and were apt to inflict them with difficulties during labour, sometimes involving the death of the infant.

Dangerous as these spirits were believed to be, however, it was thought that the group dwelling at each sacred place had made a promise to the claimant of the surrounding area to leave him and his heirs unmolested. The members of the lineage accordingly felled the timber growing close by without anxiety, convinced that they would enjoy protection.[1] The only exception was when one of them had recently been indulging in sexual intercourse. The spirits hated women so intensely that a man who had the faintest smell of one lingering about him was offensive to them. Men who had been

[1] It was impossible at this late stage to discover the relation which existed between the spirits and a man who regularly cultivated the soil with his father instead of with his maternal uncles.

sleeping with their wives took the precaution of keeping at a distance, and young husbands always made their gardens as far away as possible.

Persons who had no claim to cultivation rights, on the other hand, imagined that any unauthorised approach to a sacred place would be fraught with danger. Not being members of the lineage, they were ignored in the contract and could expect no favours. Remnants of this fear linger to this day, especially among the women, who usually prefer when walking about in the bush to take the safer routes even if heavily laden. The village idiot, who lost his wits after a severe illness in about 1938, is presumed by many to owe his condition to having cut bamboo for a fishing rod from the vicinity of a haunted forest pool.

The proper course when a person suspected that the wrath of the spirits might have been aroused was to make a sacrifice. Sometimes he did this immediately, but in general he postponed the analysis of his past actions till the next time he was ill. If he remembered trespassing on land where there was an abode of hostile spirits, he caused a message to be sent to the owners. Begging pardon for the offence, he entrusted a small collection of valuables to them, perhaps a couple of boar's tusks or a short string of dogs' teeth, with a request that these might be offered to the spirits as a means of appeasing their anger. The leader of the group carried the valuable to the sacred place, where they remained hanging from a tree for a couple of days. By this time the spirits were thought to have taken their essence, and the outer form was returned. Forgiveness was now assured, and lack of improvement in the man's health was accepted as proof that other forces were at work and that a new course of action must be followed.

Gase', now an old man, told me that during his childhood he was once inflicted with acute inflammation of the throat. At first nobody took any notice of the complaint, but eventually, after he had lost his voice, his father enquired where he had been playing during the last few days. The boy thought for some minutes and then recalled that when passing through the neighbouring settlement of Gwado he had thrown a stone at a bird and missed. From where he was standing at the time, he said, there was some chance that the stone might have gone beyond the limits of the village into the pool at the base of the waterfall on the Bula River. This must be the explanation, the father decided, and within an hour he had arranged for one of the men from Gwado to hang some dogs' teeth on a bush alongside the waterfall. 'From that moment,' Gase' concluded, 'my throat started to improve.'

The sky dwellers were believed to be responsible for the bad weather which was always to be expected during the height of the trade-wind season, in July and August, but for prolonged storms at any other time the land spirits were blamed. If heavy seas day after day made fishing impossible therefore, or if flood rains threatened the crops, it often happened that an elder who was partial to sea food, or one whose gardens were in the greatest peril, or even one who wished to create a favourable impression amongst his fellows, would try the effect of a gift of pork on the beings who dwelt in the sacred place on his land. After the pig had been ceremonially carved a plateful was carried to them, but the villagers ate the rest of the meat. These occasional storms seldom lasted longer than a week, and there was little chance of the sacrifice failing to achieve its object.

Land spirits were also venerated as the source of much of the magic. To cement the agreement giving protection to particular ancestors, it was supposed that they handed over a number of their spells. These formed a valuable part of the man's fortune and were transmitted to his heirs along with his land rights.

As a mark of appreciation for the gift, the lineage adopted the name of one of the spirits as its battle cry and ceremonial greeting. There was no idea apparently that the call would bring supernatural aid in time of peril, but it was felt that the word had a peculiar appropriateness for rallying purposes. A man surrounded by the spears of his enemies was fortified by a reminder of the spirits of his land and of what they had done for his ancestors.

Spirits of the Dead

The relatives were summoned as soon as anyone became gravely ill, and it was unusual for them to be absent at the time of death. The great lamentation which went up informed the other villagers of what had happened, and from then till after the body was buried all work had to cease.

The members of the dead person's immediate family gashed themselves with knives in the agony of their grief and sometimes tore the
lobes of their ears, making the wearing of ornaments afterwards
impossible. Often, too they destroyed some of their property—perhaps by chopping down coconut palms or driving an axe through the
bottom of a canoe.

Meantime some of the women shaved the corpse, bathed it, and
arrayed it in new garments for the lying-in-state, which was arranged
to take place in one of the larger houses. The body rested in the
centre surrounded by the weeping family, but the remainder of the
floor space was cleared to make room for the rest of the community,
who now paid short visits to express respect and sympathy. All the
adults, youths, and girls attended, but the children were excluded
for fear that the chill of death might seize them. As a sign of grief
the visitors beat their breast and pounded their ears with coconut
shells till their cheeks and neck were lacerated and swollen.

The family continued to weep without rest during the whole of
the night, alternately embracing the corpse and flinging themselves
on the floor. For several hours, too, the villagers sang dirges. As
many as could be accommodated packed into the house, and the rest
seated themselves on the verandah or under the eaves.

Burial took place the following morning. The job of preparing
the grave, which was usually dug in front of the residence, fell to
the distant relatives, who so far had had no prominent part to play.
The hole was only about three feet deep, but the body was wrapped
up tightly in a thick covering of mats to prevent the smell of decom-
position becoming apparent in the village. A small basket of taro
was set at the side before the earth was replaced to furnish nourishment for the soul on the journey to its new home. A hut was then
built on top, and to this the members of the family retired to continue their mourning. Kinsmen gave them food, most of which had
to be eaten raw, and also fuel sufficient to keep a fire burning constantly in order that the body might be kept warm. Mourners were
forbidden to wash, and the men were also not allowed to shave.

At length, after an interval of from one to three months, depending on the dead person's status, a feast brought the period of
seclusion to a close. The heirs furnished the pigs and taro, squan-
dering much of what they would otherwise have inherited. Funeral
feasts were distinguished from all others by the fact that the

food was roasted on an open fire instead of being boiled or steamed.

The soul, which had so far been hovering around the village, was now thought to have taken its last farewell. The natives had no belief, however, in a single afterworld where all the departed were assembled: the doctrine was that each one went to dwell with the particular land spirits which had previously granted him their protection. The tie with these beings was thus presumed to last for ever —the persons whom they allowed to approach them in life took up residence with them after death. I was unable to discover for certain what happened to the souls of the women but gathered that if they were single they joined the land spirits of their parents and if married they went to those of the husband.

It follows that the lineage had reason to regard its sacred place as doubly hallowed. Here not only were its land spirits congregated but also the souls of its ancestors, the men who in times past had belonged to the group, tilled the same ground and carried out the same magical rites.

Yet although the two sets of spirits lived side by side, they were clearly differentiated. Their supernatural power was equally extensive but was exercised in a different way. Ancestral spirits never became incarnate as eels or reptiles, for instance, and, far from inconveniencing mortals with bad weather, they preferred to help them with large hauls of fish and increased herds of pigs.

As a return for their kindness, a basket of fish was presented to them every time a big catch was secured and a plate of pork whenever a pig not consecrated to another spirit was killed.

The ancestral spirits sometimes inflicted the living with disease, it is true, but here again there was a difference. They were concerned on such occasions with punishing not trespass, which left them unmoved, but such breaches of custom as neglect of kinship obligations and wilful setting aside of marriage rules; further, they ignored strangers and struck only at their descendants, the persons who were normally immune from the wrath of the land spirits. The whole group was considered to be at fault for allowing the offence to take place, and all had in consequence to pay the price. Responsibility was thus attributed to the ancestors only when two or three members of the lineage fell ill simultaneously. The sacrifice of a pig was considered to be sufficient to assuage the anger and secure a renewal of goodwill.

Lonely Female Spirits

Deaths of adults, unless they were killed in battle, were generally thought to be the result of sorcery, and the survivors not infrequently sought out the man alleged to be responsible and put him to death. The Busama infant-mortality rate, as in other parts of New Guinea, was, however, so high that such a doctrine might have had serious disruptive effects if it had been extended to young children. There was accordingly an alternative belief in childless spirits which were supposed to make a practice of kidnapping the souls of babies.

Continual precautions had to be taken. Thus when leaving her baby at the edge of the garden the mother always made a loud noise by banging two sticks together to frighten away any spirit which might have been hiding close by, and when sitting on the beach she was careful to see that no tiny footprint was left in the sand to attract unwelcome attention. She refrained from venturing on the sea, too, till the child was at least a year old. In the depths of the ocean one of the spirits was supposed to lurk in the form of a giant octopus whose long arms could clutch infants no matter how tenderly they might be nursed.

If the baby was fretful or irritable the mother thought that one of the female spirits was either frightening it by making faces or already attempting to take away its soul. She retired to the dwelling and had an older child periodically scatter hot ashes round about. At night, too, blazing fires were kept burning just outside the doors to prevent the spirit from going inside. If there was still no improvement the services of a magician were sought to recover the stolen soul. He took his spear to a rocky promontory and murmured a spell to conjure the spirit to appear. As soon as it was visible to him he flung the weapon, causing it to drop the soul in fright. He then made his way as speedily as possible to the village and returned the missing soul to its owner with the aid of incantations and magical herbs.

Spooks

Such beings were of little significance beyond serving as the explanation for the profound dread which the natives had for the dark. Spooks were not considered to have any power to harm humans but were supposed to take delight in frightening them. To this end they banged doors in empty houses, rustled the leaves on calm days, rolled stones down hillsides, and jumped from behind patches of shadow at night. Such manifestations, besides being alarming in themselves, were regarded as the forerunners of misfortune. If at the time someone in the village was seriously ill, it was taken for granted that he would probably die.

The Male Cult

The foundation of the cult was the belief that the sexes were in substance different. Men, it was claimed, were akin to the spirits and could at certain times acquire the same sanctity, a state indicated by the expression *dabung*, a close equivalent of the Polynesian *tapu*. Women, on the contrary, were outside the spirits' pale—they were essentially profane and could never attain sacredness. Contact between the two was accordingly held to be ritually dangerous and likely to lead to loss of virility. The cult had as object the overcoming of this disability and bringing about the restoration of ritual purity.

The most vital of the ceremonies was concerned with blood letting, the means adopted for removing the women's contaminating influence. The penis, as the organ which penetrated the female body, was the obvious choice for the cut.

Incising the penis, apart from the pain and inconvenience involved —the gash had to be of some depth—was not to be undertaken lightly. Maleness was now renewed to the full, and, as a result, the affinity with the spirits was at its height. Because of the supernatural forces present, a period of preparation was necessary beforehand and some days of seclusion afterwards. During these times all contact with women was prohibited, and the patient lived in the club house. Diet taboos were also imposed, and various restrictions had to be observed. Fluids were barred, for instance and thirst had to be quenched by sucking a piece of sugar cane. Further, if the food permitted could not be eaten raw—and this was considered to be preferable—it had to be roasted on an open fire: in no circumstances could it be prepared in the normal manner by steaming or boiling.[1]

[1] Women were on two occasions subject to the same diet taboos—when mourning and when set apart after first menstruating. The loss of a kinsman

The operation was supposed to be performed at more or less regular intervals, but many men, probably the majority, were apt to delay until jolted into remembrance of their growing impurity by an attack of illness. They then retired to take the preliminary precautions. These were considered to be complete after two days, and at dawn on the third the men went to a lonely spot on the beach armed with an obsidian knife. They allowed the blood to drip into the sea and afterwards bound up the wound with leaves.

Most important undertakings also involved a preparatory incision to ensure that defilement would not bring about disaster from weakness or any other cause. Warriors purified themselves before a raid, weavers before the manufacture of a seine, builders before the erection of a new club house, and gardeners before engaging in collective cultivation to furnish supplies for a feast.

Other ceremonies of the cult involved the impersonation of supernatural monsters. The women and children were told that these were like enormous crocodiles but were never allowed to approach. Instead, on hearing the monsters' 'voices', they had to run into hiding, reputedly on pain of death. The noise was in fact made by bullroarers.

The myth giving the origin of bullroarers relates that their special properties were discovered accidentally in a village near Mount Yambi, at the mouth of the Waria River, to the south. One of the women when chopping firewood struck off a chip which flew into the air with a whirring noise. Picking it up, she discovered that it had a slight twist, which she rightly concluded was responsible. She thereupon bored a hole through one end, attached a piece of string, and returned home twirling it round her head. The husband, interested, borrowed it to show his friends in the club, first warning her to make no mention as yet of what had happened. The men agreed that here was an object which could well be incorporated into their cult, from which hitherto they had had difficulty in keeping the members of the other sex. They would say that it was the voice of a spirit, they decided, which women were forbidden to look upon. The difficulty was that one woman had already seen it and would no

was supposed to have the effect of pulling them to the brink of the spirit world; and the ceremonial associated with first menstruation was obviously based on that carried out at the initiation of youths, to be discussed in the next section. But women were never regarded as *dabung*.

doubt laugh at them as humbugs. It was accordingly declared that she must be killed. The husband was at first reluctant, but at length gave his consent when promised a substitute. He sent a message to her to bring his supper, and as soon as she stepped on the ladder of the house the men despatched her with their spears. The body was buried in secret, and the rest of the women were told that she had been eaten by a fearsome spirit monster. From that time onwards the men alone possessed the bullroarers.

The story may perhaps give the impression that the hoaxing of the women was uppermost in the men's minds when carrying out their ritual. From my experience in other New Guinea communities where pagan rites are still performed I am convinced that, although this aspect of the matter cannot be ignored, it would be a mistake to pay too much attention to it.

Every club had two bullroarers, both named, a 'male' about thirty inches in length and a 'female' somewhat shorter, often only a foot. The surfaces of both were engraved with designs of mythological significance. They were preserved in a carved bowl on a special shelf and when removed for a ceremony were reverently painted with ochre and decorated with leaves and feathers.[1]

One of the chief occasions for the impersonation of the monsters was when a headman wished to put a taboo on certain kinds of food as a prelude to a feast. A rite to summon them from a lair underground was carried out some time beforehand, and from then till the date of the feast the consumption of coconuts or bananas and the killing of pigs were forbidden. They appeared, too, if a new club was to be erected or if a leading man of a neighbouring community was ill or had died, when it was said that they had come to mourn because his kinsmen had not taken better care of him.

The bullroarers themselves were also put to special uses. A headman wishing to communicate with another village usually entrusted one to the messenger as an indication that he was on official business.

[1] The leaves most commonly used in ceremonies, as elsewhere in Melanesia, were those of the *Cordyline* (wrongly identified as *Dracaena* in some of the older literature). I suspect that the main reason for the choice is the distinctive crimson colouring of so many of the varieties (Croton leaves, either red or yellow, are also of religious importance in many areas). It may be significant also that a loop of long *Cordyline* leaves is usually the most convenient means of transferring live coals from a neighbouring hearth when a new fire is to be kindled.

The holy object gave him immunity from attack, for to kill or wound him would have been sacrilege. When an alliance or a truce had been concluded between two settlements, too, several bullroarers were exchanged to cement the relationship. It was said that if treachery occurred afterwards, the guilty parties were likely to be the victims of supernatural vengeance.

Initiation

Youths were excluded from the cult until physically mature, when they were put through a series of tests first and formally initiated. So much food had to be provided for the accompanying feasts, however, that the appropriate ceremonies could seldom take place oftener than at intervals of ten years. The younger lads involved were therefore only about fifteen, whereas the eldest were more than twenty-four. The headmen gave the word as they had to supply most of the pigs and taro.

After certain preliminaries (see above pp. 135–136), the villagers selected two old men to undertake the arduous duties of guardians during the tests. Once these had been chosen a large building was erected in the bush to house the boys. This had to be fairly substantial as they remained there for some months. A meeting then decided which lads were ready. Each had to be sponsored by a man who had himself been initiated at the last ceremonies, so that he was at most only a decade older than his ward. The pair subsequently became bond friends and were at all times mutually considerate and helpful.

On the day fixed for the beginning of the ordeals the various sponsors sought out their wards. The youths had to climb on the men's backs, and the party left the village for the house in the bush in procession. Meantime the older men had lined up along the track, taking with them firebrands, sticks tipped with fragments of obsidian, and bundles of nettles. These they used to administer a sound thrashing as each boy passed by. The sponsors did not escape unscathed, and by the time the house was reached everyone was covered with blood.

The guardians received the initiands, at this stage known as *saga*, and told them that during the next few months they would be tried out to see whether they were fit to be fed to the monsters. If they proved worthy there would be no cause for fear, as they would pass through whole and be evacuated. But anyone who failed to measure up to the requirements would remain fast in the monster's belly and never be heard of again. The tests included further beatings, being kept awake for several days on end, and partial suffocation. Huge fires were lit inside the house and green boughs piled on top. The doors were then kept tightly closed till everyone was practically insensible.

During this period, which lasted for upwards of three months, the boys were only allowed to eat minute portions of the coarsest types of food either raw or roasted. All liquids were forbidden, though if they were thirsty permission was occasionally granted for them to chew a piece of sugar cane provided by the sponsors. The mothers and sisters handed over plates of delicious stews daily, but these were taken by the elders. There was also a ban on leaving the house at any time except just before dawn, when each youth had to bury his faeces in a deep hole. The guardians kept a watch to see that he did not wash himself afterwards.

At length the day arrived for the summoning of the monsters. Word had been sent out to the neighbouring villages, and a vast concourse of people was by this time in attendance. They remained until the last rite ended, causing severe strain on their hosts' resources.

The drama continued with the pretence that the monsters lived underground, and a hole was accordingly dug from which they could emerge. At first only a faint humming was heard, and the women murmured amongst themselves that the tree roots must be scraping the creatures' flanks. Soon afterwards a man covered with earth went along to the village to announce how deep the monsters had been but that they had at last appeared. The humming now became louder, till in the end the countryside rang with the booming of dozens of bullroarers.

The boys had to listen for a few days, and the guardians then brought them out and showed them with much impressive ritual, how the noise was made. A poisonous fish was later flourished in front of their mouths, and they were warned that if a word of what had been disclosed crossed their lips they would perish as assuredly as if they had swallowed a deadly toxin.

The revelation was followed by the incision rite. This time the boys were cut by one of the guardians, though on subsequent occasions each person operated on himself. A long low shed had been built to represent one of the monsters, and the man waited inside with his knife. The lads were taken in turn, each one being carried on the back of his sponsor, who also served as a support while the gash was made. The blood, as the first which they had shed, was especially sacred, and the sponsors gathered it in leaves for use later as face paint.

The men spoke of the wound as the mark of the monster's teeth while the boy was being swallowed. Informants stated that at times some of the candidates bled to death or died as a result of the cut becoming poisoned and that occasionally those who had offended the guardians by their weakness or disobedience were deliberately put to death. The bodies were buried in the bush and the mothers informed that the monsters had failed to evacuate their sons.

The hosts now made ready a great feast, supposedly for the entertainment of the monsters but in fact for the guests. The youths, however, were hurried back to the shelter, where they were subject to the same taboos as before. They remained shut up until the wounds were quite healed, generally a couple of months. Different men took turns swinging the bullroarers day and night, and it is claimed that the lads barely slept on account of the noise. At the same time, no further tests were held, and instead the guardians delivered long moral homilies. Respect must always be paid to the elders, they said, and it was necessary for everyone to bear in mind that he now had a binding obligation to help his various kinsfolk, those on the mother's side as well as those on the father's side. They made a great point also of the rule that sexual intercourse outside marriage was forbidden and urged the lads to avoid entanglements by concentrating on their work and refraining from sitting for long gossips in the houses of others.

Before the boys could emerge the monsters had to be sent back underground, a rite accompanied by another feast for which hundreds of pigs were slain. The villagers liked to boast that so much food was provided that a large quantity had become rotten before it could be eaten.

Now called *gwale*, the youths next day went to a stream and were given a ceremonial bath by their sponsors. Richly painted and decorated, they were then led one by one into the village, where the women welcomed them with tears of joy. A secular feast, which all could share, had in the meantime been prepared and a platform erected outside one of the ceremonial houses. On this the boys sat while their relatives danced and sang songs in their honour.

This concluded the celebrations, and the guests made their farewells and departed. One duty alone remained, a purely private matter for the boys' families. Most of them liked to show their appreciation of the sponsors by showering them with gifts.

Social Consequences of Initiation

The rites made a drama of the lads' change of status. Their childhood came to an abrupt close, and, after a period when they were under close observation, their manhood had an even more violent beginning. The obvious intention was to impress upon them that irresponsibility must now give way to the earnest fulfilment of obligations to the kinsfolk and to the community.

When giving me details of what used to take place the older men always dwelt longest on the belabouring of the boys during the ride on the sponsors' backs to the place of seclusion. The ostensible function was said to be the encouragement of growth by magical means, but they invariably added that the beating was of extra importance as a demonstration that authority rested in the hands of the senior generations. Whether or not the blows were administered with sadistic abandon it is now impossible to say, but everyone insisted that this was so.

Women's Ceremonies

Just as men reached the highest levels of sanctity when renewing their masculinity by incising the penis, so women gravitated towards the lowest depths of the profane when their femininity was at a maximum during childbirth and menstruation. Yet though at such times the two sexes travelled in opposite directions and ended up poles apart, they had one thing in common: both were wrenched out of the ordinary world of everyday. The women no less than the men were therefore subject to restrictions—they had to avoid all contact with males and were forbidden to eat certain foods. A club house into which they could retire was lacking, but the difficulty was overcome by preventing the menfolk from visiting the family dwelling.

As the time for the wife's delivery approached the husband pulled the floorboards aside and dug a hole underneath to receive the placenta and the blood. These preparations concluded, he withdrew to wait on the beach or at some other convenient spot. The woman was attended by certain of her female relatives, who brought firewood, water, and clean mats. Progress was announced from time to time, and as soon as the child was born they sent a message to the father telling him of its sex. He was not permitted to see it as yet, however, or to go near the house.

The mother remained in the house for about a week, devoting all her attention to the care of the infant. The only food permitted, in contrast with the raw or roasted vegetables eaten by men under a taboo, was hot soup, preferably made from the shoots of young sago palms, which her husband and brothers were expected to provide on each alternate day. At length, if she was considered to have regained her strength fully her kinswomen went out with their nets to catch a dish of freshwater fish. After she had eaten these her seclusion ended. She was allowed to come out of the house into the village, and the husband could now examine his offspring and nurse it for a few minutes.

The girl's entry into womanhood at her first menstruation was something of an event. The accompanying ceremonies were not unlike those carried out at the initiation of the boys. At the same time, they were not nearly so elaborate, and, as only one girl passed through at a time, there was no general disturbance of village life.

On the first appearance of the blood the girl was ordered to bed. As well as being chilled in fact, she was considered to be ritually cold. Re-heating was achieved by massage with warm oil in which charmed ginger roots had been steeped. The mother continued the rubbings for several days, during which the patient did not sit up.

This was the beginning of a period of seclusion lasting for six or seven months. The girl went outside only to answer the calls of nature, and at such times she wore a shroud of mats. If the father or brothers wished to remain in the dwelling she lived in a small compartment in one corner, but the men usually preferred to stay outside and eat and sleep in the club.

Unlike the youths, the girl was not called upon to undergo any ordeals, but she was forbidden to wash or drink water, and her diet was also confined to raw or roasted foods. Three or four companions attended to her wants.

When at last the father considered that he had enough supplies for a small feast, he announced to his relatives that the time for emergence had come. The next morning the companions took the girl to a stream for a ritual bathe. An old woman went with the party, and on the completion of the toilet it was her duty to give a certain amount of elementary instruction in sex. Using a gourd or a green banana, she told of the male organs of generation and showed the girl how the penis would be inserted in her vagina. The demonstration always ruptured the hymen.

A member of the train carried the girl back to the village. Many persons, men as well as women, stood in readiness, and as the two appeared they were beaten lightly with the stalks of ginger plants. They were afterwards expected to become bond friends.[1]

The feast took place on the following day. The girl, known now as an *aku'wi*, was painted and decorated with all the family ornaments for the occasion. The food was displayed in front of the house with a mat on the ground before it. To this she was led by her brothers, who protected her from observation with a screen of mats until she was seated and arranged to the best advantage.

When menstruating later, women were not confined so strictly to the house, though they rarely came outside. The beach was barred for fear that fish might afterwards smell the contamination on the canoes drawn up above high-water mark and keep their distance. Gardening and the preparation of family meals were also forbidden, and, to tide the husband and children over, the neighbours sent provisions. The women cooked for themselves but limited their meals to hot broth.

---

[1] Male bond friends called one another *nengga'*, the kinship term used by men married to two sisters. The girl and her attendants also addressed each other as *nengga'*; but she called her bond friend *ise'*, the reciprocal of which is *sangung*. *Ise'* and *sangung* are not kinship terms.

Sorcery

Three types of black magic were recognised—*mwi'sinang*, resulting in illness only; *katon*, leading to the annihilation of entire populations; and *bula*, bringing about the death of particular individuals.

Mwi'sinang.

Each minor ailment with which the people were commonly afflicted had one or more systems of magic associated with it. Thus there were systems to cause tropical ulcers and cure them afterwards; systems to cause and cure diarrhoea; systems to cause and cure conjunctivitis; and so on. Nearly everyone in the community has a knowledge of at least one system, a fact which he did not as a rule attempt to conceal. The details of the rites, however, especially the spells which had to be chanted, were carefully guarded from all but the legal heirs, who learnt them as part of their heritage.

The chief use of such magic was to prevent theft from palm groves and orchards. The trees were often planted at a considerable distance from the village where no watch could be kept, and to protect them the owners carried out the first of their rites. They then hung a warning sign on a bush close by or twisted it around one of the trunks to inform the potential thief that from thenceforth he meddled at his own risk. If he was undeterred and stole any of the nuts or fruit, it was thought that he would certainly be taken ill.

Spells to cause disease were also used as a means of taking vengeance when an offence was committed by a fellow villager—failure to pay a debt perhaps, destruction of property, or borrowing tools without first asking permission. The members of the community were linked together by such a never-ending chain of reciprocal obligations that an open breach would usually have been inexpedient, and persons who considered themselves to have been injured preferred to punish the offender in secret through their magic. The necessary rites were carried out in the depths of the forest over a leaf or some other convenient substance, which was then buried in his garden or thrown on his bed. He himself was unaware of what had occurred, but the magician was satisfied because convinced that sickness would follow.

It is possible that persons with a guilty conscience may occasionally have imagined themselves into illness. But New Guinea is not a healthy country, and as few drugs are obtainable the average villager today spends at least a fortnight or three weeks confined to his bed every year. Subsequent events must accordingly have confirmed the magicians in their belief—sooner or later the culprit always suffered. The disease with which he was afflicted was sometimes different from the one intended, but this was not regarded as of much consequence. The magic had worked itself out in a new way, or another person who had been wronged had used more powerful spells.

The fact that rites could be performed by stealth meant that the villagers sometimes resorted to them also for the satisfaction of private grudges. The victim, that is to say, was innocent of offence and ought not to have been expected to pay any penalty. His ignorance was on such occasions his protection. Being unconscious of the enmity which his conduct had aroused, he had no suspicion that magical forces might have been directed against him.

The normal treatment for minor illnesses was to have the remedial rites performed. Persons who were aware of having trespassed on a sacred area or who felt that an incision of the penis might be due had recourse first to the appropriate religious ceremony, but in ordinary circumstances no further action was taken than to request the assistance of a man with a knowledge of the correct magic. Any one of them served the purpose, and it was not regarded as necessary to locate the person actually responsible for the onset of the complaint. Natural resistance was generally in itself sufficient to ensure recovery, and once again the current belief received apparent corroboration.

Katon.

This was the most lethal sorcery of all and was thought to be capable of wiping out everyone in a village. It was only employed with the consent of all the elders, and then solely against a neighbouring settlement which had given serious offence.

Each village in the locality had one or two *katon* sorcerers, men who had inherited the spells from a brother of their mother. So deadly was this form of magic that during their apprenticeship they were compelled to withdraw from the rest of society to a cave in the forest, where they lived for upwards of a year on a diet of uncooked food.

The essential ingredient of *katon* sorcery, apart from the spells, was a length of a species of creeper which when left in the sun gradually disintegrates into powder. If the elders agreed that the sorcery was to be carried out the magician collected his creeper and that night journeyed to the outskirts of the offending settlement. Having lit a fire, he murmured incantations over the stalks and cut them into short lengths. These he held over the flames one by one till they were ignited, when he hurled them in the direction of the houses. If by chance a night bird cried while the ceremony was in progress, he was doubly certain that the mission would be crowned with success.

It is said that within a couple of days one of the women began to sicken, to be followed later by everyone whom she had touched, then by everyone with whom they had been in contact, till in the end not a single healthy person remained. If steps were not taken to have the magic undone, death carried them all off within a few weeks. Anxious to prevent such a catastrophe, the offenders sent compensation for their misdeed to the group which they had injured, with a message also to the headmen to have mercy. The latter called a meeting to decide whether the gifts were acceptable, and if it was agreed that this was so the sorcerer was ordered to undo his work. He bespelled a length of sugar cane and chopped it into four pieces, one for himself and one each for a man, a woman, and a child from amongst the wrongdoers.

Bula.

This is the familiar sorcery of food remains, common throughout the primitive world. The magician collected a few crumbs which had fallen to the ground while his victim was eating a meal and later, in the privacy of his house or the forest; recited spells over them. The man began to feel pains soon after, but it was believed that death could not take place till the food had been burned. The only hope of a cure was to find the sorcerer and persuade him to neutralise the magic by putting the crumbs into cold water.

The headmen and one or two other persons of importance were supposed to have *bula* spells. The net specialists and the stone-working specialists alone were excluded—black magic would have been incompatible with the white magic which they were called upon to perform. If a man wished to become a sorcerer and had not inherited the necessary knowledge he could buy it for a large fee from someone more fortunately placed who was willing to sell.

PAGAN RELIGION

As with *katon*, the main purpose of *bula* was to score off the inhabitants of other places. To aim it at a fellow villager would normally have been the height of folly—the sorcerer would have been depriving himself of a helper and the group of a warrior. It was one of the duties of the headmen, however, to rid the community of trouble makers and habitual criminals; and leaders were occasionally suspected also of bewitching possible rivals who were beginning to be as wealthy as themselves.

People fell back on the *bula* explanation for illness only after simple home treatment by sacrifices, the incision of the penis, and remedial magic had failed to effect any improvement. The patient then began to cast about in his mind to discover whether anyone in a neighbouring community might have a grievance against him. If he came to the conclusion that this was so, he persuaded one of his kinsmen who was friendly with the man in question to make a few discreet enquiries. Confirmation of the suspicion was followed by a plea that the crumbs might now be placed in cold water, a request which was seldom, if ever, refused. The questioner was often met with a blank denial, nevertheless, and a further search had then to be made. In cases where this was still unsuccessful, and the patient began to recover, it was taken for granted that the sorcerer must have relented of his own accord. If, on the other hand, death took place, the only possible conclusion for the relatives was that the food had been burned.

Here then was a theory which could be put forward on practically every occasion when anyone save a young child had died. (For infants another reason was given; as has been mentioned, they were thought to have attracted the attention of lonely spirits. There is some probability, too, that *katon*, was held responsible for serious epidemics.) The villagers even supposed that *bula* was at work when a man died as the result of some misadventure, such as a fall from a tree, the bite of a snake, the wreck of a canoe, or goring by a wild boar. Had he not been bewitched his hand would have kept a firm hold, the snake would have wriggled away, the canoe would have outsailed the storm, and the boar would have been less fierce.

It is important to note that there was never at any time a suggestion that the dead man might himself be to blame either for ignoring the sacrifice due to an offended land spirit or for delaying the incision of his penis. These remedies were within the same easy reach as the drugs in our home medicine cabinets and were tried out, like them, during the early stages of the illness while there was still hope of a speedy recovery.

One may presume that *bula* magic was actually performed, but there is considerable doubt about whether it was as common as was generally believed. For the native, however, death was in itself proof that the rites had been carried out—had they not been, the person would have been still alive. The kinsmen were accordingly filled with rage against the sorcerer believed to have been responsible: they desired to make him pay in full for what was, to their way of thinking, unjustifiable homicide.

The first requirement was the man's identification, a job for which a diviner had to be called in. He had several methods at his disposal, each involving the conjuring of the spirit of the dead into some object. A series of questions was then put to it, phrased in such a way that the answer was a simple 'yes' or 'no'—'Did the man who killed you come from the west?' 'Does he live in Gwado?' and so on. The commonest object was probably a stunned eel, and a convulsion at the appropriate moment was accepted as an affirmative. A trochus shell was also used. It was poised on the base of an upturned pot of conical shape, where it stayed in position for 'yes' and fell off for 'no'. Again, some men employed a length of bamboo containing one of the dead person's ornaments: this remained still for 'no' but rolled about their hand to indicate 'yes'. It seems that gossip had usually fixed on the name beforehand, and that all the diviner did was to give confirmation, an easy task when every method was so susceptible to manipulation.

The elders decided what was to be done. They sometimes organised a raid to put the alleged sorcerer to death immediately, but more usually, for fear of causing a war, they asked the headmen to arrange for him to be bewitched in his turn.

Magic and Specialisation

Many different methods of fishing were practised, but seining was the most popular and probably on a yearly average supplied half the total catch. Each net was technically the property of a single individual, though, as I have explained in an earlier chapter, there was no possibility of his rounding up a shoal without a team of helpers to man the canoes and pull on the ropes. The significant fact was that ownership, and in consequence leadership, were based on a knowledge of the magic carried out while the netting was being manufactured—the man who performed the rites automatically took the finished seine, and persons who were ignorant, no matter how wealthy they might be, could never hope to do so. The spells were inherited in the normal way and before death were always taught to one of the sisters' sons, who thereby became in due course the owner-leader. I have observed that in other communities the abandonment of magic as a result of Mission influence has led to disappearance of seines even before the weaving skills were forgotten. The Busama can no longer make nets but are lucky in that a few natives have enough money to purchase them.

The owner of the seine had to organise and direct its repair and renewal as one of his main duties. He carried out regular inspections and gave the word for holes to be mended, for sections to be replaced, and, if required, for a whole new set to be woven. It was his job also to decide when it was to be taken out, which areas were to be fished, how the members of the team were to arrange themselves, and what proportion of the haul each was to receive. Of necessity he became thoroughly acquainted with the winds and the tides and the feeding habits of the different kinds of fish and an expert at predicting changes of weather.

The value of a director for an undertaking of this sort requiring communal effort cannot be over-emphasised. The chances of damage through neglect or carelessness were reduced by the equipment being made the responsibility of one man—his property was at stake. The background of skill and knowledge was also an advantage, and the fact that the right to give orders was recognised meant that everyone was kept informed of exactly what he had to do.

Membership of the team depended partly on kinship with the owner, partly on descent from persons who had belonged to the group in the past. The team not only fished with the seine but was under the obligation of providing either labour when a new one was made or supplies for the feast with which its completion was celebrated.

The making of a new net was a highly ceremonial business, for, apart from the specialist ritual of the owner, the workers, about thirty in all, were under strict taboos from the time when the materials were first gathered till the final feast. They lived apart in a special house on the beach eating only roasted vegetables and drinking no water, and, after the task was completed, they had to incise their penis.

Warfare was another enterprise in which leadership was bound up with the hereditary possession of special magical knowledge. There were half a dozen war generals in the village, each of whom had inherited a spirit familiar from his ancestors. This being was represented by a carved stone figure about a foot high over which spells were recited when an expedition was contemplated. The incantations translated the spirit to the enemy settlement, where it clubbed all the menfolk, making them 'heavy with sleep like blocks of stone' so that they could be taken by surprise. The only risk was that if a watch had been set the heavy tread of the spirit gave warning of its intentions.

The choice of a general for a particular campaign rested with the assembly of elders. They took various factors into consideration, such as knowledge of the geographical features in the vicinity of the enemy village—what sort of cover was available and where hazards and defences might have been placed—familiarity with the habits of the people, natural sagacity, and proven ability to inspire followers. Once the man was named he had complete authority and was implicitly obeyed.

On the evening before the day fixed for the attack the general had the duty of divining the probable result and, if success was assured, of endowing the weapons of his band with the magical ability to find the target. He filled a pot with a mixture of water, a small piece of excrement, bespelled ginger, and other herbs, and round it fixed the spears. The warriors lined up in the background while he lit the fire and kept watch on the liquid. If it boiled first on the side where the warriors stood success was a foregone conclusion, and he dipped the spears in one by one. But if instead the bubbles appeared on the other side the party returned home. The ceremony was then repeated on the next day, and, if necessary, on the day after. Not until defeat had been prophesied three times was the project abandoned.

The general was also skilled in reading omens, and as the band proceeded by stealth through the jungle he had to watch for the signs given by certain birds and reptiles.

Other leaders whose position depended on magic were the men

in charge of the overseas trading voyages and of the quarrying of stone to be ground into adzes.

The explanation for the absence of a special gardening magician to discharge the functions of agricultural leader is that the staple crop can be grown throughout the year. Gardening magicians are to be found only in places like the Trobriands, where there is an annual rhythm of agricultural work, with a regular season for planting and another for harvesting. Most of the Busama possessed individual systems of gardening magic, however, with spells to make the plants grow, spells to repel the wild pigs, and spells to keep insect pests and plant diseases in abeyance.

Village Magic

The systems of magic which were individually owned, apart from those concerned with gardening and health, related to fishing with line and hook, to hunting, and to beauty. Love magic may appear to be a striking omission, but its absence will be readily understood in the light of the Puritanical sexual code and the privilege claimed by the elders to arrange all the marriages.

Mention must also be made of a number of magical taboos, especially those associated with the care of young children, so many of whom died during their first couple of years. No one was permitted to kindle a fire or light a cigarette with embers taken from a house in which there was a baby, for example, for fear that it might contract a fever. The excrement of infants had to be burned, too, lest by being trodden about it should cause a rash to appear. Finally, the parents had to avoid eating certain kinds of fish—those with large scales which might result in skin diseases, those with prominent eyes lest the child should develop a cast, and so on. Similar taboos related to gardening, fishing, and hunting—the men refrained from going out in a canoe for a few days after eating pork, and if hoping to spear a pig they always pretended that a rat was the quarry.

Religion and Daily Life

I drew attention earlier to the link between the social organisation and the religion. The men who owned and worked the same areas

229

of land were united by a common bond with certain ancestral and
other spirits, and those who joined together for some of the bigger
enterprises belonged to a single club and had a similar ritual relationship with the mythical monsters. Co-operation for daily tasks was
thus not merely a social matter: behind lay the full force of the supernatural. The various leaders played a dual rôle, too, taking charge
of both secular and spiritual matters. The headmen, as well as presiding over the village assembly, acted as chief sorcerers and had
the final say in calling up the monsters from the underworld for
initiation and other ceremonies; and the director of the seining team
and the war general were alike expert magicians. Even the differenti-
ation of male and female was given religious backing, for the one
was held to be sacred and other other profane.

The curious attitude to sex calls for further comment. The basis
for it, I believe, was the women's social status. They were so prominent in community life that the men fell back on a cult as a means of
self assertion.

A comparison with Wogeo Island, where there is a similar
culture except that the women are of still greater importance, is
in this connection instructive. The theory here is that contact is
equally perilous for both, and the women in consequence have a
separate cult to themselves founded on menstruation, the natural
function which, they say, obviates the need for a cleansing operation.
The incision of the penis is regarded as an imitation of their monthly
periods and is commonly spoken of by the same term. The men
ignore most of the ceremonies of this rival cult with great ostentation but, in the end exasperated, bring the biggest of them to a
close by falling upon those taking part and driving them home with
sticks and stones. The leading women retaliate, though only when
by themselves, by saying that they know all about the initiation
monsters but have no objection to their husbands deluding themselves with the belief that they have a close secret.

The myth relating how everything originated with the sky
dwellers served as a means of elevating and consecrating the accepted
standards of behaviour. The ideals of conduct, it was insisted, had
been ordained not by men such as we are but by superhuman
creatures who were above and beyond criticism. Custom, that is to
say, acquired a mystical value which made the slightest murmur of
complaint an act of blasphemy. The man who followed established

traditions must have felt that he was playing his allotted part in the divine purpose of the universe.

Some of the customs had features which are to our way of thinking barbarous, but in those concerned with the relations of fellow villagers the keynote was always loyalty. Persons who lived only a few miles away may have been treated as enemies and killed for sorcery or for no reason at all as opportunity offered, but near neighbours were trusted kinsmen and friends to be supported if necessary at the cost of ease and convenience. Within certain narrow limits, then, it may be asserted that the sky spirits gave a charter which we would ourselves accept as moral.

Additional moral sanctions were provided by some of the other beliefs. Property rights were preserved, for instance, by the doctrine that the land spirits were concerned to punish trespass and by the faith in black magic as a means of bringing thieves to book. Again, the ancestral spirits were supposed to harry their descendants when marriage rules had been disregarded or kinship obligations remained unfulfilled. On the other hand, there was no invocation of supernatural penalties against either the murder of a relative or adultery. Perhaps these offences were adequately condemned by being treated as evil customs forbidden by the sky spirits; although adulterers, in any case, had little chance of escaping the avenging spears of the wronged husband and his kinsfolk.

Much has already been written about the general effect of magical and religious rites, and it will suffice to say here that in Busama as elsewhere these gave the natives confidence that, in spite of all the unforeseen difficulties against which no practical measures could be taken, their desires would in the end be achieved. The recitation of spells and the elimination of what were supposed to be contaminating influences by means of an incision assured the success of many of the enterprises, sacrifices to the land spirits brought about the return of good weather, offerings to the ancestors secured fine hauls of fish and abundance of pigs, and more magic guaranteed recovery from illness. Further, if the unexpected happened and the patient perished, the survivors were able to take comfort from the funeral ceremonies, which not only allowed due outlet for their grief but also reaffirmed their hopes for immortality by insisting that death was but the beginning of a new life on another plane.

Chapter Twelve

CHRISTIANITY

'The ledger of the Almighty is strictly kept, and every one of us has the balance of his operations paid over to him at the end of every minute of his existence.'—THOMAS HENRY HUXLEY, in a letter to Charles Kingsley, September 23, 1860.

I T is a commonplace that the religious beliefs of the West have been modified as the social environment has changed. The casual reader is familiar with our varying interpretations of the ideals of Christ through successive centuries, and Saint Simeon Stylites seeking grace on a pillar would be as out of place in this decade as Aimee Semple McPherson in the year of our Lord 400. Striking differences exist even in the contemporary scene amongst followers of the same creed: the narrow Catholicism of Ireland is in marked contrast with the indulgent polytheistic Catholicism of the two Sicilies.

Fifty years of civilised influences have so altered the way of life in New Guinea that the pagan religions could scarcely have survived intact even if direct efforts to undermine them had been avoided. The Missions, however, have been attempting to turn the people into members of one or other of the European sects, Lutheran, Catholic, Anglican, Methodist, and so on. Yet, because local conditions are unlike our own, the results have been only partially successful. Busama Christianity is one of the many compromises between what has been inherited from the past and what is taught today.

Outstanding losses include the male cult. Men and women never

CHRISTIANITY

sit together, but there is no ceremony from which women are excluded even when menstruating. The linkage with the social organisation has also disappeared. The differences between the lineages and between the clubs are not reflected in the new rituals, and everyone now attends the same services in honour of one God and His son.

The presence of several Missions in the same area has sometimes aggravated old rivalries. This in Guadalcanal I found that the three opposed parties in Longgu village—population 170—were members respectively of the Anglican, Baptist, and Roman Catholic Communions. But New Guinea is divided into Mission zones, in each of which, with minor exceptions only a single society operates.[1] The clash between Busama-Lutu and Busama-Awasa thus cannot be emphasised by the religious observances.

Busama has also avoided the struggles, common in other parts of the country, between Church and secular leaders for control of village affairs. The Mission representatives have here refrained from interference, and Bumbu was the only luluai to set himself against organised Christianity. Again, no conflict has yet taken place over the authority of European and native Mission leaders. Such quarrels seem to be a feature only of communities where the work of conversion has been in progress over a long period, as, for example Tonga.[2]

I shall give the history of the Busama Mission and the formal background of belief and practice, but much of the chapter will be devoted to a consideration of morals. The present code, ostensibly new, approximates closely to that of pagan days; so the notion of conscience, for instance, is based directly on ideas about *maya*

[1] Rivo Island, near Madang, is one of the exceptions. 'Of the 300 natives, 150 were converted to Lutheranism and the rest to Catholicism, with the result that the two groups barely speak to each other. They have even gone so far as to construct a fence in the middle of the tiny island, and each group has given the other to understand that it wishes no visiting to take place on either side of the fence.' (A. L. Gitlow, *Economics of the Mt. Hagen Tribes*, New York, 1947, p. 11).
Rivo seems to prove the truth of Voltaire's contention, quoted earlier in another context (p. 163), that if there were two religions they would be at one another's throats.
[2] B. Thomson, *Diversions of a Prime Minister*, Edinburgh, 1894. Cf. also B. G. M. Sundkler, *Bantu Prophets in South Africa*, London, 1948.

233

(p. 131), shame at being found out in an unworthy act, and the views on confession are similar to the doctrines concerned with the incision of the penis.

The Lutheran Mission

Simultaneously with the German annexation of north-eastern New Guinea in 1884 the Lutherans established a station at Finschhafen on the tip of the Huon Peninsula. The field of endeavour at first included two Administrative Districts, Morobe and Madang, but the latter was handed over to the United States branch of the parent Church in 1920, when Australia received its mandate for the Territory of New Guinea from the League of Nations. The original organisation continued to function in Morobe till the Japanese invasion in 1942. Several of the missionaries escaped by being sent to Australia, but nearly all who remained were killed. After the war arrangements were made for the District to be in the care of the Americans from Madang.[1]

Even after 1920 many of the missionaries spoke no English, and in intercourse with administrative officers and other residents they had to employ pidgin. Direct financial support was received from Germany, too, right up to 1939, though these funds were supplemented by profits from trade stores and plantations.[2]

The stage was well set for the Mission to become unpopular with all clases of Europeans. The commercial community feared it as a rival, and officials distrusted its political influence. There was added

[1] Three Catholic societies were at work in other parts of the Territory prior to 1942, the Holy Ghost Mission, the Divine World Mission, and the Marist Mission, all largely staffed by German nationals. To these a fourth has now been added, the Australian branch of the Franciscan Order. The other Australian Missions were the Methodists in northern New Britain and New Ireland, the Anglicans in southern New Britain, and the Seventh Day Adventists at various points on the mainland. The last two were comparatively late arrivals. Other Protestant denominations have opened stations in the highlands of the mainland during the last two years.

[2] Unlike some of the Catholic societies, which used the earnings from plantations for other fields, the German Lutherans kept all their money in the country.

The Americans, realising the dangers of a vested interest in cheap native labour, have determined to make a change and perhaps use the plantations for educational purposes. The seriousness of the risk has been referred to above (p. 199).

concern, too, because there was no other body at work to counteract possible un-Australian doctrines—all the natives in Morobe who wished to be Christian had to become Lutherans and be instructed by Germans. Many of the staff were proved to have been members of the Nazi Party and were interned in 1939, but it appears that the suspicions harboured against others were without foundation. I did not find any trace of anti-British propaganda in Busama.

The bond between the natives and their missionaries was particularly close. The fact that these men went to the trouble of learning a vernacular counted for much but of greater importance apparently was their lack of racial prejudice. Anthropologists are also without feelings regarding colour—they could scarcely do their work efficiently otherwise—and it is significant that after my attachment to the Army Native Administration unit had come to an end with my discharge from the Forces I received several requests by letter to return to Busama not as a member of the Government but of the Lutheran Mission. 'We do not think you are a white man from Australia,' one of these ran. 'You are a black man from New Guinea. So come home and be our missionary. Never mind about the Bible.' (I had not at this period been invited by the Administration to revisit New Guinea, and there seemed to be small prospect of my seeing my native friends again.)

The Mission in Busama

The earliest efforts of the Mission were concentrated on the villages near Finschhafen, and no move towards the western side of the Huon Gulf took place for twenty years. A block of ground was then purchased at Mala'lo, and shortly afterwards a permanent station was set up to cover the strip of coast from the Markham to Siboma, half-way to the Papuan border, together with the hill country comprising the lands occupied by the Kaidemoe, Kai, and Kaiwa.

Progress at Busama was especially rapid, and by 1920 all save four of the old men had been baptised. Most of the villagers of today have therefore been Christians for a lifetime. Polygamy, one of the classic problems for early missionaries, had been abandoned long since, and no one would now contemplate setting up an establishment with a second spouse. Divorce presented no difficulties as it was in the past never practised.

CHRISTIANITY

The actual work of conversion in the different villages was entrusted to 'black missionaries', as they are called (*yaengwaga*), selected natives of outstanding personality who had already been taught the Christian doctrines. A 'black missionary,' generally a man from the Bukawa' area, was detailed to each settlement, and he or a successor remained in residence till it was agreed that the inhabitants were able to stand on their own feet. A small committee of elders, referred to as the *giyobwaga*, was then elected to take over the running of local church affairs. The Busama congregation received their independence during World War I and from that date were permitted to send 'black missionaries' from amongst themselves to work in the hinterland.

With the 'black missionaries' came teachers to set up village schools. These continued to be drawn from Bukawa' till the Japanese invasion, when education had to abandoned. The Mission believed, rightly as events proved after the reopening of the schools in 1945, that natives without local ties would have greater authority with both parents and children. (Foreign teachers were re-introduced in January 1947.)

Neither 'black missionaries' nor teachers received a salary, but each Christmas all converts were called upon to make an offering according to their means, and the sum collected was then divided. Every worker as a rule received three or four pounds. In addition, teachers were allowed to use the pupils for work in the gardens on specific days, and from time to time the parents collaborated to clear areas for them to plant.

A tribute must be paid to the Lutheran education system, which was unquestionably superior to that provided by the majority of Missions in the south-west Pacific. I have stated that everyone is able to read and write in Yabim and work out simple sums in arithmetic. Elementary hygiene and geography are also taught in most village schools, and many natives, as well as owning vernacular New Testaments, hymn and prayer books, have two or three publications to read in leisure moments. One deals with anatomy, another with geography, and there are several collections of folk-tales and descriptions of pagan ceremonies.[1] The main criticism

[1] The contrast in the approach to geography between Busama and Segoya, a Seventh Day Adventist village which I visited in 1944, was striking. In Busama every child can draw a reasonably accurate sketch of New Guinea, but in the

which I would make is that the need in the higher grades for instruction in a European language was not appreciated. The absence of English training was, of course, inevitable when the missionaries themselves could not speak it.[1]

The devotion of the teachers is also commendable. They reopened the schools in 1945 without European supervision and carried on against enormous difficulties. Practically all the furniture and materials had been destroyed, and in several villages instruction in writing had to be given with pointed sticks in the sand.

Four years were spent in the village school, with classes every morning. Only one course was given at a time, and if a child was just too young to enter at the beginning he had to wait the full period before being accepted. This scheme had the immense advantage of enabling the teacher to concentrate his energies.

From the village school the best male students—no higher education was provided for girls—went to the boarding establishment at Mala'lo. Here the instruction, which was of higher grade, was under the care of the white missionary. The Mission garden, cultivated by the boys themselves, furnished food for weekdays, but on Saturdays and Sundays the pupils went home to their parents.

Two years at Finschhafen followed for the most brilliant. In this school technical training was given, and one Busama graduate developed such skill that he was able to superintend the erection of an aeroplane hangar at Salamaua from a blueprint.

Those who intended to become teachers spent two more years at the senior college at Hopoi, near Bukawa', where the instruction had a more specifically religious basis.

Every village had its school buildings and a church for the celebration of daily prayers morning and evening. Services were usually conducted by one of the elders, the *giyobwaga*, but occasionally these gave way for the teacher or anyone else who expressed the wish to be responsible. On Sundays, however, all who lived within walking

Segoya school not a single pupil could name more than two local towns. Yet the Segoya were familiar with maps, for a chart of the Holy Land was hanging on the wall. Again, in Segoya the children could add and subtract only with numbers, not with objects; but they knew the names of the Books in the Bible and could recite them in order.

[1] The American Lutherans established a high school at Lae in 1947 where English is now taught. My friend Ida' from Busama has been transferred to the staff as head master.

distance assembled for worship at Mala'lo. The sermon was in earlier years delivered by the European missionary, but latterly a number of the more spiritually minded of the natives were ordained as pastors, and it then became customary for one or other of these to share the duty. On the departure of the missionary at the end of 1941 a couple of these pastors took charge of the station. The services continued till the bombing of the area by Allied planes in 1943.

Each settlement aimed to have its church built of corrugated iron on a framework of sawn timber. Prestige supplied the motive, and it was a matter for boasting if the structure had cost several hundred pounds. That the architecture was both ugly and unsuitable for the climate was a matter of no importance. Altar furniture, including crucifixes, images of angels, and candlesticks, were fashioned by native workmen but were for the most part as repulsive as the erections which housed them. Forsaking traditional forms, the carvers adopted the naturalistic style developed towards the end of the nineteenth century in Europe, and it seems a pity that so many of the figures survived the ravages of war.

The degradation of native art has unfortunately occurred everywhere in the Pacific but is the more to be regretted here because the work of the people was in pagan days unique. Despite modern 'improvements' the thatched dwellings still retain much of their beauty; moreover, they are so perfectly adapted to the tropics that it is difficult to understand how anyone, native or European, could prefer an iron shed. The old style of sculpture, however, has been practically abandoned, surviving now, apart from museums, only in a few carvings made for sale to tourists (Plate 16a).[1]

Contrary to the general belief, the Lutheran missionaries were not responsible for the suppression of the old arts: several, in fact, condemned the use of corrugated iron. But to achieve a continuance of the tradition positive encouragement would have been necessary. It is not too late for a renaissance, and the authorities of the new Mission might invite some of the aged men who still retain their skill to teach the young people in the schools.

[1] Vide R. Firth, Art and Life in New Guinea, London, 1936; R. Linton, P. S. Wingert, and R. D'Harnoncourt, Arts of the South Seas, New York, 1946; and F. D. McCarthy, 'Designers of the Huon Gulf', Australian Museum Magazine, Vol. IX, No. 11, pp. 359–364.

CHRISTIANITY

As an example of what can be done the Kwato Mission, near Samarai in Papua, may be cited. A scheme has recently been introduced here to preserve the old art for adaptation to new uses. Thus the patterns formerly carved on paddles and drums now serve as linocuts for blocking fabrics. The church at the main station of this Mission is one of the finest I have seen. The end walls are of rough-hewn stone—into which several of the masons have cut their private marks—but the rafters rest in native. fashion on pillars along the sides, and the shingle roof has a saddleback and forepeak like the local dwellings.[1]

The Basis of Christianity

The Bible is regarded as the fundamental document: everyone reads it, everyone quotes it, and I was constantly referred back to it. Much of it is dismissed as padding, however, much is of little interest, and some is incomprehensible. I found myself under the necessity of enquiring therefore which are the most important sections, the parts believed to contain the essential elements of the faith. The best answer to this question was contained in the summary which Ida', then head teacher of the Busama school, gave to his pupils when the classes were re-assembled.

The most noteworthy feature of the account is the way in which Israel is translated to the New Guinea setting. This is not wanton distortion but the inevitable reaction of a people who know little of any social order but their own. It must be remembered, too, that the early Hebrews were comparatively primitive and thus had more in common with the natives than with ourselves. The picture painted by Ida' may even be in the material sense close to the truth. Pontius Pilate looks slightly curious in the guise of a District Officer, however, and Roman soldiers masquerading as police boys are still more surprising. God Himself is also changed—He appears as a person not unlike a village headman, and the struggle with Satan resembles a contest between rival leaders. But the most homely touches are the identification of the Jewish authorities with the

[1] This building may be compared with the concrete-and-corrugated-iron cathedral at Dogura, the seat of the Anglican Bishop of New Guinea, aptly described by a District Officer of my acquaintance as an example of neo-Norman with a late north-Queensland roof.

luluais and the shortening of the name of doubting Saint Thomas to the more familiar Tom.[1]

The place which we see before us now was once a swamp, Ida' began; there was no dry land, no sea. Men had not been created yet, and everything was in darkness. But God and His angels were there, living up in heaven, and one day He looked out and decided to make a change. First He separated the water from the mud, so laying the ground bare, and then He placed the sun and the moon on top to give light by day and by night. The earth was now like the beach, all sand and rocks. Next the trees and plants were created, and afterwards came the animals, the fish, and the birds.

God saw that His work was good and was sorry that there was no one to enjoy it. He accordingly took pottery clay and shaped a figure in His own image. Kneeling, He blew into the model's nose, and a living man arose. This was Adam, who walked and talked just like God. The breath blown into his nostrils became his soul, something belonging to God which we all of us possess.

Adam was lonely with no one to talk to, and God thought that it would be fitting for him to have a companion. One day when the man was asleep a rib was taken from his side, and from this bone the woman Eve was fashioned. God told them that the world had been made for them to live in and that the trees, the plants, the animals, the fish, and the birds would serve them. One tree, though, which He indicated, had to be left alone, and they were warned not to go near it.

Now before all this happened Satan, the headman of the angels, had had a quarrel with God. He had been jealous of God's name and reputation and wished to be the leader himself. This plot was discovered in time, and God banished Satan from heaven, sending him outside into hell. This made Satan angry, and, hearing what was said to Adam, he thought he saw a chance to even things up.

At this time all the animals were friendly, and snakes walked about like cats. Satan turned himself into a snake and approached Eve. 'Good afternoon,' he said. 'Are all these things yours?' 'Yes,' she

---

[1] Reference to the story of Adam and Eve as told me in pidgin in another part of the country is relevant here. The narrator, having reached the point where the woman is discovered for the first time, stated that Adam arose and said, 'Good afternoon'—exactly the remark he would have made to a stranger had he been a native of New Guinea.

replied, 'except for the tree in the middle, which belongs to God. We aren't allowed to gather any fruit from it; but the fruit from the rest we may eat.' 'That's silly,' Satan answered. 'God is afraid of you. He knows that if you pick the fruit from the middle tree you'll be His equal. You try it and see.'[1] Eve thought this might be true, so she picked some and took a bite. The taste was good, and she carried one along for Adam to share. The two of them had broken God's command. That is how shame and trouble began.

Adam and Eve were now afraid—they knew that God would soon be aware of what they had done. For the first time they were ashamed of their nakedness and tied leaves around their waists.

Sure enough, when God came as usual to enjoy the cool of the evening His eyes were flashing with fire. 'You Adam and you Eve have disobeyed Me, and now you will be punished,' He told them. 'I shall send you out of this garden into the jungle and set angels at the fence to see that you do not return. You will be hungry and must earn your food by sweat, and the animals which before were gentle will now attack you. You will grow old, become diseased, and die. And because you began it, Eve, your sufferings will be the greater. You will have the pangs of childbirth, and every time an infant is born to you I will bring you near to death. Go, away with you from my sight! Not till a man arises who can crush the head of the serpent, which will now crawl forever on its belly, shall you see My face again.'

Weeping, and with heads bent down, the two fled, knowing that their fate was deserved. They had now to toil hard from dawn till dusk and even then were sometimes hungry. Ill feeling grew up between them also, and many times they quarrelled and fought. Satan still whispered in their ears, and often they followed his evil counsel.

In time they had two sons, Cain and Abel. It was Cain's job to look after the pigs, and Abel took charge of the gardens. They felt so weak that they determined to seek God's aid with sacrifices, Cain offering a pig and Abel taro and greens. By this means they thought they might be given aid to resist Satan. But God knew that Cain was already evil, and when the sacrifices were burnt, though the smoke from Abel's fire ascended, a wind came and blew that of Cain along the ground. Cain was angry at the sight and smashed his brother's

[1] Another man telling this story reported Satan as saying that after eating the fruit she and Adam would be dressed like God in coats, trousers, and boots.

head with a club. Bloodshed, as well as shame and trouble, had come into the world.

Adam and Eve had other children, and, as there was still no one. else, the sons had to marry the daughters. We are all of us descended from them.

The account continued with several of the Old Testament stories, but I shall omit these here. Special stress was laid on the incidents involving direct intervention by God, as, for example, the saving of Noah and his family, the provision of the substitute sacrifice for Isaac, the dividing of the waters of the Red Sea, and the furnishing of the Israelites with food and water in the wilderness. These were an indication that He remembered His people despite their forgetfulness. I enquired about the laws set forth in the Books of Exodus and Leviticus but was informed that these had reference only to the Jews and that we could ignore them. God's own rules, written on the slabs of stone presented to Moses, were only ten in number.

A comment of the pastor, who was present when Ida' and I were discussing Noah, may be quoted. The economic inferiority of the peoples of New Guinea, he stated, is to be accounted for by the curse put upon Ham after he had laughed at his father's nakedness. White men are descended from Shem and Japheth, the favoured sons, whereas the natives are descended from the wrongdoer. I expressed horror at any such notion and delivered a short anthropological lecture on the insignificance of race differences. The analogy which I used was the different labels on tins of corned beef. Some tins, I pointed out, had white paper on the outside and some red paper, but the meat inside was identical. This figure of speech was soon being repeated around the village, where it so caught the public fancy that a popular District Officer was nicknamed 'Bully Beef'.

Before beginning the story of the New Testament Ida' gave a few preliminary explanations. At the time of the creation, he said, God divided Himself into three, the Father, the Son Jesus Christ, and the Holy Spirit (*ngalau dabung* or, more usually, Spiritus Sanctus).

Jesus saw how wicked men had become, he went on, and wished to help them. To appear in divine form, however, might not have been convincing, and he preferred to be born rather as an ordinary person. He chose the young Jewess Mary as his mother and entered into her womb. She later became the wife of a man named Joseph.

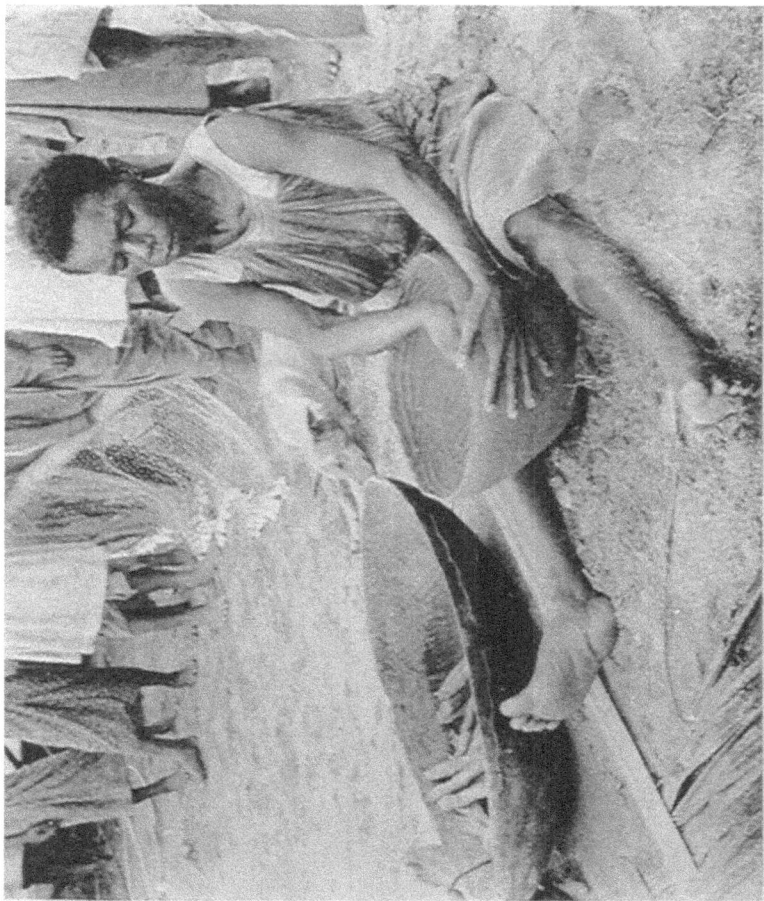

13. Potmaker of Lababia village. The bowl containing the rolls of clay came from the Tami Islands

14. Dance by the residents of Busama in Buakap village. The performers are in circular formation, with the women in pairs on the outside and the men in the centre

Palestine, the country of the Jews, had shortly before this been taken by the Romans, who had set up their own system of Administration, and during Mary's pregnancy it so happened that the District Officer issued an order that everyone must assemble at the Government station in Jerusalem for a census. So many people attended that the only shelter which Joseph could find was a cow shed, and here Jesus was born. The building was not even clean— it was covered with dung and smelt abominably—but that night a great light shone down from heaven, and all the angels sang.

Some wise men in the east saw this light. They consulted their books and found that a new king had appeared, the man who it had been foretold would crush the head of Satan. They accordingly filled their baskets with presents of soap, powder, flowers, and fragrant bark and set out to pay their respects. On the way they enquired of Herod, the reigning king of Israel under the Romans, where the new monarch was to be found. He knew nothing of the matter and, hearing the prophecy, became afraid for the supremacy of his family. Calling his followers together, he instructed them to go through the community killing all the new-born infants.

The wise men presented their gifts and returned home by a different road. After their departure Joseph had a dream in which Herod's scheme was set forth. Taking Mary and Jesus, he fled to the distant country of Egypt and there remained till Herod perished of the worms which God had sent to eat away his flesh in vengeance for the massacre of the babies. Jesus grew up in a village named Nazareth. Joseph was a carpenter who built houses, work at which the boy became expert. He was a model of obedience, not like the children of Busama, and carried out all the orders of his parents. His lessons he mastered so well that one day when his father and mother took him to the Mission even the head teachers wanted to ask him questions.

At length, when Jesus had reached manhood, he remembered the task which he had come to do. Taking nothing with him, he left home and began preaching the word of God in the manner of the 'black missionaries' of today. Soon he had gathered twelve disciples, who followed him everywhere. These men were the first Christians.

There is no need for me to relate here the account which Ida' gave of Christ's ministry, though it should be stated that the dismissal of

Satan in the wilderness and the baptism by John received particular attention and that far greater stress was laid on the miracles than the teachings. The fact that some of the disciples were fishermen gives the natives a marked fellow-feeling for them, and there was much local colour in the accounts of the storm on the sea of Galilee and the miraculous draught.[1] The most popular of the miracles, however, are the raising of Lazarus and, because of the local interest in food, the feeding of the multitude.

The final episodes of the story began with the last supper, when Jesus and his disciples met to celebrate the festival of the Passover, the occasion when the Israelites escaped having their firstborn sons slain by marking their doors for the guidance of the angel of death with the blood of sacrificial pigs. It is for this reason that blood is a special symbol, said Ida', the token that God is prepared to help us. But for Christians the last supper is still more important as the origin of Holy Communion. Jesus asked the disciples to keep the ceremony up after his death as a means of remembering him. The wine, he said, would represent the blood which he was about to give freely as a final sacrifice to make all further offerings unnecessary.

Shortly after this the false Judas, one of the disciples, betrayed Jesus to the police for thirty shillings, and he was taken before the District Officer, Pontius Pilate, for trial. Pilate's wife, however, had had a dream in which the prisoner's real name and identity were revealed, and she accordingly urged him to have nothing to do with the case. He accepted the warning and handed Jesus over to the Jewish luluais who nailed him to the cross, according to local custom.[2] 'You can do miracles,' they laughed. 'Why, then, don't you save yourself?' But he only prayed to God for their forgiveness. After he had drawn his last breath there was a great earthquake, and the sun was blotted out.

Joseph of Aramathea, a follower of Jesus, begged the District Officer for the body and carried it to his new cemetery, where he put

---

[1] I was interested to find that the remark to Peter that he should go and catch a fish when worried about his tax was phrased as a rebuke—how else could a fisherman expect to earn money? This may have been what the evangelist intended, and the interpretation of the words as an announcement that another miracle would occur is perhaps incorrect.

[2] There is a mistake here. The local custom was stoning, which the Romans would not countenance. Crucifixion was a Roman practice.

it in a cave. Pilate stipulated, however, that two policemen must be on guard at the entrance to make sure that the disciples did not steal the corpse in order to claim that the promise to rise again had been fulfilled.

Three days later, Mary, the disciples, and some of their friends visited the grave to paint the body. They found the sentries asleep and the stone at the mouth of the cave rolled away. Within were two angels, but Jesus had vanished. Shortly after he appeared to Mary in the form of a man visiting his garden with digging stick and basket. She failed to recognise him until he explained who he was. Various appearances followed, and all the disciples save Tom were soon convinced. Tom refused to believe till he had put his fingers on the wounds in Jesus's body.

The last time that the risen Jesus showed himself was when the disciples were assembled on the top of a mountain. He told them all to become missionaries and to spread over the world preaching the word of God, baptising all who were prepared to accept it. Then a cloud came down and took him back to heaven.

The men returned to Jerusalem to await a message which Jesus had foretold would come to them from God. One afternoon a great light appeared, and they saw a white pigeon flying over their heads. This was the Holy Spirit which had descended to give them strength.

Mission work started in Palestine, but the disciple Peter eventually went to Rome, where he also was crucified. By this time there were others to take his place, especially Paul, who never saw Jesus but had received a visitation from God. With Rome as the main centre, the word was carried first to France, then to England, then to Germany, and finally to New Guinea.

The Existence of God

The fact that the Bible is vouched for by the missionaries, the only Europeans who as a class have taken the trouble to cultivate the natives' friendship, is accepted as proof of its historical accuracy. No longer do confirmed pagans ask embarrassing questions, and it is too early as yet—and the people are still too ignorant—for the development of informed scepticism. Native Christians are thus in the same state as our own ancestors of mediæval times—they are harried neither by perplexity nor doubt and accept Holy Writ as the inspired word of God. 'Jesus died and came back to life,' my informants used to say. 'For us that is enough.'

I had to assume the rôle of the doubting Tom myself here and demand evidence. Allowing that the Gospels are the authentic accounts of eye-witnesses, what Mary and the others saw may have been a ghost, I insisted. Many Busama had told me of visitations from the spirit world, and perhaps the risen Christ was an apparition. For answer I was referred to the miracles. If Jesus had been an ordinary person this might have been so; but he had already demonstrated his divinity by changing water into wine, healing the blind, feeding the five thousand, and exorcising evil spirits.

'How you can go on arguing like this I don't understand,' Ida' reproved me. 'You know that God still intervenes in our affairs just as He did in the days of the Old Testament. Haven't we told you of men near death who have at once taken a turn for the better after confessing their sins? Aren't the Christian Australians and Americans beating the heathen Japanese? And if you want final confirmation there's yourself. Aren't you God's instrument? You've said that you might have gone anywhere for your work. Well, wasn't it He who sent you here? He knew we needed someone to dismiss the evil official Bumbu, who was preventing the reopening of our churches, and He picked on you to do it. That was why the pastor chose for his first sermon the text, "The grace of God which bringeth salvation hath appeared to all men" (Titus ii, 11).'

Having been placed on so lofty a plane, I could not argue that the miracles have their parallel in the claims of native magic and European science and that intervention by the ancient spirits was not unknown. I therefore turned to other aspects of my problem.

Christian Dogma

The wording of God's curse when He expelled Adam and Eve from the Garden of Eden indicates acceptance of the belief in original sin. All our present pains, it is thought, can be traced back directly to the offence of our first parents. Preaching at a funeral, an elder once stated that evil came into the world when Eve ate the forbidden fruit. She swallowed a mouthful, and quarrelling, stealing, and dishonouring of relatives followed. 'If she had only closed her ears to Satan,' he concluded, 'we wouldn't have the Government here. Offenders must be punished—everyone knows that—if no notice were taken of them they'd only continue their evil deeds. But without crime there'd be no criminals, and that would mean nothing for District Officers to do.'

At the same time, it is claimed that everyone has salvation within his reach. God gave us rules to follow, and if we obey the Commandments we are certain in the end to see His face. The choice is our responsibility—we are free to do good or evil as we please, just as Eve was free to leave the fruit alone or pluck it. So if confronted with a sum of money in an empty house we can either steal it or put it out of sight on a high shelf to await the return of the owner. But if we are tempted the proper course is to concentrate steadily on the appropriate Commandment, thereby ensuring divine assistance. The first thought of wrongdoing is Satan's chance. 'Take a risk,' he whispers, 'no one will know.' God is prepared to help only if called upon, and if we listen to Satan He abandons us.

The difficulty of reconciling this interpretation with the concept of an omnipotent but all-loving God had apparently never occurred to the natives, and they had some difficulty in answering my queries. If He is really concerned about our well being, I wanted to know, why does He allow us to be tempted? Or why is it that we are not endowed with such strength that we can always resist? Everyone was convinced that there must be some explanation but hung back for the pastor and teachers to supply it.

At length, after much cogitation, Ida' tentatively ventured the suggestion that perhaps the struggle in heaven had never taken place—the Bible, indeed, makes no reference to it. This would not do, I said, for the Crucifixion must also be accounted for. God can do everything and yet allowed His only son to suffer a cruel death. Jesus's appearance on earth was his own doing, was the reply. God wanted to destroy mankind as He had previously wiped out Sodom and Gomorrah, but His son persuaded Him that one more attempt must be made to bring them to a full realisation of what might lie in store.

This brought us back to where we had begun, as everyone soon realised—the contradiction of a God of love and a God of vengeance. A long debate, to which half the village contributed, followed, and the solution ultimately put forward was that men have been designed with freedom of action. This is God's plan, which we have to accept. He could have given us more strength had He wished, but we have enough to resist if we try and therefore have no reasonable grounds for complaint. In such circumstances the second chance which Jesus gave us is clearly an abiding mercy.

It will be noted that no reference was made to the Holy Spirit. This is characteristic. The Spirit appears once or twice in the Bible account but is otherwise almost ignored.

My next enquiries were directed towards discovering something about heaven and hell. I took as my starting point an engraving in general circulation entitled 'The Broad and the Narrow Ways'. A relic of the Evangelical movement in Europe, this showed on one side a wide road leading past drinking saloons and gaming tables to a bonfire and on the other a tiny track leading uphill past Gothic churches to the foot of a rainbow. The whole thing seemed somewhat out of place in New Guinea.

Nobody had much to say about heaven, and I gathered that it was for most persons a nebulous sort of place where the dead for ever sit in idleness eating and singing hymns. Hell is rather clearer, though several informants were careful to make it plain that the torments were more metaphorical than real. Nga'gili' made a great joke of the account which was given us in pidgin by a visitor who must have had a more fundamentalist upbringing. The souls of the wicked would be licked by great tongues of flame, said the man, and when the devils brought them a drink the mugs would be found to contain 'bloody kerosene, that's all'. This was absurd, laughed Nga'gili'. True, hell was probably far too warm for comfort, and the food was bad, but the torture consisted not in Satan's pitchfork but in the consciousness that one had erred and must carry one's sins in one's heart for ever. The body is burned not by flames of fire but by shame and remorse.

The general terms used by the pagans of old for 'spirits', *balum* and *ngalau*, are usually reserved now for visible manifestations of the supernatural world. For 'soul' the Christians have the word *katung*, the 'shadow' or 'mirror image'. This is the part of God which is in us all, the breath given to Adam when he was created out of clay.

Liberated after death, the soul passes to *lamboam*, the spirit world of the pagans, there to await the day of judgment and the separation of the sheep and the goats. *Lamboam* is also the name for hell, but for heaven a new term has been coined, *undambi*, from *un*='far away' and *dambi*='near'.

The marked contrast between the attitude of the Busama to the after-world and that of the Wogeo deserves a word. Unlike the Busama, the Wogeo when I first lived with them in 1934 had had little to do with Europeans. The life beyond the grave is in Busama a frequent topic of conversation, but in Wogeo it was seldom mentioned. The difference can be attributed to insecurity following on the collapse of old customs. The Wogeo had as yet no consciousness of belonging to a world which was fast vanishing—it did not occur to them that their spirits might not be worshipped after death and that their ways of doing things would soon be outmoded. In Busama, on the contrary, a revolution is in progress, and all are aware that change will go on. These natives are accordingly impelled to grasp at a personal immortality.

Ceremonies

Attendance at Mala'lo on Sundays is practically obligatory, and, in addition, everyone is expected during the week to be present at morning and evening services in the village. The most vital celebrations, however, are baptism and Communion.

Except in cases of illness, when a ceremony is performed at once, infants are not baptised individually. Before the war a general christening service took place at Mala'lo at approximately yearly intervals, and all the children born since the last celebration were put through together. Even then it was insisted that the community must be 'straight' beforehand, and if anyone had committed a serious sin within recent months a public meeting took place to decide whether postponement was necessary. Representatives of the churches from the other side of the Gulf as well as the local elders took part, and the verdict reached was that of the natives themselves. The views of the white missionary naturally had some influence, but he refrained from imposing his will upon the congregation. In former times it was he who conducted the service, though latterly the ordained native pastors sometimes took over the task. Because of the war there was no baptism between 1941 and 1946.

CHRISTIANITY

The rite commemorates Jesus's sojourn on earth, and the use of the water serves as a reminder also of Noah's escape from the flood and of the preservation of the Israelites first from the pursuing Egyptians in the Red Sea and later by death from thirst in the wilderness. The fact that the virtuous were saved bears witness of God's love—we too may attain salvation if we allow our sins to be washed away in the rivers of repentance. Children are tarnished by the offences of Adam, but, being so young, are in a sense blameless. Baptism for them symbolises their dedication to a new life: they are now marked as the servants of the Lord.

A comparison is made between the circumcision of the Jews and the corresponding mutilation practised by the pagans at initiation ceremonies. Baptism fulfils the same sort of function, it is said, but is a more appropriate way of denoting membership of a religious group.

Communion is in many respects similar. This ceremony is another annual event, and the same discussion takes place first to determine whether the worshippers have been living according to the standard set forth in the scriptures. The aim, too, is identical—wiping out the past and consecrating the erstwhile sinner to a new life. There is even a parallel between the wine and the water as symbols of divine potency and mercy. The wine represents the blood of Isaac, the blood smeared on the doors to give protection from the angel of death, and the blood of Jesus shed upon the Cross.

Before partaking of Communion it is essential to be freed from the stain of guilt, a process achieved by confession in private to the missionary or an ordained pastor. The penitent expresses his contrition and a determination to forsake evil in the future, and prayers are then recited begging for his absolution. To attend without confessing would be certain death: God is not mocked and refuses to tolerate those who have not repented. 'I will wash mine hands in innocency;' sang the psalmist, 'so will I encompass Thine altar, O Lord' (Psalms vi, 26).

The celebration is conceived by the natives as a meal at which the faithful are the guests. In ordinary life one is invited to share food only by relatives and friends, the persons on whom one can depend for support and assistance, and to be bidden to God's table is thus interpreted as an earnest of His goodwill. Those present are reassured that, provided the necessary conditions are fulfilled, He will now be ready to stand at their side in all their difficulties.

CHRISTIANITY

As with baptism, there is an appeal to the precedent established by the Israelites and the pagans, both of whom were in the habit of making offerings to secure favours. Cain and Abel lit their sacrificial fires, and Mary and Joseph brought pigeons to the temple; and the ancestors made regular presentations of pork to the spirits. But just as the incision of the penis has been replaced by ceremonial washing, so Communion has taken the place of sacrifice. Jesus gave himself up to be slain as the last offering, and all that Christians have to do now is to pledge themselves to follow his teachings.

Easter passes without much comment, and Christmas is looked forward to mainly as a secular festival.[1] A big gathering of all the Gulf villages takes place at Mala'lo or one of the other stations, and there is a feast at which the quantity of food rivals that of the old pagan ceremonies. Dances have been forbidden, but games are arranged to take their place, and church services and hymn singing occupy several hours of each of the two or three days till the visitors return home.

Other occasional ceremonies take place at the consecration of a new house, canoe, or seine. There is a dignified gathering of all the persons interested, and the pastor recites a prayer and invites the assembly to sing a hymn. At the only service of this kind which I attended, in the village of Buakap, the people's attitude of earnest reverence was most marked. Proceedings took place under the trees near the beach, and the fact that the dogs and fowls were wandering about unmolested amongst the worshippers bore witness to how much religion is part of normal existence. It is not something which the natives keep within the four walls of the church on Sundays—God is everywhere, in the village, in the bush, and on the sea.

The purpose of these rites is to secure a 'blessing' on the work. The owner of the house interprets this as good health and abundant food supplies, the owner of the canoe as safety on overseas voyages, and the owner of the net as great hauls of fish.

[1] Easter and Christmas rituals in the Western Churches are to a large extent derived from the spring and winter festivals of our own heathen ancestors. In the tropics, where neither spring nor winter occurs, these can have little meaning. (See E. E. Kellett, *History of Religions*, London, 1933, Chap. VII, for an account of the way in which early Christianity absorbed elements from the religion of Rome and of the Germanic tribes. 'Every conquest introduced a touch of heathenism;' he says, 'the vanquished in some measure took the victors captive.' The process continues.)

Christianity and Conduct

The Decalogue is regarded as the ultimate guide, and it is always asserted that those who keep the Commandments are certain after death of admission into the kingdom of heaven.

The rules are separated into categories. The first group relates to purely religious observances; then one prescribes proper respect for parents and, by implication, all other relatives; then a trio deals with murder, theft, and slander; and a final group is concerned with sexual offences.

The first series enjoins abandonment of the heathen deities, active acceptance of the scriptures, and due reverence for God.[1] To pay the appropriate honours it is necessary to attend all the services, including the occasional celebrations of Holy Communion. For many years after the establishment of the Mission emphasis was also laid on the sanctity of Sunday, and, if the stories are true, the Lord's Day in Busama must have been as dull as Sabbath in Aberdeen. It is reported that when one man went fishing a large crowd assembled on the beach and smashed the canoe on his return, an action which might have resulted in their imprisonment had he cared to tell the District Officer. People are more liberal today, and, although the taboo continues on heavy work, such as gardening, house building, or shaping canoes, there is no objection to a carrying out such jobs as mending leaky thatch, repairing nets, and renewing the lashings of outrigger floats. At the same time, discretion is advisable, and the workers try if possible to remain in the semi-seclusion provided by their verandah or a grove of trees. Children, too, are warned not to be boisterous in their play till the afternoon, when church is over. Because of the ban on labour, Sunday is now the favourite day for visiting, and after attendance at Mala'lo many persons accompany friends from other villages to their homes.

Great significance is attached to the Commandment relating to the care of parents, for filial devotion is a feature of the culture. As is to be expected in a community with a classificatory system of reckoning kin, there is a spread-over from the members of the family to other

---

[1] 'Thou shalt not take the name of the Lord thy God in vain' is usually ignored, possibly because the natives are not given to blasphemy and in Court are seldom required to take an oath.

relatives, and a younger brother who disobeys an older kinsman and a nephew who neglects an uncle are both likely to be reproved for 'breaking the law of God'.

The prohibition of murder, theft, and slander is also approved. In ancient times children were brought up to be loyal to fellow villagers, and the dangers arising from giving offence and quarrelling were pointed out from the earliest years. Respect for the property of others was a necessity, too, in a settlement which was without locks and bolts, and parents took pains to train their offspring not to meddle.

Yet the old insularity and parochialism are barely beginning to be broken down, and, though no one would today dream of raiding the people living in other places, only amongst the 'black missionaries' is there much thought of the universal application of all the Commandments and of the brotherhood of mankind. Stealing from 'foreigners' in the labour compound, or from a European, is thus regarded by some, if not as commendable, at least as unlikely to imperil the immortal soul.

The rules which the Busama really take to their hearts, however, are those relating to sexual irregularities. Adultery has always been treated as a most heinous offence, and, as I have pointed out, in the past a man who had an affair with a married woman was put to death. Intercourse before marriage was only slightly less grave, and the seducer if caught was speared in the upper arm or thigh. The natives admit that there is no backing in the Commandments for their extreme attitude, and when pressed for Biblical authority the pastor and Ida', after much study, produced two verses from the Epistles— 'If thou marry thou hast not sinned; and if a virgin marry she hath not sinned' (1 Corinthians vii, 28) and 'Mortify therefore your members which are upon earth; fornication, uncleanness, inordinate affection, evil concupiscence, and covetousness, which is idolatory' (Colossians iii, 5).

Comparison may be made between the reaction of these natives to Mission teachings relating to sex and those of the Trobriand Islanders. In Busama Christianity serves to confirm the traditional code and is in this respect markedly successful. But in the Trobriands, as Methodist missionaries have admitted to me, the failure has been a dismal one. These latter natives, unlike the Busama, were before marriage almost completely free—and in spite of fifty years of missionary endeavour they still are. During a visit to the Trobriands

CHRISTIANITY

I asked the Court Interpreter why the islanders were so heedless of Mission morality. 'There is nothing in the Commandments to say that unmarried people should avoid intercourse,' was his reply. 'We accept the Bible and follow it.' I thereupon quoted the two passages, which I still remembered. 'That's only Paul!' he exclaimed. 'God's orders and Paul's opinions are two different things.'

The Busama elders of today have such a phobia about sex that they see it in everything, even the attractive custom, universal in New Guinea, of wearing flowers in the ears and in the hair.[1] Dancing is condemned as a temptation to 'immorality', and the Mission can have little trouble in inducing them to ban it from the village.

A certain amount of dalliance is bound to go on, however, no matter how much the older generation tries to prevent it, and in my opinion the lighter festivals make no difference. This was apparently also the view of the pagans in times gone by: they did not imagine that the virginity ideal was incompatible with the encouragement of physical display.

I have said already that the ban may also have serious social repercussions. Dances used to be the highlight of village life, looked forward to for months beforehand and ecstatically enjoyed when at last they took place. Without them existence has become flat and dull, and the result is that the youths are bored and rush away to find excitement in European employment.

Finally, the prohibition of dancing is another blow at native art. New Guinea dances could be a fine contribution to the world. Given the right setting and proper rehearsals, they are as moving and inspiring a spectacle as the better known exhibitions from Spain, India, and Java. It is surely not sentimental to urge their preservation. My impulse is to repeat to the Mission the words of the Emperor Charles V to the Chapter at Cordoba when several of the central arcades of the mosque were pulled down to make room for an Italianate cathedral. They had built something which could have been put up anywhere, he said, and spoilt something the like of which existed nowhere else.

[1] Once when I was out walking in Wogeo my companion picked two flowers from a hibiscus bush, one for himself and one for me. Having placed his own in the hole in the lobe of his ear without thinking, he turned to help me. At that point the remembrance that my ears were not pierced occurred to him, and he wanted to know where, then, did a white man wear his flowers.

The Virtues

I used to remind my informants that the Commandments deal exclusively with the sins of the flesh, to which Jesus was always lenient. He did not admonish the woman taken in adultery but told her to go and sin no more. Yet he had a great deal to say about the sins of the spirit, especially pride, and condemned these with great emphasis.

To make this point clear I quoted the parable of the Pharisee and the publican (Luke xviii, 10–14). 'The Pharisee stood and prayed thus with himself, God I thank thee that I am not as other men are, extortioners, unjust, adulterers, or even as this publican. I fast twice in the week, I give tithes of all I possess. And the publican, standing afar off, would not lift up so much as his eyes to heaven, but smote upon his breast, saying, God be merciful to me a sinner. I tell you this man went up to his house justified rather than the other; for everyone that exalteth himself shall be abased; and he that humbleth himself shall be exalted.'

This was an unfamiliar approach, though once my informants realised the significance of the passage they all assured me that pride and vanity are the poisons of the soul and that the man who is puffed up is already walking down the road to hell. Yet when in other contexts I asked for a list of the main sins pride was invariably omitted; further, the pastor's account of some of the confessions, given without the names of the penitents, made no mention anywhere of such a fault.

The explanation is probably to be found in the attitude to wealth, which is distributed in order to enhance status. The giver of a feast certainly eats little of the food provided for his guests, but his abstention is ostentatious, and his left hand is only too clearly aware of the alms which his right is doing (Matthew vi, 3).

With the concentration on display, it is scarcely to be expected that humility should be a Busama virtue. On the other hand, the beauties of generosity are constantly accented, and the parable of the Good Samaritan and the thirteenth chapter of the first Epistle to the Corinthians ('Though I speak with the tongues of men and of angels and have not charity, I am become as sounding brass or a tinkling cymbal') are probably the most frequently quoted passages in the New Testament.

CHRISTIANITY

The expression used for 'charity' and 'love' is *tita' giwing nganu*. All emotional states are expressed in physical terms, and the literal translation is 'internal-organs-excrement to-be-with truly'. A native speaking of charity, however, no more has his bowels actually in mind than an Englishman thinks of a piece of bleeding tissue when he talks of having 'lost his heart'.

The primary application of *tita' giwing nganu* was to the mutual regard of bond friends, who were required to be 'closer than brothers'. The minds—bellies, excrement—of such persons were together in utter completeness. The expression is extended also to the affection of close kinsfolk who are especially demonstrative towards one another. Ida' told me of the love of his mother's brother Buasi', who had reared him after the death of his parents. 'Whenever I come home from Hopoi on a holiday,' he said, 'Buasi' always killed the largest pig. And not once did he ask for a gift in return. That is charity.'

The only occasion when I heard *tita' giwing nganu* applied to members of the same family was in reference to a widow who, from her great affection for her dead husband, refused to remarry. This suggests that the word carries a slight flavour of full-measure-pressed-down-and-running-over, an impression which is confirmed by the standard example which is always quoted to illustrate what Saint Paul meant by Christian charity. The man concerned was a 'black missionary' stationed in the Markham valley who, knowing the risk which he was taking, lost his life in attempting to recover the body of a member of his flock from a deep well.

Yet while there is full recognition of generosity in the abstract, the natives are keenly aware of the advantages which accrue from it. Filial love, they say, must be earned, and to secure the appreciation of persons to whom one is less closely related it is necessary to strive harder still. One must share one's food with them and assist them with their work; then, having ensured their affection, one is certain when the need arises of a return in kind. 'If you're away from home and your kinsmen write to say they're thinking of you,' said Nga'gili', 'that's just ink and paper—there's nothing in it. To prove what they say they must send you presents. (You must send them money too, of course.) Again, if friends come it's not the soft words that count; no, it's the betel, the coconuts, and the cooked food. Look, it's like this. If I want something from you, you give it to me;

256

and if you want something from me, I give it to you. It's that which makes us brothers, not me calling you *nga'dua* and you calling me *lasing.*' (These are the terms for older and younger brother.)

The Busama approach, then, is a practical one, and friendliness is lightly regarded unless translated into action. The natives would agree with Michael Mont in Galsworthy's *Modern Comedy* that 'Pity is tripe'—that sympathy for a blind beggar means a coin as well as a kind word.

In our own society tolerance is the last thing to be hoped for when the residents of a small village are talking amongst themselves without critical strangers being present. In New Guinea, too, there is so little to discuss that the foibles of the neighbours are a favourite topic, and not much patience is shown towards those with an unusual point of view. Yet it is a fact that, though the Busama feel superior about their culture, they do not look upon other methods of doing things with the disdain of the travelling Englishman or Australian. They have grown up in a country where customs differ from district to district. Languages come to them readily, and every boy of fourteen is at home in three, his own, Yabim, and pidgin. I heard few complaints against the Mission for its selection of Yabim for instruction, and the inevitable modification of the local speech is usually a matter for comment but not regret.

The constant repetition of the Commandments—they are recited every day at the evening service—gives the impression at first that the religion of the native today is wholly negative, a compound of taboos.[1] Closer study reveals that this view is incorrect and that there is also a positive side. The Sermon on the Mount is treated as of less consequence than the Laws of Moses, but the fact that some of the virtues are encouraged and that all the preacher's energies are not taken up in thundering against the vices leads to the conclusion that if the founder of Christianity were to visit Busama he would recognise his handiwork.

[1] The Old Testament is easier for natives to understand than the New just because it is based on a series of concrete prohibitions—do not do this, this, and this, and entry into heaven will be assured. The stress on the taboos also furnishes a reason for the success of the Seventh Day Adventist Mission, a never-ending source of amazement to many Europeans. Giving up pork, certain kinds of fish, tobacco, and Saturdays is a hardship, but this is the sort of demand which the pagan religions made and is also much simpler than becoming as simple as a little child, turning the other cheek, and praying for one's enemies.

257

Conscience

The pagan religion did not recognise conscience. The nearest approach was the notion of *maya*, the word used for the shame or embarrassment felt by a person discovered in irregular behaviour. A percentage of the population seems to have accepted the traditional standards from a conviction of their reasonableness, but it must be admitted that the impression to be gained from many is that this shame is associated more with annoyance at being found out than with feelings of remorse. In a study by the late Stephen Lehner, a missionary authority, it is even stated that *maya* 'never inhibits anyone unless the culprit is afraid of being seen'.[1]

A person oppressed by shame is said to flush or turn pale and to cast his eyes on the ground, and after a serious breach he may go into retirement for a time. But such sensitivity is often the result of combined fear of possible penalties and annoyance at stupidity rather than the outcome of feelings of degradation. This is indicated by the remarks of the man Po'gwi' when I enquired was he not ashamed to have undertaken the adulterous intrigue about which he was then giving me details. 'Why should I have been ashamed when we began?' he wanted to know. 'I didn't realise we were going to be discovered. The husband wasn't suspicious for a long time. It was only after the women told me she'd been questioned that I became anxious. I started wondering at once would she confess or go on putting him off. She was steadfast enough, but the fellow set a trap and caught us. That was when I had *maya*—I was sad and worried then. I realised that I was tangled like a fishline which had been pulled up carelessly, and I was angry with myself for being such a fool as to be seen. Everyone would now point me out as an adulterer, I thought. Yes, I certainly hung my head when the husband began having his say.' Yet the knowledge that he was in employment at Salamaua was a comfort, he went on. There was no necessity for him to face the villagers and suffer their condemnation in person.

---

[1] S. Lehner, 'Maja', *Journal of the Polynesian Society*, Vol. XLI, pp. 121–130. Cf. also H. I. Hogbin, 'Shame', *Oceania*, Vol. XVII, pp. 273–288.

In primitive conditions, where everyone knows everybody else's business, secret sinning is difficult, and it follows that *maya* is tolerably effective in achieving the maintenance of moral standards. In more complex conditions, however, it is by itself insufficient.

15. Dancer with hand drum.   His garment is made from painted
bark cloth : and he is also wearing a headdress of feathers, small
cowrie shells, and dogs' teeth, together with a breast ornament of
dogs' teeth

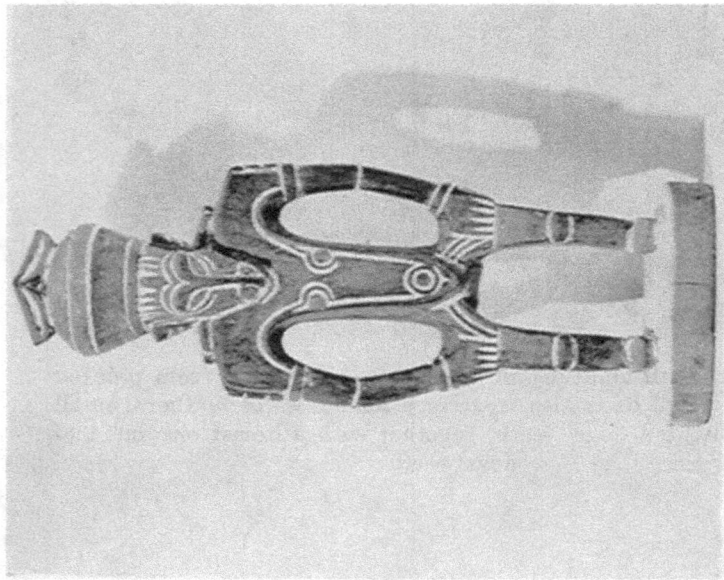

16a. Tami Island figure in the traditional style of the Huon Gulf. The figure is 15 inches high and, except for the whitened base, is painted dark grey. The inlay is lime, with the highlights (hair, eyes, nipples, etc.) picked out in red ochre

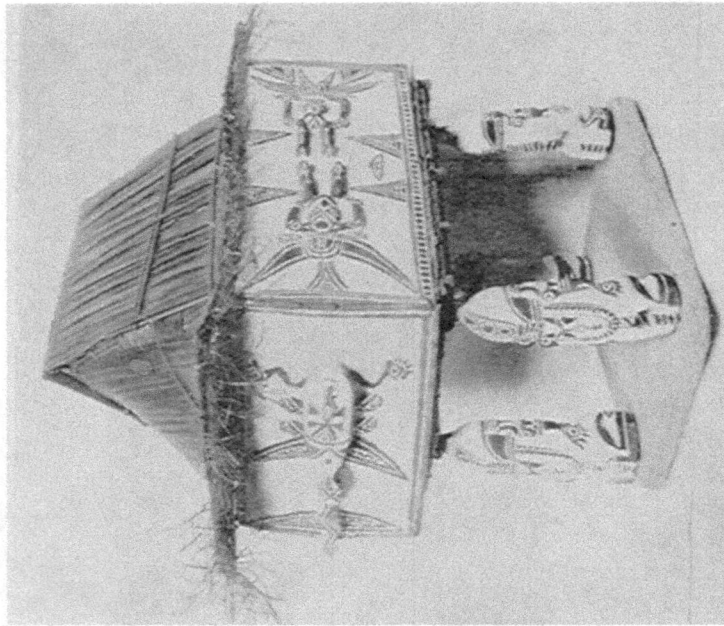

16b. Model of a club house in the traditional style (courtesy of Australian Museum, Sydney)

Confirmation of this statement of the situation was provided in the following month when it was revealed that at this very moment Po'gwi' had been involved in a similar affair with another married woman. There was no evidence of his being ashamed at the time of our conversation, though when found out he was as abashed as he had then said he was on the earlier occasion.

For Po'gwi' and others like him it would probably be true to say that the idea of conscience still has little meaning.[1] Missionaries have done their best to explain it, nevertheless, using different words according to the context. The commonest expressions are *tita'-kika-eng*='his inside tears him asunder violently', and *ngalilum*= 'inside', either alone [2] or with various combinations, including *aweng ngalilumnga*='voice inside',[3] *ngalilum pali'pali'*='inside weak',[4] *ngalilum ngatutu'*='inside heart beats' (that is 'anxious', 'worried',[5] and *ngalilum wapa'*='inside heavy', 'mourning'.[6]

It is difficult to say how many, but a number of persons share the disregard of Po'gwi' for the Christian ethic—or perhaps one should rather say his failure to appreciate it. At the opposite extreme is the small handful of converts who have absorbed the missionaries' teachings completely. These men, headed by Ida' and the pastor, have nearly all studied for a long period at one of the colleges. Their sincerity may be gauged from the statement of Ida' that on one occasion when he became aware that he had sinned the main reason for his sorrow was a realisation of his impaired relations with the Deity.

[1] Cf. A. Cruden, *Complete Concordance to the Holy Scriptures*; 'Conscience is the testimony and secret judgment of the soul, which gives its approbation to actions which it thinks good, or reproaches itself with those which it believes to be evil: or it is a particular knowledge which we have with us of our own deeds, good or evil, arising out of the general knowledge of the mind, which shews us what is good or evil, and Conscience tells us when we have done the one or the other.'

[2] E.g. Titus i, 15: 'their mind and conscience is defiled' (*ngalilum ngatimui*= 'inside dirty').

[3] E.g. Romans ii, 15: 'their conscience also bearing witness.'

[4] E.g. 1 Corinthians viii, 7: 'their conscience being weak.'

[5] E.g. 1 Corinthians x, 25: 'asking no questions for conscience' sake.'

[6] It should be noted that these words also retain their pre-Christian uses. Po'gwi' employed *ngalilum ngatutu'* to describe his anxiety when the husband became suspicious and *ngalilum wapa'* for the despair after the adultery had been discovered. Again, a woman worried about a sick child speaks of her *ngalilum ngatutu'*, and if it dies she is *ngalilum wapa'*, 'grief stricken'.

CHRISTIANITY

The majority of the villagers occupy an intermediate position. They claim to be Christians and salt their conversation freely with Biblical texts but by 'conscience' understand little more than a transference of *maya* to a different plane. They are ashamed now not only from fear of the disapproval of their fellows but also from dread of the wrath of the Lord. The 'inner voice' speaks to them of the all-seeing eye and of God's awareness of hidden actions; yet, if asked what is implied by their glib talk of forfeiture of grace, they tell only of the risks of hell. Like Po'gwi', their goodness is dependent upon expediency, though the fact that they believe in divine retribution may well mean that it is somewhat more consistent.

Retribution

Sin is said to have a defiling effect: it makes the soul unclean. The passage, 'He that is without sin amongst you, let him cast the first stone at her' (John viii, 7), is translated, 'He that is pure inside, let him cast the first stone at this woman.'

Those who are besmirched are believed to have cut themselves off from God, and, if the problem is being discussed in the abstract, one is informed that they have to be put outside the Church. In practice, however, official judgments are given only in cases of adultery and seduction, a fact which supports the earlier statement that in the native mind the sexual sins loom largest. The culprit remains more or less in Coventry until such time as his offence has been expiated—for a particularly glaring adultery over a year may be required—when he approaches the pastor, expresses his contrition, and begs for re-admittance.

I one day remarked that this procedure seemed to me to be directly contrary to the instruction to judge not lest we should ourselves be judged. I spoke of a missionary of my acquaintance in the Solomons who, when reproved by a colleague for taking no action against some natives who had stolen his supplies, had answered simply, 'It pleases me to forgive them'. Such conduct was stupid, my hearers replied. As the thieves remained unpunished they would repeat their evil actions and so end in hell, whereas a scolding might have led to their reformation. Ida' also referred, rather inappropriately, to the fate of Hophni and Phinehas (1 Samuel ii–iv). God told the High Priest to punish them for stealing a sacrificial offering, and when the order was ignored what happened? They were killed in battle on the same day. I countered this with a further reference to the woman taken in adultery. Nothing had happened to her, but instead the accusers were rebuked. Here was a special case, someone interrupted, and no conclusion could be drawn from it. Had Jesus counselled stoning her the men would have murmured against him and protested that he came here to kill people.

'So in your opinion Jesus behaved as he did through fear of what people might say about him?' I asked.

This question finished the discussion for the time, but the pastor visited me later and stated that after much thought he had decided that suspension from the Church could be justified on the analogy of the action taken by a gardener to protect his taro. 'The man clears a patch of ground and plants his suckers,' it was explained. 'But he doesn't build the fence yet—he waits first to see whether the wild pigs come near. If they don't, then he doesn't bother. But once a wild pig eats some of the corms he puts up a fence to save the rest. Well, sending the sinner away is just like that: it is the same as the fence. He's reminded of what he's done and goes no farther. If we left him alone, sin would consume his soul completely like the wild pig eating the taro. And don't forget that the rest of the congregation has to be considered. Failure to punish one sinner would soon lead to everyone imitating him.'

Once a person is cut off from God he is exposed to divine vengeance and must face the consequences. The most serious danger is illness or accident, and the villagers are always inclined to suspect a secret sin if they hear of someone being stricken down suddenly. Once when I was making a visit to Salamaua a member of the party shook his head as we passed the war cemetery and murmured that it was a dreadful thing for all these men to have perished so young, but no doubt God would have shielded them from the bullets of the enemy had they not been guilty of wickedness.

Again, when news was brought that the youth Laho, who was suffering from pneumonia, had wandered off into the bush in delirium, Sali, the man to whom I was talking at the time, immediately exclaimed, 'This is punishment for an offence! He must have done something to make God angry with him'. He then went on to say that some years before while he was a student at Mala'lo the same thing had happened to a fellow pupil, who had been found in the jungle dead. Later, when a search was made of the youth's belongings, a letter was discovered proving conclusively that he had been arranging meetings with one of the girls.

The death of Imata' gave rise to similar suspicions. This man suddenly went blind after over-exerting himself carrying a heavy load for several miles. Rushed to hospital, he died within a few days. A post mortem revealed heart disease, but the natives were positive that, although nothing was known against him, hidden wrong-doing was responsible.

In the gossip which followed the funeral of Imata' I learnt a number of incidents which seemed to prove that death is the wages of sin. The case most frequently quoted concerned a woman who was killed by a falling tree while on her way to the gardens. Everybody had thought her virtuous, but, frightened by what had occurred, one of the men confessed that he had been carrying on an intrigue with her. Several references were also made to sinners who had been gored by wild pigs when out hunting, and I heard, too, of an adulteress who had died giving birth to a still-born infant and of a husband who survived only a year after admitting his unwillingness to forgive his once faithless but now contrite spouse.

The case of a woman from the neighbouring village of Gwado demands special mention, indicating as it does that a person's sins may be visited on other members of the family (cf. p. 178, footnote). She was subject to fits and on this occasion had collapsed into the fire and had been seriously burned. Her husband, a notorious and flagrant adulterer who had twice been suspended, was at once blamed. 'This is your trouble,' his brother-in-law told him fiercely. 'My sister is paying for your misdeeds.'

Of particular interest also is the insane woman from Buakap. Till middle age she had been normal but then contracted an illness which left her brain affected. This was God punishing her for opposing the marriage of her daughter to the man approved by the kinship group, I was told. As I was unaware of a Biblical prohibition on the expression of such disagreement, I enquired in what her sin lay. 'She disobeyed the Commandment bidding us respect our relatives,' was the reply.

Crop failures, either through the depredations of wild pigs or insect pests, may also be put down to supernatural causes, though a distinction is drawn here between divine vengeance on the one hand and laziness or bad workmanship on the other. The difference was made plain by an incident related by Ida' concerning a village near Finschhafen. One of the men went on a pleasure jaunt to an island a few miles off the coast, and during his absence pigs began to eat his taro. His friends made a smoke signal to recall him, but he either did not see it or ignored it, and on his return the garden was ruined. 'I know I have sinned in the past,' he cried, 'but God ought to have listened to my prayers and protected my food supplies. I went to church every morning specially to ask Him.' The villagers told him not to be a fool. If he wanted to remain away for so long he should have built stronger fences.

As in other parts of the Christian world, however, the wicked in Busama sometimes flourish like the green bay tree. The crowning instance was Bumbu. He and his son Mayeng, who was almost as much to blame, enjoyed perfect health and were involved in no accidents. What of divine justice in cases like this, I wanted to know: why were these two men not smitten as they stood? It might be well for me to turn to the parable of the wheat and the tares was the rejoinder (Matthew xiii, 24–30: 'In the time of harvest I will say to the reapers, gather ye together first the tares, and bind them in bundles to burn them: but gather the wheat into my barn'). God had marked Bumbu and Mayeng for vengeance in His own good time either in this world or the next. No one could hope to escape for ever, and perhaps even then plans were being made.

It happens also at times that the virtuous are cast down. They are themselves prone to make comparisons with Job and claim that they have been chosen on account of their outstanding merit to have their patience tried, but other villagers usually dismiss such misfortunes as bad luck.

The fact that many diseases have a 'natural' origin is acknowledged, and an endeavour is often made to discover how the infection spread.[1] Thus an epidemic of pneumonic influenza which swept

---

[1] The Government hospital and dispensary, formerly located at Salamaua but now transferred to Lae, and the Mission hospital at Finschhafen are popular for ailments requiring brief and sure treatment, such as acute yaws, malaria, dysentery, and tropical ulcers; but few village natives are willing to seek medical care if there is risk of their having to remain away from home for a long period.

through the village late in 1945 was traced back to the arrival of a party of returned labourers, then to the compound at Lae, and ultimately to European troops. In general, illnesses of which the onset is slow are placed in the category of 'merely sickness'. So although the collapse of Imata' from heart disease, as recorded above, gave rise to suspicion of misconduct, there were no probings after the death of the chronic invalid Damani a week later.

Confession

Everyone is liable to error, and an opportunity for making peace with God by means of confession is provided before the administration of the Sacrament. True Christians, however, are not expected to postpone self examination for occasions of such rarity—they should practice regular contemplation and decide whether they have been following the path laid down. If their actions have not come up to the accepted standard, and they feel that their soul may be sullied, then the proper procedure is to confess at once. 'Blessed are they that mourn,' one of the elders stated, refers to those who, realising their fault spontaneously, become ashamed before God and wish to bring themselves into harmony with Him once more. They approach the pastor and request him to pray for their forgiveness. The confession takes place in private and is treated as a solemn confidence even if others have been involved in the misdeed, but before granting absolution the pastor issues a warning that there must be a genuine desire to do better.

In cases where remorse is delayed till after the discovery of the offence, confession is clearly unnecessary. There is then a delay before the visit is made to the pastor—often, as has been indicated, the man is put outside the Church—but ultimately a petition is made and similar prayers offered up.

The notion of a spiritual spring cleaning is familiar, though the beliefs about what constitutes defilement and the method of its removal are an innovation. The men were in the past supposed to seek ritual purification regularly by incising the penis, even if in fact most of them waited till reminded of their duty to the world of the supernatural by an illness or the thought of the uncertainty or danger in some forthcoming enterprise.

CHRISTIANITY

For most of the Christian flock, the pastor admitted, confession also is the child of fear; for every penitent who was in good health, he said, there were at least four who waited for a grave illness or until they were about to embark on some perilous undertaking. No doubt was expressed concerning the efficacy of death-bed contrition, but the delay was deplored. Disease is God's reminder of the road ahead, but the real Christian should need no such warning.

A message summoning the pastor is sent as soon as the patient begins to realise that he may not recover, and he then recounts his past actions in case one of them should be responsible for his condition. I was present by invitation at two such recitals and am convinced that on each occasion the sick man looked upon the admission of his faults as a form of insurance against dying—or, if the worst happened, against being consigned to everlasting damnation. The pastor concluded his supplications, however, with a reminder that he was not begging for the man's life but only for the forgiveness of his sins. 'Thy will be done, not ours,' he prayed, 'but this Thy servant is truly sorry for having forsaken Thy ways.'

Some men take the precaution of settling outstanding quarrels with their relatives or other members of the community. Dahungmboa when laid low with pneumonia, for example, sent word to his sister's husband Gamung. The two had had a disagreement and had not spoken for several months. Dahungmboa recited two verses from the fifth chapter of the Gospel according to Saint Matthew as a greeting—'If thou bring thy gift to the altar, and there rememberest that thy brother hath aught against thee; leave there thy gift before the altar and go thy way; first be reconciled to thy brother and then come and offer thy gift.' He had been ill for five days, he continued, and though I was giving him the new sulfa medicine, perhaps he might still die. Before asking for God's mercy he wished to express regret to Gamung for having nursed hatred for so long. The two men then shook hands, and Gamung gave an assurance that he felt no resentment.

Just as hidden sin may lead to sudden death, so repentance is believed to be followed on occasion by spectacular recovery. Gingmamboa, one of Dahungmboa's kinsmen who had been sitting in the background, at this point came forward and reminded us of his restoration to health a couple of years before. Although he had waited till his disease was further advanced before admitting the purchase of love magic from a visitor, God heard his cry and from that moment decreed that he should not die.

At a later date Ida' told me of a still more wonderful experience in which he had been involved at the Mission at Hopoi. A friend of his, Jeremiah by name, an indentured labourer working on a plantation nearby, was bitten by a snake and found by his fellow workers on the roadside in a state of collapse. They carried him to the labour lines for treatment, but in spite of the efforts of his employer he grew steadily worse. After a time everyone began to give up hope, and it was decided to send for his closest associates. When Ida' arrived the man was breathing feebly and had a barely perceptible pulse. 'This seemed strange,' he related. 'People attacked by poisonous snakes usually die quickly, but Jeremiah had been lingering for some time. So I thought this was perhaps the hand of God.' He accordingly took up a New Testament and read aloud the second chapter of the Gospel according to Saint Mark in which Jesus told the man sick with the palsy that his sins were forgiven and to take up his bed and walk. Turning to his friend, he then asked him had he any wrong to confess. 'Yes, yes,' was the barely audible reply. 'I have committed adultery four times.' This was the turning point, and three days later the man was back at work. But after a few months he contracted another illness. Ida', visiting him in hospital, enquired whether he had returned to his evil ways. He sorrowfully nodded and the next morning was found dead.

An extract from a tract written by the Reverend Stephen Lehner shortly before his death is relevant to the discussion (*It is God Which Worketh to Will and Do*, New Guinea Mission Board, United Evangelical Church of Australis, 1946). 'Gideon handed me his life story. According to that everything was in order. But . . . a certain evasiveness made me dubious. He took sick. Suffering from a peculiar headache he almost raved at times. We cry, "Lord have mercy upon this student". Several weeks passed on. Eventually, after a lesson on a portion of the Gospel of Saint Mark, in which was shown that only after open confession of guilt God's grace would fully do its work, Gideon came to me by night. Somewhat shamefacedly he handed me pages of writing. Another biography. He asks, "*Bingsu*—my teacher— pray for me". We did so. According to the second biography the life of this young man is quite different from that which he first handed in. Serious moral lapses hitherto unconfessed burdened his soul.

They were the cause of his evasiveness, and in consequence of his inner strife probably led to sickness. After he had unreservedly confessed all and received absolution he felt free. The spell was broken, the sickness disappeared, and he felt a happy man.

'There is another student. . . . Gradually I noticed him becoming more quiet. Often I asked myself what could have come over Lingkato. Often I tried to cheer him up but a spirit of despondency seemed to have come over him. He too took sick. An attack of pneumonia. But he recovered, nursed attentively by my wife. He realised that apart from the devoted nursing it was God's kindness that granted him another lease of life. Once, when I visited him and sat with him, he said, "Teacher, tonight I will visit you". As erstwhile Nicodemus, stealthily he came hiding a bundle under his arm. He opened up the package: two bush knives, a tomahawk, several smaller knives, pencils, and a sixpence came to light. Quite overcome, he said: "See, all these things I have stolen, the knives and the axe years ago, and the sixpence from a classmate. This and that belong to the villagers here and there. Please return them to their owners. I know, teacher, that my sickness was God's call to me to be absolutely truthful. Always when you were giving lessons the voice cried in me, Lingkato, you are a hypocrite. Always I tried to drown this voice because I was ashamed to confess my failings. But now I know that if Jesus is really to be my Lord, the unclean spirits must first be driven out. And I will be his own." We knelt in prayer, and, comforted, he returned to his house cleansed from an evil conscience. Thus the Holy Spirit is at work preparing himself chosen vessels from amongst the heathen.'

Pagan Survivals

Mission converts today, when giving their views in broad daylight, usually speak of the old spirits with derision. Such things have no existence, I was told; they were the figments of the ancestors' imagination. It was also denied that the various ceremonies had the effects claimed, and the long continuance of the rites through the ages was cited as proof of the ignorance of the poor benighted heathen.

When questioned during the night, however, few of the natives were so positive. Most persons have an inordinate dread of darkness, and, although the notion of all-powerful beings was ridiculed, they reluctantly admitted to a lingering suspicion that perhaps, after all, there may be spooks which lie in wait to dart from behind a heavy patch of shadow and frighten passers-by out of their wits. Several men claimed to have seen such apparitions, and, whenever the opportunity arose for them to repeat their hair-raising experiences, credulous bystanders always urged them to tell more. It is not surprising to find, then that the old reluctance to undertake journeys on dark nights should still persist; further, if by chance anyone is overtaken by dusk while still some distance from home he makes a long detour around the cemetery. The spirit pool a mile to the west of the village, a perfect spot for bathing, is also avoided unless a European happens to be available to give protection.

The pastor and one or two others who have had a long training in the Mission become angry if anyone mentions such fears in their hearing. God would be justified in administering punishment for such foolishness, they insist. Ida' told me of his desire to imitate a missionary who locked a terrified pupil out of the dormitory, making the lad spend the night in the bush to test whether the spirits could harm him.

This small group of enlightened natives also dismiss magic as an illusion, but the majority are convinced that it worked. When during a discussion of the subject I spoke of the Wogeo spell of invisibility, used by raiding parties to enable them to sneak on the enemy unobserved, one of the men present remarked that he had had a demonstration of how effective such formulæ could be. Some years before, he said, while he was working in one of the towns, some of his friends from the Aitape district recited a few phrases and then managed to burgle a liquor store without being detected. Even the police on watch did not see them. (I suspect that the thieves took the additional precaution of bribing the guard with the promise of a share in the loot.) Again, a woman charged in court with adultery gave as her defence that she had no alternative as the man touched her on the arm with charmed oil.

The fact that the Mission looks upon the performance of magic as a sin was put forward as grounds for believing in its efficacy. If magic were a fraud the missionaries would laugh, one man assured me. 'But they don't; instead, they become enraged. The spells are prayers to Satan, that's why. You know how strong Satan is and that he's always waiting to undo God's work.'

CHRISTIANITY

The rites carried out by the Busama ancestors have long since been abandoned, nevertheless, and it is today impossible to record a single local spell. But the natives have many contacts with people who are less sophisticated than themselves. Vast areas of New Guinea are as yet untouched by missionary endeavour, and when the young men from such places enter European employment they often bring a battery of magical knowledge with them. In the artificial conditions of the compound spells associated with agriculture, fishing, and the weather have no place, and one seldom hears them mentioned. Sorcery, on the other hand, is in a different category; it can be used to terrorise anyone who retains a belief in it. Many of the villagers recounted unpleasant experiences on the goldfields and in the towns, particularly with natives from the backward Sepik and Aitape areas.

The case which I shall quote here was related by Nga'gili'. The details are typical, except that he happens to be one of the few unbelievers. While working as a labourer on the mining field at Wau he was approached by an orphaned Kaidemoe lad. A Sepik native had begged the boy to become his lover and had given him presents, but he was unwilling to indulge in homosexual practices and sought the advice of Nga'gili'. 'Refuse to go,' he was told. The next evening, however, he came home from work to find that his belongings had been carried off to the man's house. Somewhat afraid, he went again to Nga'gili', explaining that if he still declined he could easily be bewitched by magic performed over his property. Nga'gili' thereupon retrieved the bundle himself and later went back with a tuft of his own hair, which he threw in the Sepik native's face. 'There, use that for your witchcraft,' he exclaimed. 'I'm not afraid of you, and in future leave the Kaidemoe boy alone, or you'll have my fists to contend with.'

Very occasionally persons taken ill in the village express suspicions against one of the neighbours, but it seems that they are always burdened with a guilty conscience or have an intense dislike for the person accused. Nga'tigeng, for example, claimed that the severe tropical ulcer on his leg was caused by Angkong, whose bush knife he had recently broken. 'It must have been Angkong,' he said. 'He was angry with me because I had no money to pay for a new knife. He probably learnt some sorcery while he was away working for the Army in Lae and is now trying it out on me.' The other members of the family laughed at the story and told him not to be silly. 'Let me hear no more of such talk,' the elder brother reproved him. 'We don't want a quarrel with Angkong on our hands. Besides, I'm sure he didn't do it. You know the sore began when you cut your leg.'

Ho'giling was also urged to keep quiet when he suggested that his attack of diarrhoea might have been the result of witchcraft carried out by Apim, who, like Angkong, had recently finished a term of indenture with the Army. 'The other night I had an argument with my wife and accused her of flirting with Apim,' he told one of his kinsmen. 'I didn't think she had really, but I was angry, and, as you know, she wanted him for a husband before her parents gave her to me. I daresay someone overheard me and went gossiping. Apim was vexed, and this is his way of making me pay for it.' 'Nonsense,' the man replied. 'Apim's a good Christian. He wouldn't do a thing like that. You must have eaten too much or had a piece of tainted fish.'

It is reasonable to suppose that Bumbu was anxious to take vengeance on all who had given evidence against him, and when two witnesses became ill shortly after the case they claimed that he was responsible. The first, Mabiyeng, had a poisoned toe, the result of an infection contracted by using an unsterilised razor blade for incising a snake bite. 'I know it's Bumbu,' he informed Ida'. 'We've always hated one another since I was a boy, and I've heard it said that he visited one of the sorcerers up at Hote' in the hills last week. He must have bought the magic then, and this is the result. Or perhaps he got it from that Aitape son-in-law of his, Tape.' Ida' calmed him down and persuaded him to go to hospital, where the toe was amputated. No more was heard of the matter on his return.

The second man, Sali, was equally convinced that Bumbu was responsible for his bout of malaria. The pastor was on this occasion summoned to hear his confession and delivered a homily on the stupidity of anyone believing in black magic. 'Even if Bumbu has made spells against you,' he finished, 'they can't do you any harm unless you're afraid of them. Sorcery works through fear—if you're frightened you'll certainly imagine yourself into an illness. But this malaria you've got is real sickness.'

Beside sorcery, love magic is also of use to the young men from the interior when they come down to work on the coast, and they cast their spells as often as opportunity presents itself for sexual dalliance. The passions of the young Christians are no less keen, but, lacking magic of their own, they are less confident of success. The difficulty is overcome by purchasing charmed material, and a brisk trade goes on in bespelled cosmetics, hair lotions, and scent. The Busama are as eager as the rest, and several men admitted having paid as much as three months' wages and more for small amounts. Po'gwi', for instance, the man with no conscience mentioned in an earlier section, gave thirty shillings for a tin containing an ounce of face paint to a friend from the Kaiwa area in the hills to the south-west when they were working together in a store at Salamaua. 'But it was worth this sum,' he stated, 'for when I had it on my face no woman I followed could resist me. Some of them actually made the first offers.' A Rabaul woman married to a Chinese trader was amongst his conquests, and one night she made an assignation with him at the back of her house while the husband was asleep on the verandah not ten yards away. The wife of a man from Buakap also surrendered herself to him, though this time, as recorded, he was discovered.

Po'gwi' gave every indication of being shocked when I asked was any of the paint left. 'I wouldn't bring it here,' he replied. 'I threw it away long ago. We Busama have all been baptised and do not carry out love magic in the village.' He may have been speaking the truth—though I have grave doubts—but there is ample evidence that many others are not as scrupulous. During my residence in the village the pastor heard no less than six confessions of purchasing love charms, and two of the culprits were fathers of young families.

The reason why magic associated with agriculture and health has been so readily abandoned is no doubt to be accounted for by the fact that prayer is an effective substitute.[1] At the formal services, it is true, the requests take the form of supplications; but many members of the congregation do their best in private to bludgeon God into manipulating nature to their advantage. When in January 1945 much of the taro was beginning to wither for want of rain the pastor prayed at the Sunday service that the Lord might have mercy on His flock. 'If the hot sun continues to burn the ground,' he lamented, 'we shall soon have no food, and without food we shall die. Give us, then, Thy blessing, we beg Thee, that Thy children may eat.' But after the weather had at last changed, and the village had enjoyed the benefit of a heavy thunderstorm, a householder with a

[1] For certain diseases also European drugs are a guaranteed cure.

large family, Gala'bo', told me that the day before, seeing all his plants dying before his eyes, he had looked up to heaven while in his garden and asked that rain might fall in the night. 'I reminded God that another day of sunshine would be disaster,' he told me, 'and if He really loves us, as the Bible says, He must do something at once.'

The same difference of attitude is apparent in sickness, when the pastor phrases his petition in some such words as, 'Thy will be done, O Lord, not ours; Thou knowest what is best for us, and we accept Thy judgment; but we beg that, if Thou art testing Thy servant, he may not be found wanting': while the relatives urge baldly, 'Spare him, O God; don't let him die; he's confessed and is sorry for what he did; there's no need to punish him further'.

Again, although public prayers are never offered up for women in childbirth, several husbands—and brothers—have admitted to making personal supplications in their anxiety. Ahipum also stated that he had a private session with God when a quarrel between the two village sections threatened to result in a brawl.

A curious prayer was that of a villager named Gamengsawa. He had been severely beaten by Bumbu not long before and his hatred of the man was burning especially fiercely. When thanking me-for my part in the Court case, he remarked that I must have been the answer to his entreaties. 'I have besought God every night to strike Bumbu dead,' he informed me. 'My belly was churned up with anger, and I wanted to have him punished. Well, God didn't kill him, but He sent you here to see that the fellow was disgraced.' Gamengsawa had clearly been using prayer as a form of sorcery.

Dr. Audrey Richards had pointed out ('A Modern Movement of Witchfinders', *Africa*, Vol. VIII, pp. 448–460) that the complexities of Western civilisation have brought new factors beyond the natives' control and that in Africa the result has been an increase in various protective rites and· more rather than less magic. In Busama the crudest fears of the past have disappeared—except during our wars death by violence no longer occurs—but here also fresh' anxieties have developed. I cannot tell how frequently magic was performed and am thus unaware of whether calls on the Deity are commoner, but it is a fact that prayer is sometimes used to meet difficulties for which there is no precedent. One man, admittedly not notable for his intelligence, confessed appealing for divine aid to ensure that the money set aside for some purchases would be adequate.

Native Independence

The policy of the Lutheran Mission was to lay the foundations of what would ultimately become an independent New Guinea Church, and the leaders frequently stated that they looked forward to the time when the European staff could be withdrawn.[1] No one would have been optimistic enough to have suggested that the preliminary work done prior to 1941 was sufficient, but the four years which followed, when the people were thrown upon their own resources, provided an excellent test for what had been accomplished.

A casual visit to Busama during the middle of 1944 would have left the observer with the impression that paganism had returned. The church and school buildings had not been repaired after their destruction by bombing, and all services and instruction were discontinued. Dance rehearsals, discouraged by the Mission, took place every afternoon, and at monthly intervals festivals were held either in the village or in one of the neighbouring settlements.

Investigation would have revealed, however, that the villagers were not to blame. The manpower situation was desperate, for so many, including the teachers, had been conscripted as labourers. With the family dwellings barely waterproof, any move to construct a place of worship was out of the question. Further, Bumbu, who at that time had supreme authority, was alone responsible for the suppression of prayers and for the dances.

The people's reaction to Bumbu's removal was one of intense relief, and that evening prayers of thanksgiving were recited. Great stress was laid on the fact that exactly a year had passed since the last religious meeting. The coincidence was regarded as a clear demonstration of God's direct intervention—He must have been waiting for the anniversary to come round.

After a day or two, joy began to be replaced by misgivings, and towards the end of a week many were in despair at the realisation of their failure to remain steadfast. The following Sunday was accordingly set aside for a service of humiliation. The passage chosen for the text was Ephesians iv, 17-25: 'This I say therefore and testify in

[1] The constitution of the American Lutheran Mission states, 'The object and purpose of the Lutheran Mission Madang is the evangelising of the natives, gathering them into congregations with an indigenous Church as a final goal'.

the Lord, that ye henceforth walk not as other Gentiles walk, in the vanity of their mind, having the understanding darkened, being alienated from the life of God through the ignorance that is in them, because of the blindness of their heart: who being past feeling have given themselves over to lasciviousness, to work all uncleanness with greediness. But ye have not so learned Christ; if so be that ye have heard him, and have been taught by him, as the truth is in Jesus: that ye put off concerning the former conversation the old man, which is corrupt according to the deceitful lusts, and be renewed in the spirit of your mind; and that ye put on the new man, which after God is created in righteous and pure holiness. Wherefore putting away lying, speak every man truth with his neighbour: for we are members one of another.'

The service turned into an emotional orgy. Over thirty members of the congregation spoke, with much weeping and beating of the breast. The tenor of all the remarks was the Busama had been weighed in the balance and found wanting. The early Christians were prepared to face wild beasts in the Roman arena rather then turn away from God, but the New Guinea converts could not stand up against a beating. What a way this was of showing appreciation of the abiding compassion vouchsafed to a people who had lost less than a dozen men during the war! 'Alas, we are miserable sinners, the most unworthy of Thy children, O Lord,' one of the elders declaimed. 'We realise that we are not fit to offer up our prayers. Yet we beg Thee to look upon us once more. Give us another chance to prove ourselves: replenish us with Thy spirit and make us new men.' 'Woe, woe, woe,' another took up the lament. 'We forgot our brothers and our sons. There they are with the soldiers, exposed to bombing and rifle fire, and we didn't think of their danger enough to pray for their safety. Forgive us, Lord, and help us to return to Thee.'

The Christmas ceremonies six weeks later developed along similar lines, and before the day was over a large number of persons had made public statements of their backslidings. Two men, for example, admitted having bought magic, another that he had conducted the practice for one of the dances, and still another that he, a church elder, had taken no steps to remonstrate with Bumbu.

A necessary condition before baptism can take place and Communion be celebrated, as was mentioned, is that serious misconduct must not have occurred for some months. Oppressed with a sense of sin, the Busama did not broach the subject for nearly a year, when elders from the other side of the Huon Gulf were invited across to give advice. No wine was available for Communion, but after much discussion it was decided that the war-time babies might be baptised early in 1946.

In this chapter I have described how Christianity came into its own again between Bumbu's disgrace and the baptism ceremony. Despite several later visits, I have restricted myself here to material collected during that particular period, while the natives were still without the guiding hand of a European missionary. The sole change which I have noted is that church attendance is now not quite as regular as in the days of stress.

Chapter Thirteen

RACE RELATIONS

'They have sown the wind, and they shall reap the whirlwind.'—*Hosea* viii, 7.

'HERE comes the *bumbum*,' I overheard someone remark to his companions as he caught sight of me approaching. This is the expression for 'white man,' but I felt that I was entitled to something more specific. I would be grateful, I told him, if in future he would use my name. 'I see what you mean,' he replied. 'We also object when we're called kanakas.'[1] Another speaker then enlightened me on the derivation of the word. *Bum*, he said, has two meanings: it is used for fish which are no longer fresh when a canoe has returned from a protracted expedition on a hot day, and it is also applied to bush pigs or plants to distinguish them from the domestic or cultivated types. The literal translation of *bumbum* is thus 'stinking wild man', a fact which, if they were aware of it, would shock a number of those to whom it is customarily applied.

Nothing is of greater importance for the future of the Busama than their attitude to Europeans, under whose tutelage they must remain for many years, and in this final chapter I shall discuss the relations between the two peoples. I shall leave the intimate village

[1] *Kanaka* is the Hawaiian word for 'man'. It was applied originally to any South-Sea-island labourer, but is nowadays used for village natives to distinguish them from employees, and also derisively for all natives.

276

circle which has hitherto supplied my material, partly because most contacts take place outside, partly because all the natives and all the whites in the country are equally involved. I shall still rely on my own observations, though the printed statements of others can now be used for corroboration..

White Prestige

A number of the whites in New Guinea have no racial prejudice and regard skin pigmentation with indifference. They are found in all classes but are most common amongst the missionaries and, to a lesser extent, the officials and independent miners. These last usually have a small labour line and learn to appreciate the native as a human being by working at his side.

Many European residents are, however, sensitive about what they refer to as 'white prestige'. To them the natives' homage is a right of race, not something to be won by sympathy, kindness, and consideration. They argue that dignity is best maintained by indifference and authority by discourtesy; and there are those who advocate brutality.[1]

The supporters of this view, like those who put forward the argument in other parts of the world, are firm advocates of segregation. 'Never talk to the boys themselves in any circumstances . . .' the Rabaul *Times* warned newcomers to the Territory in a special article in its issue of August 27, 1926. 'Apart from your house boys and boss boy, never allow any native to approach you in the field or on the bungalow verandah.'

Several members of ANGAU during the war attempted to impose the principles of 'white prestige' on the troops. In some bases they were so successful that orders were issued that natives must not travel in jeeps, where of necessity they would sit in close proximity to a European, unless on Army business. I learnt afterwards that my action in allowing a native servant to accompany me in a staff car to the airfield when we were about to catch a plane gave rise to criticism. What I should have done was to order a special truck for him: it was better to use up petrol than to endanger the status of Europeans. But the most significant illustration of the popular attitude

---

[1] Cf. S. W. Reed, *The Making of Modern New Guinea*, op. cit., pp. 243–252.

occurred in Madang immediately after its recapture. The town was in ruins, and soldiers and natives were at work clearing up the mess. Two tanks were installed near the wharf for drinking, both full of the same chlorinated water but labelled respectively 'European personnel' and 'Natives only'. As I passed one morning I heard the ANGAU officer in charge of the natives roundly abusing a private who had gone to the wrong tap. 'Have you no pride of race?' he asked. 'Don't you realise that this water is for coons?'[1]

All coloured persons fall under the ban irrespective of their background and education. The Airways line which maintains the service to Australia at one stage yielded to local pressure to the extent of refusing to carry natives who were being sent away to complete their training as teachers. An appeal to the management in Sydney soon led to the removal of the prohibition, but the students, though charged full fares, still received none of the meals served to the other passengers. More recently a grave scandal occurred in one of the towns when a member of the club took along as his guest a visiting medical practitioner of Filipino origin. In the subsequent recriminations it was said by some that they saw no difference in inviting this man and a labourer from a plantation.

The situation has many parallels with Victorian England, when those born into the upper class used to put forward the notion in all seriousness that their privileges were divinely ordained. 'Towards our inferiors,' a contemporary volume of etiquette stated complacently, 'by keeping them at a safe distance, we merely maintain ourselves and them in the rank in which a Higher Power has placed them.' Arguments against native advancement have similar echoes. It is no use giving labourers higher pay, for example, because they would spend the money on trash (see above p. 201, footnote), and no use shortening their hours to allow them more time for vice.[2]

[1] Such distinctions were sometimes made on medical grounds (the natives are a reservoir of tropical diseases), but this was not so in Madang. (Cf. S. W. Reed, *op. cit.*, p. 246: 'Natives never enter white stores except on errands for their masters. When they do, they always use a side entrance.' The bakery in Lae serves natives, who form the bulk of its customers, through a window. One sometimes sees a queue waiting in the rain while the commodious shop is empty.

[2] Cf. Lord Hailey, *African Survey*, Oxford, 1945, p. 1,219: 'When the President of the Royal Society could urge in 1807 that the education of the labouring classes would be prejudicial to their morals and happiness, his logic differed

RACE RELATIONS

The use of the word 'boy' for the native is indicative of the rôle to which he is assigned. He is expected to revere the white man in the way that a child looks up to his elders. The *Pacific Islands Monthly*, a journal representing commercial interests published in Sydney for circulation in Oceania, was most scathing when in 1947 the Administrator gave orders that the expression must not in future appear in official documents.[1] 'Some old hands are laughing and some are jeering over the latest fatuousness,' an article stated. '"Boy" to indicate a coloured man is as old as pidgin English itself, and there is nothing offensive or derogatory in it. . . . The Government circular ties in with various incidents which have been received with derision in the Territories—the reception at Government House luncheon table of Papuan ex-POW's, for instance, and the official handshaking when representatives of the natives are being greeted.' 'To what absurd lengths planners will go in evolving Government policy: what next?' added a writer in another part of the same issue.

'Boy' is justified by some with the argument that the Melanesians are incapable of mental development after the age of twelve. These are the persons who oppose education as ridiculous waste of public funds.[2] 'We learn with pleasure that the seven natives who were being sent to Australia [for medical training] did not go owing to representations made by the Citizens' Association,' wrote the Editor of the Rabaul *Times* in the issue of February 1, 1929. 'This should go a long way towards satisfying those who expressed their indignation, and the number is legion.' Facilities for giving the instruction in New Guinea did not exist, and the project had for the time being to be abandoned.

The natives' inferiority is also forced upon them by the way in which they are addressed. A high Army officer who was visiting New Guinea from Land Headquarters at Melbourne in the war years asked me after we had been messing together for a few days

from that of the South African farmer mainly in the terms in which it was expressed.'

[1] *Pacific Islands Monthly*, August 1947.
The residents of New Guinea, like those of other Colonial outposts, are often out of touch with what is taking place elsewhere. In 1948 a settler defended the word 'boy' in my presence on the ground that it was recognised as 'the proper term for a native in Shanghai, Batavia, and Cairo.'

[2] S. W. Reed, *op. cit.*, p. 189, noted 'the definite hostility of Europeans to the natives being given any education at all'.

whether I always spoke as I had then been doing to my servant. When I wanted to know in what way I had seemed to be peculiar, he replied that I was the only person he had so far met who did not make a practice of raising his voice. Many Europeans also sprinkle their remarks liberally with such epithets as 'coon,' 'boong', and 'bloody black bastard'.

Rough speech is sometimes accompanied by the use of strong-arm methods. 'As soon as the natives here are made to work the healthier they will be, and the less call there will be for the expenditure by the Government on large quantities of medicine for the curing of native ailments, which are nothing more nor less than pure laziness on the part of the kanaka,' the Rabaul *Times* commented on March 22, 1929. 'In addition to making him healthy it will also make him honest, though there is no getting away from the fact that corporal punishment will have to be applied here until the kanaka is taught that honesty is the best and most painless policy.'

The current viewpoint may be gathered from an item published in the *Pacific Islands Monthly* of August 1945. 'All the old hands in the Territories are chuckling over the story of how Sergeant C. of ANGAU presented a souvenir walking-stick to Eddie Ward,' the report began. The then Minister for External Territories, the Honourable E. J. Ward, was at the time on a tour of New Guinea. As the stick was being handed over, the donor noticed that the end was split. 'Oh, I'm sorry it's damaged,' the reporter quoted him as saying. 'I must have done that when I whacked that coon this morning.

'The Australian Minister bridled and snorted. "When you did what?" he demanded.

'C. suddenly realised that he was in the sensitive presence of officialdom, which says that fuzzy-wuzzies are our black brothers, whose bottoms must in no circumstances be caned. But it was too late. He explained gently that circumstances occasionally arose when it was necessary to whack a recalcitrant native. . . .

'(The) boys were lined, in the presence of grave and senior officers, and interrogated. They frankly admitted that Masta C. had caned the behinds of a couple of lads guilty of persistent absenteeism and that they deserved punishment.

'Did they wish to make a complaint. . . .? asked senior officers. The labourers said coyly that they did not.'

RACE RELATIONS

The report then goes on to tell derisively of Sergeant C's transfer
to another unit. It concludes with this paragraph. 'A booklet
entitled *You and the Native*, prepared by the Allied Geographical
Section, Southwest Pacific Area, was placed in the hands of every
officer and non-com. serving in the Pacific Islands. . . . And here are
the exact words of Section 91 of the booklet, outlining the best way
of treating natives: "There may be a bad egg who deliberately defies
you, just to try you out. There is only one thing to do in these
circumstances. Crack him." ' The author of the booklet, which was
specially written for the Geographical Section, had lived in Papua
for twenty years.

A paragraph in an article by a reporter of the Sydney *Sun* newspaper is also illuminating ('Way to Islands' New Order is not
Smooth,' June 9, 1948). 'In Port Moresby a few days ago a
schooner skipper was urging newcomers to read a sweat-streaked
clipping. It was an editorial from the *Pacific Islands Monthly*, only
newspaper of the islands. Under the heading, "Brown Brother in
South Pacific Administration," the *P.I.M.* wrote: "Why cannot the
nations of this world understand that for the majority of the coloured
races there is only one law which the masses understand—the law of
the clenched fist?" "Everybody here knows that is true," the skipper
said. The skipper had been fined £5 for kicking a native in the
pants.'

Suitable comment is provided by the remark of an Army signalman stationed near Busama when he asked me would I reprimand a
native who was working for his unit as a linesman. 'Yako has been
rude,' I was informed, 'but he's a good boy, and we don't want to
send him in to have his arse kicked by ANGAU. They're such cruel
bastards.'

Assault has always been a penal offence, but the natives express
doubts about the disinterestedness of the justice meted out; they
claim that some magistrates make a practice of punishing coloured
offenders with greater severity than those of European origin.[1]
Comment was especially critical during 1948 after a party of natives
guilty of being drunk were sentenced to pay £10 or in default to
serve three months in gaol. Some time before, it was pointed out, a

[1] In 1948, however, a magistrate who had grossly exceeded his powers was
sentenced to imprisonment for three years.

white man charged with bad language and resisting arrest had paid only £5.[1]

ANGAU Instruction D.S., No. 9, 3.XI.43, is relevant here. 'If a member of the field staff conducting the inspection of [a plantation] possesses the necessary authority, he should deal immediately with charges laid against the labourers by an employer. No proceedings will be taken, however, against an employer until a full report has been submitted to this Headquarters and an instruction received that proceedings are to be instituted.'

Causes

Economic factors account in part for the prevailing attitude of the Europeans. Industry, as organised in New Guinea at present, depends upon the cheap labour which the local inhabitants provide. Native advancement is therefore resisted in some quarters because the white man's pocket would suffer and his livelihood be endangered.

The cultural gap separating the two peoples may also have some effect, for neither is able to appreciate the values of the other. Yet in the neighbouring Solomons I have never seen native medical practitioners received socially even though their educational standard is higher than that of many of the white residents; and the average European in Africa is not noticeably liberal towards university-trained negroes.

Of greater weight is the fact that the Europeans are a tiny minority. A rising is unthinkable while things remain as they are, and many persons fear any change lest it should hasten the day when the whites will be thrown out. The insularity of the average settler has been

[1] The dates of the offences were August 9, 1947, and December 29, 1947. The European was charged with resisting a police officer in the execution of his duty and also with using indecent language. When the case came up for hearing he did not appear on call, and watch-house bail was ordered to be estreated, £2 10s. in each case. Convictions were recorded and no other penalty was imposed. The cases attracted the attention of others besides the natives. In April 1948 the sentence passed on four Europeans guilty of drunkenness varied from a fine of £10 or six weeks' imprisonment to a fine of £15 or two months' imprisonment.

mentioned, but the establishment of the Republic of India has not passed unnoticed.

Sexual jealousy may be involved: certainly the young labourer, naked except for his loin-cloth, is a better physical specimen than his employer is as a rule willing to acknowledge. At the same time, I have found no trace of the American stereotype of the sensual black man continually seeking to rape the pure white woman. Bedrooms in the towns may be 'boy proofed,' but everyone recognises that the cause of this inconvenience is not the native as such but the system which deprives him of normal access to members of the opposite sex.[2]

Native Reactions

Before the war those who scorned to be intimate with the native used to cite his behaviour as proof that he accepted his inferiority. Save in the vicinity of such towns as Rabaul, where what were called 'radical notions' were beginning to circulate, his manners, it was pointed out, were excellent. He knew his place—was self effacing and obedient and neither answered back nor defended himself from cuffs and kicks.

In those days, however, power was in the hands of the Europeans, and the people had to pay lip service. Many of them knew from experience how unpleasant the consequences of refusal were likely to be. But even then one had only to gain their confidence to realise the absence of any spontaneous regard for the white man. The natives are acute observers and soon sum up the character of all with whom they come in contact. The worthy earned praise, but others were despised or, if they were not dangerous, laughed at. These last were often mercilessly lampooned in dances and semi-dramatic performances.

[1] Cf. J. Dollard, *Caste and Class in a Southern Town*, Yale University Press, 1948.

[2] Sexual approaches by European women to natives are very rare. The Busama with whom I was sufficiently intimate to discuss the matter denied that they ever take place, but the Wogeo elders think it necessary to warn their young men of the danger involved in yielding to a white woman's advances.

Relations between European men and native women are largely confined to areas where pre-marital intercourse is customarily approved. S. W. Reed, *op. cit.*, pp. 246–247, however, says that 'addressing a native woman in the street is regarded as tantamount to an admission of having an affair with her'.

RACE RELATIONS

It is possible that the Europeans may have been confused by the remarks which were so frequently dropped expressing envy for their knowledge. The fact to be noted here is that this was attributed to opportunity: nowhere was it looked upon as a fundamental quality associated with a light skin.[1] Indeed, the least sophisticated natives considered themselves to be the white man's intellectual equal. The story of the outwitting of the cunning overseer who had a glass eye has since the early days been as popular in remote villages as in hotel bars. This relates how the man left the eye on a post, telling his labourers that it would keep watch on them during his absence. They waited till he had gone some distance and then covered it with a hat. Europeans tell the tale as an illustration of the natives' stupidity; the latter tell it to demonstrate their own sagacity.

The groups living in the interior, where information about our economic system has not yet penetrated, ascribe superiority of modern equipment to magic. Various new religious cults which have as their object the diversion of the goods and money to native channels are the direct outcome of this conviction.[2] A belief that ceremonies can serve as a substitute for science may be irrational, but a number of parallels from the recent history of Europe and Australia immediately come to mind. As the natives' experience has grown, the importance of technical efficiency and of training to achieve it has come to be appreciated, and in the coast villages there is an increasingly urgent demand for better educational facilities. 'If the Australians would only send us more teachers,' one of the Busama lamented, 'we'd be turning out our own engineers, doctors, and aeroplane pilots.'

'White prestige', in point of fact, had the reverse effect from what

---

[1] The Busama pastor who referred to the New Guinea peoples as descendants of Ham (see p. 242) was, I believe, unique.

[2] *Vide* L. P. Mair, *Australia in New Guinea, op. cit.,* pp. 64–66; G. Hoeltke, 'Die Mambu Bewegung in Neuguinea', *Annali Lateranensi,* Vol. V, pp. 181–219; and F. E. Williams, *Vailala Madness,* Anthropological Report of Papua, No. 4, Port Moresby, 1924, and 'Vailala Madness in Retrospect', *Essays presented to C. G. Seligman* (edited by E. E. Evans-Pritchard), London, 1934, pp. 369–380. Such cults are a feature of culture contact all over the world; see A. L. Kroeber, *Anthropology,* London, 1948, pp. 437–440; B. G. M. Sundkler, *Bantu Prophets in South Africa, op. cit.;* A. C. Cato, 'A New Religious Cult in Fiji', *Oceania,* Vol. XVIII, pp. 146–156; C. S. Belshaw, *Island Administration in the Southwest Pacific.* London, 1950, pp. 126–129; etc.

was intended, and the result was not respect but resentment. Though normally concealed, this flared up on occasion to bitter animosity. An instance was the unrest, culminating in a near riot, when a native member of the New Guinea Infantry Battalion was found dead one morning early in 1945 with no mark of violence on his body. The board of enquiry was satisfied that he had accidentally electrocuted himself and that no one was to blame, but his companions were for a long time convinced that the officers had murdered him. Such a suspicion would have occurred to no one had the relations between the two races been satisfactory. The younger Europeans, however, had been carefully schooled by their superiors in all the usual prejudices. The majority of these latter were old residents of the Territory.[1]

The active support which a few natives gave to the Japanese is attributable in some instances to pique at European pretensions. A statement made in 1943 by Professor D. W. Brogan in his book *The English People* sums up the situation. 'All the British peoples share the "Anglo-Saxon" colour prejudice which, whether it is a new phenomenon or not, and whether it is increasing or diminishing, is still a mighty force weakening the political and moral power of all English-speaking peoples. . . .' he writes. 'However much the Chinese may hate or the Indians may fear the Japanese, there must be few Asiatics who have not been tempted to think of Pearl Harbour and Singapore with just a little gratification. Such gratification, of course, is a luxury which neither Indians nor Chinese can afford, but people sometimes indulge in feelings beyond their means.'

The ungracious behaviour of the people in the towns used to be ascribed to agitators from overseas steamers, but a more likely explanation is that these natives had opportunities for earning money without entering regular European employment and were

[1] I had accounts of this incident from both the whites and the natives. A version published later in the Sydney *Sun* newspaper blamed 'irresponsible whites and negroes' (August 30, 1945).

The Lutu-Awasa quarrel and other intra-village disputes may be the direct outcome of 'white prestige'. Anger against the whites, unable to find open expression, has perhaps been turned against members of the natives' own group. The subject is discussed, against the American background, in J. Dollard, *Caste and Class in a Southern Town*, op. cit., and *Frustration and Aggression*, Yale University Press, 1939. B. G. M. Sundkler, *Bantu Prophets in South Africa*, op. cit., develops the theme—see especially p. 173.

either no longer obliged to hide their resentment or were taking the whites as a model. They disdained to show the most casual courtesies, and a stranger asking directions or seeking some slight assistance, as, for instance, if a car refused to start, to quote from my own experience, was answered with the utmost incivility.

Brutality filtered downwards, too, and was as common in the villages as on the plantations. It is arguable that the traditions of olden days may have been in part responsible, but there are plenty of European examples to follow. The worst offenders were the native police, and innumerable cases occurred of village officials being struck and village women raped.

It appears that some of the old German missionaries tended to take as their guide the Christ who drove the merchants and money changers out of the temple with a scourge of small cords in preference to the Christ who advised turning the other cheek.[1] These also had their imitators, and natives spreading the Gospel sometimes used methods no less ferocious than those adopted by the police.

One even met the occasional native who adopted his master's attitude to alien races. I twice during the war heard labourers sneering at negroes as 'boong belong America.'

Whatever may have been said in the past, however, no one would be so foolish as to regard the present situation as proof of the success of discrimination. The so-called radical notions have now spread far and wide, and Europeans are painfully aware that the old esteem, or what they took to be esteem, is no longer forthcoming. The people display no great keenness to enter employment, and they report assaults, ask for high wages, and strike when these are refused. The Administration also has a problem with deputations requesting the provision of more teachers, the introduction of new crops, and the setting up of some form of local government. A meeting of village officials at Finschhafen in 1946 threatened mass resignations if the demands were not granted.

Perhaps the chief reason for the change is that for the time being the natives are independent. Cash is more plentiful than it used to be in 1939, and many persons have a substantial banking account. Good wages were earned during the war, when the able-bodied men were conscripted, high prices were paid by the troops for curios, and

[1] S. W. Reed, *op. cit.*, p. 238.

generous payments have been handed over as compensation for war damage. The supply of goods in the trade stores, on the other hand, is still somewhat meagre, and there is little incentive to go on piling up more money.

The old hands, however, lay the sole blame on the Army. The troops, they say, 'spoiled' the natives, a statement which can only be answered with the query, spoiled them for what?

Certain ANGAU officers may have done their best with safeguards, but the Australian soldier was as a rule unimpressed and mixed with the people on terms of comparative equality. Friendships were established, and I know of several instances where letters are still being exchanged. The soldier's job was not at stake—the lad who accused ANGAU of cruelty was just the type who, as a labour overseer in peace instead of a signalman in war, would himself have been ready to kick the backside of anyone who was impertinent—he and his companions appeared to be in a huge majority, and sexual jealousy could not be involved because the only white women in the country were a few Army nurses. The xenophobia which is usually regarded as characteristic of Australians is bound up with protection of living standards, and if these are not threatened there is frequently an impulse to champion the underdog.[1] The Indonesian Republic has always had the Australian workers' support, for instance, and only the more expensive restaurants in Australia favoured by white Americans issued a ban in war-time on negroes. Another factor of importance was that the native carriers and stretcher bearers had won admiration for their work on the Kokoda trail and in the Salamaua and Ramu River campaigns. The press of the day habitually referred to them as fuzzy-wuzzy angels, and a poem with this as its title was enormously popular. Finally, some of the troops probably enjoyed stepping into the shoes of Lady Bountiful. Considerable psychological satisfaction can be derived from distributing largesse, especially at low cost, and the natives accepted such simple gifts as a packet of cigarettes or a tin of meat with pathetic gratitude.

With the many thousands of Americans the people had little direct contact. Nearly all the campaigns for which carriers were required were fought by Australians, native troops took no active

[1] Professor W. K. Hancock notes in his book *Australia* the tendency both to exalt the humble and meek and to put down the mighty from their seat.

part in operations till fairly late when most of the Americans had left, and Australians always acted as overseers for the labour gangs in the United States' bases. The presence of negroes was, however, of immense importance. They were convincing evidence, it was thought, of the truth of the earlier contention that coloured peoples, if given the chance, could rise to the same economic level as whites. The New Guinea natives were naturally unaware that race riots and lynchings take place in America.

Conversation with Australian soldiers had the effect of widening the native horizon, but it must be admitted that the new vision of the world is often seriously distorted. The troops had little realisation of the cost of financing native development and no notion at all of the difficulties involved in bringing about a social revolution. Their misconceptions were transmitted to their hearers, thus adding fuel to the fires of indignation which had already been kindled. It is manifestly impossible for any plantation to pay unskilled employees at the rate of one pound per day, the figure sometimes asked for, and the Administration with the best will in the world cannot hope either now or in the foreseeable future to establish a school with a European teacher in every village, build a road and maintain transport to every remote centre, or give every householder a saleable crop to grow and arrange for it to be marketed.

Conclusion

The Reports which used to be submitted by the Administration each year to the League of Nations had much to say about the way in which native progress was being fostered. The achievements, nevertheless, were comparatively slight. One difficulty was lack of funds, for New Guinea, like most colonies in the pre-war period, was expected to pay its way from its own revenues, which were necessarily small when the country was as yet undeveloped and the inhabitants still primitive. But the Australian Government has at last begun to take up its responsibilities, and grants are now being made available. It has thus been possible to inaugurate the Education service and to make extensions to the Departments of Native Affairs, Public Health, and Agriculture.

A new approach is evident, too, in the Administration. Inspired

RACE RELATIONS

by the Administrator and some of the senior officers, numbers of the field staff are determined to end the stagnation of the past. Detailed plans have been drawn up, and the initial steps for their implementation are being taken.

The ultimate success of any scheme must largely depend on whether the natives' confidence has been secured. 'White prestige' has failed in New Guinea as it has everywhere, and something else is called for. The obvious substitute is an assumption that every human being, no matter what his colour, has essential dignity which is entitled to respect. Good manners must then follow, and, as Burke pointed out, manners are more important than laws. 'Upon them, in large measure, the laws depend,' he said. 'The laws touch us here and there and now and then. Manners are what vex or soothe, corrupt or purify, exalt or debase, barbarise or refine us, by a constant, steady, uniform, insensible operation, like that of the air we breathe.'

The Editor of the London *Observer* recently told his readers that Africa could never be a white continent and that only the most careful attention to race relations could save it from being a continent where no white man is welcome (May 8, 1949). This is true also of New Guinea. Australia has a million potential friends at her northern gateway, and it largely rests with the Europeans already resident in the Territory whether they become friends in fact—or enemies.

APPENDICES

Appendix A

VITAL STATISTICS

The natives do not keep an exact record of their ages, and those quoted are only approximate.

CENSUS OF OCTOBER 1, 1944

	Males	Females	Total
Infants (under 3)	27	22	49
Children (3–13)	92	105	197
Adolescents (14–20)	50	19	69
Young adults (21–45)	94	102	196
Older adults (over 45)	27	40	67
Total	290	288	578

Of this number 51 males (26 adolescents, 25 young adults) were absent in employment.

The Army had a category of 'effective males', which was taken to include all able-bodied men between the apparent ages of 16 and 45, exclusive of village officials, Mission workers, and fathers with four or more young children living. Thirty effective males were left in the village, and the 51 labourers thus represented 60·3 per cent. of the total. Of these 8 were married but had no children, 8 had one child each, 5 had 2 children each, and 4 had 3 children each.

Prior to 1944 Busama and Gwado (population 51 on 1.x.44)

figures were recorded together. The following are the births and deaths for the previous seven years:

	Births		Deaths	
	Males	*Females*	*Males*	*Females*
13.x.37–12.x.40	15	13	11	14
13.x.40–19.iii.44	35	28	22	33
20.iii.44–30.ix.44	13	9	14	9
Total (13.x.37–30.ix.44)	63	50	47	56

The net gain in the period was therefore 16 males; but there was a loss of 6 females. (The death-rate for Gwado, where a community originally from the interior now lives close to the sea, is certainly higher than for Busama.)

CENSUS OF OCTOBER 1, 1945

	Males	*Females*	*Total*
Infants	30	27	57
Children	95	110	205
Adolescents	48	19	67
Young adults	92	102	194
Older adults	26	40	66
Total	291	298	589

Of this number 33 males (15 adolescents, 18 adults) were absent in employment. These represented 43 per cent. of the total effective males.

Births and deaths (Busama only):

	Births		Deaths	
	Males	*Females*	*Males*	*Females*
1.x.44–30.ix.45	8	14	7	4

Net gain in one year: 1 male, 10 females.

CENSUS OF MAY 5, 1947

	Males	*Females*	*Total*
Children (under 16)	142	129	271
Adults (over 16)	167	179	386
Total	309	308	617

APPENDIX A

I was not on this occasion present and give only the figures recorded.

Births and deaths (Busama only):

	Births		Deaths	
	Males	Females	Males	Females
1.x.44–4.v.47	22	14	4	4

Net gain in 2½ years: 18 males, 10 females.

Absentees 31.i.48:

Labourers	42 (plus	2 wives and	4 children)			
Teachers	5 (,,	5 ,,	,, 15	,,	)
Black missionaries	2 (,,	2 ,,	,, 2	,,	)
Mission trainees	5 (,,	2 ,,	,, 2	,,	)
Total	54 (,,	11 ,,	,, 23	,,	)

FIGURES ON JANUARY 31, 1950

No census had been taken since 1947. The births and deaths, as recorded by the Mission teachers (on whom Government officials have to depend), were as follows:

	Births		Deaths	
	Males	Females	Males	Females
5.v.47–31.1.50	32	11	14	14

Net gain in 2½ years: 18 males; but there was a loss of 3 females.

The population of the village was therefore 327 males and 305 females, a total of 632.

The gain since 1.x.44 was 37 males and 17 females, a total of 54 (9·3 per cent.). The proportion of females of reproductive age must have fallen, and the increase is unlikely to continue at the present rate.

Absentees 31.i.50:

Labourers	55 (plus	5 wives and	7 children)		
Teachers	6 (,,	6 ,,	,, 12	,,	)
Mission trainees	3				
Government trainees	4				
Total	68 (,,	11 ,,	,, 19	,,	)

Of the 55 labourers 10 had been away for more than 3 years, 16 between 2 and 3 years, 10 between 1 and 2 years, and 19 less than 1 year. The last group included a number who intended to be absent for only a few weeks or months.

Appendix B

FOOD SURVEYS

Gardens were measured by pacing, with the pace length carefully checked.

1. CONDITIONS ON SEPTEMBER 30, 1944

Acreage

Total area under cultivation		8½ acres
Area planted during:	September	7,347 sq. yd.
	August	3,547 sq. yd.
	July	6,207 sq. yd.
	June	9,162 sq. yd.
	May	4,900 sq. yd.
	April	5,993 sq. yd.
	March	2,975 sq. yd.

Yield

Every 9 sq. yd. contained approximately 24 plants; and the average weight of each corm, if it is dug up at the end of 6 or 7 months, is 6·4 oz. (weight when not yet prepared for cooking).

The potential harvest was:

October	3,184 lb.
November	6,392 lb.
December	5,227 lb.
January	9,771 lb.
February	6,685 lb.
March	3,802 lb.
April	7,837 lb.

Consumption

At this stage 512 persons were resident in the village. To feed these the equivalent of 414 full rations was required (the infants

296

needed no taro and the children and aged persons only three-quarters of a full ration each).

Full ration 4½ lb. taro daily (my estimate; but see below).
Full ration for 414 for 30 days 55,890 lb.

In October there would be enough taro for 1·7 days
November   ,,   ,,   ,,   ,, ,, 3.9 days
December   ,,   ,,   ,,   ,, ,, 2.8 days
January   ,,   ,,   ,,   ,, ,, 5.2 days
February   ,,   ,,   ,,   ,, ,, 3·5 days
March   ,,   ,,   ,,   ,, ,, 2 days
April   ,,   ,,   ,,   ,, ,, 4·2 days

Army authorities had been supplying sufficient rice, biscuits, and meat for 12·3 days in every month. Sago had been available for 5 days in every month but was becoming scarce. The people had therefore to eke out 20 days' supplies over 30.

These figures were forwarded to Army HQ., and the issue was increased by 50 per cent.

2. CONDITIONS ON AUGUST 31, 1945

Acreage

Total area under taro cultivation   38 acres
Area planted during: August   20,322 sq. yd.
                      July   21,857 sq. yd.
                      June   25,077 sq. yd.
                      May   24,804 sq. yd.
                      April   24,142 sq. yd.
                      March   19,333 sq. yd.
                      February   24,124 sq. yd.
                      January   24,238 sq. yd.

Yield

The potential harvest was:

September   48,500 lb.
October   48,200 lb.
November   38,700 lb.
December   48,200 lb.
January   49,600 lb.
February   50,200 lb.
March   43,700 lb.
April   40,700 lb.

APPENDIX B

Consumption

At this stage 420 full rations were required (56,700 lb. every 30 days).

In September there would be enough taro for 25.7 days
October   ,,   ,,   ,,   ,,   ,,   25·5 days
November ,,   ,,   ,,   ,,   ,,   20·5 days
December ,,   ,,   ,,   ,,   ,,   25·5 days
January   ,,   ,,   ,,   ,,   ,,   26·3 days
February   ,,   ,,   ,,   ,,   ,,   26.6 days
March   ,,   ,,   ,,   ,,   ,,   23.3 days
April   ,,   ,,   ,,   ,,   ,,   21·7 days

Practically no sago was available.
The authorities continued to issue supplies till December.

3. CONDITIONS ON JANUARY 31, 1947

Acreage

Total area under taro cultivation		65 acres
Area planted during:	January	44,000 sq. yd.
	December	42,000 sq. yd.
	November	42,500 sq. yd.
	October	39,500 sq. yd.
	September	37,000 sq. yd.
	August	33,000 sq. yd.
	July	31,500 sq. yd.
	June	30,000 sq. yd.
	May	36,000 sq. yd.

Yield

Each taro corm, if dug up at the end of 8 or 9 months, as was now possible, weighs approximately 11 oz.

The potential harvest was:

February	66,000 lb.
March	55,000 lb.
April	57,800 lb.
May	60,500 lb.
June	67,800 lb.
July	72,400 lb.
August	76,100 lb.
September	77,000 lb.
October	80,700 lb.

APPENDIX B

Consumption

At this stage 460 full rations were required (62,000 lb. every 30 days).

In February there would be a surplus of   4,000 lb.
March   „   „   „ deficit of   7,000 lb.
April   „   „   „   „   „   4,200 lb.
May   „   „   „   „   „   1,500 lb.
June   „   „   „ surplus of   3,800 lb.
July   „   „   „   „   „ 10,400 lb.
August   „   „   „   „   „ 14,100 lb.
September „   „   „   „   „ 15,000 lb.
October   „   „   „   „   „ 18,700 lb.

Sago was available to make up the deficits of March, April, and May.

4. CONDITIONS ON JANUARY 31, 1948

Acreage

Total area under taro cultivation		95 acres
Area planted during:	January	57,000 sq. yd.
	December	80,900 sq. yd.
	November	86,900 sq. yd.
	October	68,000 sq. yd.
	September	31,200 sq. yd.
	August	29,300 sq. yd.
	July	30,500 sq. yd.
	June	35,000 sq. yd.
	May	40,000 sq. yd.

Yield

The potential harvest was:

February	73,000 lb.
March	64,000 lb.
April	56,000 lb.
May	54,000 lb.
June	67,000 lb.
July	125,000 lb.
August	169,000 lb.
September	146,000 lb.
October	106,000 lb.

APPENDIX B

Consumption

At this stage 460 full rations were required (62,000 lb. every 30 days).

In February there would be a surplus of 13,000 lb.
March   „   „   „   „   „   2,000 lb.
April   „   „   „   deficit of   6,000 lb.
May   „   „   „   „   „   8,000 lb.
June   „   „   „   surplus of   5,000 lb.
July   „   „   „   „   „   63,000 lb.
August   „   „   „   „   „   107,000 lb.
September   „   „   „   „   „   84,000 lb.
October   „   „   „   „   „   44,000 lb.

5. CONDITIONS ON JANUARY 31, 1950

Acreage

Total area under taro cultivation 106 acres. (A week earlier the figure would have been 108, but two acres had been destroyed in a single night by pigs.)

Gardens on the Buang River must be distinguished as the land here had not been tilled for a generation, and the yield was therefore high. The average weight of each corm, instead of 11 oz., was 13 oz.

		Buang gardens	Other gardens
Area planted during:	January	34,000	28,000 sq. yd.
	December	32,000	27,000 sq. yd.
	November	32,000	27,000 sq. yd.
	October	34,000	28,000 sq. yd.
	September	35,000	29,000 sq. yd.
	August	23,500	16,000 sq. yd.
	July	24,000	15,500 sq. yd.
	June	36,000	30,000 sq. yd.
	May	35,000	27,000 sq. yd.

Yield

The potential harvest was:

			Total
February	75,800	49,500	125,300 lb.
March	61,300	55,000	116,300 lb.
April	52,000	28,400	80,400 lb.
May	50,900	29,000	79,900 lb.
June	75,800	53,200	129,000 lb.
July	73,700	51,300	125,000 lb.
August	69,300	49,500	118,800 lb.
September	69,300	49,500	118,800 lb.
October	73,700	51,300	125,000 lb.

APPENDIX B

Consumption

At this stage 480 full rations were required to feed the villagers (64,800 lb. every 30 days).
Surpluses for pig feeding and export, if there were no accidents, would be:

February	60,500 lb.
March	51,500 lb.
April	15,600 lb.
May	15,100 lb.
June	64,200 lb.
July	60,200 lb.
August	54,000 lb.
September	54,000 lb.
October	60,200 lb.

NOTE

A nutrition survey conducted by the Australian Institute of Anatomy, Canberra, early in 1947 found that the natives were not eating 4½ lb. taro daily. At the same time, their intake was only 1,223 calories, whereas their requirements, as estimated by the survey, were 2,500 calories for a male adult and 2,100 for a female adult. Food was at this period still short, and during the month which the party spent in the village many persons lost weight.

The average daily consumption (cooked weight) was as follows:

Taro	18·2 oz.	Cucumber	0.2 oz.	Yams	0·4 oz.
Sago	1·9 oz.	Bananas	0·3 oz.	Rice	0·2 oz.
Coconut	0·6 oz.	Maize	0·1 oz.	Growing shoots	1.1 oz.
(stated to be underestimated)		Pit	0.4 oz.	Other fruits	0·13 oz.
Greens	4 oz.	Pawpaw	0.2 oz.	Animal protein	0.9 oz.

Raw taro loses 30 per cent. of its weight when prepared for cooking: 18·2 oz. cooked therefore represents 26 oz. raw.

The diet was deficient by 32·8 per cent. in calories, 66·3 per cent. in protein (animal and vegetable), and 50 per cent. in calcium: it was adequate in thiamine and more than adequate in ascorbic acid.

See *Report of the New Guinea Nutrition Survey Expedition* 1947, Canberra, 1950.

Appendix C

WAR DAMAGE CLAIMS

The following are typical:

TANGAPI': House (£15), spectacles (£2), 5 enamel basins (15*s*.), clothing (8*s*.), scissors (4*s*.), chisel (4*s*.), axe (5*s*.) miscellaneous household goods (7*s*.). Total £19 3*s*.

ANGKI: 3 pigs (£8), enamel basin (3*s*.), wooden bowl (10*s*.). Total £8 13*s*.

ALINGAM: 7 pigs (£6 10*s*.), large canoe (£1 10*s*.), 2 planes (19*s*.), saw (10*s*.), chisel (4*s*.), saucepan (6*s*.), clothing (16*s*.), 6 coconut palms (£3). Total £13 15*s*.

AWAGING: Pig (£3), 2 enamel basins (6*s*.), saucepan (8*s*.), lamp (6*s*.), kerosene (4*s*.). Total £4 4*s*.

MADULU: House (£15), pig (£3), bicycle (£7), 2 clay pots (8*s*.), 2 woven bags (£1), 2 coconut palms (£1). Total £27 8*s*.

APILUM: House (£15), 8 clay pots (15*s*.), 3 trade boxes (£1), 4 coconut palms (£2), books (12*s*.). Total £19 7*s*.

MOALI': House (£15), cash (£13 8*s*.), bicycle (£7), 2 benzine irons (£2 10*s*.), 3 bush knives (15*s*.), axe (5*s*.), 8 wooden bowls (£3), saucepan (5*s*.), clothing (£2 5*s*.), miscellaneous household goods (£2). Total £46 8*s*.

NGA'GALI: House (£15), 2 pigs (£6), 20 chickens (£4), 2 bush knives (10*s*.), 3 axes (15*s*.), saw (10*s*.), awl, chisel, hammer, rule (together 15*s*.), 13 saucepans (£1 5*s*.), 2 enamel basins (7*s*.), 8 clay pots (£1 5*s*.), 4 blankets, cups, clock, 2 lamps, mosquito net, frying-pan (together £4), clothing (2s.), 12 woven bags (£2), books (£1), hunting dog (£1 10s.). Total £38 19s.

KAMBOLANG: House (£15), cash (10s.), canoe (£1 10s.), clay pot (6s.), lamp (6s.), frying-pan (2s.), clothing (£1 4s.), 6 mats (18s.), kerosene (4s.). Total £20.

GAI: Pig (£3), 6 chickens (£1 4s.), saw (10s.), pliers (7s.), fishing lines (5s.), wooden bowl (8s.), clothing (16s.), 6 coconut palms (£3). Total £9 10s.

Appendix D

DAILY WORK SCHEDULES

Details of how each of three persons spent three of their days are given. The first, Ida', is a school teacher with a wife and young family; the second, Danto, has a wife and young family; and the third, Kwasangwi, is the wife of Ida'. On each occasion I supplied a watch, notebook, and pencil.

Ida' is thoroughly familiar with our way of reckoning time, and his record can be accepted without question. Danto was probably accurate to within a few minutes, but Kwasangwi, unused to a watch, may have sometimes erred, especially in the afternoons, when Ida' was not there to keep a check.

The weather was uniformly fine; sunrise was at 6 a.m. and sunset at 6 p.m.

The total number of hours worked includes travelling time (approximately one hour per day) as a full load was carried on each occasion.

I. IDA'

9.X.45	19.X.45	23.X.45
5.55 a.m. Rose 6–6.15 a.m. Prayers. 6.15–6.25 a.m. Chatted.	6. a.m. Rose. 6–6.20 a.m. Prayers. 6.20–6.30 Made plans for fishing in evening.	6.10 a.m. Rose. 6.15–6.30 a.m. Prayers. 6.30–7.20 a.m. Discussed village affairs with pastor.

APPENDIX D

9.x.45	19.x.45	23.x.45
6.25–7 a.m. Breakfast.	6.30–7 a.m. Breakfast.	7.20–7.30 a.m. Breakfast.
7–8.30 a.m. Planned work with wife and chatted with neighbours.	7–7.40 a.m. Chatted with neighbours.	7.30–9.5 a.m. Walked to forest to collect poles for new house (accompanied by helpers).
8.30–9.55 a.m. Walked to gardens, collecting areca nuts on the way.	7.40–8.15 a.m. Walked to gardens.	
9.55–11.10 a.m. Stacked rubbish into heaps with wife.	8.15–10 a.m. Stacked rubbish into heaps with wife.	9.5–9.30 a.m. Rested.
11.10–11.15 a.m. Rested.	10–10.10 a.m. Rested.	9.30–3.15 p.m. Brought poles from forest to beach (no rests).
11.15–12 noon. Dug holes for wife to plant taro.	10.10–12.10 p.m. Dug holes for wife to plant taro.	3.55–4.5 p.m. Prepared poles to be floated to village.
12–12.10 p.m. Bathed.	12.10–1.15 p.m. Walked home (inc. 30 mins. to bathe and chat).	4.5–4.20 p.m. Walked home.
12.10–12.30 p.m. Burnt rubbish.		
12.30–1.20 p.m. Lunch and rested.	1.15–2 p.m. Lunch and prepared for school.	4.20–5 p.m. Served helpers with food (ate nothing himself).
1.20–1.55 p.m. Walked home.		
1.55–2.5 p.m. Prepared for school.	2–5.25 p.m. Taught school.	
2.5–5 p.m. Taught school.		5–6 p.m. Made fishing spear.
5–6.15 p.m. Dinner and rested.	5.25–6 p.m. Read.	6–7.15 p.m. Chatted.
6.15–10.45 p.m. Village meeting.	6–6.15 p.m. Dinner.	7.15–7.30 p.m. Prayers.
	6.15–6.30 p.m. Prayers.	7.30–8 p.m. Dinner.
10.45–11 p.m. Prayers.	6.30–12 midnight. Fished.	8–9.30 p.m. Prepared school lessons.
11 p.m. Retired.	12.10 a.m. Retired.	9.30 p.m. Retired.
Total time spent working: 7 hrs. 25 mins.	Total time spent working: 13 hrs. 35 mins.	Total time spent working: 8 hrs. 35 mins.

APPENDIX D

2. DANTO

18.x.45	22.x.45	26.x.45
5.45 a.m. Rose.	5.50 a.m. Rose.	6 a.m. Rose.
6–6.15 a.m. Prayers.	5.55–6.10 a.m. Prayers.	6.10–6.25 a.m. Prayers.
6.20–6.40 a.m. Breakfast.	6.10–7.30 a.m. Chatted.	6.25–7 a.m. Chatted.
6.40–7.15 a.m. Walked to gardens.	7.30–8.5 a.m. Breakfast	7–7.30 a.m. Breakfast.
7.15–11.15 a.m. Felled trees for new garden.	8.5–9 a.m. Walked to forest.	7.30–8.5 a.m. Chatted.
11.15–11.30 a.m. Rested.	9–9.20 a.m. Rested.	8.5–8.50 a.m. Walked to gardens.
11.30–12.45 p.m. Felled trees.	9.20–1.45 p.m. Helped haul log for canoe.	8.50–9.5 a.m. Rested.
		9.5–11 a.m. Planted taro.
		11–11.15 a.m. Rested.
		11.15–12.30 p.m. Planted taro.
12.45–1.30 p.m. Lunch and rested	1.45–2 p.m. Lunch.	12.30–2 p.m. Lunch and rested.
1.30–1.45 p.m. Walked to another garden.	2–3 p.m. Helped tow log to village.	2–3.30 p.m. Collected lashings for canoe.
1.45–3 p.m. Burning off.	3.30–5 p.m. Helped prepare meal for workers.	3.30–3.45 p.m. Bathed.
3–3.15 p.m. Bathed.		3.45–4.30 p.m. Walked home.
3.15–4 p.m. Walked home.		4.30–6.5 p.m. Chatted.
4–5.15 p.m. Helped relative to repair house.	5–6.30 p.m. Dinner and rested.	6.5–7 p.m. Dinner.
5.15–6 p.m. Repaired lures.	6.30–8 p.m. Chatted.	7–7.25. Chatted.
6–6.45 p.m. Chatted.	8–8.15 p.m. Prayers.	7.25–7.40 p.m. Prayers.
6.45–7.30 p.m. Dinner.	8.15–9.30 p.m. Chatted.	8–1 a.m. Fished.
7.30–10 p.m. Chatted.		
10 p.m. Retired.	9.30 p.m. Retired.	1.15 a.m. Retired.
Total time spent working: 8 hrs. 5 mins.	Total time spent working: 8 hrs. 20 mins.	Total time spent working: 10 hrs. 25 mins.

APPENDIX D

3. KWASANGWI

31.x.45	12.xi.45	17.xi.45
5.45 a.m. Rose.	5.50 a.m. Rose.	5.50 a.m. Rose.
5.45–6.5 a.m. Made fire and cleaned house.	5.50–6 a.m. Made fire.	5.50–6.15 a.m. Made fire and cleaned house.
6.5–6.20 a.m. Prayers.	6–6.15 a.m. Prayers.	6.15–6.30 a.m. Prayers.
6.20–7.15 a.m. Cleaned house and fed children.	6.15–6.35 a.m. Fed children.	6.30–7 a.m. Fed children.
7.15–7.30 a.m. Breakfast.	6.35–7.15 a.m. Cleaned house.	7–7.15 a.m. Breakfast.
7.30–7.40 a.m. Filled water-bottles.	7.15–7.25 a.m. Breakfast.	7.15–7.45 a.m. Walked to garden.
7.40–8.15 a.m. Walked to gardens.	7.25–7.45 a.m. Filled water-bottles.	7.45–11.30 a.m. Planted taro.
8.15–11.5 a.m. Stacked rubbish.	7.45–8.15 a.m. Walked to gardens.	11.30–12.15 p.m. Dug taro and gathered wood.
11.5–11.15 a.m. Rested.	8.15–12.5 p.m. Planted taro.	12.15–12.25 p.m. Bathed.
11.15–12.55 p.m. Planted taro.	12.5–12.50 p.m. Cooked lunch.	12.25–1 p.m. Walked home.
12.55–1.15 p.m. Lunch.	12.50–1.30 p.m. Lunch.	1–3.50 p.m. Minded sick neighbour's baby.
1.15–2.10 p.m. Planted taro.		
2.10–2.30 p.m. Walked to another garden.	1.30–2.45 p.m. Dug taro and gathered wood.	3.50–4 p.m. Chatted.
2.30–3.40 p.m. Dug taro and gathered wood.	2.45–3.5 p.m. Bathed.	4–4.30 p.m. Wove string bag.
3.40–4.5 p.m. Rested.	3.5–3.35 p.m. Walked home.	4.30–6 p.m. Prepared dinner.
4.5–4.30 p.m. Walked to to beach.	3.35–3.45 p.m. Rested.	
4.30–5.5. p.m. prepared vegetables.	3.45–4.15 p.m. Wove string bag.	
5.5–5.25 p.m. Bathed and washed clothes.	4.15–6 p.m. Prepared dinner.	6–6.15 p.m. Washed up and filled water-bottles.
5.25–5.40 p.m. Walked home.	6–6.30 p.m. Dinner.	6.15–6.30 p.m. Dinner.
5.40–7 p.m. Prepared dinner and fed children.	6.30–8 p.m. Village meeting.	6.30–7.10 p.m. Chatted.
7–7.30 p.m. Dinner.		7.10–7.25 p.m. Prayers.
7.30–7.45 p.m. Prayers.	8–8.15 p.m. Prayers.	
7.45–9.15 p.m. Chatted.	8.15–9.20 p.m. Chatted.	7.25–9 p.m. Chatted.
9.15 p.m. Retired.	9.20 p.m. Retired.	9. p.m. Retired.
Total time spent working: 10 hrs. 25 mins.	Total time spent working: 10 hrs. 25 mins.	Total time spent working: 11 hrs. 35 mins.

Appendix E

WORK DIARIES

I. DIARY FOR FOUR MEN FROM SEPTEMBER 11 TO OCTOBER 30, 1945

The men were Ahipum, who has a large family and other dependants; Alingam, who has a small family and one other dependant; Gwaleyam, who has a small family; and Dahungmboa, who has only a wife and child.

I have presumed that the average working day is about eight or nine hours, but when night fishing is carried out from four to six hours must be added.

More time was spent in building than is usual as the village was being re-constructed; and less time was spent in agriculture owing to the lack of taro suckers.

It should be noted that work is interrupted by rain far more frequently in late June, July, and August.

Date	Ahipum	Alingam	Gwaleyam	Dahungmboa
Sept. 11	Planting.	Helping to make net.	Visiting Govt. station (private business).	Planting.
12 (Half day lost by rain.)	Entertaining visitors.	Visiting hospital with sick child.	Fishing.	Fishing.
13 (Village meeting at night.)	*Morn.* Shaping relative's canoe. *Aft.* Fishing.	*Morn.* Planing planks for relative's house. *Aft.* Fishing.	*Morn.* Chipping relative's canoe. *Aft.* Fishing.	Helping relative build house.

308

APPENDIX E

Date	Ahipum	Alingam	Gwaleyam	Dahungmboa
Sept. 14 (Village meeting at night.)	Fishing.	Fishing.	Fishing.	Fishing.
15	Clearing.*	Clearing.	Planting.	Clearing.*
16	SUNDAY.	SUNDAY.	SUNDAY.	SUNDAY.
17	Clearing.	Fishing.	Clearing.	Morn. Clearing. Aft. Odd jobs.
18	Clearing.	Odd jobs.	Fencing.	Planting.
19	Morn. Adzing planks for own house. Aft. Odd jobs. Night. Fishing.	Fishing.	Odd jobs. Night. Fishing.	Morn. Odd jobs. Aft. Fishing.
20	Morn. Clearing. Aft. Fishing.	Planting.	Fishing.	Fishing.
21 (Village meeting at night.)	Visiting Govt. station (private business).	Helping relative prepare feast.	Helping relative prepare feast.	Morn. Chipping relative's canoe. Aft. Fishing.
22	Clearing. Night. Fishing	Clearing. Night. Fishing.	Clearing. Night. Fishing.	Planting. Night. Fishing.
23	SUNDAY.	SUNDAY.	SUNDAY.	SUNDAY.
24	Burning off. Night. Fishing.	Burning off. Night. Fishing.	Burning off. Night. Fishing.	Burning off. Night. Fishing.
25	Morn. Helping relative build house. Aft. Idle.	Fishing.	Idle.	Morn. Clearing. Aft. Planting.
26 (Village meeting at night.)	Planing planks for own house.	Fishing.	Helping relative build house.	Fencing.
27	Morn. Odd jobs. Aft. Idle.	Morn. Preparing garden. Aft. Idle.	Morn. Clearing. Aft. Planting.	Morn. Planting. Aft. Idle.
28	VISIT OF DISTRICT OFFICER TO CHECK VILLAGE BOOKS.			
29 (Half day lost by rain.)	Odd jobs. Night. Fishing.	Chipping relative's canoe. Night. Fishing.	Chipping relative's canoe.	Idle. Night. Fishing.
30	SUNDAY.	SUNDAY.	SUNDAY.	SUNDAY.
Oct. 1	Planting.	Planting.	Planting.	Hunting.
2	Clearing.*	Clearing.*	Morn. Chipping canoe. Aft. Entertaining visitors.	Cutting tree for relative's canoe.
3 (Half day lost by rain.)	Idle.	Odd jobs. Night. Fishing.	Idle. Night. Fishing.	Helping drag log to village. Night. Fishing.
4	Helping relative build house.	Visiting Lae.	Visiting Lae.	Helping relative build house. Night. Fishing.

* Indicates that the work occupied longer than the usual 8–9 hours.

309

Date	Ahipum	Alingam	Gwaleyam	Dahungmboa
Oct. 5 (Village meeting at night.)	Feast for returned relative.	Visiting Lae.	Visiting Lae.	*Morn.* Feast for returned relative *Aft.* Fishing.
6	Adzing planks for own house. *Night* Fishing.	„ „	„ „	Planting. *Night* Fishing.
7	SUNDAY.	„ „	„ „	SUNDAY.
8	Clearing.*	„ „	„ „	Clearing.*
9	Clearing.	„ „	.„ „	Clearing.*
10	At funeral.	„ „	„ „	At funeral.
11	Clearing.*	Clearing.*	Idle.	Clearing.
12 (Village meeting at night.)	*Morn.* Cleaning roads. *Aft.* Erecting guest hut.	*Morn.* Cleaning roads. *Aft.* Erecting guest hut.	*Morn.* Cleaning roads. *Aft.* Erecting guest hut.	*Morn.* Cleaning roads. *Aft.* Erecting guest hut.
13	*Morn.* Odd. jobs *Aft.* Idle. *Night.* Fishing.	Fishing.	Visiting Govt. station (private business.	*Morn.* Chipping relative's canoe. *Aft.* Idle. *Night.* Fishing.
14	SUNDAY.	SUNDAY.	SUNDAY.	SUNDAY.
15	Planting.	Planting.	Preparing for guests.	Preparing for guests.
16	Shaping canoe for relative.	*Morn.* Planting. *Aft.* Fishing. *Night.* Fishing.	*Morn.* Burning off. *Aft.* Fencing.	Burning off. *Night.* Fishing.
17		MISSION CONFERENCE		
18	Shaping canoe for relative.	Cutting posts for own house.	Visiting store.	*Morn.* Chipping relative's canoe. *Aft.* Idle.
19	*Morn.* Clearing. *Aft.* Planting.*	Cutting posts for own house.	Clearing.	Fencing.
20	Idle.	Cutting posts for own house.	Entertaining visitors.	Ill.
21	SUNDAY.	SUNDAY	SUNDAY.	Ill.
22	Visiting store.	Clearing. *Night.* Fishing.	Clearing. *Night.* Fishing.	Ill.
23	„ „	Clearing.*	*Morn.* Fishing. *Aft.* Odd jobs.	Ill.
24	Burning off.	Helping drag log for relative's canoe.	*Morn.* Building own house. *Aft.* Idle.	Ill.
25 (Village meeting at night.)	Idle.	Cutting posts for own house.	Odd jobs.	Ill.
26	Shaping canoe for relative. *Night.* Fishing.	Building own house.	Cutting posts for own house.	Ill.
27 (Half day lost by rain.)	Attending meeting.	Helping relative build house.	Cutting posts for own house.	Ill.

* Indicates that the work occupied longer than the usual 8–9 hours.

Date	Ahipum	Alingam	Gwaleyam	Dahungmboa
Oct. 28 29 (Half day lost by rain.) 30	SUNDAY. Attending meeting. At funeral.	SUNDAY. Helping relative build house. At funeral.	SUNDAY Ill. Night. Fishing. Night. Fishing. At funeral.	Ill. Ill. Ill.

Tabular analysis of preceding diary:

Activity	Number of Days			
	Ahipum	Alingam	Gwaleyam	Dahungmboa
Garden work	13½	10½	10	14
Fishing	2	6½	3½	4½
Hunting				1
Building own house	2½	4½	2	
Building house for relative	2	2	2	2
Working on relative's canoe	4	2	1½	3
Working on relative's net		1		
Odd jobs	2	1½	2½	1
Attending day meetings	1			
Government work	1	1	1	1
Preparing for guests	½	½	1	1
Entertaining guests	½		2	
Feasting relatives	1			½
Visiting (inc. store)	3	6½	9	
Mission conference	1	1	1	1
Ill			½	8
Idle	4	2	3	2
Funerals	2	1	1	
Raining	3	3	3	
Sundays	7	7	7	7
Total number of days	50	50	50	50
Nights spent fishing	10	8	3	7
Night meetings	7	6	6	6
Extra long days	6	3		3

Percentage of total number of days spent in different activities:

Gardening	24	Sundays	14	Fishing	9
Canoe making	9	Visiting	9	House building	8½
Raining	6	Idle	5½	Ill	4
Entertaining	3½	Odd jobs	3½	Funerals	2½
Hunting	½	Govt. work	½	Conference	½

APPENDIX E

Percentage of working time spent in different activities:

Gardening	44	Fishing	16	Canoe making	16
House building	15	Odd jobs	7	Hunting	1
Govt. work	1				

In addition, 14 per cent. of the nights (43 week days) were spent fishing.

2. A DIARY FOR EIGHT MEN FROM OCTOBER 11 TO 24, 1945

The times given in the following diaries are approximate only and are liable to error: none of the persons concerned was under continuous observation.

The figures support certain generalisations: (1) that married men work harder than youths; (2) that married men who have been in employment soon settle down to family obligations on their return; (3) that youths who have been in employment are at first not adjusted to village life, and (4) that in course of time these youths also begin to shoulder their responsibilities.

Date	Married men of 40–45 with families and other dependants. Both resident in the village continuously. (Time in hours)		Married men 25–30 with one child each. Both returned to village after indenture one week previously. (Time in hours)	
Oct. 11	Clearing. 10	Clearing. 9	Clearing. 8	Clearing. 6½
12	Working on roads. 3 Preparing for guests. 3½	Working on roads. 3 Preparing for guests. 3½	Working on roads. 3 Preparing for guests. 3½	Working on roads. ½ Preparing for guests. 1 Fishing. 7
13	Odd jobs. 3 Night fishing. 5	Fishing. 8 Odd jobs. 1	Clearing. 8	Planting. 6
14	SUNDAY.	SUNDAY.	SUNDAY.	SUNDAY.
15	Planting. 9	Planting. 8½	Burning off. 6	Fishing. 6
16	Chipping canoe for relative. 6 Odd jobs. 1	Planting. 6½ Fishing. 4	Helping build relative's house. 7	Helping build relative's house. 7 Fishing. 4
17	MISSION CONFERENCE			
18	Chipping canoe for relative. 6½ Odd jobs. 1	Carrying posts for own house. 7	Fishing. 6	Odd jobs. 4
19	Clearing. 14	Carrying posts for own house. 8	Clearing. 8½	Planting. 8
20		Carrying posts for own house. 8	Odd jobs. 3 Fishing. 4	Burning off. 8

312

APPENDIX E

Date	Married men of 40–45 with families and other dependants. Both resident in the village continuously. (Time in hours)		Married men 25–30 with one child each. Both returned to village after indenture one week previously. (Time in hours)	
Oct. 21	SUNDAY.	SUNDAY.	SUNDAY.	SUNDAY.
22	Visiting store. 9	Clearing. 9½	Planting. 7	Fishing. 6
23	Visiting store. 9	Hauling canoe log. 7 / Odd jobs. ½	Visiting to buy taro suckers. 6	Making thatch. 7
24	Clearing. 10	Clearing. 10	Planting. 7 / Fishing. 3	Planting. 4 / Fishing. 3
Total hours worked (11 work days).	90	93	80	70

Date	Unmarried men aged 20 who had been back in the village for 9 months. (Time in hours)		Unmarried men aged 20 who had finished their terms of indenture one week previously. (Time in hours)	
Oct. 11	Clearing. 9	Clearing. 9	Sitting about and gambling.	Pleasure visit.
12	Working on roads. 3 / Preparing for guests. 5	Working on roads. 2½ / Preparing for guests. 4	Working on roads. 1 / Preparing for guests. 2	Pleasure visit.
13	Planting. 7	Planting. 3 / Fishing. 5	Fishing. 5	Fishing. 5
14	SUNDAY.	SUNDAY.	SUNDAY.	SUNDAY.
15	Planting. 8	Planting. 7	Planting. 5	Planting. 5
16	Fishing. 4	Fishing. 4	Pleasure visit.	Lounging about.
17	MISSION CONFERENCE			
18	Carrying posts for relative's house. 7	Carrying posts for relative's house. 8	Fishing. 4	Fishing. 5
19	Fishing. 4	Planting. 9	Gambling.	Clearing. 9
20	Helping relative build house. 7	Helping relative build house. 7½	Helping relative build house. 5	Lounging about.
21	SUNDAY.	SUNDAY.	SUNDAY.	SUNDAY.
22	Planting. 6 / Fishing. 3	Hauling log for relative's canoe. 5	Hauling log for relative's canoe. 5	Hauling log for relative's canoe. 5
23	Clearing. 8	Helping relative build house. 8	Lounging about.	Lounging about.
24	Odd jobs. 3 / Fishing. 4	Planting. 4 / Fishing. 3	Fishing. 3	Fishing. 5
Total hours worked (11 work days).	78	79	32	34

313

Appendix F

HOUSEHOLD GARDENS

HOUSEHOLD A

This consisted of 3 adults and 2 children. Rations were therefore required for 4½ adults, an amount of 608 lb. taro every 30 days.

When the average weight of each corm was 6·4 oz., as it was in August 1945, 570 sq. yd. would have had to be cultivated to produce this harvest. When the weight was 11 oz., however, as it was from the end of 1946 onwards, 332 sq. yd. sufficed.

	Planted in:	
	January 1945	380 sq. yd.
	February–March 1945	700 sq. yd.
	April–May 1945	800 sq. yd.
	June–July 1945	1,000 sq. yd.
	August 1945	500 sq. yd.
	May–June 1946	1,000 sq. yd.
	July–August 1946	1,100 sq. yd.
	September–October 1946	1,200 sq. yd.
	November–December 1946	1,200 sq. yd.
	January, 1947	900 sq. yd.
	May–June 1947	1,600 sq. yd.
	July–August 1947	1,400 sq. yd.
	September–October 1947	1,300 sq. yd.
	November–December 1947	1,700 sq. yd.
	January 1948	1,100 sq. yd.

HOUSEHOLD B

This consisted of four adults, who required 540 lb. taro every 30 days. The acreage needed in 1945 was 506 sq. yd.; and in 1947–1948 300 sq. yd.

APPENDIX F

Planted in: January 1945   400 sq. yd.
February–March 1945   300 sq. yd.
April–May 1945   400 sq. yd.
June–July 1945   900 sq. yd.
August 1945   500 sq. yd.
May–June 1946   980 sq. yd.
July–August 1946   900 sq. yd.
September–October 1946   1,000 sq. yd.
November–December 1946   1,000 sq. yd.
January 1947   600 sq. yd.
May–June 1947   1,700 sq. yd.
July–August 1947   1,600 sq. yd.
September–October 1947   1,450 sq. yd.
November–December 1947   1,950 sq. yd.
January 1948   1,000 sq. yd.

HOUSEHOLD C

This consisted of 4 adults in August 1945 and of 6 adults from January 1947 onwards. The amount of taro required was 540 lb. in 1945 and 810 lb. in 1947–1948. The acreage needed in 1945 was 506 sq. yd. and in 1947–1948 440 sq. yd.

Planted in: January 1945   300 sq. yd.
February–March 1945   700 sq. yd.
April–May 1945   800 sq. yd.
June–July 1945   850 sq. yd.
August 1945   450 sq. yd.
May–June 1946   1,100 sq. yd.
July–August 1946   1,000 sq. yd.
September–October 1946   1,500 sq. yd.
November–December 1946   1,400 sq. yd.
January 1947   800 sq. yd.
May–June 1947   1,800 sq. yd.
July–August 1947   1,900 sq. yd.
September–October 1947   1,850 sq. yd.
November–December 1947   2,500 sq. yd.
January 1948   1,200 sq. yd.

HOUSEHOLD D

This consisted of 6 adults and 2 infants, who required 810 lb. taro every 30 days. The acreage needed was 760 sq. yd. in 1945 and 440 sq. yd. in 1947–1948.

Planted in: January 1945   650 sq. yd.
February–March 1945   1,250 sq. yd.
April–May 1945   1,400 sq. yd.
June–July 1945   1,400 sq. yd.
August 1945   750 sq. yd.
May–June 1946   1,450 sq. yd.

21*   315

APPENDIX F

Planted in : July–August 1946   1,400 sq. yd.
September–October 1946   1,600 sq. yd.
November–December 1946   1,600 sq. yd.
January 1947   900 sq. yd.
May–June 1947   3,100 sq. yd.
July–August 1947   2,800 sq. yd.
September–October 1947   900 sq. yd.
November–December 1947   2,900 sq. yd.
January 1948   1,200 sq. yd.

Appendix G

TIME AND LABOUR IN HOUSE BUILDING

The dwelling to which the following figures refer was when complete 40 feet long by 14 feet wide. Over 7 weeks elapsed between the felling of the first tree and the driving of the last nail, but during this period many days were occupied with other tasks. The number of persons engaged in constructional work is given, but I found it impossible to record simultaneously the number who cooked food for them.

Task	Number of days	Number of workers
Cutting posts, stumps, ridge, beams, purlins, and braces	2	7 men
Bringing timber to village	1	21 men
Erecting framework	½	6 men
Cutting bearers, joists, rafters, and battens	1	6 men
Bringing timber to village	1	15 men
Completing framework	1	9 men
Cutting palm leaf and other thatch material and bringing to village	1	9 women
Making thatch	1	13 men
Fixing thatch	½	10 youths
Cutting palmwood and bringing to village	1	22 men
Making flooring	½	8 youths
Cutting planks	10	5 men
Planing planks	2	9 men
Fastening plank walls	½	4 men
Total number of days worked	23 (out of a total of 46, 7 of which were Sundays)	
Total man-days worked	199	

At least 25 more man-days were taken up with cooking.

Index

Administration, 2, 6, 23, 39, 59, 60, 102, 107, 118, 140, 150, 151, 155, 157–168, 173, 174, 177, 181, 183, 187, 190, 191, 192, 199, 201, 203, 234, 235, 247, 277, 286, 288. See ANGAU; Courts; Labourers; Luluai; Murray, J. K.; Officer, District; Tultul; Village council; Village court.

Administrator, see Murray, J. K.

Adultery, 136, 141, 142, 143, 146, 156, 161, 162, 166, 167, 169, 188, 189, 191, 192, 195, 231, 255, 258, 259, 260, 261, 262, 266, 268, 271; and Christianity, 252–254.

Affines, 49

Africa, 97, 164, 184, 205 n., 272, 282, 289

Aggressiveness, 115–117, 132. See Fighting.

Agriculture, 2, 17, 18, 36, 37, 38, 39, 40, 42, 54, 55, 56, 57, 60–71, 81–84, 97–113, 119–125, 127–130, 136, 144, 153, 154, 157, 189, 192, 198, 205, 206, 209, 229, 236, 241, 261.

Ahipum, 32, 64, 98, 119, 120, 132, 133, 140, 154, 155, 160, 161, 168, 272.

Alcohol, 190, 268, 281, 282

Americans, 5, 8, 11, 19 n., 234, 235, 246, 283, 285 n, 287, 288

ANGAU, 6–10, 13, 15, 151–160, 277, 278, 280, 281, 282, 287.

Army, and race relations, 279–281, 287, 288. See ANGAU; Conscription.

Art, see Carving; Dances.

Asini', 15, 27, 28, 81, 88, 89, 91, 145, 146, 148

Atrocities 8 n., 9, 156

Australia, 2, 4, 19, 155, 157, 165, 167, 186, 200, 201, 234, 235, 246, 257, 278, 279, 284, 287, 288, 289

Awasa, 28, 29, 30, 99, 115–117, 121, 132, 148, 149, 233, 285. See Sections.

Ballet, see Dances.

Bananas, 56, 66, 73

Banks, 20, 22, 23

Baptism, 244, 245, 249–251, 271, 274, 275

Barry, J. V., 19

Barter, 83–95, 224, 244

Bateson, G., 26 n., 205 n.

Bathing, 40, 41, 217, 218, 221

Bedding, 55, 56

Belshaw, C. S., 164 n., 284 n.

Betel nut, 56, 57, 60, 74, 123

Bible; see Christianity.

Birth, 61, 129, 219, 220, 241, 272

Blood feud, see Fighting.

Blood, ritual, 213, 214, 218, 244, 250. See Male cult.

Boat, 21, 155

Bonito, see Fishing.

Bowls, carved, 21, 31, 47, 49, 50, 82, 90–94, 103, 127. See Gift exchanges; Trading.

Bride price, see Marriage.

Brogan, D. W., 285

Brown, G. St. J. Orde, 184 n.

Brutality, 152, 277, 280, 281, 283, 286. See Atrocities.

Buakap, 15, 16, 28, 81, 88, 89, 91, 137, 138, 139, 251, 262, 271

Buangs, 3, 28, 63, 64, 100

Buasi', 25, 29 n., 64, 145, 146, 147, 148

Building, see Club; Houses.

Bukawa', 27, 28, 32, 86, 88, 102, 113, 204, 236, 237

Bull roarers, 214–218

Bumbu, 7, 8, 19, 32, 117, 151–163, 165, 166, 181, 185, 233, 246, 263, 270, 272, 273, 274, 275

319

Busilim, 33, 134, 139, 140 n.
Buso, 69, 81, 87

Calendar, 34–39, 87, 206, 209
Cannibalism, 147
Canoes, 16, 18, 19, 21, 41, 53, 55, 58, 59, 61, 70, 75, 77, 78, 79, 81, 90, 100, 114, 123, 128, 140, 141, 174, 189, 251, 252
Capell, A., 25 n.
Cargo cult, see Religious cults, new.
Carpenter, see Crafts.
Carving, 32, 130, 135, 228, 238, 239
Cash, see Money.
Cato, A. C., 284 n.
Census, 15, 35, 243
Charity, Christian, 255–257
Chickens, see Fowls.
Chief, 150, 151. See Headman; Luluai.
Chinese, 285
Christianity, 39, 71, 87, 93, 148, 158, 166, 232–275; Bible, 236–248; dogma, 246–249; ceremonies, 249–251; conduct, 252–254; virtues, 255–257; conscience, 258–260; retribution, 260–264; confession, 264–267; pagan survivals, 267–272. See Missions.
Christmas, 236, 251, 274
Church, see Christianity; Missions; Sunday.
Circumcision, see Male cult.
Civil disputes, see Quarrels; Village court; Village meetings.
Clan, see Club; Lineage; Sections.
Clements, F. W., 45, 66 n.
Climate, 4. See Calendar.
Clothing, 29, 55, 56, 103, 137, 187, 188, 196, 241
Club (house and group), 31, 32, 49, 97, 113–118, 120, 127, 128, 130, 131–135, 140, 174, 180, 192, 193, 205, 207, 213, 214, 215, 220, 221, 230, 233
Club head, 118, 122, 123, 128, 130, 131–135, 139, 140, 141.
Coconuts, 43, 47, 48, 55, 73, 100, 118, 127, 136, 139
Colour prejudice, 235, 242. See Race relations.
Commandments, Mosaic, 166, 179, 242, 247, 252–257, 262

Communion, 244, 249, 250, 251, 252, 264, 274, 275
Compensation, for injury, 143–145, 224; for war damage, 19–23, 188, 287
Conception theory, 104
Confession, 234, 246, 250, 255, 264–267, 270, 271, 272, 274
Conscience, 222, 233, 258–260, 267, 269. See Shame.
Conscription, 8, 9, 10, 12–15, 156, 273, 286
Consecration, 251
Cooking, 41, 46–50, 55, 57, 58, 127
Cordyline, 215 n.
Council, village. See Village council.
Courts, 115, 146, 154, 155, 158, 159, 160, 167, 192, 244, 252, 268, 281, 282. See Village court.
Cousins, cross, 49, 97, 108
Crafts, 21, 77, 78, 79, 185, 224, 237, 238, 239
Credit, see Debt.
Crime, 116, 134, 135, 141–145, 166, 167, 168, 225, 247
Crops, export, 97, 200 n., 286, 288. See Agriculture.
Cruden, A., 259 n.
Cults, see Male cult; Religious cults, new.
Culture heroes, see Spirits.
Currency, see Money.

Dances, 59, 136–139, 145, 151, 153, 158, 188, 191, 219, 251, 254, 273, 274, 283
Death, 59, 102, 129; and Christianity, 262–267; and pagan religion, 209–213, 215, 218, 231; and sorcery, 222–226
Debt, 122, 123, 125, 126
Decker, J. A., 184 n.
Defence, see Fighting.
Defilement, see Blood, ritual; Confession; Male cult.
Descent, 108, 109. See Matriliny; Patriliny.
Diet, see Food.
Disease, 29, 35, 122, 186, 187 n., 199, 201, 241, 249, 278; and Christianity, 261–267; of children 212, 213, 229; and pagan religion; 208, 211, 212

Disease—*continued*
  214, 215, 223, 231; and sorcery, 222–226, 270
Disloyalty, 11, 12
Disputes, see Courts; Land tenure; Quarrels; Village court.
District Officer, see Officer, District.
Diviner, in fighting, 228; in sorcery, 146, 226
Division of labour, sexual, 55–61.
Division, social. See Awasa; Lutu; Sections.
Divorce, 235
Dollard, J., 283 n., 285 n.
Dracaena, 215 n.
Dreams, 43, 244
Drinking, 50, 23, 215, 217, 221, 228, 278. See Alcohol.

Easter, 251
Eating, see Food; Manners in eating.
Education, see Schools.
Eggs, 43, 48
Elders, see Relations between generations.
Employment, see Labourers.
Epidemics, 225, 263, 264
Etiquette, see Manners in eating.
Exchange, see Barter; Gift exchanges; Market; Trading.
Exogamy, 114
Expiation, Christian, 260–267
External Territories, Minister for, 19, 165, 199, 200, 202 n., 280

Family, 98, 126, 133, 206, 210, 253, 257, 262. See Club; Household; Lineage.
Father, 103–111, 192, 193, 220
Feasts, 46, 55, 79, 114, 123–141, 151, 210, 220, 227, 255; abandonment of, 135, 137; arranging, 126–128; Christian, 251; club, 130; dance, 136–139; importance of, 123–126; initiation, 135, 136, 216–219; occasions for, 128–130
Fienberg, D. M., 97 n.
Fighting, 55, 59, 87, 97, 136, 145–149, 180, 190, 191, 195, 199, 206, 214, 216, 226, 228. See Aggressiveness; Quarrels.
Finschhafen, 82, 91, 234, 237, 263, 286

Firth, R., 83 n., 238 n.
Fishing, 37, 39, 40, 41, 45, 55, 57, 74–77, 92, 93, 98, 114, 123, 140, 167, 169, 205, 206, 209, 211, 244, 252; net, 39, 55, 75, 76; seine, 21, 43, 44, 75–77, 226–228
Fly Islands, 88
Food, 39, 41–53, 61–75, 81, 97, 153, 157, 159, 167, 188, 189, 198, 210, 211, 213, 215, 217, 220, 221, 224, 244, 255; and nutrition, 44, 45; preparation of, 40, 41, 46–53; resources, 42–44; restrictions, 44–47, 51; social attitude to, 118–123; and trade, 81–95; and war, 15–18; and wealth, 118–123. See Feasts; Gift exchanges; Manners in eating; Taboo.
Fortes, M., 102 n.
Fowls, 16, 18, 55, 57, 187
Friendship, bond, 147 n., 216, 221, 256
Fruits, 43, 46, 48, 54, 57, 73, 153, 187
Funerals, see Death.
Furniture, see Tools.

Gaiwaku, 28, 29
Galsworthy, J., 257
Gambling, 190
Gaol, see Prison.
Gardens, see Agriculture.
Gawa', 25, 27, 28, 116
Generations, see Relations between generations.
Generosity, 84, 85, 121, 122, 123, 133, 255, 256
Germans, 4, 11, 29, 123 n., 150, 151, 155, 234, 235, 286
Ghosts, see Spirits.
Gift exchanges, 41, 83–95, 121–123, 256. See Trading.
Gi'lahi, 33, 153
Gitlow, A. L., 135 n., 233 n.
Gods, see Spirits.
Goldfields, 5, 7, 93, 152, 185, 186, 189, 195, 269
Government, see Administration; ANGAU; Luluai; Officer, District; Murray, J. K.; Tultul.
Groves, W. C., 81 n.
Guests, see Visitors.
Gwado, 28, 208, 262

Gwaleyam, 33, 101, 102, 105, 107, 121, 134, 139, 140 n., 152, 154, 159, 160, 161, 162, 168, 169, 172, 175, 176

Haddon, A. C., 24 n., 25 n.
Hailey, Lord, 164 n, 184 n., 278 n.
Hall, R. A., 26 n.
Hancock, W. K., 287 n.
Harnoncourt, R. d', 238 n.
Headman, 118, 123, 126, 128, 135–145, 147, 148, 162, 185, 206, 215, 216, 224, 225, 226, 230, 239
Health, Department of, see Disease.
Heroes, culture, see Spirits.
History of Busama, 27–29, 102 n.
Hoeltke, G., 284 n.
Homosexuality, 190–192, 269
Honour, see Reputation.
Hornbill, 147.
Hospitals, see Disease.
Household, 65, 97–99, 115, 117
Houses, 6, 17–19, 30, 31, 55, 56, 58, 61, 79, 80, 97, 102, 103, 114, 128, 141, 161, 187, 189, 194, 198, 205, 220, 221, 251, 252
Hunter, M., 184 n.
Hunting, 55, 57, 102, 205

Ida', 32, 120, 139, 178, 180, 239, 242, 243, 246, 247, 253, 256, 259, 260, 263, 266, 268, 270
Illness, see Disease.
Incest, 154, 157, 158, 161
Incision, see Male cult.
India, 283, 285
Indonesia, 289
Infantry Battalion, Native, 12, 285, 287
Inheritance, 99, 100, 102, 103, 209, 210, 222, 223, 227
Initiation, 104, 108, 135, 145, 147, 151, 193, 216–219, 230; for women, 219–221
Inquest, 226
Interest (investment), 124, 136, 137
Investment, 124, 136, 137
Isom, 7, 9, 10, 117, 152, 154, 155, 156, 172–174

Jabêm, see Yabim.
Japanese, 6–11, 12, 152, 153, 156, 234, 236, 246, 285
Justice, see Courts; Village court.

Kaberry, P. M., 205 n.
Kai, 27–30, 92, 93, 116, 235
Kaidemoe, 27, 28, 92, 93, 100, 116, 235, 269
Kaiwa, 27, 29, 235, 271
Kanaka, 276, 280
Kate (Kâte), 26
Keane, A. H., 24 n.
Kellett, E. E., 251 n.
Kila, 27, 81, 87–89, 91, 145–148
Kinship, 3, 63, 65, 77–79, 96–117, 179, 180, 193, 211, 231, 250, 253, 256, 262. See Affines; Club; Cousins; Lineage; Matriliny; Parents; Patriliny; Relations between generations.
Kroeber, A. L., 284 n.

Lababia 69, 81, 87
Labour, division of. See Division of labour.
Labourers, 7, 9, 12–14, 17, 24, 29, 42, 93, 94, 95, 98, 119, 131, 151, 152, 156, 160, 167, 253, 254, 264, 266, 268–271, 277, 278, 280, 282, 284, 285–288; and marriage, 183; female, 183, 184; indenture, 185, 186, 191, 199–202; repatriation of, 185, 186; contracts of, 186, 199–203; reasons for becoming, 186–189; compounds, 189–191, 269; and sexual morals, 188–191; returned, 191–199; and village ceremonies, 196–199; conditions of today, 199–203.
Labu, 3, 15, 16, 28, 30, 81, 90, 91, 99, 111, 116, 145, 146, 147, 148
Lae, 5, 10, 13, 14, 15, 18, 19, 28, 32, 52, 66, 83, 86, 87, 94, 99, 153, 158, 162, 195, 197, 203, 263, 264, 269, 278
Laiwamba, 28, 116, 146
Land tenure, 99–113, 144, 182, 207–209, 229–231; disputes, 177, 178
Language, 25–27, 86, 206, 235, 237, 257. See Gawa'; Kate; Pidgin English; Yabim.
Laukanu, 69, 70, 81, 84, 87
Law, see Courts; Land tenure; Village court.
Laziness, see Relations between generations.

Leadership, 118–149, 226, 230, 233. See Club head; Headman; Luluai; Magic; Tultul.
League of Nations, see Mandates Commission.
Lehner, S., 204 n., 258, 266
Lineage, 63, 97, 99, 112, 115, 117, 205, 207–211, 233
Linton, R., 238 n.
Local government, 165, 286. See Village council; Village court.
London *Observer*, 289
Love, see Charity; Marriage.
Loyalty, 11, 12
Luluai, 7, 8, 32, 33, 115, 116, 121, 150–163, 181, 192, 233, 240, 244; paramount, 151
Lutheran Mission, see Christianity; Missions.
Lutu, 27, 29, 30, 99, 102, 113, 115–117, 132, 148, 233, 285. See Sections.

Magic, 209, 212, 219, 220, 222–226, 246, 274, 284; and Christianity, 266, 268–272; and leadership, 226–229. See Sorcery.
Mair, L. P., 184 n., 284 n.
Mala'lo, 28, 29, 165, 204, 235, 237, 238, 249, 251, 252, 261
Malaria, 29, 35, 263 n., 270
Male cult, 135, 204, 213–219, 225, 228, 231–234; and Christianity, 250, 251, 264
Malinowski, B., 66 n., 83 n., 118 n., 205 n.
Mandates Commission, 4, 151, 234, 288
Manners in eating, 46, 48–51, 120, 122, 128
Market, 54, 94, 95, 153. See Trading.
Markham River, 3, 4, 5, 12, 27, 28, 35, 67, 81, 146, 190, 235, 256
Marriage, 84, 87, 111, 114, 115, 118, 119, 121, 128, 129, 140, 142–144, 148, 154, 172–175, 189, 191, 192, 195, 206, 211, 221, 229, 231, 262. See Affines.
Masalai, see Spirits, of land.
Matriliny, 99–111, 120, 121, 193, 218, 227
Mats, 40, 41, 82–94. See Gift exchanges; Trading.

McCarthy, F. D., 238 n.
Mead, M., 205 n.
Meals, 48–51, 250. See Food.
Meanness, see Generosity.
Meat, see Pigs.
Melanesian physical type, 24–26
Men's house, see Club.
Menstruation, 104, 129, 219, 220, 221, 230, 233; for men, 230
Minister for External Territories. See External Territories, Minister for.
Missions, 11, 26, 29, 32–35, 39, 60, 67, 70, 71, 87, 93, 94, 120, 123, 135, 137, 148, 157, 158, 163, 165–168, 178, 183, 184, 187, 188, 199, 204, 227, 232–239, 243, 245, 249, 252–257, 260–263, 266, 268, 269, 273–277, 286; native officers of, 236–239; rivalries, 162, 163, 233. See Christianity.
Mitchell, Sir P., 97 n.
Moiety, 116 n.
Money, 2, 19–23, 64, 76, 83–86, 90, 91, 97–99, 118–124, 129, 130, 136, 137, 143, 152, 155, 160, 162, 184, 185, 187, 188, 190, 193, 196, 197, 198, 203, 208, 209, 244, 256, 285–288. See Wages.
Moon, see Calendar.
Morobe District, 5, 21, 26, 30, 234, 235
Mother right, see Matriliny.
Mother's brother, see Matriliny.
Murder, 136, 141, 142, 145–148, 166, 226, 231, 241, 242, 252, 253
Murphy, J. J., 26 n.
Murray, Sir H., 201
Murray, J. K., 164 n., 200 n., 201 n., 279, 289
Music, see Dances.
Myths, 206, 214, 230

Names, 33
Native currency, see Money.
Nazi Party, 235
Negroes, American, 11, 283, 285–288
Neuhauss, R., 204 n.
New Caledonia, 24
New Hebrides, 24
Nga'gili', 32, 104, 125, 126, 133, 153, 160, 173, 176, 248, 256, 269
Nga'sele', 33, 193
Nutrition, 44 45. See Food.

Officer, District, 10, 11, 15, 21, 29, 30, 78, 112, 115, 141, 150–163, 164, 166, 167, 168, 170, 177, 178, 181, 182, 192, 195, 239, 242, 244, 247, 252.
Officials, see Club head; Headman; Luluai; Officer, District; Tultul.
Oliver, D. L., 100 n., 119 n.
Opinion, public, see Public opinion.
Oratory, 171
Ordinancs, 165, 166, 186, 187, 190.
Orion, 37
Ornaments, 93, 137, 188, 210, 221
Orphans, 120, 134, 135, 140, 256
Ownership, see Land tenure; Leadership.

Pacific Islands Monthly, 201 n., 279, 280, 281
Papua, 4, 11 n., 13, 19, 25, 26, 186, 201, 235, 239, 281
Parents, 35, 41, 45, 51, 55, 134, 135, 167, 178–180, 196, 212, 252, 256. See Father; Patriliny.
Patriliny, 99, 111, 207 n., 218
Payment, see Gift exchanges; Market; Marriage; Retaliation; Trading.
Physiology theories, 44, 45
Pidgin English, 7, 26 n., 86, 150, 151, 159, 181, 182, 185, 192, 195, 196, 234, 240, 248, 257, 279
Pigs, 8, 19, 21, 43, 50, 55, 57, 67, 69, 84, 85, 92, 93, 98, 103, 118, 120, 121, 122, 123, 124, 125, 128, 129, 130, 136, 138, 139, 144, 158, 161, 182, 209, 210, 211, 216, 218, 231, 241, 244, 256
Pim, Sir A., 97 n.
Platters, see Bowls, carved.
Pleiades, 35–38
Police, 9, 10, 155, 156, 159, 177, 187, 190, 239, 245, 268, 282, 286
Polygamy, 235
Population, 5, 17, 71, 111, 115, 117, 189
Pork, see Pigs
Port Moresby, 4, 196, 281
Potatoes, sweet, 42, 44 n., 66, 82, 90, 92, 93
Pots, 21, 48, 49, 52, 70, 81–95, 103, 127, 206. See Gift exchanges; Trading.

Prayers, 41, 169; and magic, 271, 272
Prices, in native trading, 83, 86, 90, 91, 93; in stores, 83 n., 197, 198
Prison, 144, 152, 156, 159, 168, 181, 200, 252, 281, 282
Profane, see Taboo.
Prostitution, 188–190
Protein, 43
Public opinion, 85, 119, 120, 126, 131, 132, 142, 144, 153, 157, 160, 166, 168, 170, 178. See Reputation; Shame.
Punishment, 140–149, 154, 166, 170, 247; and Christianity, 248, 260–267. See Death; Disease; Sorcery.
Purification, see Birth; Blood, ritual; Male cult.
Pygmies, 24

Quarrels, 115, 136 141, 167, 168, 174, 175, 222, 241, 246, 253, 265

Rabaul, 4, 6, 7, 150, 180, 190, 271, 283; Times, 277, 279, 280
Race relations, 42, 235, 242, 276–289; attitude of Europeans, 277–283; attitude of natives, 283–288; sexual, 283, 287
Racial types, 24, 25
Rainbow, 207
Rainfall, 4, 35. See Calendar.
Rape, 190, 286
Ray, S. H. 25 n.
Read, K. E., 12 n., 165 n.
Reciprocity, see Gift exchanges; Kinship.
Recruiters, labour, 185, 186, 188, 200
Reed, S. W., 26, 184 n., 277 n., 278 n., 279 n., 283 n., 286 n.
Relations between generations, 167, 174, 179, 180, 184, 189, 191–196, 216, 218, 219, 243, 252
Religious cults, new, 162, 284
Repentance, see Confession.
Reputation, 85, 119, 120, 121, 126, 131–135, 139, 152, 153, 160, 166, 168, 255
Responsibilities of young, see Relations between generations.
Retaliation, 85, 141–149, 240. See Sorcery.

Rice, 44 n., 48, 120, 125, 130, 138, 139, 153, 157
Richards, A. I., 272
Rivalries, church and state, 162, 163; mission, 233. See Fighting; Headman.
Roads, 39, 59, 166, 167, 169
Ross, Father, 135 n.

Sacrifices, 207–211, 225, 231, 241, 244, 251, 261
Sago, 42, 47, 48, 58, 60, 71–73, 121, 123, 127–129, 136, 138, 139, 143, 220
Salamaua, 3, 5, 6, 7, 9, 10, 12, 15, 27, 30, 81, 82, 84, 87, 88, 92, 152, 156, 158, 160, 168, 177, 195, 196, 197, 237, 261, 263, 271, 287
Sanctions, moral, 231
Satan, see Temptation.
Savings, see Banks.
Schapera, I., 184 n.
Schools, 21, 22, 29, 32, 40, 41, 94, 95, 157, 165, 167, 169, 178, 179, 184, 189, 190, 193, 196, 199, 200, 202, 236, 237, 238, 243, 273, 278, 279, 284, 286, 288
Sculpture, see Carving.
Seasons, see Calendar.
Sections, 115–117, 132, 272. See Awasa; Lutu.
Seduction, 143, 146, 154, 157, 158, 161, 166, 167, 169, 172, 173, 174, 181, 188, 189, 191, 192, 218, 260, 262, 271; and Christianity, 252–254
Segregation, racial, see Fishing.
Seine, see Fishing.
Seligman, C. G., 24 n.
Sex, instruction in, 221. See Adultery; Homosexuality; Labourers; Race relations; Seduction; Women.
Shame, 85, 86, 119, 120, 121, 126, 131–135, 139, 153, 166, 168, 233, 234, 241, 248; and Christianity, 258–260
Siassi Islands, 82, 87
Siboma, 69, 70, 81, 87, 88, 235
Sin, 178, 246, 248, 249, 252, 253–255, 258, 260–268, 275; original, 246, 250
Slander, 144, 252
Solomon Islands, 19, 20, 24, 100 n., 116 n., 119 n., 163, 164 n., 181 n., 194, 195, 233, 260, 282

Sorcery, 136, 142, 144, 146, 147, 155, 156, 190, 195, 222–226, 230, 231, 269, 272
Soul, 240, 248, 249, 260 264
Spells, see Magic.
Spirits, sky, 206, 207, 230, 231; of dead, 209–211, 226, 231, 245, 247, 248; familiar, 228; female, 212; of land, 207–209, 231, 268; of male cult, 213–219; spooks, 212, 213, 225, 267, 268
Stealing, see Theft.
Strikes, 286
Sun, see Calendar.
Sunday, 39, 70, 187, 188, 237, 238, 249, 251, 252, 271, 273
Sundkler, B. G. M., 233 n., 284 n., 285 n.
Sweet potatoes, see Potatoes, sweet.

Taboo, 213–221, 227, 229; and children, 229; Christian, 252, 257 n.; food, 135, 136, 213, 215, 217, 218, 220, 221, 223, 228; menstrual, 221; sexual, 207
Tambaran, see Spirits, of male cult.
Tami Islands, 81, 87, 91
Tapioca, 42, 73
Taro, see Agriculture; Food.
Taxation, 166, 181, 188, 197
Taylor, J. L., 19
Temptation, 241, 247
Theft, 143, 144, 166, 167, 175–177, 190, 195, 222, 246, 247, 252, 253, 261, 267, 268
Thomson, B., 233 n.
Time, 34, 41, 42, 102 n. See Calendar.
Tobacco, 56, 57, 60, 66, 74, 82, 92, 93, 188, 190, 198
Tolerance, 257
Tools, 21, 27, 31, 55, 56, 79, 92, 93, 94, 103, 116, 140, 187, 188, 196, 197, 198, 199, 228, 229
Trade stores, 8, 29, 48, 50, 64, 69, 70, 83, 92, 93, 103, 131 n., 175, 176, 187, 188, 234, 278 n., 287
Trading, 55, 59, 64, 69, 70, 81–95, 145, 148, 186, 206, 228, 229; with Europeans, 94, 187, 196
Treasury, village, see Village treasury.
Trobriand Islands, 66 n., 118 n., 229, 253, 254

Tultul, 7, 32, 115, 116, 118, 140, 150–163, 181
Tuna, see Fishing.

United States, see Americans.

Values, see Prices.
Vegetables, see Agriculture; Food.
Vendetta, see Fighting.
Vengeance, see Fighting; Sorcery.
Village, history of, 27–29, 102 n.; description of, 29–32; population of, 30
Village council, 21, 164–182
Village court, 164–182
Village meeting, 99, 133, 141–145, 166–182, 193, 224, 228, 230
Village officials, see Club head; Headman; Luluai; Tultul.
Village treasury, 21, 165 n.
Visitors, 52, 71, 87, 89, 93, 99, 111, 119, 120, 127, 128, 136, 137, 138, 139, 217–219, 252
Voltaire, 163, 233 n.

Wages, 182, 184–187, 190, 193, 196, 197, 200–202, 236, 271, 278, 286, 288
Wakop, 64, 147, 148
Wamasu', 15, 28, 29
War, Pacific, see ANGAU; Army; Conscription; Infantry Battalion; Japanese.
Ward, E. J., 280
Warfare, see Fighting; War, Pacific.
Warner, W. L., 205 n.

Warrior, see Fighting.
Wealth, see Food, Money.
Weapons, 93, 146, 288
Webb, Sir W., 8 n.
Wedgwood, C. H., 195 n.
White prestige, see Race relations.
Whiting, J. W. M., 26 n.
Williams, F. E., 205 n., 284 n.
Wilson, G., 184 n.
Witchcraft, see Sorcery.
Wogeo, 45 n., 112, 205 n., 230, 249, 254, 268, 283 n.
Women, and children, 44, 45, 61; and Christianity, 232, 233, 241; and fighting, 146, 148; treatment of, 174, 175, 178–180; and pagan religion, 207, 211, 213–215, 219–221, 230; and prestige, 61; and property, 102, 103; and schooling, 237; and status, 113; and wage labour, 183, 188–190; and work, 39–41, 46, 52, 54–61, 68, 72, 75, 76, 86, 88, 89, 153, 210
Work, see Agriculture; Canoes; Club; Division of labour; Houses; Fishing; Labourers; Women.
Worthington, E. B., 97 n.

Xenophobia, 287

Yabim, 26, 27, 29, 86, 181, 182, 236, 257
Yams, 42, 48, 66, 82, 90, 92, 93.
Youth, see Relations between generations.

For Product Safety Concerns and Information please contact our EU
representative GPSR@taylorandfrancis.com
Taylor & Francis Verlag GmbH, Kaufingerstraße 24, 80331 München, Germany